The shaping o

Within a variety of historical contexts, T_ most important tasks that states have confronted – namely, how to protect their citizens against the short-range as well as the long-range dangers their polities confront in the present and may confront in the future. To be successful, grand strategy demands that governments and leaders chart a course that involves more than simply reacting to immediate events. Above all, it demands that they adapt to sudden and major changes in the international environment, which more often than not involve the outbreak of great conflicts but at times demand recognition of major economic, political, or diplomatic changes. This collection of essays explores the successes and failures of great states attempting to create grand strategies that work and aims to achieve an understanding of some of the extraordinary difficulties involved in casting, evolving, and adapting grand strategy to the realities of the world.

Williamson Murray is Professor Emeritus of History at The Ohio State University. He has been the Centennial Visiting Professor at the London School of Economics, Secretary of the Navy Fellow at the Navy War College, Horner Professor of Military Theory at the Marine Corps University, and Harold Johnson Professor of Military History at the Army War College. At present he is a defense consultant and commentator on historical and military subjects in Washington, D.C. Murray is coeditor of *The Making of Peace* (2009, with James Lacey); *The Past as Prologue* (2006, with Richard Hart Sinnreich); *The Dynamics of Military Revolution, 1300–2050* (2001, with MacGregor Knox); *Military Innovation in the Interwar Period* (1998, with Allan R. Millett); and *The Making of Strategy* (1996, with Alvin Bernstein and MacGregor Knox).

Richard Hart Sinnreich retired from the U.S. Army in 1990. His active service included field artillery commands from battery through division artillery; combat in Vietnam; teaching at West Point and Fort Leavenworth; and assignments on the Army, Joint, and National Security Council staffs as assistant to the Supreme Allied Commander Europe and as the first Army Fellow of the Center for Strategic and International Studies. He helped establish and subsequently directed the Army's School of Advanced Military Studies and has published widely on military and foreign affairs. Since retiring from the Army, he has worked as an independent defense consultant for both private industry and government agencies and as the regular defense columnist for the *Sunday Constitution* in Lawton, Oklahoma.

James Lacey has served for more than twelve years as an infantry officer on active duty and is recently retired from the Army reserves. He is a widely published analyst and Professor of Strategy at the Marine Corps War College in Quantico, Virginia. He has written several works on the war in Iraq and the global war on terrorism. He also teaches graduate-level courses in military history and global issues at Johns Hopkins University. Lacey was an embedded journalist with *Time* magazine during the Iraq invasion, traveling with the 101st Airborne Division. He has written extensively for many magazines, and his opinion columns have been published in the *National Review, The Weekly Standard, The New York Post*, the *New York Sun, Foreign Affairs*, and many other publications. He is the author of *Takedown: The 3rd Infantry Division's 21-Day Assault on Baghdad* (2007), which has been hailed as "a major and successful effort to fill in one of the major blank spots in our knowledge of Operation Iraqi Freedom"; *Pershing* (2008); and *Keep from All Thoughtful Men* (forthcoming). He is coeditor of *The Making of Peace* (2009).

The shaping of grand strategy

Policy, diplomacy, and war

Edited by

WILLIAMSON MURRAY
Ohio State University, Emeritus

RICHARD HART SINNREICH
Independent Scholar

JAMES LACEY
Marine Corps War College

CAMBRIDGE
UNIVERSITY PRESS

CAMBRIDGE
UNIVERSITY PRESS

32 Avenue of the Americas, New York, NY 10013-2473, USA

Cambridge University Press is part of the University of Cambridge.

It furthers the University's mission by disseminating knowledge in the pursuit of education, learning, and research at the highest international levels of excellence.

www.cambridge.org
Information on this title: www.cambridge.org/9780521156332

© Cambridge University Press 2011

This publication is in copyright. Subject to statutory exception and to the provisions of relevant collective licensing agreements, no reproduction of any part may take place without the written permission of Cambridge University Press.

First published 2011
Reprinted 2014

A catalog record for this publication is available from the British Library.

Library of Congress Cataloging in Publication data
The shaping of grand strategy : policy, diplomacy, and war / edited by Williamson Murray, Richard Hart Sinnreich, James Lacey.
   p.   cm.
Includes bibliographical references and index.
ISBN 978-0-521-76126-0 (Hardback)
1. World politics – 18th century.   2. World politics – 19th century.   3. World politics – 20th century.   4. Strategy – History – 18th century.   5. Strategy – History – 19th century.   6. Strategy – History – 20th century.   7. Strategic culture – Case studies.   I. Murray, Williamson.   II. Sinnreich, Richard Hart.   III. Lacey, Jim, 1958–
D217.S44   2011
327.1–dc22   2010037125

ISBN 978-0-521-76126-0 Hardback
ISBN 978-0-521-15633-2 Paperback

Cambridge University Press has no responsibility for the persistence or accuracy of URLS for external or third-party Internet Web sites referred to in this publication and does not guarantee that any content on such Web sites is, or will remain, accurate or appropriate.

Dedicated to

General James Mattis
United States Marine Corps

Mentor, Leader, and Student of History

Contents

Contents

Contributors

Jeremy Black
University of Exeter

Colin S. Gray
University of Reading

Marcus Jones
U.S. Naval Academy

James Lacey
Marine Corps War College

John A. Lynn II
Northwestern University

Williamson Murray
Ohio State University,
  Emeritus

Richard Hart Sinnreich
Independent Scholar

1

Thoughts on grand strategy

WILLIAMSON MURRAY

What keeps big systems integrated? Can they go on getting bigger and bigger? How much do communications media matter? How far can globalization go? How does systems-failure begin to appear? From the reign of Hadrian, the Roman empire, gigantic system that it was, stopped getting bigger, more integrated, more complicated, stopped providing so many opportunities, stopped improving the possibilities of change and innovation. Maybe it was enough that the positive trends faltered; maybe they started to go into reverse. No one noticed for generations, but the pace and nature of change had altered for ever. The big labels, Greek, Roman, Christian, remained but concealed increasing chaos.[1]

We might begin our examination of the issues involved in grand strategy with an effort to describe what we mean by the term. Over the centuries, some governments and their leaders have attempted to chart a course for their nations that has involved more than simply reacting to the course of events. In most cases they have confronted sudden and major changes in the international environment, often resulting from the outbreak of great conflicts, but at times involving economic, strategic, or political alterations that threaten the stability or even existence of their polities.

Yet, grand strategy is a matter involving great states and great states alone. No small states and few medium-size states possess the possibility of crafting a grand strategy. For the most part, their circumstances condemn them to suffer what Athenian negotiators suggested to their Melian counterparts in 416 BC about the nature of international relations: "The standard of justice depends on the equality of power to compel and that in fact the strong do

---

[1] Danny Danziger and Nicholas Purcell, *Hadrian's Empire: When Rome Ruled the World* (London, 2005), pp. 287–288.

I

what they have the power to do and the weak accept what they have to accept."[2]

But if great states have choices that their smaller cousins do not, then the concomitant burden they must bear is what one might best describe as *overstretch*. Quite simply, overstretch is an inevitable part of the landscape in which great states exist. They have no other avenue but to address a wide variety of vital interests in the economic, political, and military spheres, some of which are contradictory by their nature and demands. Those vital interests will inevitably present threats either in the immediate present or to the state's long-term survival. General James Wolfe, victor on the Plains of Abraham before Quebec City in 1759, described conflict best with the short aphorism "War is an option of difficulties."[3]

The same is even truer for grand strategy. In a world where great states confront overstretch, they must make hard choices. Thus, in the end, grand strategy is more often than not about the ability to adjust to the reality that resources, will, and interests inevitably find themselves out of balance in some areas. Strategy is about balancing risks. But above all, it is about insuring that the balance is right in those areas that matter most. And in times of great stress, it is also about adapting national focus on the international environment to those areas of overstretch that threaten the polity to the greatest extent.

What distinguishes leaders who have attempted to develop and execute a grand strategy is their focus on acting beyond the demands of the present. In other words, they have taken a longer view than simply reacting to the events of the day. Nor have they concentrated on only one aspect of the problem. Instead, in times of war, while they may have focused on the great issue confronting them, such as Lincoln's effort to maintain the Union in the great Civil War that enveloped North America, that vision has recognized the political, economic, and diplomatic framework within which the conflict was taking place.[4]

There is, one must admit, considerable confusion of grand strategy with policy, military strategy, and strategies to achieve this or that specific goal.

---

[2] Thucydides, *History of the Peloponnesian War*, trans. Rex Warner (London, 1954), p. 402. There are two exceptions to the rule. Both the Swiss and the Finns were able to exercise a certain independence that allowed them to maintain a grand strategic framework: the former by balancing great powers off against each other; the latter, by creating the distinct impression in the minds of the Soviets that they were willing to fight to the last man and woman in defense of their independence.

[3] Fred Anderson, *Crucible of War: The Seven Years' War and the Fate of Empire in British North America, 1754–1766* (New York, 2000).

[4] Thus, in discussing the goal of his grand strategy (namely, the preservation of the Union, as he was about to issue the Emancipation Proclamation), Lincoln commented, "If I could save the Union without freeing *any* slave I would do it, and if I could do it by freeing *all* the slaves I would do it; and if I could do it by freeing some and leaving others alone I would also do that." Quoted in Stephen W. Sears, *The Landscape Turned Red: The Battle of Antietam* (New York, 1983), p. 166.

Grand strategy is none of these, but to one extent or another, it consists of all of them. It demands a recognition of and ability to react to the ever-shifting environments of war and peace. Thus, the day-to-day decision making that drives policy making must be involved in the execution of grand strategy. The latter will envelop military strategy and diplomatic strategy. Nor must grand strategy ignore the other issues that invariably confront leaders who are in a position to develop and execute it. However, it also demands that statesmen encompass within their view of the larger goal the pieces of bureaucratic decision making, policy, and specific strategic approaches. Thus, those who develop a successful grand strategy never lose sight of the long-term goal, whatever that may be, but are willing to adapt to the difficulties of the present in reaching toward the future. Above all, at the same time that they have maintained a vision focused on the possibilities of the future, they have adapted to the realities of the present.

Those who are interested in the subject of grand strategy must understand that much of the flesh and muscle that went into its creation and maintenance in its various forms is lost to the pages of history. To a considerable extent, the past remains an unrecoverable land, where time has muted or obscured the relationships, hatreds, and calculations of those who made decisions. As one of the leading historians of the rise of Britain to mastery over the world's oceans has noted about the creation of Britain's strategy during the War of Spanish Succession:

> [The proximity of the major military and political players in London during the winter when strategy was made] makes the process of strategic formulation almost unrecoverable for the historian, at least in its more interesting aspects. Parliamentary debates and gossip remain, but thousands of other informal discussions in saloons, taverns, dinner parties, balls, and random encounters are lost. Unofficial correspondence exists only when key figures retreated to their country estates or were otherwise absent, and official documents tend to reflect decisions rather than the processes that created them. The compromises, trade-offs, and private deals characteristic of advanced systems of clientage are often lost to recorded memory. Decisions were usually compromises, and those who dissented could only grumble and criticize until victory dismissed their complaints or misfortune made them next year's policy.[5]

In fact, those who have developed successful grand strategies in the past have been much the exception. The affairs of man as recorded by historians seem nothing more than one long catalogue of crimes, follies, and egregious

---

[5] William S. Maltby, "The Origins of a Global Strategy: England from 1558 to 1713," in Williamson Murray, MacGregor Knox, and Alvin Bernstein, eds., *The Making of Strategy, Rulers, States, and War* (Cambridge, 1992), p. 163.

errors.[6] Wars begun with little or no thought of their consequences, assumptions unchallenged in the face of harsh reality, the possibility of second- or third-order effects casually dismissed with the shrug of a shoulder, and idle ignorance substituted for serious considerations have bedeviled the actions of statesmen and generals over the course of recorded history. During much of the past, a strategic framework, much less a grand strategy, has rarely guided those responsible for the long-term survival of polities either in a political or military sense.

And so the inevitable question that should concern American policy makers and military leaders – much less the polity as a whole – is simply put: is there even the possibility of charting a grand strategy for a United States that at present confronts monumental challenges to its security?[7] Is there a strategic path that would protect the United States, its interests, and its values more effectively than simply reacting to the next great crisis? If so, what does history suggest about how those few in the past who have done so have thought clearly and coherently in setting out a course to the future? In other words, how have first-rate statesmen and their military and diplomatic advisers developed effective approaches to grand strategy in meeting the demands of the present as well as those of the future?

The history of the past century certainly underlines the importance of a coherent approach to grand strategy, one that is flexible, realistic, and above all connects means to ends. It warns, however, that this has rarely been the case. In an article examining military effectiveness and the impact – or lack thereof – of a coherent strategic approach over the years from 1914 to 1945, this author and his colleague Allan Millett argued:

> No amount of operational virtuosity... redeemed fundamental flaws in political judgment. Whether policy shaped strategy or strategic imperatives drove policy was irrelevant. Miscalculation in both led to defeat, and any combination of politico-strategic error had disastrous results, even for some nations that ended the war as members of the victorious coalition. Even the effective mobilization of national will, manpower, industrial might, national wealth, and technological know-how did not save the belligerents from reaping the bitter fruit of severe mistakes [at this level]. This is because it is more important to make correct decisions at the political and strategic level than it is at the operational and tactical level. Mistakes in operations and tactics can be corrected, but political and strategic mistakes live forever.[8]

---

[6] The title of Barbara Tuchman's book, *The March of Folly*, encapsulates much of mankind's historical record.
[7] For a general examination of strategy as a process over the course of human history, see Murray et al., *The Making of Strategy*.
[8] Allan R. Millett and Williamson Murray, "Lessons of War," *The National Interest*, Winter 1988–1989.

UNDERSTANDING GRAND STRATEGY

No simple, clear definition of grand strategy can ever be fully satisfactory. The closer one comes to understanding what it entails, the more one sees how complex and uncertain in historical terms are the aspects that encompass its making and use. One might adapt a comment by Clausewitz to our purpose of developing a theoretical understanding of grand strategy:

> The second way out of this difficulty is to argue that a theory need not be a positive doctrine, a sort of *manual* for action. . . . It is an analytical investigation leading to a close *acquaintance* with the subject; applied to experience – in our case [strategy] – it leads to thorough *familiarity* with it. The closer it comes to that goal, the more it proceeds from the objective form of a science to the subjective form of a skill.[9]

Grand strategy involves some willingness and ability to think about the future in terms of the goals of a political entity. Yet, those who have been most successful at its practice have also recognized that the "future is not foreseeable" and consequently have been willing to adapt to political, economic, and military conditions as they are rather than as they wish them to be. Above all, grand strategy demands an intertwining of political, social, and economic realities with military power as well as a recognition that politics must, in nearly all cases, drive military necessity.[10] It must also rest on a realistic assessment and understanding not only of one's opponents but also of oneself.[11] There is rarely clarity in the effective casting of grand strategy because, by its nature, it exists in an environment of constant change, where chance and the unexpected are inherent.[12] Thus, simply thinking about developing a concept of grand strategy demands not only a deep understanding of the past but also a comprehensive and realistic understanding of the present.

---

[9] Carl von Clausewitz, *On War*, trans. and ed. Michael Howard and Peter Paret (Princeton, NJ, 1976), p. 163.

[10] The German military in the First World War consistently rejected strategic and political concerns in what its leaders consistently posited as "military necessity" – a concept they used to override all political and strategic concerns. In this regard, see Isabel V. Hull, *Absolute Destruction, Military Culture and the Practices of War in Imperial Germany* (Ithaca, NY, 2005).

[11] Sun Tzu's most justly famous aphorism is that "if you know the enemy and you know yourself, you need not fear the results of a hundred battles." Sun Tzu, *The Art of War*, trans. and ed. Samuel B. Griffith (Oxford, 1963), p. 84.

[12] One of the most important contributions to our understanding of international relations, diplomatic and strategic history, and the conduct of war has been the impact of non-linearity. For its implications for history and political science, see John Lewis Gaddis, "International Relations Theory and the End of the Cold War," *International Security* 17, no. 3, Winter 1992/93.

Grand strategy may be as concerned with avoiding war as with fighting it, although there are times when there is no alternative to conflict.[13] War avoidance was certainly a basic principle of Byzantium's approach to grand strategy, at least from the death of Justinian in 565 AD.[14] Thus, one should not assume that grand strategy is only a matter of war; some of the greatest successes of grand strategy have been wars not fought, the most obvious of which was the Cold War.[15] Moreover, miscalculations of grand strategy in peacetime, such as Neville Chamberlain's policy of appeasement and its execution, can lead to catastrophic results not only in peace but in the initial conduct of military operations, although the latter, not surprisingly, are far easier to see with historical perspective than the former.[16]

History is essential to any understanding of the present; only the past can clarify and elucidate the factors, trends, and political and economic frameworks that have made the present and will certainly drive the future. Moreover, grand strategy demands a recognition of unpleasant realities and a willingness to challenge one's own assumptions and the myths and truisms of one's own culture – normally not characteristics of the human race in general or of its political or military leaders in particular, who generally prefer pleasant and comfortable illusions to the stark truths of reality.

Given their importance, one might suppose that grand strategy and strategy would be the subjects of innumerable books and studies. In fact, they have not been. The greatest book on war, Thucydides' *History of the Peloponnesian War*, presents a deep and thorough examination of grand strategy, among a number of other crucial issues.[17] However, the Western historical canon is largely silent on the subject until Machiavelli, and even he is largely focused on stratagems for the individual ruler to follow in the pursuit of internal and external power. Jomini concerns himself mostly with the geometry of war, although he was finally forced to admit that Clausewitz was

---

[13] This was the case with the response of the Western Powers in dealing with Hitler's Nazi Germany in the 1930s.

[14] This is the main theme in Edward Luttwak's book on the grand strategy of the Eastern Roman Empire.

[15] See, among others, John Gaddis, *Now We Know: Rethinking Cold War History* (New York, 1998); and *The Cold War: A New History* (New York, 2006).

[16] Neville Chamberlain's decisions to surrender Czechoslovakia in September and October 1938, while maintaining Britain's leisurely pace of rearmament, underlines how crucial decisions of grand strategy in peacetime can be. For further discussion of the military and strategic results of Munich, see, among others, Williamson Murray, *The Change in the European Balance of Power, 1938–1939: The Path to Ruin* (Princeton: Princeton University Press, 1984), chaps. 7 and 8.

[17] One of the more bizarre aspects of modern historiography is the argument among ancient historians that there was no understanding of strategy in the Greco-Roman world. For a refutation of such nonsense, simply refer to the speech given by King Archidamnus in Book 1 of Thucydides' great history: *The History of the Peloponnesian War*, pp. 82–86.

right that war is a matter of "the continuation of politics by other means."[18] The great Prussian theorist himself admits, at the beginning of *On War*, that policy and strategy represent the crucial drivers and determinants of human conflict; however, because his subject is the phenomenon of war, his work discusses these subjects only peripherally.

Nor is grand strategy described better by more recent theoretical approaches such as Alfred Thayer Mahan's work on sea power; Guiliho Douhet's work on air power; or British pundits Basil H. Liddell Hart's and J. F. C. Fuller's theories of the indirect approach and armored warfare.[19] Each of these authors focused his attention on specific aspects of the technological attributes of war, although Mahan and Liddell Hart were willing to use historical examples effectively to support their arguments. Only Julian Corbett, the great British naval thinker, was willing to draw on Clausewitz for understanding the fundamental nature of war as a means to understand the role of naval conflict in grand strategy.[20]

In the twentieth century, the subject of grand strategy as a topic for rigorous historical examination first appears in serious form in Edward Meade Earle's classic *Makers of Modern Strategy*, which, not surprisingly, appeared at the midpoint of America's participation in the Second World War.[21] Of the voluminous official studies of the two world wars commissioned by the various governments involved, only the British undertook a deep study of their performance at the level of grand strategy.[22] America's official histories were far less coherent and, in the end, less satisfactory in their efforts to discuss U.S. grand strategy.[23] Their examination of the war was more about military strategy and decisions involving the employment of military forces than about American grand strategy.[24]

---

[18] "We see, therefore, that war is not merely an act of policy but a true political instrument, a continuation of political intercourse, carried on with other means. What remains peculiar to war is simply the peculiar nature of its means." Clausewitz, *On War*, p. 99.

[19] Douhet's major works were not translated into English until after the Second World War, although translations of his articles were available at the Air Corps Tactical School in the 1930s. For Basil Liddell Hart's views on the subject, see *Strategy* (London, 1929).

[20] See Julian Corbett, *Principles of Maritime Strategy* (Mineola, NY, reprint, 2004).

[21] Edward Meade Earle, ed., *The Makers of Modern Strategy* (Princeton, NJ, 1943). It was reedited by Peter Paret in 1984 in a far less satisfactory volume, *The Makers of Modern Strategy* (Princeton, NJ, 1984).

[22] See the outstanding six-volume series dealing with British grand strategy in the Second World War, published by Her Majesty's Stationery Office from 1957 to 1972. The most outstanding volume in the series is Michael Howard, *Grand Strategy*, vol. 4, *August 1942–September 1943* (London, 1972).

[23] For examples of the American approach to the analysis of grand strategy, see Maurice Matloff, *The United States Army in World War II – The War Department: Strategic Planning for Coalition Warfare, 1943–1944* (Washington, DC, 1959).

[24] In fact, many of the discussions in the Green Books, as the Army's official histories are known, are flawed by faulty assumptions and sloppy research. The clearest example is their almost complete silence on the strategic debates that took place in late 1942 over

Why then, considering the importance of the topic, has the subject of grand strategy proven so peripheral in the literature of war and peace? There appear to be several explanations, none of them entirely satisfactory but useful nevertheless. Grand strategy lies at the nexus of politics and military strategy and thus contains important elements of both. Moreover, it exists in a world of constant flux, one in which uncertainty and ambiguity dominate. And the international environment will more often than not have its say, as national opponents take the most inopportune moments to change their policies, while internal and ideological factors also have a vote.

Thus, the *Weltanschauungen* (worldviews) of statesmen and military leaders alike – a major determinant in the formation of any grand strategy – will come under constant assault from the ever-changing environment within which they work. One does not make effective grand strategy entirely as one would like but rather according to the circumstances in which a national polity finds itself. Finally, as noted earlier, great states possess considerable wiggle room in the casting of grand strategy, but small states have virtually none.[25]

A part of the problem in understanding grand strategy – or for that matter strategy of any kind – lies in the belief of most historians and commentators that it represents an enunciated set of goals and principles to which statesmen and military leaders adhere in a consistent fashion. However, historical examples of marches toward clear goals are less than enlightening, one example being the disastrous trajectory of the Third Reich. From his beginnings as a street agitator in Munich to his dismal end in a bunker in Berlin, Hitler possessed a coherent, carefully thought-through, long-term grand strategy from which he rarely deviated in the course of his rise and fall – although in his early years in power, he was willing to make temporary adjustments such as with his signing of the Non-Aggression Pact with Poland in 1934. Initially, Hitler's strategy brought Nazi Germany great military and diplomatic triumphs, but within those successes lay the seeds of catastrophe, because Hitler's conception of grand strategy and the assumptions on which it rested led straight to the invasion of the Soviet Union and his declaration of war on the United States.[26] In fact, although the goals of grand strategy may

American mobilization and the nation's ability to support the buildup of ground forces as well as the argument, entirely fallacious, that George Marshall argued for a landing on the coast of northwest France in 1943 at the Casablanca conference. For a refutation of such views, see James Lacey, "Economic Foundations of American Military Strategy, 1940–1943," Ph.D diss. University of Leeds, 2009.

25 In the cold, dark words of the Athenian negotiators on the island of Melos in 416 BC, "in fact the strong do what they have the power to do and the weak accept what they have to accept." Thucydides, *History of the Peloponnesian War*, p. 402.

26 Far and away the best books on Hitler's grand strategy – its origins, its development, and its end – are Gerhard Weinberg, *A World at Arms: A Global History of World War II* (Cambridge, 1994); and MacGregor Knox, *To the Threshold of Power, 1922/33*, vol. 1, *Origins and Dynamics of the Fascist and National Socialist Dictatorships* (Cambridge, 2007).

be clear, the path to achieving them is invariably tortuous and uncertain, a reality that has inevitably led to great difficulties.

In fact, the best analogy for understanding grand strategy is that of how French peasant soup is made – a mixture of items thrown into the pot over the course of a week and then eaten, for which no recipe can possibly exist.[27] In thinking about the soup of grand strategy, recipes and theoretical principles are equally useless. What works in one case may well not work in another. In various strengths, grand strategy consists of leadership, vision, intuition, process, adaptation, and the impact of a nation's particular and idiosyncratic development and geographic position, but in no particular order or mixture.[28]

Geography, historical experience, and culture have all invariably exercised a heavy, but often unseen, influence over the making of national grand strategy, but individuals and their own particular abilities to upset every seemingly rational calculation represent a factor that statesmen rarely seem to command. In other words, Murphy's law works at every level.[29] This is particularly so because what appears rational to the leaders of one national group inevitably reflects their own cultural biases.[30] Thus, one must think of grand strategy in terms of an idiosyncratic process rather than a specific, clearly thought-through approach to the world. When successful, it almost invariably involves the choices and guiding hands of individuals, for better or worse, rather than an effective bureaucratic system. Thus as a human endeavor, it is suffused with the idiosyncrasies that mark all of humanity's decision making.

The two greatest grand strategists of the nineteenth century, Abraham Lincoln and Otto von Bismarck, are cases in point. Neither individual began his course with a clear idea of his route or the political and international framework within which he was going to have to work. Both had specific long-term goals in mind: Lincoln, the preservation of the Union; Bismarck, the political security, internal as well as external, of the Prussian monarchy. Both found themselves remaking and even extending their goals. Lincoln, for his part, turned to emancipation of the South's slaves, which was not a part of his original agenda, as an essential component of the preservation of the Union.[31] Bismarck eventually turned to unifying the "Germanys," southern and northern, to secure Prussia.

---

[27] This analogy, used in a different context, and apparently used often by General William E. Depuy in various briefings, was passed along to the author by General Don Starry, U.S. Army (ret.).

[28] For a discussion of these issues, see Murray and Grimsley, "Introduction, On Strategy," in Murray et al., *The Making of Strategy.*

[29] The law posits that if something can go wrong, it will go wrong.

[30] This reality makes the whole concept of the "rational actor," on which so much of American political science rests, completely irrelevant to any real understanding of the world.

[31] In this case, Lincoln's decision to issue the Emancipation Proclamation had as much to do with undermining the economic stability of the Confederacy and bucking up the North's

Perhaps the most important factor that one needs to recognize when thinking about grand strategy is that the decisions that constituted it in the past confronted considerable ambiguities in the international environment. That recognition is crucial because the uncertainties of the present are little different in their fundamental nature from those that have confronted statesmen and military leaders throughout history. As the Bible clearly underlines, mankind peers into the future "through a glass darkly" – a reality that Winston Churchill caught so brilliantly in his history and memoir of the First World War:

> One rises from the study of the Great War with a prevailing sense of the defective control of individuals upon world fortunes. It has been well said, 'there is always more error than design in human affairs.' The limited minds of the ablest men, their disputed authority, the climate of opinion in which they dwell, their transient and partial contributions to the mighty problem, the problem itself so far beyond their compass, so vast in scale and detail, so changing in its aspects – all this must be considered [in understanding the outbreak of war in 1914].... Events... got onto certain lines and no one could get them off again.[32]

For this reason alone, grand strategy is easier to recognize after the fact, when events have clarified the landscape, uncertainties have disappeared, and only historians remain to pick over the bones. The balancing act that statesmen confront between the means available and the ends desired disappears, and only its results drive the conventional wisdom of historians. What appeared difficult and complex when statesmen were charting an intelligent course in a complex and uncertain environment now appears simple and obvious in the aftermath of events. Herein lies the great danger in historical analysis: again, to paraphrase Clausewitz, grand strategy may appear to be a simple matter, but given the enormous uncertainties within which it must work and the prevailing forces that work on it, its execution is exceedingly difficult.[33]

The remainder of this chapter examines a series of issues to tease out the factors involved in grand strategy. The discussion is not meant to be prescriptive but rather to suggest the realm of possibilities in which success and failure in grand strategy have rested in the past. Some of the questions which should frame an examination of grand strategy are: How has geographic position influenced the making of grand strategy? How has the nature of government influenced its development? What has been the role of alliances or unilateralism in its success or failure? Finally, are there examples

---

morale and strategic situation as it did with his belief that slavery represented a moral wrong. But politics and grand strategy are matters of the practicable.

[32] Winston S. Churchill, *The World Crisis* (Toronto, 1931), p. 6.
[33] Clausewitz comments on the fundamental nature of war: "Everything in war is very simple, but the simplest thing is difficult." Clausewitz, *On War*, p. 119.

of great powers which have gained or maintained their position only because they possessed a coherent grand strategy?

Of particular importance to those who are interested in grand strategy, its articulation, and its success or failure is the context within which it has occurred. No theoretical construct, no set of abstract principles, no political science model can capture its essence.[34] That is because grand strategy exists in a world of flux. Constant change and adaptation must be its companions if it is to succeed. Not only does it find itself under the pressures and strains of the politics and processes of decision making, but the fact that the external environment can and often does adapt will inevitably affect the calculations of those who attempt to chart its course. The goals may be clear, but the means available and the paths are uncertain. Exacerbating such difficulties is the reality that grand strategy demands intuitive as much as calculated judgment.

Geography and grand strategy

The specific factors that will inevitably affect the formulation and execution of a grand strategy are easy to describe. Geographical position is perhaps the most obvious and important. Those who have been responsible for making grand strategy in the United States and Britain have found their worldviews fashioned in a fundamentally different way from those who have led Continental powers. In particular, they have enjoyed the inestimable advantage of the sea's protection, an advantage that has allowed them time to prepare for future engagements or to accept defeats that no Continental power could accept.

The vastly different paths that the British Empire and the French Republic took in June 1940 reflected not only their differences in leadership but also their differences in strategic perspective. The French saw the defeat of their armies as representing the end of possible resistance; the British, no matter how dismal matters looked in June 1940, could look at the long-term strategic possibilities. Part of the explanation lay in the great differences in how the Continental powers and the British viewed the ocean. To both the French and the Germans, Dunkirk and the English Channel represented the end of military operations. To the British, Dunkirk simply provided access to one of the great highways that cross the world's seas – in this case, a highway that led to southern England but one on which the Germans were

---

[34] Clausewitz puts the matter simply: "All the positive results of theoretical investigation – all the principles, rules and methods – will increasingly lack universality and absolute truth the closer they come to being positive doctrine. They are there to be used when needed, and their suitability in any given case must always be a matter of judgment. A critic should never use the results of theory as laws and standards, but only ... *as aids to judgment.*" Ibid., p. 183.

completely unprepared to tread.[35] It was via this highway that the British and Americans would return to France on the 6th of June 1944.

But it is also the combination of geography and its accompanying historical background that plays such a crucial role in the development and articulation of grand strategy. In the 1930s, Liddell Hart argued that the First World War, with its commitment of a massive British Expeditionary force to the Continent, had represented an aberration in traditional British strategy.[36] Supposedly, in the past, the British had followed a strategic path, which he termed *limited liability*, in which Britain's leaders had committed only minimal forces to the Continent while attacking their Continental opponents on the periphery. Michael Howard's counterargument was perceptive and historically accurate:

> It was ... precisely the failure of German power to find an outlet and its concentration in Europe, its lack of any possessions overseas, that made it so particularly menacing to the sprawling British Empire in two world wars and which make so misleading all arguments about "traditional" British strategy drawn from earlier conflicts against the Spanish and French Empires, with all the colonial hostages they had offered to fortune and the Royal Navy.[37]

Yet, there is a certain grain of truth to Liddell Hart's argument. In previous wars against its Continental enemies, Britain's position, separated from the European continent, had allowed British statesmen to husband their resources – allowing their allies to bear the brunt of fighting on the continent – and to draw on the resources of the world beyond the European continent. In the First World War, however, the nature of German power broke the Czarist Empire and, nearly, France. Britain had no choice as the war proceeded but to step in with steadily increasing ground forces on the Continent. In the Second World War, the matter came closer to the traditional wars Britain had fought in the past in that the Red Army bore the brunt of the terrible battles that finally wore down the Wehrmacht. But the burden of committing substantial ground forces to the Mediterranean, fighting the Battle of the Atlantic, committing major forces to the defense of India, and waging Bomber Command's great effort against the German home front hardly represented Liddell Hart's idealized "British way of war."

In the largest sense, geographic position has led both the British and American polities to think of grand strategy in terms of the projection of

---

[35] Field Marshal Wilhelm Wilhelm Keitel, not exactly the brightest light in the German pantheon of military leaders, described the crossing of the English Channel in summer 1940 as representing "no more than a river crossing." The chief of the general staff, General Franz Halder, also remarked on 4 July 1940, about crossing the Channel: "method: Similar to large-scale river crossing." Franz Halder, *The Halder War Diary, 1939–1942*, ed. Charles Burdick and Hans-Adolph Jacobsen (Novato, CA, 1988), p. 221.

[36] See, particularly, Basil Liddell Hart, *The British Way in Warfare* (London, 1932).

[37] Michael Howard, *The Continental Commitment* (London, 1972), p. 32.

military power. In terms of the European continent, the problem of project-ing power has been less of a problem for the former given the close proximity of the British Isles to France and the Low Countries. That reality has also made the British more sensitive to who controls the Low Countries, a major factor in English grand strategy as early as the reign of Queen Elizabeth I. Not surprisingly, the British discovered themselves deeply torn by the strate-gic overstretch created by the Continental threat raised by Germany and the strategic demands raised by a worldwide empire.

With the acquisition of the Philippines in the late nineteenth century, the United States confronted the need to defend imperial possessions on the far side of the Pacific, a task that its politicians were congenitally unprepared to meet. But in the larger sense, when the United States finally awoke to its responsibilities in the early 1940s – an awakening greatly aided by its enemies – the grand strategy that it pursued in winning the hot war of 1941–1945 and then the Cold War required the projection of its vast military power across the world's greatest oceans.[38]

Grand strategy is as much the prisoner of history as of geography, although both are inextricably intertwined. For the leaders of the German Reich in the first half of the twentieth century, the inheritors of Prussia in every sense, the catastrophe of 14 October 1806, when Napoleon's Grand Army destroyed the Prussian army in a single day at the double battle of Jena/Auerstadt, had burned itself into the memories of those responsible for defending the Prusso-German state. In Bismarck's case, when Prussia went to war in 1864, 1866, and 1870, the iron chancellor went to extraordinary lengths to stack the odds thoroughly in Prussia's favor so that its army had only one opponent against whom to fight at a time.

His successors, however, still under the influence of the historical memory of what had happened in 1806, proceeded to divide strategic and political concerns from what they defined as "military necessity." Thus, in 1914, desperately fearful of the two-front war they would confront as a result of their geographical position, the Germans struck at France through Belgium in the hopes they could end the war in the west before the Russians could mobilize. Their operational gamble failed on the Marne, while the invasion of neutral Belgium insured that Britain's waffling cabinet would commit its nation to a war on the Continent and create the potential for a long war that Germany had little chance of winning.

The Germans also suffered one other major defect that resulted from their placement at the heart of Europe. Although they understood their neighborhood of Central Europe, they knew little about the world that

---

[38] A reality that has forced American strategists to emphasize logistics as the equal of combat power – a concern that its opponents over the past century have had to confront to a considerably lesser degree.

lay beyond the continental confines of their world. Surprisingly, given how close Britain was to the Reich, the leaders of the Kaiser Reich understood almost nothing about the nature of British politics and staying power. In late July 1914, with German troops poised to invade Belgium and Luxemburg, the German chancellor remarked to the British ambassador that the treaty guaranteeing Belgium's neutrality was just a "scrap of paper."[39] That tactless and inept remark was sufficient to push those in the British Cabinet, who were unsure how Britain should act, into supporting the declaration of war on Germany. But beyond the British Isles, the Germans were literally at sea. In December 1941, shortly after the Japanese attack on Pearl Harbor, Hitler asked his assembled staff where the great American naval base was located. Not a single one of the admirals, generals, or staff officers knew, an astonishing state of affairs for people who held pretensions of conquering the world.[40]

If geographic position has been particularly important in the peculiar fashion with which the Germans have addressed the problems raised by grand strategy, it has also factored into the way Russians view the strategic world. Although the vast expanses and endless steppes that characterize Russian territory have provided them the ability to trade space for time in war – time which has then brought the savage Russian winter into play – that openness has, at the same time, made them the victims of savage invasions, the first of which, in the thirteenth century by the Mongols, destroyed a flourishing civilization. That catastrophe was followed five centuries later by the invasion of the Swedes under Charles XII in the Great Northern War, which came close to undoing Peter the Great's efforts to build a modern state out of the savagery of Muscovy. In the following centuries, Napoleon's invasion of 1812 and Hitler's Barbarossa inflicted incalculable sufferings on the Russian people. Small wonder, then, that Russian grand strategy has been characterized by a deep paranoia and suspicion of the external world, a paranoia that the Soviet Union's Communist ideology only served to exacerbate.

The nature of government and grand strategy

In the centuries before 1789, the nature of polities played a less important role than it has since the French Revolution introduced mass politics into history's course. In the great world wars that took place in the eighteenth century, statesmen and their military advisers – in the case of Prussia, one

---

[39] Holger H. Herwig, *The First World War: Germany and Austria-Hungary, 1914–1918* (New York, 1997), p. 30.

[40] Dr. Horst Boog of the Militärgeschichtliche Forschungsamt passed this story along to the author in the early 1980s.

and the same – decided grand strategy with little or no reference to public opinion. "In the eighteenth century, in the days of the Silesian campaigns, war was still an affair for governments alone, and the people's role was simply that of an instrument."[41] Only in the case of Britain did the House of Commons represent opinions beyond those determined by the small group at the center. But even then, the young monarch George III felt confident enough of his own prerogatives to remove William Pitt, the author and designer of the grand strategy that had resulted in the victories of 1759, the *annus mirabilis* that had created a worldwide empire that would last for nearly two centuries.[42]

But the cabinet wars of the eighteenth century entirely disappeared with the wars of the French Revolution and Napoleon. Clausewitz caught that terrible transition to the modern world well before the academic historians who attempted to unravel the course of events between 1789 and 1815:

> Suddenly war again became the business of the people – a people of thirty millions, all of whom considered themselves to be citizens. . . . The people became a participant in war; instead of governments and armies as heretofore, the full weight of the nation was thrown into the balance. The resources and efforts now available for use now surpassed all conventional limits; nothing now impeded the vigor with which war could be waged, and consequently the opponents of France faced the utmost peril . . .

> War, untrammeled by any conventional constraints, had broken loose in all its elemental fury. This was due to the people's new share in these great affairs of state and their participation, in turn, resulted partly from the impact that the Revolution had on the internal conditions of every state and partly from the danger that France posed to everyone.[43]

Clausewitz then continued on to point out that part of the success the French were to gain over the next quarter century in conquering one nation after another rested on the failure of the other European powers to understand either the threat or the kind of wars in which they found themselves: "Not until statesmen had at last perceived the nature of the forces that had emerged in France, and had grasped that new political conditions now obtained in Europe, could they foresee the broad effect all this would have on war; and only in that way could they appreciate the scale of the means that would have to be employed, and how best to employ them."[44]

---

41 Clausewitz, *On War*, p. 583.
42 For a brilliant examination of the course of the Seven Years' War as well as its grand strategy, see Anderson.
43 Clausewitz, *On War*, p. 592.
44 Ibid., p. 609.

The French Revolution introduced into the equation of the making of grand strategy the modern religion of ideology. Along with that thread came nationalism. At the end of the Napoleonic Wars in 1815, the Congress of Vienna attempted to put those two genies back into the bottle.[45] Its efforts achieved a modicum of success, but in the end, the tide was irreversible. The revolutions of 1848 did much to unleash the drives that had sparked the events of 1789–1815. But 1789 was the grandfather of the ideological state and its leaders. As one commentator has noted:

> By 1791 the French Revolution had created what Lenin, much later, memorably described as "dual power" – an anomaly ended by coup d'état. In the France of 1791, the unsatiated revolutionary factions of the *Assemblée Nationale* and their supporters in the streets as yet lacked the capacity or will to seize power by force. They also lacked the preeminent organizational tool of later professional revolutionaries, Lenin's centralized, conspiratorial, implacable 'party of a new type.' But they nevertheless laid siege to France's post-1789 constitutional monarchy and to its ministers. And they found, step by step, debate by impassioned debate, a road to power. The road they found was war.[46]

The full and terrible denouement would come only with the First World War, when the aftereffects of the French Revolution combined with the Industrial Revolution to create modern war in its full horror.[47] The ideological successors to the French Revolution found war an attractive means to the larger ends toward which their grand strategies aimed. They proved all too effective at the waging of war with their ability to mobilize and deploy the vast material and manpower resources that the modern state possesses. Luckily for humanity, they proved less capable in the realm of grand strategy. In fact, the ideology that provided the Nazis and the Soviets – and to a lesser extent, the Italian Fascists – with the ruthless vision and determination to crush internal opposition to their rule made them, at the same time, less able to adjust their grand strategies, deeply influenced – as well as warped – as they were by ideological vision, to the realities of a rapidly changing world.

This factor proved even more true of the Nazis than of the Soviets. The enormity of Hitler's success in taking a broken nation devastated by the Great Depression and in six years making the German Reich the most powerful nation in Europe provided the Germans, including too many at the

---

[45]   For an excellent discussion of the efforts at the Congress of Vienna to put the twin genies of liberalism and nationalism back into the bottle, see Richard Hart Sinnreich, "In Search of Military Repose: The Congress of Vienna and the Making of Peace," in *The Making of Peace, Rulers, States, and the Aftermath of War*, ed. Williamson Murray and Jim Lacey (Cambridge, 2009).

[46]   Knox, *To the Threshold of Power*, p. 13

[47]   For a discussion of this factor, see MacGregor Knox and Williamson Murray, *The Dynamics of Military Revolution, 1300–2050* (Cambridge, 2001), chap. 1.

higher levels of government, with the belief that Hitler as a leader was incapable of error. The withdrawal from the League of Nations, the return of the Saar, rearmament, the remilitarization of the Rhineland, the *Anschluss* with Austria, the Munich triumph, and the occupation of rump Czechoslovakia all reinforced Hitler's belief as well as that of those around him that he was a strategic and political genius.[48] The military successes of 1939 and 1940 reinforced those beliefs. As Keitel, summing up what even Germany's more intelligent senior military leaders were coming to believe, announced, "Hitler is the greatest warlord of all time."[49]

Throughout this period, Hitler adjusted to the vagaries of fortune but never deviated from his larger goal of creating an Aryan Europe, *judenfrei*, with the great land mass of Eastern Europe under German control and with those Slavs who survived the murderous attention of the SS condemned to eke out an existence as helots.[50] The nature of German planning for the invasion of the Soviet Union rested on the belief that once the Wehrmacht had "kicked in the door" of a Soviet Union ruled by Jewish-Bolshevik subhumans in the opening weeks of military operations, "the whole rotten structure will come crashing down."[51] But when the first serious threat to that assumption appeared on the horizon with the failure of Barbarossa in December 1941, Hitler reacted with his decision to declare war on the United States on 11 December 1941.[52]

Hitler's view of the United States was equally tinged with contempt for what he regarded as a mongrelized nation in which various inferior races had intermarried with the Aryan immigrants to form a corrupt polity ruled by Jews.[53] But the Führer was not the only senior leader who dismissed the Americans. Both Admiral Erich Raeder, commander in chief of the Kriegsmarine, and Admiral Karl Dönitz, commander of U-boats, spent much of the summer of 1941 trying to persuade Hitler to declare war on the United States with arguments that such a declaration would bring Germany victory in the Battle of the Atlantic.[54] The result of such minimization of American

---

48 Part of the explanation for Hitler's success had to do with craven behavior of the other European nations, which refused to stand up to Germany's aggressive moves and which, to a surprising extent, subsidized the early buildup of the German war economy. In the case of the former, see Murray, *The Change in the European Balance of Power*, especially chaps. 6–9; for the latter, see Adam Tooze, *The Wages of Destruction: The Making and Breaking of the Nazi War Economy* (New York, 2006), esp. chaps. 2 and 3.

49 Ian Kershaw, *Hitler*, vol. 2, 1936–1945, *Nemesis* (New York, 2000), p. 300.

50 For Hitler's ideological view and its influence on his politics and strategy, see E. Jäckel, *Hitlers Weltanschauung* (Tubingen, 1969).

51 Alan Bullock, *Hitler: A Study in Tyranny* (New York, 1964), p. 652.

52 Why he did so is discussed in Williamson Murray and Allan R. Millett, *A War to Be Won: Fighting the Second World War* (Cambridge, 2000), pp. 135–136.

53 For Hitler's view of the United States, see Weinberg, *A World at Arms*, pp. 86–87.

54 See Holger H. Herwig, *The Politics of Frustration: The United States in German Naval Planning, 1889–1941* (New York, 1976), pp. 228–230.

potential was that when Hitler declared war on America, the navy was enthusiastic, while the army and *Luftwaffe*, admittedly confronting a disastrous situation on the Eastern Front, paid not the slightest attention.

If Hitler's ideology blinded him to the potential strengths of the Soviet Union and the United States throughout the war, Stalin's miscalculation in his grand strategy about the nature of Nazi Germany and the threat that it posed to the Soviet Union must be counted as one of the most disastrous strategic mistakes in history – one that entirely resulted from an analysis based on his Marxist ideology.[55] Basically, Stalin refused to take Hitler's ideology seriously, even though Mein Kampf and innumerable statements uttered throughout the 1930s made clear that one of the Führer's principal aims was to gain *Lebensraum* (living space) in the east. Instead, Stalin appears to have regarded Hitler and his Nazi regime as the stooges and puppets of German capitalism.

To the Soviet tyrant, the Nazi emphasis on living space and racial issues was a mere smokescreen to disguise the aims of those who were really running the Reich – the captains and plutocrats of German industry. Consequently, having gained control of central and western European industry, there was no reason for the masters of the Third Reich to desire further aggrandizement to the east, especially when the Soviets were flooding the German war economy with masses of raw materials and foodstuffs, the last goods train crossing into German-occupied Poland only two hours before the German invasion began.

Thus, sure that the Germans had no rational (from his point of view) reason for trashing the Nazi-Soviet Non-Aggression Pact that the two dictators had signed in August 1939, Stalin refused to believe the intelligence warnings that not only his agents but also those of the British provided. On the morning of 22 June 1941, as German troops were already driving deep into Soviet-held territory, Soviet foreign minister Vyacheslav Molotov plaintively complained to the German ambassador, "Surely, we have not deserved that."[56] And in every respect, Molotov was right: the Soviet Union had lived up to its agreement to the exact letter and more.

The one silver lining in the catastrophe that now almost overwhelmed the Soviet Union was that after the defeats of 1941, Stalin and his new crop of more competent military advisers were never again to underestimate

---

[55] It is now clear that in signing the Nazi-Soviet Non-Aggression Pact in August 1939, Stalin believed that the capitalist world would fight itself to exhaustion, as had been the case in World War I, and leave the Soviet Union and its Red Army to pick up the pieces. The collapse of France caught the Soviets by surprise, but Stalin and his henchmen never seemed to have caught on to the fact that they were in mortal danger. After all, even if Hitler were to decide to move east, his soldiers, largely consisting of German workers and peasants, would surely rebel.

[56] Gustav Hilger and Alfred Meyer, *The Incompatible Allies* (New York, 1953), p. 336.

the German danger or the toughness of their opponent. Thus, through-out the terrible struggle, as the Red Army forced the Wehrmacht back at immense cost to both sides, Soviet military strategy fit hand and glove with Stalin's grand strategy, which aimed to insure that Soviet power and influence reached as deep into the Balkans and as far west as possible.

Inherent in Stalin's grand strategy was a deep distrust of his allies, Britain and the United States, which their delay in creating a second front only served to exacerbate.[57] But Stalin's distrust rested on ideological grounds as well, and the Cold War that ensued was entirely the result of the Soviet resumption of its ideological struggle against the Western Powers once the problem of Nazi Germany had been removed.[58] Thus, Stalin's grand strategy guided military and political strategy in the conduct of operations on the Eastern Front toward preparing the Soviet Union for the eventual struggle that must ensue with the capitalist West.

What of the making of grand strategy by democratic governments? Here the record suggests that in times of crisis, such governments may possess an important advantage, namely, that the leaders of such governments must pay attention to political factors to a greater extent than is the case in tyrannies, especially the modern ideological variety, where the ruler, and thus his idiosyncratic *Weltanschauung*, is all seeing and all knowing. Perhaps it has also been the give-and-take of democratic and republican regimes that has provided the school for leaders with the kind of vision, guided by constructive political dialogue, that allows effective grand strategy to emerge.

The list of such leaders is indeed impressive: the two Pitts in Britain in the eighteenth century to deal with the great wars with France; George Washington in the American colonies during the War of Independence; Abraham Lincoln in the United States during the Civil War; Georges Clemenceau in France during World War I; and Winston Churchill in Britain and Franklin Roosevelt, Harry S. Truman, and Dwight Eisenhower in the United States during World War II and the Cold War.[59] One common thread unites these individuals: a sophisticated understanding of history and what a close reading of its lessons suggested about the "other."

---

[57] The lack of a second front was entirely the result of the actions of the Soviet Union, which had stood by in the spring of 1940 and watched the Western Front disappear. And then Molotov had passed along to the German ambassador his government's heartfelt congratulations for the *Wehrmacht*'s success on news of the French surrender.

[58] For a straightforward examination of the origins of the Cold War, see Colin Gray, "Mission Improbable, Fear Culture, and Interest: Peace Making, 1943–1949," in Murray and Lacey, *The Making of Peace.*

[59] For the crucial importance of political leadership that is capable of thinking in terms of the long-term rather than just in terms of military necessity in times of great crisis, see Eliot A. Cohen, *Supreme Command: Soldiers, Statesmen, and Leadership in Wartime* (New York, 2003).

Yet, there are two caveats to the preceding observation. Representative regimes do not appear quite so capable of pushing to the top great leaders who can think in terms of a grand strategy when the challenges and threats are not so obvious and the situation is not so desperate. The election of James Buchanan, perhaps the worst American president in American history, in 1856 is a case in point.

Moreover, democratic governments have, in the past, shown some penchant for demagogy. Thucydides describes Cleon, the chief villain in his view of the decline of strategic leadership in Athens after the death of Pericles, in the following terms: "He was remarkable among the Athenians for the violence of his character."[60] But Cleon was merely the harbinger of worse to follow. Thus, in the period after the death of Pericles, Athenian leaders proved incapable of developing a coherent grand strategy but instead floundered from one policy to another, without any clear strategic goal or direction to guide their decision making:

> His successors, who were more on a level with each other and each of whom aimed at occupying the first place, adapted methods of demagogy which resulted in their losing control over the actual conduct of affairs. Such a policy [or lack there of], in a great city with an empire to govern, naturally led to a number of mistakes, amongst which was the Sicilian expedition... because they were so busy with personal intrigues for securing the leadership.... In the end it was only because they had destroyed themselves by their internal strife that they were finally forced to surrender.[61]

But one should not forget that it has not only been ancient republics that have displayed a penchant for demagogy. After all, Senator Joseph McCarthy and a number of other similar unbridled demagogues dominated the American political scene for nearly five years, from the end of the 1940s to the beginning of the 1950s.

Whatever the deficiencies of democratic and republican regimes – and they certainly may fall victim to incompetence, an inability to understand the nature of the opponent, and a considerable degree of self-delusion – they have the advantage that failed leadership is almost always open to replacement. In other words, there are alternatives. The most obvious case in the twentieth century was the replacement of Neville Chamberlain by Winston Churchill on 10 May 1940, on the day, ironically, when the Wehrmacht came west. Churchill had been a harsh critic of the government's policy of appeasement throughout the 1930s but had then become a member of the

---

[60] Thucydides, *History of the Peloponnesian War*, p. 212.
[61] Ibid., p. 164.

cabinet as First Lord of the Admiralty on the outbreak of the conflict – an outbreak for which Chamberlain's policies had failed Britain.[62]

But matters hardly improved in the first months of the war, which *Weserübung*, the devastating invasion of Norway and Denmark by the Germans, underlined to everyone, especially since Chamberlain had stated only a few days before the invasion that "Hitler had missed the bus."[63] The result was that Chamberlain's government suffered a stunning reversal in the House of Commons, and Chamberlain finally laid down his office. He handed over to Churchill a disastrous strategic situation that was soon to lead to the complete collapse of Britain's position on the Continent. Nevertheless, Churchill would display not only leadership but a deep sense of grand strategy based on his deep knowledge of history, which would save Britain, if not the Empire.

The importance of individuals to the making of grand strategy

Perhaps the most important factor in the development and execution of successful grand strategy has been leadership at the top. We shall shortly examine two of the foremost examples of great leaders in the modern age, leaders who were able to articulate a grand strategic vision and then execute that vision through a successful conclusion.[64] But it is well to consider the words of Thucydides about the man whom he regarded as the greatest of grand strategists in his own time, namely, Themistocles, simply to underline that inherent ability may be the clearest explanation for success in the sphere of leadership and grand strategy:[65]

> Indeed, Themistocles was a man who showed an unmistakable natural genius; in this respect he was quite exceptional, and beyond all others deserves our admiration. Without studying a subject in advance or deliberating over it later, but using simply the intelligence that was his by nature, he had the power to reach the right conclusion in matters that have to be settled on the spur of the

[62] In this respect, see particularly Murray, *The Change in the European Balance of Power*, esp. chaps. 8–11.

[63] Admittedly, Churchill was the First Lord of the Admiralty, but from October 1939, he had argued that the Royal Navy should immediately mine the Norwegian Leeds, which not only would have made a German invasion of Norway impossible but would also have deprived the German war economy of its much-needed supply of Swedish iron ore, which, in the winter months, had to be transshipped through the northern Norwegian port of Narvik. For further discussion of these issues, see Murray, *The Change in the European Balance of Power*, pp. 341–347.

[64] One of the essays in this volume examines perhaps the greatest of all modern strategists: Winston Churchill.

[65] Themistocles was the great Athenian statesman who saved Athens and Greece from the massive Persian invasion of 480 BC.

moment and do not admit of long discussions, and in estimating what was likely
to happen, his forecasts of the future were always more reliable than those of
others.... To sum him up in a few words, it may be said that through force of
genius and by rapidity of action this man was supreme at doing precisely the
right thing at precisely the right moment.[66]

And the record of Themistocles is indeed impressive. After the Battle of
Marathon in 490 BC, he persuaded the Athenians to forego an immediate
windfall from their silver mines to build a fleet to meet the possibility of
a Persian invasion. He persuaded the Spartans and Athenians to form an
alliance when the invasion came. He persuaded the Greeks to stand firm at
Salamis, even after Athens had fallen to Xerxes. At that point, he tricked the
Persians into fighting a great sea battle, to their considerable disadvantage.
Then, after the defeat of the Persians, he persuaded the Athenians to build
the long walls to Piraeus, which protected Athens from any Spartan attack
and, finally, was instrumental in creating the great alliance system on which
the Athenian Empire was eventually based.

Yet, the ability to think in terms of grand strategy is not necessarily a
matter of simple natural genius, at least in the modern age. Two of the
most skilled practitioners of grand strategy in history practiced their art in
the nineteenth century. Through successful adaptation to the ever-changing
strategic and political frameworks they confronted, Abraham Lincoln and
Otto von Bismarck fundamentally changed the direction of history. Above
all, they were masterful politicians who understood the environment in
which they were operating far better than their contemporaries.

There were, of course, considerable differences in personality and background: the first was a quintessential American politician, the second an
autocrat, but the essential point is that both were students of history, and
both were extraordinarily good judges of their opponents as well as their
supporters. Both adapted their strategic framework to fit the overall political
and military realities of the conflicts in which their nations were involved.
And in both cases, their strategic framework shifted as they adapted their
assumptions to reality or what new possibilities opened up. We might also
point out that most of Lincoln's contemporaries tended to underestimate
his shrewdness, intelligence, and toughness throughout his lifetime, a reality
that he embraced because it allowed him that much more latitude in pursuit
of his goals.[67]

In Lincoln's case, his initial conception, when he assumed the position of
president of a union that had already broken apart, was that it would take
a few easy victories over Confederate armies to persuade the great majority

[66] Thucydides, *History of the Peloponnesian War*, p. 117.
[67] We might note that Eisenhower was also underestimated by most in both his military and
      political lives, a condition which he, too, accepted.

of Union sympathizers in the South to return to the old flag. By summer 1862, the realities of the battlefield and Southern resistance had altered his understanding of the political and strategic landscape sufficiently for him to issue the Emancipation Proclamation, which not only ended all hope of reconciliation but was a direct declaration of war on the South's economic and political system.[68] General Ulysses S. Grant, himself a skillful strategist and evaluator of the political scene, put the factors behind the gradual but radical adaptation of Union strategy to the realities of the war accurately in his memoirs:

> Up to the battle of Shiloh I as well as thousands of other citizens believed that the rebellion against the Government would collapse suddenly and soon, if a decisive victory could be gained over any of its armies. Donelson and Henry were such victories. An army of more than 21,000 men was captured and destroyed. Bowling Green, Columbus and Hickman, Kentucky, fell in consequence, and Clarkesville and Nashville, Tennessee, the last two with immense amounts of stores, also fell into our hands. The Tennessee and Cumberland Rivers, from their mouths to the head of navigation, were secured. But when confederate armies were collected which not only attempted to hold a line farther south, . . . but assumed the offensive and made such a gallant effort to regain what had been lost, I gave up all idea of saving the Union except by complete conquest.[69]

The result was what one historian has accurately described as the "hard war," best characterized by the signs left by Sherman's troops in their march to the sea, who derisively renamed every Southern village they passed through "Chimneyville" – an accurate description of what they left behind.[70]

Throughout his presidency, Lincoln maneuvered with great care through the shoals of the Constitution while at the same time insuring the continued loyalty of the War Democrats to the cause of Union. The latter factor led him to appoint a number of War Democrats to important commands during the war, most of whom, with the exception of "Black Jack" Logan, proved less than impressive in the field but who were essential to keeping the pro-war coalition together until the Confederacy collapsed. As Grant recognized in his memoirs, while these political generals made his life much more difficult as the commander in chief of the Union effort in 1864, they were essential to Lincoln's reelection that November against the pusillanimous former commander of the Army of the Potomac, George McClellan.

---

[68] For the evolution of Lincoln's strategy, the best places to start are James McPherson's works, in particular; *Battle Cry of Freedom: The Civil War Era* (Oxford, 2003) and *Tried by War: Abraham Lincoln as Commander-in-Chief* (New York, 2008).

[69] Ulysses S. Grant, *Personal Memoirs of U. S. Grant*, vol. 1 (New York, 1885), p. 368.

[70] Mark Grimsley, *The Hard Hand of War: Union Military Policy toward Southern Civilians, 1861–1865* (Cambridge, 2008).

Bismarck's strategic goals at the beginning of his tenure as Prussia's chancellor were straightforward: internally, to solve the constitutional impasse between his king and the *Reichstag*; and externally, to achieve for Prussia dominance over the north German states. To achieve the latter aim, he was perfectly willing to allow the Austrians to create a condominium over the south German states, which, after all, possessed a Roman Catholic population, one characterized by the values of *schlamperei*, in contrast to the good, solid values of Prussia's Protestants.[71]

But Austria refused to cooperate, and Bismarck found himself involved in an unwanted war, the Seven Weeks' War of 1866, which quickly resolved itself in the crushing defeat by Graf von Moltke's armies against those of Austria.[72] The quick peace that followed – quick enough to rob Prussia's generals of a parade down Vienna's thoroughfares, a decision for which they never forgave Bismarck – allowed Prussia to establish direct control over northern Germany and a loose alliance with the south German states now that Austria was excluded. Within a matter of months, he discovered that this settlement could only prove impermanent because the French were dabbling extensively in south German affairs, while all too many in Vienna regarded the settlement of 1866 as a matter that they could eventually overturn.

Bismarck then instigated the Franco-Prussian War, which solved the problem of the south German states by creating the Kaiser Reich, the new German state, which only the iron chancellor himself was capable of running.[73] Bismarck's external efforts appeared complete, and unlike all too many victors in war, he was content to leave the roulette table with his winnings. It is true that in 1875, fearing the extraordinarily quick recovery of the French, he briefly considered preventative war. But his own fears about the unintended and unpredictable consequences of another war as well as the clear warnings from the other major European powers that they would not stand aside led Bismarck to reconsider. For the next decade and a half, he was content to manipulate peacefully the European scene from Berlin, understanding that any further conflicts on which Germany might embark could entirely undo the political work he had created.

---

[71] For an outstanding account of Bismarck's political and strategic policies and how he adapted his strategy to the actual conditions he confronted, see Marcus Jones, "*Via victoribus*: Bismarck's Quest for Peace in the Franco Prussian War, 1870–1871," in Williamson Murray and Jim Lacey, eds., *The Making of Peace, Rulers, States, and the Aftermath of War* (Cambridge, 2009).

[72] For the most recent book on the Seven Weeks' War, see Geoffrey Wawro, *The Austro-Prussian War: Austria's War with Prussia and Italy in 1866* (Cambridge, 1996).

[73] For the origins and the political, strategic, and operational courses of the war, see Michael Howard's magisterial account, *The Franco-Prussian War* (New York, 1969). For an excellent study of the war itself, see Geoffrey Wawro, *The Franco-Prussian War: The German Conquest of France, 1870–1871* (Cambridge, 2003).

Lincoln and Bismarck displayed the ability to adapt their strategic and political assumptions and perceptions to the ever-changing strategic land-scape that confronted them.[74] What makes them extraordinary is how they adapted. Both understood history; both listened to, observed, and judged shrewdly those who worked for them; both understood the political and strategic environments as environments that never remain static but are always in flux; both intuitively understood that there were second- and third-order effects that resulted from their actions; and both were willing to accept and learn from their mistakes. And finally, Lincoln and Bismarck rarely, if ever, reinforced failure.

We might make a final note on the conduct of grand strategy and leader-ship: exceptional leadership and understanding by individuals like Lincoln, Bismarck, Churchill, Roosevelt, Truman, and Eisenhower is much the excep-tion. Instead, most leaders of states, as the introduction to this essay under-lined, have shown a penchant for superficial, immediate, short-term gains over the long-term interests of the state. Moreover, most have been unable to shake an emphasis on self-promotion. Others have either allowed the tide of day-to-day events to overwhelm them or have marched forward toward some distant goal without the willingness to recognize the changes in the international environment or the weaknesses of their own positions. Above all, most political and military leaders have been unwilling to recognize their opponents as skillful, adaptable enemies.

Alliances and grand strategy

In a dangerous and uncertain international environment, in which states attempt to maintain a modicum of security from external threats to their positions, alliances have proven to be of decisive importance. More often than not, they have involved a group of states threatened by a greater power; such alliances have inevitably involved the short-term interest of survival above all else. As Churchill commented in June 1941 when Hitler attacked the Soviet Union, he would have made a pact with the devil, if necessary, to defeat the Third Reich.

Not surprisingly, states that have aimed at the overthrow of the interna-tional order have proven far less skilled at maintaining alliances. In most cases, such states have regarded allies merely as appendages to their own concepts of grand strategy, available for military tasks and perhaps for eco-nomic support and to be provided at the victory banquet with a few scraps from the table. Moreover, such states often have used alliances as simply an expedient to extend their own reach. Thus, Napoleon allied his French Empire with Spain but then, in 1808, tossed the alliance aside and occupied

---

[74] And here it is worth emphasizing how rapid those changes were.

the country. Similarly, in 1807, Napoleon allied France with Czarist Russia at the Peace of Tilsit, but when the Russians proved unwilling to enforce their promised embargo on British goods, Napoleon invaded Russia. Like Hitler, Napoleon possessed a massive dose of megalomania in his makeup; and in the end, megalomaniacs are incapable of maintaining any coherent approach to allying themselves with other powers.

For Hitler, Fascist Italy appeared a welcome diplomatic ally in the mid-1930s.[75] But the attraction of Italy had more to do with Mussolini's adventures in Abyssinia, Spain, and Albania, which served to divert the attention of the Western Powers away from the steadily increasing and more serious threat that the Third Reich represented.[76] But Italy increasingly became a hindrance to Hitler's military strategy, while the Germans consistently ignored the interests of their ally in an off-handed and casual fashion.[77] Without informing his Italian allies, Hitler ordered large German forces into Rumania in early October 1940. An outraged Mussolini commented to his foreign minister, Galeazzo Ciano:

> Hitler always faces me with a *fait accompli*. This time I am going to pay him back with his own coin. He will find out from the papers that we have invaded Greece.[78]

The result was the ill-fated Italian invasion of Greece in late October that entirely upset the Balkans at a time when the Germans were planning for the invasion of the Soviet Union and which forced a major diversion of the Wehrmacht into Southeastern Europe in spring 1941.[79]

On the other side of the ledger is the impressive record formed by alliances of powers who group together against the threat of a hegemonic state. Interestingly, one finds the great island powers at the heart of most such coalitions over the past two centuries. At the heart of British, and even earlier, English, grand strategy has been the aim to prevent any major European power from

75 In terms of how the Nazi behavior toward their allies, including Italy, fell in with the abysmal performance of the Kaiser's Reich in how it treated its allies, especially Austria-Hungary throughout the First World War, see Herwig, *The First World War*.
76 For the foreign policy of the Third Reich during the 1930s, see Gerhard Weinberg, *The Foreign Policy of Hitler's Germany*, vol. 1, *Diplomatic Revolution in Europe, 1933–1936* (Chicago, 1970), and vol. 2, *Starting World War II, 1937–1939* (Chicago, 1980).
77 For the course of German-Italian relations, see particularly MacGregor Knox, *Mussolini Unleashed, 1939–1940: Politics and Strategy in Fascist Italy's Last War* (Cambridge, 1982).
78 Galeazzo Ciano, *The Ciano Diaries, 1939–1943*, ed. Hugh Gibson (New York, 1946), p. 300.
79 While historians have come to the conclusion that those operations against Greece and Yugoslavia did not upset Barbarossa's timetable – the Germans would not have been ready until mid-June anyway – it certainly did increase significantly the wear and tear on the panzer units which participated in the Balkan campaign and which then formed the bulk of the armored and motorized infantry divisions assigned to Army Group South.

dominating the Low Countries, but the subtext has been the aim of preventing any Continental power from creating a hegemony across the channel. How Britain handled those alliances of the willing represents a substantial portion of the explanation for how the British emerged as the dominant power in Europe for much of the nineteenth century.

Perhaps no incident better emphasizes the brilliance of Winston Churchill's great ancestor John Churchill, Duke of Marlborough, as a grand strategist, who understood the importance of allies, than that which occurred in early August 1702.[80] On that day, Churchill had maneuvered the combined Anglo-Dutch army into a position where the allies were ideally positioned to smash the French army of Marshal Louis François, duc de Boufflers, which was marching directly across their front. However, the Dutch deputies, who controlled whether their troops would fight, refused to authorize a battle and allowed the French to escape from their predicament. Three times over the course of that year, and twice in 1703, Marlborough caught the French in a similarly desperate situation, and each time, the Dutch refused to fight.

On all these occasions, the great duke refrained from exploding at Dutch pusillanimity, although on one occasion, he did force the deputies to watch as the French extracted their forces from their hopeless situation. What Marlborough understood was that Britain absolutely depended on its allies the Dutch, the Austrian Hapsburg monarchy, and the German states to fight the overwhelming power of Louis XIV's French monarchy. And for more than a decade, during which time he served as both the commander of allied armies and Britain's diplomatic representative to the governments of the Allied powers in the Hague, Vienna, and assorted other courts, Marlborough provided the grand strategic as well as military guidance that eventually humbled France. Despite his reputation as a great captain, Marlborough's greatness lay even more in the humility, tact, and understanding with which he handled his allies. While all the Allied powers desired to see the destruction of the French threat, they also possessed significantly different goals and wartime aims, and that was a reality of which Marlborough took full cognizance in his planning and conduct of Britain's grand strategy.

During the 250 years that followed Marlborough's political and military triumphs in the War of Spanish Succession, British leaders assembled great coalitions, first against the French and then against the Germans. William Pitt the elder guided the grand strategy and alliance system that destroyed France's worldwide empire in the Seven Years' War. William Pitt the younger

---

[80] Written in the 1930s, Winston Churchill's masterful four-volume history of the Duke of Marlborough's career still ranks not only as one of the greatest histories in English but also as one of the greatest pieces of English literature written in the twentieth century. Some historians, including this one, believe that it prepared Churchill to handle the great trials of alliance politics during the course of the Second World War.

and his successors cobbled together the great coalitions that finally brought Napoleon down in 1815. In 1914, Britain's statesmen held the allied cause together long enough to exhaust the Germans and bring the Americans in to help in finishing the job. And finally, the British under Churchill were the glue that held the prime minister's Grand Alliance together in the crucial years of 1941 and 1942.

In all these historical examples, we can see the grand strategy of the British – and eventually the Americans – at work. Yet, we should not allow ourselves to be deluded into believing that successful alliances work seamlessly and without friction.[81] That is simply not the way alliances work, given the reality that they consist of individuals from vastly different cultures, including military subcultures. Moreover, more often than not, those political and military leaders possess war aims, political conceptions, and worldviews that are inevitably in conflict with those of their allies. Thus, the making of any grand strategy within the context of an alliance, even under the most desperate conditions of war, demands compromise, the sacrifice of cherished assumptions, and a deep understanding of allied concerns, aims, and fears.

The sustaining of grand strategy

History does suggest that there have been periods during which great powers have been able to maintain dominance over the international scene for sustained periods of time. There are two such interesting case studies in the history of the West, but each reflects peculiarities in the international environment that are unlikely to recur in the future. The Roman Empire stands out as the clearest example of a combination of grand strategy and dominance that lasted for over two centuries, while the British Empire maintained its position of dominance over the world's oceans from 1763 to the beginning of the twentieth century. In both cases, it was not the failure of the grand strategy that brought about a decline but rather shifts in the external environment to which those two polities had to react.

In the case of the Romans, the establishment of the principate by Augustus ended a century of internal turmoil in the Republic. Nevertheless, the form of government possessed serious deficiencies not only in terms of the transfer of

---

[81] A number of books have been highly critical of the level of cooperation and personality clashes among British and American generals in the last years of World War II; not surprisingly, David Irving heads up the list with *The War between the Generals: Inside the Allied High Command* (London, 1993). In fact, such differences are inherent in the nature of military forces consisting of leaders from very different backgrounds. For the most realistic look at the relationships between the British and American military leaders and the development of Anglo-American grand strategy, see Mark A. Stoler, *Allies and Adversaries: The Joint Chiefs of Staff, the Grand Alliance, and U.S. Strategy in World War II* (Chapel Hill, NC, 2006).

power but also in that Augustus's new constitution was nothing more than a disguised tyranny, which, in the hands of weak or incompetent emperors, represented a threat to the empire's political stability.[82] On the other hand, Augustus created a grand strategic framework for dealing with the external environment that would last over two centuries. In doing so, he reduced the number of legions from the approximately 60 that he and his rival Antony had mobilized for their climactic battle to 28. Evidence that Augustus and his advisers had carefully calculated the balance between means (what the empire could afford) and ends (the defense of Rome's frontiers) is the fact that over the next 250 years, the number of legions varied between only 28 and 30.

Although written records have largely disappeared, and the historians of the time were more interested in the internal happenings of the various imperial courts, Roman actions over this period indicate a coherent grand strategy aimed at protecting the frontiers through a combination of secure borders; diplomacy; manipulation of potential threats on the other side of the border; and naked military force when necessary. Augustus himself pursued a ruthlessly aggressive policy that brought Rome to the Danube, cleaned up Spain and the Balkans, and created a strategic border resting on the Rhine and the Danube in Europe and in the deserts and mountains east of Syria.

Initially, Augustus and his advisers considered that the Elbe might be a more effective northern barrier, while also providing the empire greater depth, but the destruction of Varus's legions at the Battle of Teutobergwald ended that effort. Here one suspects that it was not so much that shocking defeat, the only significant one the Romans would suffer against the Germans over the course of the next three centuries, but rather the logistical difficulties of supplying an Elbe defense system that persuaded the Romans to settle for the Rhine border.[83]

Following Varus's defeat, the Romans turned to a grand strategy toward the northern barbarian tribes that mixed diplomacy, grants to friends of Rome, sophisticated policies that divided the tribes and turned them against each other, and ruthless military campaigns when they became a threat. Early in the second century AD, when the Dacians established a state in what largely comprised modern Transylvania that threatened the stability of the Danubian Valley, the Romans responded with all of the aforementioned approaches. When none of the more peaceful sufficed, the soldier-emperor

---

[82] For the political results of Augustus's reforms, see Ronald Syme, *The Roman Revolution* (Oxford, 2002).

[83] What exacerbated those logistic difficulties was that Gaul, with its relatively advanced agriculture, could relatively easily supply the Rhine defenses, but German agriculture was at best subsistence because the moldboard plow had yet to be invented.

Trajan responded with the ruthless campaign of subjugation that his great column in Rome commemorates.[84]

The continued success of the British Empire relied on a different grand strategy from the one developed by Augustus. Its origin lay in the actions of freebooters, adventurers, and those unwilling to accept the life doled out on the British Isles by a subsistence economy. It also had much to do with two military factors. On one hand, Britain's strategic position forced its politicians to focus on the establishment of an effective and, eventually, dominant navy. On the other, in the mid-seventeenth century, Europe went through a revolution in its military organizations. In effect, the reintroduction of Roman discipline allowed the European states to maximize the potential of technological changes occasioned and driven by the introduction of gunpowder in the fourteenth century.[85]

In the repeated contests that took place among the European states throughout the next one hundred years, the British enjoyed the important advantage that they could concentrate as their first priority on the control of the world's seas, while the priority of their opponents on the Continent had to be their armies. The Seven Years' War was decisive, for by that point, the British had developed an overwhelming tactical and operational superiority virtually everywhere on the world's oceans that was rarely challenged, and only once successfully: at the Battle of the Virginia Capes that sealed the fate of Lord Cornwallis's army at Yorktown.[86]

Britain's position as undisputed mistress of the world's oceans in the eighteenth century not only played to her mercantile dreams but also served to unleash the Industrial Revolution. The combination of the two provided the financial glue that held together the great coalition that finally destroyed Napoleon's empire. For the next century after the Congress of Vienna, Britain's naval, financial, and industrial superiority combined with skillful diplomacy to establish the *pax Britannica*. Admittedly, the British were much helped initially by the exhaustion of the Napoleonic Wars and then by the focus of the Continental powers on their immediate concerns.

Even the appearance of imperial Germany need not have disturbed Britain's position, except that its third ruler and a national mood bordering on megalomania created a threat not only to the stability of Europe but even

---

[84]   A cast of the column, made by the Italian government on the outbreak of World War II, is viewable in easy-to-follow sections in the Victoria and Albert Museum in London. Its depiction of the Roman Army on active campaign is thus far more accessible than is the case of the column in Rome.

[85]   For the symbiosis between technological developments and military developments, see particularly William H. McNeil, *The Pursuit of Power, Technology, Armed Force, and Society since* AD *1000* (Chicago, 1982).

[86]   For the rise of Britain to dominance over the world's oceans, see particularly Paul M. Kennedy, *The Rise and Fall of British Naval Mastery*, 2nd ed. (New York, 2006).

to Britain's naval superiority, which the British could not ignore.[87] From a period of general ambivalence and isolation from the day-to-day affairs of Europe, the British then found themselves swept up by the terrible challenge that the Germans represented. Churchill quite accurately described the fatal results of the events of summer 1914 in the following terms: "Events got on to certain lines, and no one could get them off again. Germany clanked obstinately, recklessly, awkwardly towards the crater and dragged us all in with her."[88] But at least Britain's strategic approach to the military, economic, and political problems raised by the war resulted in a situation where "we tried our best to steer our country through the gathering dangers of the armed peace without bringing her to war or others to war, and when these efforts failed, we drove through the tempest without bringing her to destruction."[89]

These two successful periods of grand strategy would not appear on the surface to be applicable to the situation the United States now confronts. In both cases, the two powers confronted an international environment that was relatively benign and in which their military power gave them enormous superiority over their potential opponents. For the Romans, the superiority of their legions was such that over the period of two and a half centuries, they suffered only one truly major defeat, one that convinced them that Germany was not worth the cost of conquest.[90] For the British, the Battle of Quiberon Bay, when Admiral Hawke drove his fleet over unchartered reefs to destroy the fleeing French fleet, ended French pretensions of being able to contest Europe's waters, much less the world's oceans, with the Royal Navy.

Despite the control that both powers exercised over their environments, they exercised caution, enlisted allies on the other side of the hill, and chose major war only as an exception. Both powers believed that they possessed a certain divine mission to rule, but that never prevented them from attempting to understand their adversaries. Both exercised considerable effort to insure that the means suited the ends toward which their strategic policies drove. On the sharp end of imperial concerns, the British were particularly good at developing an understanding of their opponents. *Going native* was something that applied to British experts on both sides of distant frontiers.

---

[87] The adaptation of British grand strategy to the Continental realities raised by Germany's new and aggressive behavior will be the theme of one of the chapters later in this volume.

[88] Winston S. Churchill, *The World Crisis* (Toronto, 1931), p. 6.

[89] Ibid.

[90] Even then, they were, on a number of occasions, to conquer Germany militarily in the sense that they crushed the opposition of the tribes, such as when Germanicus Caesar, nephew of the emperor Tiberius, executed a massive punitive expedition to avenge the defeat of the Teutobergwald and the destruction of Varus's three legions.

Yet, nothing in life is static. The environment changed drastically for the Romans in the third century, and the difficulties occasioned by barbarian invasions, the rise of a new and more dangerous Persian Empire in the east, deep internal dissensions within the army, and economic collapse brought the empire to its knees. The Roman Empire recovered in the late third century AD, but not in sufficient strength to survive the onslaught at the end of the fourth century. As Churchill suggested, the British Empire survived the First World War, but only with the help of its European allies and the United States. The terrible conflict that followed twenty years later did manage to break the empire, but at least, as we shall see in a later chapter, Britain and its constituent parts survived in bringing its enemies down to defeat, again with significant help from its allies.

CONCLUSION

Americans have proven that they, too, can follow a consistent and coherent grand strategy. As early as 1946, in his "long telegram," George Kennan had laid out the nature of the Soviet threat and the response that would best lead to a modification in the behavior of the Soviet Union. In the following year, he published his famous "Mr. X" article in *Foreign Affairs*, and in 1948, he commented:

> The Soviet leaders are prepared to recognize *situations*, if not arguments. If therefore, situations can be created in which it is clearly not to the advantage of their power to emphasize the elements of conflict in their relations with the outside world, then their actions, and even the tenor of their propaganda to their own people, *can* be modified.[91]

In retrospect, Kennan was correct; containment and the inherent internal contradictions of the Soviet economic system resulted in the collapse of the late 1980s. The end was not foreseeable, nor was the tortuous path that America's grand strategy followed between 1947 and 1989. Yet, despite the failures and the faulty choices made at times, the framework remained sufficiently in place to see the Cold War through to its astonishing end. And therein lies the rub, because the great advantage the United States possessed throughout the period of the Cold War was that the Soviets consistently provided more than sufficient proof they represented a moral and strategic threat to America and its allies.

At present, Americans confront the most confusing and uncertain strategic environment in their history.[92] It may also be the most dangerous to the

---

[91] Quoted in John Lewis Gaddis, *We Now Know: Rethinking Cold War History* (Oxford, 1997), p. 36.

[92] For the nature of that strategic environment, its ambiguities and uncertainties, its historical framework as well as the range of potential trouble spots that the United States and its

well-being of their republic, but only history will unravel the full extent of the potential threats the nation confronts at present.[93] The major problem is that the current environment provides no clear, certain threat such as those posed by Nazi Germany and the Soviet Union.

Yet, the past also suggests that the nation's survival may well depend on its political and military leaders establishing a strategic vision that moves beyond the immediate challenges that the present raises. As this essay has stressed, such a vision and framework of grand strategy must rest first and foremost on an understanding of the past. History provides a number of crucial elements necessary to craft realistic strategic expectations. It is not so much the direct lessons of the past that are germane to think about the future; rather it is the understanding of the ambiguities and uncertainties that political and military leaders have confronted in the past and will confront in the future that is the basis of any successful grand strategy. The problem for Americans in thinking about the issues involved in a grand strategy's development and execution is that there are no easy, simple solutions; there are no silver bullets.

[93] military forces might confront in the coming decades of the twenty-first century, see Joint Forces Command, "The Joint Operational Environment," Norfolk, VA, November 2008. Certainly the American Civil War and World War II posed threats to the continued existence of the United States. Whether any of the current or potential threats will represent such direct challenge to the nation is impossible to say at present.

2

The grand strategy of the *grand siècle*:
Learning from the wars of Louis XIV

JOHN A. LYNN II

When still young, Louis XIV received condescending advice that he ought
to pursue the best interests of the state. To this, he replied autocratically,
"L'état, c'est moi!"[1] Like one of the imposing state portraits of this impressive monarch by Charles Le Brun or Hyacinthe Rigaud, the response testified
to Louis's imperious nature. His reign encompassed most of the seventeenth
century, an era acclaimed in French memory as *le grand siècle*, the great
century, when France enjoyed cultural and political preeminence in Europe.
Reflecting the splendor of his epoch, Louis adopted the sun as his emblem,
a symbol linked in classic mythology with the god Apollo, who drove the
chariot of the sun across the sky to illuminate the world. Thus, Louis was
known as *le roi Soleil*, the Sun King. When constructing his magnificent
palace at Versailles to represent his personal grandeur, he emblazoned it
with images of his magnificence in the arts, governance, and war.

To draw lessons from such a monarch and such an era requires care; it was
another age, distant not only in years but also in principles. Yet, although
Louis XIV fell victim to errors of substance and style specific to him and his
times, others of his missteps still have relevance for those concerned in the
United States with the formation of grand strategy in the present and future.

The task of this chapter differs sharply from the author's previous works
on the wars of Louis XIV.[2] Those sought first and foremost to describe

---

[1] "The state, it is I!" This is supposed to have happened when a sixteen-year-old Louis faced
down the parlement of Paris in April 1655. Although widely believed, the story may well be
apocryphal, but the tale survives because it encapsulates the political personality of Louis
XIV.

[2] Along with a number of articles and chapters, the author's most extensive publications on
warfare in the age of Louis XIV include the following books: *Giant of the Grand Siècle:
The French Army, 1610–1715* (Cambridge, 1997); *The Wars of Louis XIV, 1667–1714*
(London, 1999); *The French Wars 1667–1714: The Sun King at War* (Oxford, 2002),

early modern military practices and institutions for their own sake, with reverence for the past's integrity. Although one can draw lessons from such an approach, its primary object is to get the history right: to demonstrate its unique and unrepeatable character. This essay draws extensively from the author's earlier works. However, the goal here is different: it is to filter the historical record to uncover what is most useful, to stress the parallels between past and present-day challenges.

Fundamentally, Louis suffered from his own arrogance, which, though hardly surprising in a seventeenth century autocrat, can be just as typical of those who lead powerful modern states. Louis abandoned a strategy based on alliances and international agreements for one based on unilateral action that increasingly isolated France. Committed to unilateralism, he tried to make his kingdom invulnerable by maintaining large military forces and building a band of the most technologically advanced fortifications to seal his borders. However, this quest for absolute security further alienated his neighbors and made war all the more probable. Louis seemed incapable of realizing how his actions were perceived; in today's terminology, he lost control of the narrative and allowed his enemies to portray him as they saw him. He might well have forestalled war by greater transparency, but he never adequately explained his defensive intentions to a suspicious Europe. Ultimately, his grand strategy caused him to overstretch the resources of France, which were insufficient to stand against all Europe, and the wars of the Sun King bankrupted the state.

Because it would be unrealistic to expect most readers, even those interested in history, to be familiar with the complex course of Louis's reign, this chapter will begin by surveying his wars. After this, it will examine themes of unilateralism, security, narrative, transparency, and overstretch. The catalog of warnings presented here is important for modern strategic thought, but one must also recognize that in terms of territorial expansion and dynastic gains, Louis knew some lasting success. For this, the chapter must finish by giving the Sun King his due. Louis changed during the long course of his life. In contrast to the arrogant assertion of his youth, Louis reportedly stated on his deathbed, "I go, but the state will always remain."

THE WARS OF LOUIS XIV

During the *grand siècle*, statesmen regarded war as a natural state of affairs, not the aberration that many consider it today. This is hardly surprising,

and *Women, Armies, and Warfare in Early Modern Europe* (Cambridge, 2008). Along with these lengthy works, one chapter will serve as a particularly important source here: John A. Lynn II, "International Rivalry and Warfare, 1700–1815," in T. C. W. Blanning, ed., *The Short Oxford History of Europe: Eighteenth-Century Europe* (Oxford, 2000), pp. 178–217.

given the prevalence of conflict: France was at war during 51 of Louis's 77 years of life. Born in 1638, Louis XIV became king at the death of his father, Louis XIII, in 1643. Because the young Louis assumed the throne as a mere boy, his mother, Anne of Austria, and the first minister, Cardinal Jules Mazarin, actually managed state affairs. Only when Mazarin, who was Louis's mentor in affairs of state, died in 1661 did the then 22-year-old king actually assume full authority. Between that point and his own passing in 1715, Louis XIV conducted five declared wars. Two of these conflicts were relatively minor – the War of Devolution (1667–1668) and the War of the Reunions (1683–1684) – but three reached major proportions – the Dutch War (1672–1678), the Nine Years' War (1688–1697), and the War of the Spanish Succession (1701–1714). Beyond these struggles, Louis also employed military force in Europe and North Africa at times when France was technically at peace.

When Louis assumed full power in 1661, France had just emerged from a period of international and civil war. It had found itself at war with Spain since the early sixteenth century. Not only a great colonial power, Spain had also used its riches to assert itself as the most powerful nation-state in Europe. It had become a globe-spanning colossus led by the Hapsburg monarchs: Charles V, who ruled as king of Spain and Holy Roman Emperor, and Philip II, who launched the Armada against Elizabeth I. In a series of wars during the first half of the sixteenth century, Spain defeated French designs in Italy, and when France sank into a series of religious civil wars between 1562 and 1598, Spain intervened by backing the extreme Roman Catholic faction.

The climax of the long struggle between France and Spain came in the mid-seventeenth century, and it ended with French triumph. The Thirty Years' War broke out in Germany in 1618, pitting shifting alliances of Protestant German princes, Scandinavian states, and the Dutch against the Austrian Hapsburgs and their Catholic German allies. Spain, still a titan when the war broke out, supported the Austrian Hapsburgs and defended Spanish interests in the Low Countries. France, although Catholic, backed the Protestant side in order to oppose Spain and assert French influence along her eastern frontier. Initially, Louis XIII and his famous first minister, Cardinal Richelieu, played their hand, not by openly entering the war, but instead by subsidizing Protestant participants such as the Swedish warrior-king Gustavus Adolphus. However, after the Swedes suffered a catastrophic defeat in 1634, Louis XIII had to enter the conflict outright in 1635, beginning 25 years of constant warfare between France and Spain. Although the Thirty Years' War ended in Germany in 1648 with the treaties of Westphalia, the fighting between France and Spain continued. In France, this clash was further complicated by the rebellion of the Fronde (1648–1653), which began as a revolt against the wartime financial levies imposed by the monarchy.

In 1659, the Peace of the Pyrenees that ended the long war with Spain registered that state's decline. In this treaty, the Spanish king, Philip IV, surrendered minor territory and gave his daughter María Teresa in marriage to Louis XIV. When Marie Thérèse became queen of France, she formally renounced her claim to any Spanish inheritance. But because this act was contingent on the payment of a large dowry which was never forthcoming, she brought with her to the altar a claim on Spanish lands should the male line of the Spanish Hapsburgs falter, which it soon did.

After a century of internal discord, the elites of France seemed ready to fall in behind the leadership of the young Louis XIV. The French wished for a great monarch, and they got one. Once firmly in charge, Louis sought to make his mark, to establish his glory. In 1665, Philip IV died and was succeeded by the sickly and deformed boy Carlos II, half brother of Marie Thérèse. Anxious to prove himself and lusting after territory in the Spanish Netherlands, Louis advanced a tortured interpretation of his wife's right of inheritance. The Sun King argued that she had a claim to territory in the Spanish Netherlands, based on a relatively obscure law from those provinces, holding that the daughter from a first marriage retained rights to inherit goods and property over a son of a second marriage – that property "devolved" on the earlier child. In 1667, Louis launched an army into the Spanish Netherlands to enforce his wife's "rights," beginning the War of Devolution. Uneasy about having a powerful and aggressive France on their southern border, the Dutch moved to limit French gains by forming the Triple Alliance with England and Sweden. These allies informed Louis that he could retain what he had already taken, most notably the city of Lille, but that he must halt his advance or they would enter the war on the Spanish side. Unprepared for a larger war, Louis reluctantly and resentfully concluded peace in 1668.

For Louis, the War of Devolution ended in frustration, not glory. The culprits were the Dutch, who, after receiving generations of French support in their struggles against the Spanish, had turned against their erstwhile French benefactors. Louis resolved on revenge while gaining the lands he coveted. He isolated the Dutch diplomatically by securing an alliance with Charles II of England and even secured the neutrality of the Hapsburg emperor Leopold I. Louis did not plan to conquer Dutch territory but simply to teach the Dutch a lesson and make them step aside so that he could pursue his goals in the Spanish Netherlands.

The initial attack by French forces in 1672 was as impressive a military campaign as Louis ever mounted. Nevertheless, while his troops soon occupied parts of the Netherlands, the Dutch staunchly refused to accept

Louis's terms and, instead, flooded their lands to stymie the French. In 1674 the French withdrew from Dutch territory in frustration. That same year the English pulled out of the war, while Spain, Brandenburg, and the Holy Roman Emperor joined the Dutch. Louis now faced the first in a series of powerful coalitions assembled by the Dutch leader William III of Orange (1650–1702). Yet, if the initial grand strategy of the Dutch War went awry, Louis XIV still had won impressive gains. A French army took the free county of Burgundy, Franche-Comté, for Louis, and the Treaty of Nijmegen awarded it to France. Further territory and towns along the border of France and the Spanish Netherlands also went to Louis. In addition, the French would occupy the province of Lorraine, which they had seized in 1670, until 1697.

Louis interpreted the Dutch War as achieving the glory he so desired; he would henceforth be known as Louis the Great. The closing years of the Dutch War also brought an important shift in French strategy. During 1675, two new advisors rose to prominence in French councils of war: the efficient but brutal minister of war the Marquis de Louvois and the incomparable master of fortress warfare Sébastien le Prestre de Vauban. Both were ultimately more interested in defense than conquest, and with Louis pleased by his success along his northern border and in Franche-Comté, the king's definition of glory shifted from conquest to preserving his gains.

But there was a catch. Vauban counseled the king to safeguard his lands by creating a strong fortified frontier. Along the border with the Spanish Netherlands, this entailed creating a double line of mutually supporting fortresses known to history as the *pré carré*, or "dueling ground." Running south from this, Louis intended to rationalize his borders to create a tougher shell. He could have done so either by pulling back from exposed salients or by pushing forward to straighten out his frontiers. Louis being Louis, pulling back was not in his nature, so he pushed forward. Diplomatic casuistry and the French law courts papered over these land grabs, known as the Reunions. Louis particularly focused on the Rhine border of Alsace, which had been violated by enemy armies during the Dutch War. Therefore, he ordered his troops to seize Strasbourg without warning in 1681. His other prominent target was the fortress city of Luxembourg, which Vauban thought vital to the defense of France. Luxembourg was a Spanish possession that the outraged Carlos II sought to retain. However, with Louis intent on having it, the result was the brief War of the Reunions, declared by Spain in October 1683. While Carlos received Dutch support, the Dutch were less adamant than the Spanish and soon helped engineer a peace that transferred Luxembourg to France. Yet, this Truce of Ratisbon (1684) did not award the fruits of the Reunions to Louis permanently but rather simply acceded to his gains for a period of 20 years. Although the Truce of Ratisbon marked the high water of Louis's success, its impermanence troubled him.

Perhaps emboldened by his use of force against foreign enemies, Louis now used violence against his own Protestant minority, the Huguenots. In 1685, determined to convert all French Christians to the Catholic faith, he annulled the 1598 Edict of Nantes that had granted toleration to the Huguenots. Alarmed both by Louis's Reunions and by his attacks on his own Protestant community, many of his German neighbors joined in the anti-French League of Augsburg in 1686.

Worried by the League and by the growing power of the Austrian Hapsburgs, Louis issued an ultimatum demanding that the Truce of Ratisbon be converted into a permanent peace by 1 April 1687. Finally, in September 1688, Louis brought on a general war when he succumbed to what historian Paul Sonnino has labeled his "fatal predilection for the preemptive strike"[3] by besieging the fortress of Philippsburg. Louis feared that he had not yet secured the Rhine frontier of Alsace, but the taking of Philippsburg would effectively seal it. Seeing this seizure as a "last campaign," a final effort to create impenetrable frontiers, Louis expected the Germans to acquiesce to his "reasonable" goals. Late that month, French troops moved against the fortress, which capitulated at the end of October. But instead of conceding the loss, German states took the field to oppose France. Louis's minister of war, Louvois, had assured his master that the resort to force against Philippsburg would result in a quick victory, but what was supposed to be a few months' blitz turned into the Nine Years' War.[4]

Caught off guard by the German response, Louis had to buy time to counter the unexpected threat he now faced. Without sufficient troops immediately available to wage a conventional campaign, he ordered his troops to devastate the Palatinate in 1688 and 1689 so that it could provide neither food nor quarters for attacking armies. Louvois directed the time-consuming task of expanding the French army to a wartime footing, building up existing units and creating new squadrons, battalions, and regiments. Meanwhile, with the French preoccupied along the Rhine, William III accepted the crown of England, landing at Torbay in November. Louis's implacable Dutch foe thus became the king of England in consort with his queen, Mary. An able diplomat, William III spearheaded a Grand Alliance of England, the Dutch Netherlands, the Holy Roman Empire, Spain, and Savoy, in addition to lesser German states.

As a result of Louis's assertive unilateral course of action over the previous decade, France stood alone. Faced by a broad coalition capable of mustering large total forces, Louis had to match and surpass them to have

[3] Paul Sonnino, "The Origins of Louis XIV's Wars," in Jeremy Black, ed., *The Origins of War in Early Modern Europe* (Edinburgh, 1987), p. 122.

[4] The Nine Years' War goes by other names, notably, the War of the League of Augsburg or the War of the Grand Alliance. This author's mentor, Andrew Lossky, always insisted on the "Nine Years' War," and in respect for him, this essay employs this title.

any hope of victory. Thus, his army swelled to unprecedented proportions, achieving its peak size in 1693. His navy also increased. Nevertheless, he ultimately had to sacrifice his navy in order to concentrate his resources on sustaining the largest army in Europe. Accordingly, after 1694 he conceded the ocean to the English and the Dutch, limiting French naval efforts on the high seas to commerce raiding. On land, Louis benefited from the services of Vauban, an absolute master of siege warfare, and François-Henri de Montmorency, Duke of Luxembourg, a highly talented army commander. As a result, Louis's armies were usually successful in sieges and virtually invincible in battle.

However, victory on campaign did not produce success at the negotiating table. Creating and maintaining his huge army overstretched the resources of France, and this grim picture was only made worse by a famine that struck France during the years 1693 and 1694. Military victory lost its influence when faced with attrition, and Louis sought peace even at the price of territorial concession. The Treaty of Ryswick, signed in fall 1697, cost the French Luxembourg and some additional gains of the Reunions; it also forced Louis to give up Briesach and his other holdings on the right bank of the Rhine, thus establishing the Rhine boundary that would remain intact until the French Revolution. Lorraine went back to its duke, although French troops were allowed right of passage through the province.

Louis felt chastised by the Nine Years' War; he had neither wanted it nor won it, at least in the sense of new territorial conquest. Moreover, the war had ruined French finances and, along with famine, brought the economy to its knees. Louis seemed to take it as a judgment of God, and he was willing to maintain the peace as a penitent. But fate confronted him with a new and unavoidable crisis.

The problem of the succession to the Spanish throne had hung over Europe since the accession of Carlos II, but after the Nine Years' War, it took precedence over all other international issues. Few had expected the malformed young king to survive for long, but he surprised Europe by lasting through his thirties. The sickly and impotent king sired no progeny, and the Bourbons and the Austrian Hapsburgs possessed the best claims to inherit the Spanish throne and lands.

Louis sincerely wished to avoid another war and so agreed to a partition treaty in 1698 that would award only Naples, Sicily, and parts of Tuscany to the Grand Dauphin, who was both son and grandson of Spanish princesses. The Hapsburg claimant, Archduke Charles, second son of Emperor Leopold I (1658–1705), would receive Milan. All the rest was to go to a weaker candidate, the son of the Elector of Bavaria, because this would avoid a Bourbon-Hapsburg war. Unfortunately, the Bavarian prince died the next year, so Louis sought another partition treaty. Here, Louis showed a moderation that seems inconsistent with his well-known pride. He willingly conceded Spain, the Spanish Netherlands, and the Indies to Charles, reserving only the Italian holdings, now including Milan, for the Grand Dauphin. William III agreed to this second partition treaty, but the emperor and Charles would not accept it, wanting everything for Charles. That is how it stood when Carlos II died on 1 November 1700.

Carlos refused to countenance any partition and dictated a will that offered the Spanish crown with all its lands to Louis's grandson, Philip of Anjou, but if Philip refused this bequest, the inheritance would go in its entirety to Archduke Charles. Carlos's offer to Philip was quite clever. Had territory gone to the Grand Dauphin, it would eventually have been incorporated into France when he or an immediate successor became king, so France would have gained. But Philip of Anjou was the second son of the Grand Dauphin and, in 1700, quite removed from any possibility of becoming king of France. Therefore, in accepting the crown for Philip, Louis XIV would advance the interests of the Bourbon dynasty but not those of France, and Spain would remain independent.

Louis thus faced an odd choice. On one hand, should he accept the will of Carlos II, he would necessarily have to fight the Austrian Hapsburgs, who would not acquiesce to being frozen out of Spain's disposition. If Louis handled the resulting conflict with finesse, the fighting could be limited; even William III would probably admit that the threat of French domination was minimal because no lands would go to France. On the other hand, if Louis turned down the will and insisted on the second partition treaty, he would still have to fight the Austrians, who would surely accept the offer to Charles. In such a fight, the Austrians would enjoy the added advantage of Spanish resources. By accepting the will, as he did, Louis actually opted for the surer path to peace, although the least territorial gains for France, even if it acquired a throne for the Bourbon family. So Philip of Anjou became Philip V of Spain.

At this point, however, Louis committed a series of arrogant acts that unnecessarily created a new alliance against him. His relatively penitent desire to avoid war after 1697 turned into an arrogant disregard for European opinion. Louis refused formally to guarantee that Philip would not succeed to the French throne, as remote as that possibility seemed to be. He distressed the Dutch by sending French troops to occupy the barrier fortresses along the northern border of the Spanish Netherlands, which were supposed to be garrisoned by the Dutch as security against French attack. This infuriated William. Then, Louis alarmed English merchants by securing the *asiento*, the exclusive right to supply slaves to the Spanish colonies, for French traders. Last, he recognized the son of the deposed James II as the rightful king of England when James II died. This represented a direct attack

on the sovereignty of William and Mary. Louis was at least guilty of being
foolishly oblivious to the way in which his actions would be interpreted. The
English and the Dutch, both led by William, now sided with the Hapsburg
emperor, ensuring another general European war.

In the larger sense, Louis had been backed into a situation that he had
done everything he could to avoid through the partition treaties. But then,
through lesser acts, he misplayed his hand badly, looking arrogant and
aggressive. The result was 13 years of war (1701–1714) that almost completely bankrupted France.

During his earlier wars, the French Army had done well; Louis was accustomed to victory. However, in this conflict, his forces suffered a number
of disastrous defeats at the hands of a pair of superb allied commanders,
the Duke of Marlborough and Eugene of Savoy. One can argue that Marlborough was the finest captain ever to lead a British army, on one hand,
and Eugene the finest to lead an Austrians army on the other. In 1704, they
joined to crush a Franco-Bavarian army at Blenheim. Other French defeats
followed: Ramillies and Turin (1706) and Oudenarde (1708). The tale of
disaster was made all the worse by a horrendous famine that struck over the
winter of 1709–1710. Faced by this woe, Louis sought peace terms in spring
1709, but the allies rapaciously escalated their demands. Surprisingly, Louis
agreed to most of them but refused the allied demand that he drive his own
grandson from the Spanish throne. Louis resolved to continue the fight, even
issuing a formal explanation of his decision to his subjects.

The fortunes of war then turned more in favor of the French. Louis finally
appointed a general of considerable talent to command in the key theater of
the war, the Spanish Netherlands. Marshal Claude Louis Hector de Villars
proved able to deal with Marlborough and Eugene at Malplaquet in 1709
and, ultimately, to defeat Eugene at Denain in 1712. French armies in Spain
under Marshals Berwick and Vendôme also scored victories. Meanwhile,
Archduke Charles's father, Leopold I, died in 1705, and then his elder
brother, Joseph I, passed away in 1711, putting Charles on the imperial
throne as Charles VI.

This immediately cooled the ardor of the British for the war. They had
little interest in re-creating the empire of Charles V, who was both Holy
Roman Emperor and king of Spain, so the cry of "No peace without Spain!"
died down. Queen Anne's representatives signed a preliminary agreement
with the French in October 1711, and in May 1712, she ordered Marlborough's successor, Ormonde, to avoid fighting the French. The treaties that
ended the war, Utrecht (1713) and Rastatt and Baden (1714), acknowledged
Philip V as king of Spain. Louis had achieved his dynastic goals but at a terrible price. The great king died the next year. One of his last comments, that
"he had loved war too well," had proven all too true.

THE UNIQUE CHARACTER OF THE *GRAND SIÈCLE*

The *grand siècle* was an age unlike our own, and the motives that underlay the grand strategy of Louis XIV were those that inspired early modern European monarchs. They are difficult to translate directly into terms that are obviously relevant to current U.S. international relations.

Above all, the Sun King was much concerned with his personal *gloire*, referring to it repeatedly. "Glory" is a dated term; in fact, there is something vainglorious and melodramatic about it today. But a more accurate translation of *gloire* is "reputation," and even today, modern statesmen hardly regard national reputation as insignificant. In the realm of foreign policy, Louis believed, "reputation is often more effective than the most powerful armies. All conquerors have gained more by reputation than by the sword." The great difference between Louis's *gloire* and modern national reputation is that the nation's glory was associated inseparably with the person of the king. Yes, there are modern rulers who also have pursued a cult of personality, but few countries have had such heads of state since Hitler and Stalin, and even these claimed to be representing a people, not simply their own interests.

In contrast, the Sun King unashamedly sought his individual glory and that of the Bourbon dynasty. Bloodlines and dynasty were key factors in a monarch's policy. In other words, the assertion of claims by inheritance and the advancement of individuals within the royal family were matters of importance, even if those interests were quite separate from those of the state. Louis himself claimed that he had rights to Spanish territory because he was the son and the husband of Spanish princesses and he fought the War of Devolution and the Dutch War to establish his glory by seizing towns and territory in the Spanish Netherlands on his northern border. His gains in these wars became part of the French state. However, he later fought the War of the Spanish Succession to enforce not his but rather his grandson's claims to the Spanish crown, even though this did not increase the lands of the French monarchy. These claims were based on carefully constructed bloodlines. Louis XIV and his wife, the infanta Marie Thérèse, were cousins whose nearly identical genealogies led back to Philip III and Philip IV of Spain.[5] The personal nature of Louis's power and his concern for dynasty contrast sharply with the modern executive organization of the U.S. government.

Another contrast lay in the importance of public opinion. Imperious Louis XIV, while sensitive to public opinion to a degree, did not make his decisions

---

[5]   Louis XIV and Marie Thérèse were cousins on both their mother's and father's sides; thus, beyond their parents, the genealogies were identical.

based on pleasing his subjects, nor did he brook political dissent. The most enduring opposition to the king's policies was expressed in terms of a puritanical Catholic theology by followers of Cornelius Jansen. Louis ultimately appealed to the papacy to silence this opposition in 1713. Political criticism of the Sun King was not to be tolerated, and when the royal tutor Archbishop François Fénelon cast doubt on the divine sanction of royal authority, he was banished from court and exiled to his bishopric at Cambrai.[6]

Louis did present his case before the public at times: in 1672, he issued a manifesto announcing his motives for war; on 24 September 1688, he published "Mémoire des raisons" prior to his attack on Philippsburg; and most important, in 1709, he circulated a letter explaining why he could not accept the terms offered by the allies and thus had to continue the war. Yet he made his decisions on the basis of his own interests and values, not in regard to popular support. As Fénelon commented in August 1710, "Our great misfortune comes from the fact that to date the war has been only the affair of the king, who is ruined and discredited."[7]

The Sun King regarded his political authority as the will of God; that is, the king was the elect of God and to be judged only by Him, not by the king's subjects. Ultimately, an all-powerful God controlled the mysteries of birth and thus the succession of rulers. The implications of this divine right of kings for Louis's foreign relations and the prosecution of wars exaggerated two characteristics of many rulers, from monarchs to presidents: first, that holding power is evidence that one has been accorded a special mission, and second, that success is a judgment that not only validates past actions but justifies continuing on that course even further. For a modern politician, this usually reflects confidence that one is correct; for Louis, it was a sign of divine sanction. Not to extend success in the former case may be an error; in the latter, it bordered on sin.

DEFINING THE FAILURE AND SUCCESS OF LOUIS XIV

Louis XIV enjoyed the longest reign of any European monarch in history, and as such, it would be surprising if his grand strategy had not evolved through different phases during the 72 years he occupied the throne. A similar span of years placed against a timeline of U.S. history would reach back to the Great Depression and carry through World War II, the entire Cold War, and 18 years of the post-Cold War era, including the Gulf War of 1991, 9/11, and the Iraq War of 2003. In fact, Louis's strategy

---

[6]   For a recent discussion of Fénelon and his criticism of Louis, see David A. Bell, *The First Total War: Napoleon's Europe and the Birth of Warfare as We Know It* (Boston, 2008), pp. 54–66.

[7]   Letter from Fénelon to the duke of Chevreuse, 4 August 1710, in Fénelon, *Lettre à Louis XIV* (Neuchâtel, 1961), p. 129.

evolved, and his wars varied in their proportions of failure and success. Fortune may well have turned on Louis during his last two wars, which brought France to the brink of financial collapse. However, even these two conflicts differed with each other in cause and onset. In the first, Louis brought on the war by his own aggression, albeit in the name of defense, while in the second, he was blameless in accepting the will of Carlos II, although he then committed a series of headstrong actions that brought together a mighty coalition against him.

Part of the idea that Louis "failed" derives from a misconception of his goals. He was not trying to subordinate all Europe to France in some grand imperial scheme. The best argument for Louis's seeking to dominate Europe applies to his handling of the crisis of 1682–1683, when he refused to support the Austrian Hapsburgs as the Ottoman Turks attacked Vienna. He turned a deaf ear to Leopold I's appeals to send troops, tried to dissuade the Poles from riding to the relief of Vienna, and actually encouraged the Turks. Had the Turks succeeded in taking Vienna and moved west, Louis XIV could have assumed the role of Europe's last best hope. But one can argue that Louis was playing a common gambit in using the Turks to counterbalance the Austrian Hapsburgs. This tactic went back to the French king Francois I (1515–1547). In the event, a combined German and Polish force drove the Turks from Vienna, and the moment passed. In the long run, Louis believed that France deserved preeminence within Europe, but dominance over Europe was not a fundamental aim of his policy.

Another more convincing argument that Louis failed follows from the horrendous economic and human cost of his wars. At the end of his reign, the French treasury was empty, the state confronted massive debt, and much of the economy was in tatters. Soon after Louis's death in 1715, the royal government went through a peculiarly French form of bankruptcy. By relying on fiscal expedients rather than attacking the fundamental problem of aristocratic tax privileges and exemptions, Louis may have doomed his successors to the French Revolution. One can only surmise the suffering imposed by his wars within France and outside its borders. One historian estimates that battle deaths among all participants in the wars of Louis XIV reached 2,200,000, with 1,251,000 falling during the War of the Spanish Succession alone.[8] Were the adjustments along the French frontier worth such a butcher's bill?

Should we take another tack and judge Louis's wars by how closely they achieved his grand strategic goals, we meet combinations of success in failure and failure in success. The original purpose of the Dutch War was to chastise

---

[8]   Jack Levy, *War in the Modern Great Power System, 1495–1975* (Lexington, KY, 1983), p. 90.

the Dutch for frustrating Louis's ambitions in the Spanish Netherlands and force the Dutch to give him a free hand there. In that Louis failed. However, he was still able to add Franche-Comté and a number of fortress towns along his northern border, including Aire, Bouchain, Cambrai, Condé, St. Omer, Valenciennes, and Ypres. Louis counted this enough of a victory to celebrate it by making it the theme for the decoration of the great Hall of Mirrors, the central space of his palace at Versailles. He had achieved success in failure. At the other end of the spectrum, Louis engaged in the War of the Spanish Succession primarily to maintain his grandson on the Spanish throne, and Philip V was, indeed, recognized by Europe as the rightful king of Spain at the end of the fighting. But this was achieved by imposing an unacceptably high cost on France. One might accurately term the war a disaster. Here, Louis suffered failure in success.

After the death of the Sun King, France was not as strong relative to the rest of Europe as it had been in 1661, but this was not simply because France was weaker; it was also because other European states had become noticeably stronger. The Austrian Hapsburgs gained much, including Hungary, from the decline of the Ottoman Turks after their defeat at Vienna. England emerged as the world's greatest naval power during the Nine Years' War and continued to rule the waves after the War of the Spanish Succession. In relative terms, France fell back to the status of one of Europe's great powers rather than being *the* great power of Europe. This decline was not the result simply of Louis's mistakes; it also occurred because of broader developments over which Louis had little control. When he took the reins of power in 1661, Spain had run her course, and the soon-to-be great powers of the Austrian Hapsburgs and England/Britain had yet to emerge at full strength. Soon, another two great powers appeared on the chessboard – Russia and Prussia – creating the balance-of-power mathematics that governed international relations in the eighteenth century and on into the nineteenth.

Seen in a broader context, there was a kind of inevitability to France's relative decline, but that does not relieve Louis and his policies of responsibility. Louis misplayed his hand, which resulted in a grand strategy that produced wars that he need not have fought, stretched French resources to the breaking point, and brought untold suffering and death to great numbers of people. Louis's real failure was not that France lost its hegemony or that he was deprived of territorial and dynastic success but rather that he paid far too great a price for the gains he did win and maintain. Limiting his European wars could have spared his finances, allowed a more rational course of reform within France, given France greater colonial success through investment in the navy, and benefited the economy and well-being of his people.

SHORTCOMINGS IN THE GRAND STRATEGY
OF LOUIS XIV

The strategic mistakes committed by Louis XIV included his particular thirst for glory, as he defined it, his penchant for a unilateral foreign policy, his quest for absolute security, and his tendency to allow arrogance to define the substance and style of his policy. These were linked to his inability later in life to forsake the image he had created for himself as a younger and more aggressive king. The perception of Louis as an insatiable conqueror inspired his enemies to forge great alliances to oppose his plans. Louis could face such coalitions only by committing himself to policies that stretched the burdens of warfare beyond what France could support.

The pursuit of glory

To modern eyes, Louis's unabashed thirst for glory would seem most damning. But the *grand siècle* expected grandeur, and the Sun King delivered. Louis was by no means exceptional in his desire for *gloire*; it was an age in which the powerful and privileged cared much for this intangible. The Frondeur, Cardinal de Retz (1613–1679), defined humanity itself in terms of *gloire*: "That which makes men truly great and raises them above the rest of the world is the love of *la belle gloire.*"[9] Mazarin, in his role of tutor and advisor to the young Louis, directed him, "It is up to you to become the most glorious king that has ever been."[10] The talented and fascinating courtier Madame de Sévigné (1626–1696) was an acute observer who regarded the desire for glory as a critical and worthwhile element in aristocratic education: "Since one constantly tells men that they are only worthy of esteem to the extent that they love glory, they devote all their thoughts to it; and this shapes all French bravery." She clearly identified *gloire* as a positive force in the aristocratic masculine code and lamented that women did not share in it. "As women are allowed to be weak, they take advantage of this privilege without scruple."[11]

Essential to a prince's *gloire* was his success in the international arena, and this meant victory in war. *Gloire* predisposed a monarch to desire war, especially a young monarch in need of establishing his own reputation. Louis admitted that it pulled at him. Accounting for his attack on the Dutch in

---

[9] Quoted in Gaston Zeller, "French Diplomacy and Foreign Policy in Their European Setting," in *New Cambridge Modern History*, vol. 5 (Cambridge, 1961), p. 207.
[10] Letter from Mazarin to Louis XIV, quoted in John B. Wolf, *Louis XIV* (New York, 1962), p. 89.
[11] Marie de Rabutin-Chantal, marquise de Sévigné, *Lettres de madame de Sévigné*, Gault-de-Saint-Germain, vol. 7, p. 394, letter of 23 October 1683.

1672, he wrote: "I shall not attempt to justify myself. Ambition and [the pursuit of] glory are always pardonable in a prince, and especially in a young prince so well treated by fortune as I was."[12] When the young man came into his own with the death of Mazarin, he was certain to try his hand at war. The Dutch statesman John de Witt foresaw the inevitable in a 1664 memoir presented to the States, or assembly, of Holland. France had "a twenty-six year-old king, vigorous of body and spirit, who knows his mind and who acts on his own authority, who possesses a kingdom populated by an extremely bellicose people and with very considerable wealth." Such a king would have to "have an extraordinary and almost miraculous moderation, if he stripped himself of the ambition which is so natural to all princes... to extend his frontiers."[13]

Should Louis be condemned for such frivolous, though deadly, concerns? Indeed were they really frivolous? For one thing, one should not dismiss the love of *gloire* as an exclusively French disease; the concern for glory was a European, not a national, obsession, to which even the staid William III succumbed.[14] For another, Louis employed the term much as modern statesmen speak of national prestige or national interest, and these are regarded as reasonable motivations today. Louis defended *gloire* with convincing authority when he wrote: "A king need never be ashamed of seeking fame, for it is a good that must be ceaselessly and avidly desired, and which alone is better able to secure success of our aims than any other thing. Reputation is often more effective than the most powerful armies. All conquerors have gained more by reputation than by the sword."[15]

Gloire was a potent weapon of intimidation and a vital deterrent. Louis was no fool: *gloire* was no mere fluff. The pursuit of *gloire*, of his personal grandeur, moreover, did not obviously compel Louis to act in ways that ran counter to the more immediate interests of his dynasty and his state. His *gloire* depended on actual achievement. As Vauban once stated, "true *gloire* does not flit like a butterfly; it is only acquired by real and solid actions."[16] Therefore, the precise role played by a concern for *gloire* in determining royal actions cannot be easily isolated, because that achievement required reasonable and rewarding policies. But it was not so much reason and reward as reputation that ruled.

12 Louis XIV in Zeller, "French Diplomacy and Foreign Policy," p. 217.
13 De Witt in Ernest Lavisse, *Histoire de la France*, vol. 7, pt. 2 (Paris, 1906), p. 281.
14 As did Leopold I and Charles XII. Ragnhild Hatton, "Louis XIV and His Fellow Monarchs," in John C. Rule, ed. *Louis XIV and the Craft of Kingship* (Columbus, OH, 1969), pp. 155–95.
15 Louis XIV in Wolf, *Louis XIV*, p. 185. In a similar manner, Vauban, who was little interested in conquest, wrote, "states maintain themselves more by reputation than by force." Vauban, in Michel Parent and Jacques Verroust, *Vauban* (Paris, 1971), p. 78.
16 Vauban, "Pensées diverses," in Albert Rochas d'Aiglun, ed., *Vauban, sa famille et ses écrits*, vol. 1 (Paris, 1910), p. 627.

A desire for glory was to be expected, but it became a liability when wielded with aggressive arrogance. Louis's sense of his own glory and of French power tempted him to go it alone in international affairs and war. At times, he either was oblivious to how his actions were perceived or seemed simply not to care. His kingdom may have been the richest and the most powerful in Europe, but it was not so dominant that Louis could take on all of Europe's other great powers without exceeding and exhausting his resources. Thus, it was not his particular interpretation of glory in itself that damned Louis but rather the blindly arrogant unilateralism it inspired. Here is another way in which French foreign policy was intensely personal because it reflected the failings of the king himself. Admittedly, one could argue that Louis's advisors, most notably Louvois, led him down the wrong path, but the king chose those advisors because they embodied the elements of his own character and policy.

Unilateralism

Of Louis's conflicts, only in the Dutch War did he seek by extensive diplomatic preparations to gain allies and isolate his foes. Louis used French money to dismantle the Triple Alliance, paying off the Swedish regency government to abandon its alliance with the Dutch and the English. He also concluded the secret Treaty of Dover (1670) with Charles II, promising him a large subsidy of 2,000,000 livres and, if needed, French troops to put down civil disturbances in England. In addition, should Charles join Louis in a war against the Dutch, he could expect an annual subsidy of 3,000,000 livres. At the same time, Louis managed to deceive the most powerful Dutch political figure at the time, Jan de Witt, assuring him that the Dutch were in no danger and that the French were open to negotiations.

Louis could count on Bavaria and Saxony acquiescing to France, and he made efforts to win over Brandenburg, although its ruler, Frederick William, the Great Elector (1620 – r. 1640–1688), eventually joined the Dutch. In a treaty in 1671, even Leopold I agreed to neutrality in case of a Franco-Dutch War, conditional on the French preserving the territorial status quo concerning Germany and the Spanish Netherlands. The projected line of French advance through the Bishopric of Liege did not violate Spanish lands and thus would keep the Spanish out of the war until Louis had neutralized the Dutch. Yet, even in the Dutch War, Louis soon found himself relatively isolated. Troubled by the French advance, Leopold concluded a defensive alliance with the Dutch in July 1672, and imperial and Hapsburg troops took the field against the French. In 1673, the Spanish, as well, joined the war against France, and in February 1674, the English concluded the Treaty of Westminster with the Dutch, ending English participation in the conflict. Louis now confronted the Dutch Netherlands, the Holy

Roman Empire, and Spain with only Sweden, Münster, and Cologne as allies.

His next major conflict, the Nine Years' War, saw an isolated France take on the Grand Alliance, which included the Holy Roman Empire, the Austrian Hapsburgs, the Dutch Netherlands, England, Spain, Sweden, and Savoy. It is arguable that he backed into a war that caught him unprepared, so it is not surprising that he went in alone. But the fact that he was caught off guard by the consequences of his own actions only testifies to his strategic blindness, a consequence of his own arrogant unilateralism and, perhaps, his putting too much faith in the awe that French power should have inspired. Awe is more easily anticipated than achieved. At the time of this war, Fénelon wrote a letter that he wisely never sent to Louis: "Not one old ally has been retained, because only slaves are wanted."[17]

From 1678 onward, the Sun King had bullied his neighbors, and it would seem that the success of one act of force simply convinced him that the next would meet with resignation as well. Given his worldview, success evidenced divine justification. And so, considering only French interests, he pressed on. His initial goal of rationalizing the French frontier became all the more urgent as he viewed an isolated France as beleaguered, surrounded by all the other great powers of the seventeenth century.

Louis interpreted the creation of the League of Augsburg and the tide of Hapsburg victory against the Ottoman Turks as indications that Germany would soon turn against him. There was both evidence and logic behind Louis's perception of the German states as his most dangerous enemies. However, neither the Sun King nor his advisors seemed to have acknowledged that French actions had isolated France or that Louis should have done something to allay European fears. He might have realized that marching into Strasbourg and taking Luxembourg by siege had inspired German enmity. Instead, Louis issued his ultimatum that the terms of the Truce of Ratisbon be made permanent and followed it by attacking Philippsbourg. In purely military terms, this attack made sense because it closed off the Rhine frontier of Alsace, but in political terms, it both alienated the Germans and went a long way toward convincing the Dutch to support William's expedition to England, with all the drastic implications this had for Louis and France. France would fight alone!

During the War of Spanish Succession, Louis enjoyed the support of Spain, but this was owing not to skillful diplomatic maneuvers but rather to the war being fought to maintain his grandson, Philip V, on the Spanish throne. Apart from Spain, Louis counted only Savoy, Portugal, Bavaria, and Cologne as allies, and even these did not stay in the French camp for long. In 1703,

---

17 Fénelon, "Lettre à Louis XIV," from Gutenberg Project site, http://www.gutenberg.org/etext/13914.

Savoy and Portugal abandoned Louis and joined the coalition of Britain, the Dutch Netherlands, the Holy Roman Empire, and the Hapsburgs. That year, coalition forces also took the lands of the archbishop of Cologne, who sought refuge in France. Then, by winning a crushing victory at Blenheim in 1704, Marlborough and Eugene of Savoy eliminated Bavaria from the war, although the Elector of Bavaria and some of his troops fled to the Spanish Netherlands, where they joined the French. Hence from fall 1704 through the end of the war in 1714, the two Bourbon monarchs had only each other and what diversionary aid they could gain from Hungarian rebels against the Hapsburgs.

Louis did not inherit his characteristic unilateral foreign policy from his mentor. Working from the premise that even a powerful France required friends, the wise Mazarin had created a network of alliances among the German Protestant states and other German principalities, such as Bavaria, which feared the Austrian Habsburgs. This put his Most Christian Majesty the King of France in league with heretics, but French policy had to be guided by reasons of state, not confessional bias, at least outside France. Because the smaller German states regarded the greater threat as a too-powerful Hapsburg emperor who might try to dominate Germany, France could pose as a defender of the liberties of the lesser states. During the negotiations that ended the Thirty Years' War, Mazarin carefully respected his commitments to weaker allies, protecting their interests even when this prolonged the negotiations instead of bringing a speedy end to the war.[18] Mazarin demonstrated that alliances between strong and weak players can work best when the former operates as a sponsor of the latter rather than treating them as dispensable junior partners.

While fighting still continued between France and Spain, Mazarin formed an alliance with neutral German states that became the League of the Rhine in 1658. France viewed the League as a way of keeping Emperor Leopold I from aiding the Spanish in the Netherlands, while the German states saw it as a way of keeping the emperor's troops from marching through their lands. The League thus served the interests of all parties and also helped to shelter the French frontier. Mazarin was so clever in forging peace in 1659 that the historian Andrew Lossky claims, "It can be said that never did France enjoy such near-perfect security on its frontiers as in the last year of Mazarin's life" – a security that it had not experienced in the preceding three and a half centuries.[19]

Louis learned the art of diplomacy under Mazarin, but he eventually followed an entirely different course. His plans to seize parts of the Spanish

[18]   Charles Derek Croxton, *Peacemaking in Early Modern Europe: Cardinal Mazarin and the Congress of Westphalia, 1643–1648* (Selinsgrove, PA, 1999).
[19]   Andrew Lossky, *Louis XIV and the French Monarchy* (New Brunswick, NJ, 1994), p. 60.

inheritance with the War of Devolution cost him the League of the Rhine, as members declined to renew their association in 1666 and 1667. Louis soon forgot Mazarin's legacy, or perhaps it would be more accurate to say that Louis eventually came to see France as powerful enough to fight alone if it had to, and this made him unwilling to accommodate the interests and outlooks of others. It required greater wisdom than Louis possessed to recognize that his security would have benefited more by tempering his strength to unite a coalition than by relying on his strength as a license to do as he wished without regard to the interests and fears of others.

Going it alone cost Louis in two ways: he blundered into wars he might otherwise have avoided, and France had to bear alone the expense of those conflicts. Louis's style of unilateral action was intrinsically arrogant; he not only chose policies guided exclusively by conceptions of his own interests but also executed them in a blustering and bullying style. Had he felt the need to conciliate allies, he might have moderated his actions and style, instead of driving his neighbors into alliance against him. Thus, multilateralism more in the spirit of Mazarin would have aided Louis in avoiding conflicts he wanted to avoid. Moreover, by securing and nurturing alliances, Louis could have diminished his enemies' resources and increased his own, lessening the huge burdens of war borne by France. This second aspect of a multilateral policy should not be seen simply as getting others to shoulder the burden because the quid pro quo of their participation requires that their views be taken seriously. The need to honor others' interests incurs the inconvenience of unwanted complexity or moderation, but it can also encourage a wisdom that avoids self-deluded policy.

There was a third problem with the isolation of France: it added to Louis's concerns that he was becoming the object of envy and would be the target of European aggression. The very unilateralism encouraged by French strength thus paradoxically bred a growing sense of vulnerability.

The quest for absolute security

Louis's unilateral actions peaked in the period between the Dutch War and the Nine Years' War. From 1678 to 1688, his determination to go it alone in fulfilling his goals grew almost to a sense that he was required to act as he did. Thereafter, defense became his obsession. After the Dutch War, for all his desire for *gloire*, Louis harbored in his heart more fear of invasion than lust for conquest. Clausewitz concluded that "it had become almost a question of honor for Louis XIV to defend the frontiers of the kingdom from all insult, as insignificant as it might be."[20]

More and more, Louis and his advisors came to view France as the potential victim of European aggression. In the words of Vauban, "almost in

---

[20]   Carl von Clausewitz in Jean Bérenger, *Turenne* (Paris, 1987), p. 514.

the middle of the most considerable powers of Christendom, she is equally in range of blows from Spain, Italy, Germany, the Low Countries, and England." A victorious France threatened to become a lightning rod, drawing to itself bolts from all quarters. Vauban believed that "France has today attained a high degree of elevation that renders her formidable to her neighbors, in a manner that they all interest themselves in her ruin, or at least in the diminution of her power."[21] In the opinion of Louis and his advisors, the Germans posed the greatest threat. In a 1684 letter to Vauban, Louvois warned against "the Germans, who from now on ought to be considered as our true enemies and the only ones from whom we can receive injury if they have an emperor who wants to mount a horse."[22] So Louis adopted a policy designed to block any invasion from the east. This defensive strategy was the creation of Louis and Louvois, with Vauban as both advisor and technical expert. Louis turned to the most sophisticated military technology of his day: fortifications. He would protect his frontiers, not by alliances, but instead with stone and iron. As previously explained, along with the *pré carré* guarding his northern frontier, Louis grabbed Strasbourg and besieged Luxembourg. Finally, his eye fell on Philippsbourg.

While Louis may have viewed his land grabs as essentially defensive in nature, Europe read them otherwise. The reasons are not hard to discover. The lesser part of the answer was style: although Louis desired security, the overbearing monarch acted as if he wanted to conquer or emasculate. But the greater part of the answer was substance, for the image of Louis with an infinite appetite for conquest grew in response to his first two wars. His rationale for both did not go much beyond his desire for *gloire* and lust for the Spanish Netherlands.

The brutal seizures of land along the French borders after 1678 subsequently reinforced European opinion. In seeking to deter his enemies by constructing "impregnable" borders during the 1680s, Louis so alarmed his foes that he made virtually inevitable the very war he sought to avoid. The Sun King never appreciated how his quest for absolute security threatened his neighbors; an impregnable France could bully them with impunity. Bridgeheads that Louis commanded on the Rhine to deny the enemy the opportunity to attack him could as easily provide him with avenues to attack them. His fortresses not only covered his frontiers but also projected French power.[23] His security must by nature compromise theirs. It was thus reasonable for those suspicious of the French to read Louis's intentions as offensive.

[21] Vauban in Alfred Rebelliau, *Vauban* (Paris, 1962), pp. 141–42.
[22] Letter from Louvois to Vauban, 28 June 1684, Service Historique de l'armée, AG, A¹714, no. 807. The full text of this quotation explains more fully that it was Alsace and the defensive line that made the Germans the enemy.
[23] It was my friend and colleague, George Satterfield, who first attached the modern strategic term 'power projection' to Louis's fortresses.

Louis believed that the Nine Years' War was imposed upon him. He saw
his opening moves as essential and defensive – the seizure of Philippsburg
to close off the Rhine and the devastation of the Palatinate to prevent the
Germans from launching an offensive. It was beyond Louis's intentions, and
perhaps beyond his control, that the short defensive war he wanted turned
out to be a long war of attrition that exhausted France.

The paradox of reputation and the need for transparency

Louis opted to go it alone, and in his arrogant autonomy, he appeared as
insatiably aggressive and insolently oblivious to the apprehension generated
by his shortsighted actions. Understandably, that apprehension drew his
anxious neighbors together.

Louis XIV's search for *gloire*, or reputation, thus proved to be paradoxical. The young king believed that to win glory, he must demonstrate his
prowess in war. This he had done by the Dutch War, after which he began to
redefine glory in terms of defense rather than conquest. But in achieving glory
through conquest, he also acquired a reputation among the other European
princes as dangerously aggressive. This reputation, further fostered by his
imperious demeanor, undermined his more defensive grand strategy because
the latter was seen not as a change in course but instead as a further quest
for territory. Fénelon believed that Louis's problems dated from his greatest
success, the Dutch War: "I cite this war in particular, because it has been
the source of all the others."[24]

As early as 1667, François-Paul de Lisola (1613–1675), a diplomat and
publicist for the Hapsburgs, warned in his *Bouclier d'estat et de justice*
against "the clearly revealed intentions of Universal Monarchy" that he
argued Louis XIV hoped to establish across Europe. Lisola's charges were
not true – Louis was not trying to bestride the continent and dictate to it –
but his actions played right into this perception. In modern terminology,
Louis lost control of the narrative, which portrayed him as a danger to
Europe, and his opponents continued to see him as such. They witnessed the
crescendo of his actions in the 1680s as justifying their fears: the land grabs
of the Reunions accompanied with brute force at Luxembourg in 1684; the
French bombardment of Genoa in 1684;[25] the revocation of the Edict of
Nantes in 1685; the campaign against neighboring Italian Protestants the
Vaudois in 1686;[26] and his ultimatum of 1687, demanding that the Truce
of Ratisbon be made permanent.

[24] Fénelon, "Lettre de Louis XIV."
[25] This bombardment by the French was in retaliation for neutral Genoa allowing the Spanish
to disembark troops and supplies there.
[26] The Vaudois of the Alpine valleys were brutally punished because Louis believed that they
were aiding French Huguenots in their escape from France.

A modern electoral system can replace national leaders periodically in an orderly manner, and new leaders can signal a change of course. Louis XIV personally directed the French government for more than 50 years, which gave French policy the appearance of continuity even when there were changes in direction. The great king might have avoided the Nine Years' War had he pursued security, not by unilateral action that aroused apprehension, but rather by forging alliances that calmed them. As Fénelon suggested in his letter to the king: "You ought not to claim that you are within your rights to retain forever certain fortresses because they secure your frontiers. You ought to seek this security by good alliances, by your moderation, or by constructing fortresses *behind* those frontiers."[27]

Moreover, he could have been more transparent in his defensive aims, which Europe misinterpreted. Transparency in grand strategy may not always be the most effective course. However, if a state's ultimate goals are essentially benign, but others portray them as threatening and aggressive, then honest transparency can serve to correct international perceptions, allay fears among those who need not feel threatened, and put the real foes on notice.

Controlling a narrative should not be simply a matter of spin or of telling more convincing lies. A strategic narrative gains in effectiveness by truth, which illuminates and explains actions. Narrative cannot be a substitute for reality, but hostile narratives can portray what is actually done as something very different from reality or intention. A desire to control the narrative can bear witness to a respect for international opinion rather than being merely a bald attempt to manipulate it.

Overstretch

Louis fell victim to a kind of strategic overstretch, although to call it "imperial overstretch" à la Paul Kennedy would be to miss a critical point. French forces were not overcommitted across a distant empire; in fact, by essentially scuttling his naval ambitions in 1694, Louis forswore overseas competition in order to fight along his frontiers in Europe. Overstretch afflicted the French monarchy in conflicts contiguous to its borders. But overstretch it still was because miscalculation born of unilateralism, arrogance, and a lack of concern for European opinion embroiled Louis XIV in wars of longer duration and greater expense than he could afford. As a result, France emerged from these struggles bankrupt, and while this exhaustion was not the only reason for the relative decline of France as a great power, it certainly was an important contributor.

---

[27]   Ibid. Italics added.

Louis found himself making commitments greater than he or his advisors had intended because the wars he fought got out of hand. The twenty-first-century descriptive dichotomy between wars of necessity and wars of choice does not really fit the wars of Louis XIV, which were in the main neither necessary nor chosen but rather the products of miscalculation. As the reality of each of his major wars refused to conform to its expected limits, Louis found himself compelled to mobilize forces of unprecedented size. The Sun King expanded the size of his wartime armies nearly sixfold over previous highs.[28] From the late Middle Ages through the mid-seventeenth century, the number of troops France mustered for war had topped out at roughly 60,000 to 80,000. There are claims that the French put 125,000 soldiers in the field during their war with Spain (1635–1659), but the most authoritative scholarship by David Parrott claims that the French never mustered more than 80,000 at any point during that conflict.[29]

With Louis's Dutch War, this number increased to a paper strength of approximately 280,000, which, even discounted to approximately 253,000 actual troops, clearly represented a major increase. Louis had isolated the Dutch at the start of the war, but they rallied and formed a coalition with the Austrian and Spanish Hapsburgs, and that required Louis to expand his army. The Nine Years' War saw the army climb to new heights; during the year of Louis's greatest effort, 1693, its paper strength rose to 447,000, a figure that in reality translated to 362,000 men under arms. This amounted to an increase in strength equal to four-and-a-half to six times the level of wartime highs before 1661.

From 1661 to 1680, the peacetime army grew at an even more rapid rate. From the mid-fifteenth through the mid-seventeenth centuries, the monarchy's peacetime forces usually stood at about 10,000 men, with a rare increase under Louis XI. Louis XIV increased this to a high of 150,000, where it essentially remained until the French Revolution. Much is made of the expansion of French forces during the revolutionary and Napoleonic eras, but in percentage terms, neither revolutionary troops totaling 750,000 men nor Napoleonic forces of approximately 600,000 even came close to approaching the expansion achieved under the Sun King.[30]

---

28 Most important, see John A. Lynn II, "Recalculating French Army Growth during the *Grand siècle*, 1610–1715," *French Historical Studies* 18, no. 4 (Fall 1994), pp. 881–906, and "Revisiting the Great Fact of War and Bourbon Absolutism: The Growth of the French Army during the *Grand siècle*," in Enrique Garcia Hernán and Davide Maffi, eds., *Guerra y sociedad en la monarchia hispanica: Política, estrategia y cultura en la Europa moderna (1500–1700)* vol. 1 (Madrid, 2006), pp. 49–74.

29 David Parrott, *Richelieu's Army* (Cambridge, 2001).

30 See, e.g., Bell, *The First Total War*, p. 7, and Yuval Noah Harari, *The Ultimate Experience: Battlefield Revelations and the Making of Modern War Culture, 1450–2000* (Houndsmill, Basingstoke, 2008), pp. 180–81.

Historians debate the impetus behind this increase. For example, Geoffrey Parker has argued that it arose in response to the spread of the new fortifications designed to resist artillery fire. He insists that such fortresses either required more troops to besiege them or absorbed more troops in their garrisons. Certainly garrisoning the extensive belt of fortifications required a large number of troops, but although this helps explain the impressive increase in peacetime forces, it cannot account for wartime highs. Those figures multiplied in response to the array of forces marshaled against Louis. As Vauban urged Louis:

> However great the forces of the kingdom, one ought not to imagine that it alone can furnish troops to guard and maintain so many fortresses and at the same time put armies in the field as great as those of Spain, Italy, England, Holland and the Empire joined together.[31]

In fact, Vauban, the great fortress engineer, urged Louis to reduce the number of fortresses held so that the king could concentrate more troops in the field to fight the Nine Years' War. In a sense, Louis took heed of Vauban's logic, if not of his conclusions. The Sun King did not cut down his fortresses and their garrisons, as Vauban proposed, but instead created a 362,000-man army to ensure his *gloire*. At that level, the army reached a breaking point in terms of the manpower and finances that the monarchy could tap.

The nature of warfare during the *grand siècle* exaggerated even further the strain of maintaining such large forces. Owing to a number of factors, decisive blows were practically unachievable. The complicated and clumsy logistics of the time slowed movement. Fortresses dampened the impact of battlefield victory by offering defeated troops a safe harbor and presenting obstacles to the momentum of victors. In such an operational environment, wars of the period dragged on into long contests ruled by attrition.[32] So the cost of armies was a product of their size multiplied by the long years they spent on campaign.

Sustaining his army demanded so much that Louis XIV had to give up his navy after 1694, but more than that, the financial needs of the army undermined the financial reforms Louis had hoped to achieve. His great finance minister, Jean-Baptist Colbert, accomplished a good deal between 1661 and the outbreak of the Dutch War. Colbert tried to resist this war because of its inevitable effect on finances, and he protested that the expense would be impossible. In response, Louis threatened his finance minister,

---

[31] SHAT, Bibliothèque., Gen. 11 (fol.), Vauban, "Les places fortifiées du Royaume," fol. 12 ver.

[32] See the discussion of war-as-process and war-as-event in Lynn, "International Rivalry and Warfare, 1700–1815," pp. 190–92 and 210. These terms contrast the style of warfare under Louis XIV (war-as-process) with the style under Napoleon (war-as-event).

"Think about it. If you can't do it, there will always be someone who can."[33] Colbert capitulated.

The outbreak of war thus brought renewed reliance on the same old varieties of financial "obfuscation and deceit."[34] Once again, the government turned to traditional abuses: sale of offices, bloated short-term bills of credit, and anticipations, that is, borrowing secured by the promise to repay loans with future tax income stipulated in advance. Such a method compromised state revenues in subsequent years, guaranteeing that still more borrowing would be required to meet expenses. Expenses for debt service soared as war continued. In 1694, 78.72 percent of government expenses went to direct military costs and only 8.07 percent to debt service, but by 1697, these percentages changed to 63.61 percent and 23.03 percent, respectively. In 1698, military outlays fell to 49.93 percent of total expenses, while debt service climbed to 50.00 percent.[35]

The French monarchy had been prone to bankruptcy in the past, but Louis staved off that fate during his reign. Yet, he left the crown so bereft of resources and mired in debt that after his death, the regency council that managed government for the five-year-old Louis XV had to institute a peculiarly French form of bankruptcy, summoning a Chambre de Justice that tried financiers for fraud and renounced much of what the monarchy really owed.

SUCCESS IN FAILURE: CONFORMING TO THE INTERNATIONAL SYSTEM

The discussion so far has stressed Louis's missteps and failures, but he also achieved an enduring share of success, particularly when measured by his own territorial and dynastic goals. Historians often compare the Sun King unfavorably with Napoleon, at least in military terms. After all, Napoleon was the king of rapid maneuvers, decisive battles, and brief wars, so much so that staff colleges still study his campaigns while ignoring the plodding and endless wars of Louis XIV. But it is sobering to remember that Louis died in bed at Versailles, still king and able to pass on his crown to his grandson. Napoleon died a prisoner on St. Helena, poisoned by one of his own entourage, while back in Paris, Bourbon kings had returned to the French throne.[36]

---

[33] Paul Sonnino, *Louis XIV and the Origins of the Dutch War* (Cambridge, 1989), p. 172.

[34] Julian Dent, *Crisis in Finance* (New York, 1973), p. 23.

[35] Phillipe Contamine, *Histoire militaire de la France* (Paris, 1997), 1:429. See the table of French expenses, p. 428.

[36] See the works of Ben Weider, who spearheaded the investigation into the death of Napoleon; Ben Weider and David Hapgood, *The Murder of Napoleon* (Bloomington, IN, 1986), and Ben Weider and Sten Forshufvud, *Assassination at St. Helena Revisited* (Hoboken, NJ, 1995).

Moreover, the France delimited by the Treaty of Paris of 1815 was smaller than the France that Napoleon seized in his military coup of 18 Brumaire in 1799. In contrast, Louis left his successor a significantly larger domain than the one he had inherited in 1643 or that he ruled in 1661. Louis was able to retain a substantial share of the territorial gains he made before 1688: (1) much of Alsace and all of Rousillon, secured by Mazarin in the Treaty of Westphalia and the Peace of the Pyrenees; (2) French gains in the War of Devolution, including Lille; (3) most of what Louis acquired in the Dutch War, including the major addition of Franche-Comté; and (4) a few additions of the Reunions – Longwy, Saar-Louis, and Strasbourg. And his grandson, Philip of Anjou, became King Philip V of Spain. Napoleon, for all his military brilliance, failed, while Louis XIV succeeded in adding territories to France that remain French to this day and in winning for the Bourbon dynasty the Spanish throne, which it still occupies.

To what did Louis XIV owe this degree of success? First, his armies were victorious much of the time. It is true that his forces suffered notable defeats at the hands of Marlborough and Eugene during the War of the Spanish Succession, but even in that war, French marshals Villars, Vendôme, and Berwick won major battles. Yet, military success did not necessarily equate with gains at the peace table because attrition played such a major role.

Most important, Louis's additions to his domains were acceptable within the give-and-take that made up the international system of his day. Paul Schroeder, the noted diplomatic historian, argues that an international system consists of "the understandings, assumptions, learned skills and responses, rules, norms, procedures, etc." that states employ.[37] The norms of the late seventeenth and early eighteenth centuries accepted struggles for discrete advantage but not wars meant to destroy other states or regimes or to decide great issues of religion or ideology. The most common rationale for war was the acquisition or retention of territory. In addition, dynastic disputes over which princely family or individual would occupy a vacated throne were the natural by-products of succession in this age of princes. The struggle for wealth also drove states to confront each other. So we encounter another paradox: Louis, perceived as trying to create a universal monarchy, achieved what he did by staying within the parameters of the international system of his day, not by shattering them.

Louis's grand strategy conformed to the tolerances of the international system that defined the *grand siècle*, with significant though modest additions that did not overturn the European balance. His greatest single addition, Franche-Comté, became French at a time when its Spanish masters could no longer hope to defend it. It was fated to be French and fell like ripe fruit to Condé's invading army in 1674. Bourbon dynastic claims to the

---

[37]   Paul W. Schroeder, *The Transformation of European Politics 1763–1848* (Oxford, 1994), p. xii.

Spanish crown were considered to be sufficiently valid that even William III recognized them in agreeing to the partition treaties of 1698 and 1700. And in 1713–1714, all Europe recognized Philip as the rightful king of Spain.

Napoleon, on the other hand, showed little regard for the international standards of his day. He reshaped and destroyed states and sought to impose his will across Europe from Spain to Russia. His rapaciousness dumbfounded rather than outwitted rival European statesmen because he operated outside the parameters of the late eighteenth century's balance-of-power system. Doubtless that system was intrinsically flawed, but it had a certain predictability, limitation, and quid pro quo. Napoleon's policy lacked all these. Moreover, lacking any clear conception of a peaceful and stable Europe, Napoleon had no long-range grand strategy. In lieu of one, he simply pursued whatever seemed the best way to score the next gain. The mixture of Napoleon's perpetual aggression with his enemies' balance-of-power behavior produced a fatal alchemy at first. Napoleon refused to be restrained by his rivals' rules, while their rules so promoted selfish action that they could not form the unified front required to halt the Napoleonic juggernaut. Ultimately, the threat of Napoleon convinced the other European powers to unite to oppose him, not only to stop but also to eradicate his conquests.

It is one thing, however, for historians to define the international system of a past epoch with the wisdom of hindsight; it is quite another for statesmen to understand the international system in their own time. Foreign policy is a game in which the players only discover the rules by playing. Nonetheless, there are ways to come closer to an understanding. First, recognize that dramatic change is likely to run into unexpected problems precisely because it is outside the parameters of the system. Second, it is probably easier to recognize what will not fly than to define with precision the limits of tolerance of the system. Third, multilateral action is more likely than unilateral action to produce a strategy consistent with those limits because it is the relations and practices among states that constitute the system itself.

POSING THE GANDHI QUESTION

The search for applicable strategic lessons to be learned from the wars of Louis XIV leads to what one might label as the *Gandhi question*: what will be the residue left by the use of violence? Gandhi preached nonviolence, which was adopted by some as a philosophy of universal love and by others only as a tactic that could be used by the morally strong but physically weak to triumph over those commanding greater force. Frankly, one can question the applicability of nonviolence outside an environment that allows those who are being abused to appeal to the higher moral standards of a greater authority beyond their attackers. However, embedded within

Gandhi's teachings is the assertion that the use of violence always has costs, even if these are not immediately apparent.

The residues of violence can take many forms. Since 1945, the two that have been most important in the American context are the capacity of violence to be counterproductive in struggles meant to win the respect and support of foreign populations and the way in which the costs and perceptions of violence undermine support for such conflicts within America itself. Killing insurgents or terrorists may well be necessary, but such violence is rarely surgical, and the almost inevitable collateral casualties among non-combatant men, women, and children fuel outrage that can raise obstacles and multiply enemies.

The costs of violence thus are often greater than the benefits, even if one succeeds in eliminating the intended targets. Even when the use of force compels short-term compliance, it can engender long-term resentment, resistance, and revenge. In addition, resort to violence by the United States in Vietnam resulted in physical and psychological injuries to American combatants as well as to their enemies. In addition, the American population was repelled by acts committed by their own sons and/or by the price paid by those troops in lives and injury. Such revulsion eventually turned the American people against a war they initially supported. The Gandhi question has cut both ways, in the effects on those attacked and on the attackers themselves.

The residue of violence that so damaged Louis XIV and his France was of another stripe: the Sun King never escaped the tenacious reputation for conquest and brutality that he earned as a result of the Dutch War. His apparent success and the glory won turned on Louis, leading to the costly disappointment of the Nine Years' War, although he had, in fact, changed his strategic goals. Certainly he did little to dispel the image his aggression created. His arrogance during the 1680s made a bad situation worse and seemed to justify those who painted him in such threatening colors. He would pay dearly for this from 1688 to 1697.

CONCLUSION

The *grand siècle* ended with the passing of Louis XIV in 1715. No subsequent French monarch would equal his influence in France or over Europe; none would surpass the radiance of the Sun King. Yet, tarnishing his brilliance, the inordinate human and financial costs of his wars stood as grim reminders of his shortcomings. Surveying his grand strategy and the pursuit of it, the present generation can take away some guides and warnings for the future.

A wiser monarch would have realized that preserving the peace relied above all on interdependence. Mazarin had pursued this route, and Louis should have as well. Louis could have benefited from a more multilateral foreign policy, based not only on French power but also on his willingness to respect the interests of his allies. Once he resolved on a defensive grand strategy, he could have buttressed his borders by "constructing fortresses behind those frontiers," as Fénelon conceded, rather than by seizing new strongpoints from his ever-anxious neighbors. In retrospect, Louis would have done better had he recognized that invulnerability was unattainable and that security would best be served by international agreements rather than by sole reliance on stone and steel. Transparency in making clear his essentially defensive goals after the Dutch War would have facilitated formation of such international agreements. Instead, Louis became the victim of a narrative that he himself fostered by his arrogance.

All good advice, but one has to wonder whether Louis XIV could have followed such a course. A child of his own times, the Sun King found himself dazzled by the pursuit of *gloire* and blinded by the aura of his own grandeur. How could such a monarch escape his own arrogance or rely on anything other than his own power? So much a product of the culture of the *grand siècle* was Louis that his failings were simply exaggerated versions of the foibles of his times; the main thing that he got right, his sense of the contemporary international system, was more intuitive than learned.

But that Louis XIV seemed oblivious to his own failings and incapable of benefiting from the lessons his missteps might have taught him does not mean that current statesmen and their advisers cannot learn from his errors. Otto von Bismarck is reputed to have declared, "Fools say that they learn by experience. I prefer to profit by others' experience."

3

Strategic culture and the Seven Years' War

JEREMY BLACK

In this essay, strategic culture emerges from the complex political situation of mid-eighteenth-century Britain as a key public mythos. This is at variance with its more common use in the literature as the context within which military tasks were "shaped."[1] The latter usage reflects discussion of distinctive ways of war[2] and draws on the authority of cultural interpretations of warfare.[3] However, the concept of strategic culture also has to address the issue of coherence and consistency in the face of the contested character of actual national interests, the ferocity of debate and the roles of politics and contingency. In short, there is a revenge of history on theory.

The very existence of strategy, strategic culture and strategic policy in the eighteenth century is highly problematic as far as some well-informed scholars are concerned.[4] They hold this delay in the development of the idea of

---

[1] Robert Jervis, *Perception and Misperception in International Politics* (Princeton, NJ, 1976); K. Booth, *Strategy and Ethnocentrism* (London, 1979); Clark G. Reynolds, "Reconsidering American Strategic History and Doctrines," in his *History of the Sea: Essays on Maritime Strategies* (Columbia, SC, 1989); A. I. Johnston, *Cultural Realism: Strategic Culture and Grand Strategy in Chinese History* (Princeton, NJ, 1995); Colin S. Gray, "Strategic Culture as Context: The First Generation of Theory Strikes Back," *Review of International Studies*, 25, 1999, pp. 49–70; L. Sondhaus, "The Strategic Culture of the Habsburg Army," *Austrian History Yearbook*, 32, 2001, pp. 225–34; Williamson Murray, "Does Military Culture Matter," in John F. Lehman and Harry Sicherman, eds., *America the Vulnerable: Our Military Problems and How to Fix Them* (Philadelphia, 2002), pp. 134–51. For valuable historical applications, see E. Ringman, *Identity, Interest and Action: A Cultural Explanation of Sweden's Intervention in the Thirty Years War* (Cambridge, 1996), and Geoffrey Parker, *The Grand Strategy of Philip II* (New Haven, CT, 1998).
[2] E.g. A. R. Lewis, *The American Culture of War* (New York, 2007).
[3] T. Farrell, *The Norms of War: Cultural Beliefs and Modern Conflict* (Boulder, CO, 2005).
[4] J. B. Hattendorf, *England in the War of the Spanish Succession: A Study of the English View and Conduct of Grand Strategy, 1701–1712* (New York, 1987); N. A. M. Rodger, "The Idea of Naval Strategy in Britain in the Eighteenth and Nineteenth Centuries," in G. Till, ed., *The Development of British Naval Thinking* (Abingdon, 2006), pp. 19–33.

strategy as reflecting the conceptual and institutional limitations of the time. However, such an approach mistakes the absence of an articulated school of strategic thinking for a lack of strategic awareness. For example, as far as the Royal Navy was concerned, there was considerable experience in balancing resources among tasks. One can see this in the detachment of squadrons from home waters for operational tasks in the Baltic and Mediterranean. Moreover, a strategy of commercial interdiction played a major role in British operations against the Dutch in the late seventeenth century, and later, in the Anglo-Spanish crisis of 1725–1727, it included a powerful transoceanic dimension. Furthermore, the planned use of naval power in international crises, as in 1730 and 1731, was wide ranging and reasonably sophisticated given the limitations of communications and logistical support at the time.

The same was true of British planning for operations on land, although here there was a greater degree of complexity because such operations involved coalition warfare, which inevitably makes the development of grand strategy more complex and difficult. Thus, there was an intertwining of military planning and diplomatic exigencies in the wars Britain waged in the eighteenth century. This is clear in the War of the Spanish Succession, in which Britain was involved from 1702 to 1713, and again in the War of the Austrian Succession, in which Britain was involved from 1743 to 1748. In the former, the great Duke of Marlborough played the crucial role not only as a superb operational commander but also in providing the diplomatic glue that provided direction to the alliance's grand strategy against Louis XIV.

Thus, an important background to the issue of strategic culture during the Seven Years' War is to appreciate that strategy existed as a concept even if the word was not used in English until approximately 1800, when it was borrowed from the French. The earliest citation to *strategy* in the second edition of the *Oxford English Dictionary* is from 1810. Moreover, as much of the scholarly discussion of the eighteenth century relates to terms not employed by contemporaries, such as the *Enlightenment*, it is difficult to see why one should not employ it in the military history of the period.

If that is one context for the subject, an understanding of strategy in a wider sense, namely as it relates to the health and strength of the country as a whole, provides a second. From this perspective, the British role in the Seven Years' War was a symptom, albeit a significant one, of a wider anxiety about the country. This may seem far removed from the habitual consideration of the conflict, but it repays attention because it helps explain the contours of contemporary public political concerns, which were an important factor in the making of strategy. These, in turn, helped drive the politics of the conflict, which will be assessed in the next section of this essay.

The anxiety referred to earlier reflected the extent to which organic theories of the state were important. There is a tendency among historians when considering the eighteenth century to emphasize mechanistic themes, not least because of the intellectual thrall of Newtonian physics, and the extent to which notions of balancing power were regarded as important. This was the case both for international relations and for domestic constitutional issues. Concerning the former, the participants in the making of grand strategy saw states as sovereign but linked as if within a machine. They conceived of this system as being self-contained and part of a static and well-ordered world. The concept rested on the model of the machine, which, in turn, they regarded as well ordered and which enabled its parts to conduct activities only in accordance with its own construction. The mechanistic concept of the system of states was well suited to the wider currents of thought, specifically Cartesian rationalism and its successors.

These currents of thought provided not only an analytical framework but also a moral context for international relations. For example, many theorists view balance-of-power politics, as generally presented, as selfishly pragmatic, bereft of any overarching rules and lacking any ethical theoretical foundations in their conduct. In practice, however, the situation was somewhat different. Throughout the eighteenth century, there was a widely expressed theory of the balance of power and rules for its politics, outlined in tracts, pamphlets, doctoral dissertations, and explanations of the reasons for the resort to war. The relationship between such theorizing and rules, on one hand, and decision-making processes, on the other, is obscure and clearly varied by ruler and minister, not to mention nation, but such discussion set normative standards that helped shape policies and responses among those who conducted policy and grand strategy.[5]

Without denying the central role of such notions, it is necessary to complement them with an awareness of the context and assumptions within which decision makers acted. These were important not so much at the level of the international system (until the nineteenth century) as at the level of the leaders of individual states. Moreover, these assumptions helped provide a dynamic component generally lacking in the more structural mechanistic themes. This dynamic component was vitalist in intention. In particular, there was a sense of the state as the expression of a nation, of the latter as linked to a national character and of this character as capable of change and prone to decay. The last named quality in part reflected cyclical accounts of the rise and fall of empires, which drew much of their authority from the commanding role of classical Rome in the historicized political thought of the period, but there was also a strong input from ideas of health. Thus,

---

[5] H. K. Kleinschmidt, *The Nemesis of Power* (London, 2000), esp. pp. 114–70, and "Systeme und Ordnungen in der Geschicht der internationalen Beziehungen," *Archiv für kulturgeschichte*, 82, 2000, pp. 433–54; A. Osiander, *The States System of Europe, 1640–1990: Peacemaking and the Conditions of International Stability* (Oxford, 1994).

the traditional sense of the nation as similar in its course to the life of an individual remained important.

This idea translated in the international sphere into a sense of nations as competitive and as under threat from challenges that were foreign as well as domestic in their causation and mechanism. Concerning the Seven Years' War, anti-Catholicism was crucial in affecting British attitudes,[6] and this is worth emphasizing because it encouraged a sense that Britain must continue the struggle even in the face of news that was negative from virtually every theatre of war, which was the case in the early days of the war.[7] Anti-Catholicism among British leaders led to a sense that their nation was engaged in an existential and meta-historical struggle.

In Britain, the politics of the conflict drew on the direction of public political concern to an extent that was not matched on the Continent. Governmental and public sensitivity to imperial issues arose in mid-century. Economic competition led to the foundation of the Anti-Gallican Association in 1745, a body that joined manufacturing and trade in its goals. By design, this competition was linked to aesthetic rivalry, which was given economic point through a conscious process of public support, particularly by the Society of Arts, Manufactures and Commerce, established in 1754. Enthusiasm for imperial expansion in Britain reflected both political positioning and the strengthening of public engagement with such expansion of the empire at the expense of Britain's enemies, especially France, as a way to ensure commercial strength and maritime destiny.[8]

In part, however, this conflation of "an empire of the seas," the traditional idea of British power, with territorial empire in North America posed serious problems in policy as well as conception. As a result, it is necessary to be cautious in presenting an undifferentiated account of British public attitudes, not least because it is unclear how extensive were prewar interests in territorial expansion.

That said, there can be little doubt that war helped powerfully to foster imperial ambitions, not only at the governmental level but also in terms of public discussion. Thus, the strategic culture altered considerably, indeed was transformed, during and by the war, as much as causing it or setting its alignment. To argue this does not deny the role of earlier interest in imperial expansion, but it does suggest a major change.

Moreover, the preceding argument does not deny the value of linking expansionism to sociocultural shifts, including a growing assertiveness on the part of the expanding middle class and the accompanying repositioning

[6] M. Schlenke, *England und das friederizianische Preussen, 1740–1763* (Munich, 1963), pp. 171–225.
[7] G. Yagi Jr, "A Study of Britain's Military Failure during the Initial Stages of the Seven Years' War in North America, 1754–1758," PhD dissertation, University of Exeter, 2007.
[8] B. Harris, *Politics and the Nation: Britain in the Mid-Eighteenth Century* (Oxford, 2002).

of trade as a political interest and sphere of discussion.[9] However, there is a need for specificity, not only in chronological terms but also with respect to the relationship between imperial expansion and differing mercantile interests. That relationship was complex, not only because of these differences but also because merchants were wary of the burdens that might arise from the need to defend an expanded empire.

Rivalry with France provided a common issue, linking diplomatic, mercantile, imperial and cultural anxieties and themes. It also resonated with a strong context of popular assumptions. This rivalry also made it both important and possible to minimize tensions between these different themes. In part, this reflected France's great prominence in European affairs. Her commercial and colonial revival after 1748, and the failure of Holland or Spain, the other leading maritime powers, to match this growth in French power, whether objectively or as far as British commentators were concerned, was important. So also was the extent to which an easing (although not ending) of Anglo-Spanish political and commercial tensions after the War of the Austrian Succession[10] helped focus British leaders on France.

This focus on France encouraged an important shift in the public imagination of Britain as an imperial power. The importance of this shift for British policy will be the prime subject of this chapter, but first it is appropriate to contrast the situation in Britain with that in France. In recent decades, there has been work on the "public space" in France. Most relates to domestic politics,[11] but there has also been consideration of foreign policy. This, however, focuses on the 1760s–1780s, and more specifically, on the unpopularity of the alliance with Austria[12] and on attitudes towards Britain.[13] This does not provide much guidance concerning France's position in the 1750s and the particular circumstances in which it went to war.

A crucial element of the latter was the unexpected character of the war that arose. Indeed, that helps ensure that there is no strict comparability between the British and French cases because for France, the key cause of war was antagonism to Frederick the Great's Prussia in 1756 among powerful figures in the French court, whereas for Britain, the focus of war

[9] K. Wilson, *The Sense of the People: Politics, Culture and Imperialism in England, 1715–1785* (Cambridge, 1995).
[10] R. Lodge, ed., *The Private Correspondence of Sir Benjamine Keene* (London, 1933); J. McLachlan, *Trade and Peace with Old Spain, 1667–1750* (Cambridge, 1940).
[11] E.g. D. van Kley, *The Damiens Affair and the Unravelling of the Ancien Régime: Church, State, and Society in France, 1750–1770* (1984); J. W. Merrick, *The Desacralization of the French Monarchy in the Eighteenth Century* (1990); A. Farge, *Subversive Words: Public Opinion in Eighteenth-Century France* (Cambridge, 1994).
[12] G. Savage, "Favier's Heirs: The French Revolution and the *Secret du Roi*," *Historical Journal*, 41, 1998, pp. 225–58; T. E. Kaiser, "Who's Afraid of Marie-Antoinette? Diplomacy, Austrophobia and the Queen," *French History*, 14, 2000, pp. 241–71.
[13] E. Dziembowski, *Un Nouveau Patriotisme Français, 1750–1770: La France face à la puissance anglaise à l'Époque de la guerre de Sept Ans* (Paris, 1998).

was France.[14] The war with Britain was less important to French policy makers and the French public at the time than was to be the case in retrospect. In part, this was because animosity to Austria was more central in the French collective memory and in part because of the stronger role of landed interests in France compared to the greater focus on maritime issues of their counterparts in Britain.[15] The result was to show clearly in the allocation of resources between the French army and navy. This contrast was even more visible in discussion between the two states.

Public opinion was, and is, open to multiple definitions. It is most helpful to think of a number of widely held opinions that lacked specific force, such as the wish to be seen to do well and the need to protect national territorial and commercial interests, together with more particular notions that were not so widely held but that were presented as public opinion by their protagonists. The application of both to the diplomatic revolution of 1756, however, was indirect, not least because of the pace of this process and the extent to which it was a response to the actions of others. The Anglo-Prussian Convention of Westminster of 16 January 1756 helped drive France into alliance with Maria Theresa's Austria. Alongside the formal Austrian approach, there was also private diplomacy that took place outside the public's view. For example, Chancellor Kaunitz approached Louis XV through his influential mistress, Madame de Pompadour, who deeply loathed Prussia's Frederick for the less than complimentary remarks he had made about her.[16]

As evidence of the weaker influence of public opinion in France, the First Treaty of Versailles, the Austro-French defensive alliance signed on 1 May 1756, specifically excluded the Anglo-French conflict, which had escalated on 18 April when French troops landed on Minorca. This was not the sort of provision that appealed in the public sphere. Austria benefited most from the defensive agreement because her position made her more vulnerable to attack than France, but France was freed for war with Britain. Moreover, the treaty stipulated that if a British ally should attack France, Austria would support her; but this was unlikely. France was not bound to support the Hapsburgs in any offensive war to gain Silesia but was obliged to provide 24,000 soldiers or money if Prussia attacked Austria. The nature of the French commitment was to be expanded, again as part of a process that was not greatly affected by public discussion.

[14]   T. R. Clayton, "The Duke of Newcastle, the Earl of Halifax and the American Origins of the Seven Years' War," *Historical Journal*, 24, 1981, pp. 571–603.

[15]   For French interest in North America, see A. Reese, *Europäische Hegemonie und France d'outre-mer: Koloniale Fragen in der französischen Aussenpolitik, 1700–1763* (Stuttgart, 1988).

[16]   L. Schilling, *Kaunitz und das Renversement des Alliances* (Berlin, 1994).

On 1 May 1757, in the Second Treaty of Versailles, the two powers negotiated an Austro-French offensive alliance directed against Prussia. France
promised an army of 105,000 soldiers for operations against Prussia and
a substantial subsidy. The terms, however, were rather those of traditional
dynastic diplomacy than of the themes of national power that were to be
more significant in public discussion later in the century. The treaty stipulated that Austria was to regain Silesia, then to cede much of the Austrian
Netherlands to Louis XV's son-in-law, Don Philip. The latter was to return
Parma, which he had gained at the close of the War of the Austrian Succession, to Maria Theresa.[17] When Austria had reconquered Silesia, France was
to gain Beaumont, Chimay, Furness, Ostend, Nieuport and Ypres, and her
troops were to be allowed to occupy Ostend and Nieuport at once. These
acquisitions would consolidate France's position on the North Sea and make
it easier for her to threaten Britain and the Dutch. Nevertheless, there was
no real popular resonance in France with the agreement. The same was true
when the alliance was reaffirmed by the Third Treaty of Versailles, signed
on 26 March 1759 but backdated to 31 December 1758.[18]

Instead, once war began, French public opinion focused on war news.
This followed a fatal trajectory. Success in the initial stages – the capture of
Minorca in 1756 and of several North American forts in 1756–1757, and
the defeat of Hanoverian forces in 1757 – gave way later that same year
to Frederick the Great's crushing victory at Rossbach and thereafter to a
series of disasters to French arms. Debate over foreign policy and the war
thus became a discussion of means rather than ends, compelling the French
increasingly to view the war in operational rather than strategic terms.

In Britain, although war news was also important, the ends were crucial in
public debate, and strategic culture was thus centrally linked to questions of
public politics. Like most discussion about a climate of opinion, the nature of
that public debate is a matter of scholarly contention. In particular, there is
disagreement about just when a commitment to overseas empire developed.
A recent account by Marie Peters emphasizes the impact of the Seven Years'
War and implies that the events on the battlefield shaped the debate:

> It was the wide interest in the events leading up to the Seven Years' War –
> prompted by and prompting a great variety of works – that first familiarized
> large numbers of people, through print with trade, colonies and empire – there
> were bursts of temporary enthusiasm for "empire," prompted by victories, in
> the late 1730s and 1740s.... But only from the mid-fifties did interest become

[17] J. C. Batzel, "Austria and the First Three Treaties of Versailles, 1755–1758," PhD dissertation, Brown University, 1974.
[18] H. Bédarida, *Parme et la France de 1748 à 1789* (Paris, 1928), and *Parme dans la Politique
Française au XVIIIe siècle* (Paris, 1930).

widespread and more sustained.... Only with the impact of the Seven Years'
War – that is of international politics – did an active and continuing public
consciousness of empire begin to be shaped in Britain.[19]

This is an important argument, although it suffers greatly from a failure
to mention, let alone assess, much of the relevant literature, especially, but
not only, that by foreign scholars.[20] Two related issues need to be raised.
First, it is important to consider the role of public debate in Britain and the
extent to which it framed or influenced policy, and, second, it is pertinent to
assess its content as well as changes in its content. These are not separate in
practice or conceptually because part of the importance of the debate was
the use politicians made of it.[21] This use (to be considered in terms of the
impact of the debate) involved drawing on aspects of the debate that seemed
relevant, pertinent or convenient (content reconsidered). Thus, an attempt
to draw the general contours, such as that by Peters, suffers from a lack of
understanding of the complexity of political resonances in the debate among
politicians.[22]

Again, this relates to the chosen model of influence. Judging a debate
to have influenced policy presupposes a linear influence process, albeit one
affected by important feedback mechanisms resulting from the attempt to
produce material for and in this debate. In this case, however, the relationship between debate and policy was more complex and less automatic than
any model can assume and thus provided more opportunity for those who
sought to shape both debate and policy. It also challenges Peters's approach
because arguments about the salience of imperial issues might therefore
appear more prominent to contemporaries in particular conjunctures, contrary to her attempt to produce a developmental model with all its associated
teleological implications.

Debate, politics and policy were thus in a complex relationship, and
describing the latter in terms of strategic culture might underplay this complexity. For example, in early 1754, the direct political impact of the shift
in public consciousness over colonial disputes, especially concerning North
America, remained limited, but by late 1754, the prevalent opinion in British
political circles was of a need to stand up to France in these disputes.
Moreover, as a reminder of the complexity of debate, politics, and policy,

[19] M. Peters, "Early Hanoverian Consciousness: Empire or Europe?," *English Historical Review*, 122, 2007, pp. 663, 667.
[20] E.g., G. Niedhart, *Handel und Krieg in der Britischen Weltpolitik 1738–1763* (Munich, 1979); M. Mimmber, *Der Einfluss Interessen in Nordamerika auf die Strategie und Diplomatie Grossbritanniens während des 18. Jahrhunderts* (Hildesheim, 1983); G. Abbattista, *Commercio, colonie e impero alla vigilia della Rivoluzione Americana: John Campbell pubblicista e storio nell' Inghilterra del sec. XVIII* (Florence, 1990).
[21] J. Black, *Parliament and the Foreign Policy in the Eighteenth Century* (Cambridge, 2004).
[22] The same is true of B. Simms, *Three Victories and a Defeat: The Rise and Fall of the First British Empire, 1714–1783* (London, 2007).

this development was not directly, or even closely, related to the more general issues of Britain's continental relations with France and other European powers. Indeed, these issues were less acute in 1754 than they had been earlier in the decade. In 1753, Anglo-French hostility still revolved around European issues, but without the political or public resonance within Britain that could lead ministers to expect support if they pressed for action.

North America had been a cause of diplomatic activity and ministerial concern for a number of years, but its sudden rise to prominence in summer 1754, with the outbreak of fighting in the Ohio Valley, came as a surprise. Yet, this prominence was politically significant precisely because it matched a powerful and politically loaded theme of public debate, one that joined, or could join, Whig critics of the (Whig) government with Tory opponents. There was frequent emphasis among political leaders on the threat from France, and these preceded the mid-1750s. In the *London Evening Post* of 27 May (os) 1749, the pseudonymous 'Camber' referred to the "encroaching ambition" of the French when warning of their moves in the West Indies. He pointed to the possible loss of the sugar trade and also drew attention to the threat to the Newfoundland fishery posed by the French recovery of Cape Breton. Pressing for efforts to separate Spain from France, *Old England* claimed on 21 December (os) 1751 that "the exorbitant power of the House of Bourbon is a subject worn . . . threadbare by my indefatigable brethren of the quill."

Such an emphasis could also serve domestic political purposes by creating the impression that the government was failing to respond and was thus part of the problem – in fact the chief threat. Ministers did indeed respond, although they shaped their response by their own attitudes and experience, and here the notion of a strategic culture can appear unduly unitary, hegemonic, and based on an unsubtle notion of influence. For example, Thomas, Duke of Newcastle, was keener on focusing on Europe, while, a rival, John, 4th Duke of Bedford, secretary of state for the Southern Department and, in 1762, negotiator of the Peace of Paris, was a supporter of 'blue water' policies. In 1749, Bedford responded to news of Spanish warships searching British merchantmen in the Caribbean by writing to Benjamin Keene, the envoy in Spain, "You know how extremely jealous this nation is of the least encroachments of this nature – the least spark of this sort must, if not timely prevented, kindle a flame."[23]

It is easy to leap from such remarks to William, Duke of Cumberland, who complained in 1757, "I am very fully convinced that the Tory doctrine of a sea-war, which we are following, will be repeated by our

---

[23] Bedford to Benjamin Keene, 6 July (os) 1749, London, National Archives, State Papers (hereafter NA. SP.) 94/136 fol. 1.

children's children."[24] Cumberland, the sole surviving son of George II, it must be remembered, was part of the politics of the situation. An opponent of William Pitt, he felt that he was starved of support in his German command because of the influence of Pitt's ideas. Cumberland sought to condemn them by labeling them Tory, although that proved a difficult case to sell to the British public.

Cumberland's deprecation of Tory policy as "doctrine" was correct but insufficient. Ideas were important, but to move to policy, it is necessary to explain their interaction with the politics of the period. Although this included a public sphere, politics also were a matter of what one might term "five men and the Duke of Newcastle." Here a crucial shift in recent scholarship has been the positive reevaluation of the role of monarchy and the impact of monarchs in eighteenth-century Britain.[25]

This provides a further parallel with Continental developments. Although elderly, George II was still fit and committed to both his royal prerogatives and his interests as Elector of Hanover, to which he paid long visits in 1753 and 1755. In Britain, the political role of the king was crucial because of the lack of collective ministerial responsibility and cabinet cohesion. Instead, ministers were appointed by, and answerable to, the king. His role was even more significant when ministries were divided and weak, and the death in 1754 of Henry Pelham, First Lord of the Treasury, began a period of instability only ended by the formation of the Pitt-Newcastle ministry in 1757.[26] Throughout that period, but particularly in 1756–1757, George II was crucial politically, and any discussion of strategic culture has to take note of him.

Personnel issues were related to complex questions of policy, and these constrained George's options. The vulnerability of the Electorate of Hanover to French and Austrian military operations insured that he did not want war with France, but the deteriorating situation in North America limited his options. Hanover was indeed vulnerable to attack in what was a fast-deteriorating international situation. Although conflict between Britain and France had broken out over the Ohio country in 1754, the two nations did not declare full-scale war until 1756. However, alongside the concern that war could break out, there was a specific worry that France might attack Hanover to pressure Britain, counteracting any British gains in North America with gains at the expense of Hanover. British leaders assumed that this would also involve an attack by France's ally Prussia, to which Hanover

---

[24]   Cumberland to Henry Fox, 23 Sept. 1757, Earl of Ilchester, *Letters to Henry Fox* (London, 1915), p. 120.

[25]   Jeremy Black, *George III* (New Haven, 2006), and *George II* (Exeter, 2007).

[26]   On Pitt's attitudes, see Jeremy Black, "Pitt the Elder and the Foundation of an Imperial Foreign Policy," in T. G. Otte, ed., *The Makers of British Foreign Policy: From Pitt to Thatcher* (Basingstoke, 2002), pp. 35–51.

was particularly vulnerable, at least until the diplomatic revolution that saw France switch allies.

In response, the British government sought to strengthen relations with Austria and its ally Russia, each of which bordered Prussia and each of which was in a position to put military pressure on Frederick. George II was associated with this policy, which had indeed been a significant theme in his views since the early 1730s. To him, the empire that counted was the Holy Roman Empire and not the British Empire, although, alongside his continued interest in Hanover, he became more concerned about the latter during the course of the war. Already, in June 1755, Robert, 4th Earl of Holdernesse, one of the secretaries of state, had written *entre nous* to Newcastle that "the King seemed overjoyed at the probable success of his measures in America,"[27] a reference to the decision to deploy more troops there to attack French positions – in short, to a militarization of policy, which was frequently George II's instinctual response.

Attempts were made by politicians (and subsequently have been by scholars) to lessen the tension between European and imperial goals in British foreign policy and to argue that they were fundamentally compatible. This was indeed the argument William Pitt the Elder made after 1758, but it does not capture George II's attitude at the opening of the war. He saw a clash in commitments and, despite his interest in North America, clearly favored the European dimension. Such a clash was particularly apparent in the mid-1750s. Nevertheless, when the war went well, George II was to press for the conquest of Canada from the French.

George II's role might appear marginal were the focus solely on the crisis for the British Empire in North America, but in fact George II's determination to keep attention directed on Europe and his Hanoverian possessions influenced both British policy and politics, which raises questions about how strategic culture is discussed. Holdernesse underlined George's determination in a letter to the diplomat Sir Charles Hanbury Williams, who had been appointed envoy to St Petersburg: "I am particularly commanded by the King to press your departure, as every day may be of the utmost consequence in the present critical state of Europe."

Similarly, a cabinet meeting recommended that the Austrian envoy be informed "that His Majesty has lately given the strongest orders for concluding, forthwith, the treaty with Russia, and greatly augmented the terms hitherto offered, both with regard to the preliminary subsidy, and to the sum to be allowed for the Russian troops, when in motion,"[28] the last a reference to the wish to deploy Russian troops in order to put pressure on Prussia. Frederick the Great regarded George II as having a great predilection for

---

[27] London, British Library Additional Manuscripts (hereafter BL. Add.) 32856 fol. 380.
[28] 11 Ap. 1755, Newport, Hanbury Williams papers; BL. Add. 32996 fol. 79.

Austria as well as considerable concern for Hanoverian interests and views. Ironically, this concern, a concern that was also to influence Newcastle's views, was to help lead to an alliance between Britain and Prussia.[29]

On 10 January 1755, George II told the newly arrived French envoy, Mirepoix, that he sought a continuation of peace, but he also spoke to him warmly about the situation in North America. Characteristically, George II presented this in terms of honor and obligation, with the monarch appearing in the traditional light of a defender of his subjects. He told Mirepoix that in response to repeated complaints from the colonists, he could not refrain from providing them with the protection he owed them. George II claimed that he had no intention of expanding his possessions, but he stated that he could not accept that others should infringe the territorial rights of his subjects, an approach that Mirepoix declared was shared by Louis XV.[30] The king, therefore, very much took the government's view.

Mirepoix claimed in correspondence that George II did not care much about the colonies and did not want war but that he had no intention of trying to improve the situation for Hanover by making concessions over North America, and, indeed, that he had no power to make such concessions,[31] which was an accurate account both of George II's position and of his views. There were suggestions that George II was capable of taking initiatives without consulting the government, but these related to less central issues such as the choice of the new envoy to Paris.[32]

In sum, George II was in line with the development of government policy in the growing crisis over North America, and British diplomatic instructions were not simply using the Crown as a fiction. Holdernesse wrote in January 1755:

> These repeated insults of the French, which, in their consequences, would end in the ruin of His Majesty's colonies, induce the King to send two regiments to America, together with some ships of war, and to give orders for raising more forces within the colonies... though the King is determined to maintain and defend the just rights of His Crown and People, His Majesty will use his utmost endeavours, that these disputes with the Crown of France, may not be productive of consequences fatal to the general peace.[33]

Turning to Frederick reflected George II's quest for security for Hanover and his perception of the state of these alliances and, in particular, his anger over Austria's strategic policy. Alongside loyalty to the Imperial constitution,

29 *Polit. Corresp.* X, 386.
30 Paris, Ministère des Affaires Etrangères, Correspondance Politique Angleterre (hereafter AE. CP. Ang.) 438 fol. 15.
31 AE. CP. Ang. 438 fol. 305, 439 fol. 169.
32 AE. CP. Ang. 438 fol. 50.
33 NA. SP. 84/468, 28 Jan.

ambivalence toward Austria characterized his reign from the outset, and it was certainly apparent in 1755. Quite apart from his battle experience at Oudenaarde in 1708, it is clear that the vulnerability of the Low Countries to French attack was an important consideration for George II, not least because it would weaken Austria's potential role in protecting Hanover against Prussia. In May 1755, there was a noticeable tone of complaint: "Every measure the King is taking with the different powers of Europe must be at a stand until Her Imperial Majesty shall come to the necessary resolution of sending, without loss of time, a strong reinforcement into the Low Countries." In clear-cut reproach, the King accused his envoy in Vienna of going native, complaining that he could not see why the envoy referred to the Austrian government as having a good disposition "when you see a refusal, on the part of the Court of Vienna, of coming into the only measure in which His Majesty's interest is concerned."[34]

Like the neutrality convention that George II had been obliged to accept as Elector of Hanover in 1741, the neutrality enforced by the victorious French by the Convention of Klosterzeven revealed the limited value to Hanover of its ruler's great-power diplomacy. The emptiness of such diplomacy without significant military force to back up George II's position (and, in 1756, the Hanoverian army had been increased to 27,146 men) had been displayed, and, unlike in 1741, this time, Hanover had been conquered with all the attendant destructiveness of war.

The French occupation of Hanover led George II to consider negotiations with Austria for neutrality of the Electorate of Hanover. This indicated the dependence of strategic culture on events. Hanoverian neutrality, however, was rejected by Pitt as likely to wreck Britain's alliance with Prussia and as posing the danger that Frederick would leave the war. Pitt indeed pressed his king hard for the rapid disavowal of the Convention.

That winter, Pitt played a major role in securing a political settlement that tied the defense of Hanover to British direction and identified it with the more popular Prussian alliance. He proposed that Britain pay the entire cost of the "Army of Observation" and, in 1758, won support for the dispatch to Germany of British troops who were to assist this army. Landing in Emden that August, British forces saw action the following year. The dispatch of this force was an important concession to George, although it also fixed Hanover as a principal in the war, ending the option of neutrality and leaving Hanover vulnerable to renewed French attacks. Nevertheless, provision for the protection of Hanover was essential to the settlement of domestic political differences in Britain, and this reflected George II's importance to the processes of making strategy.

[34] NA. SP. 80/196 fols 56–57.

By the close of George II's reign in 1760, the Royal Navy had smashed the French navy (at the battles of Lagos and Quiberon Bay, both in 1759) and also captured much of the French Empire, most dramatically Québec in 1759. Thus, Britain had become the dominant European power in South Asia and North America. George II was proclaimed in verse for British victories, and indeed war patriotism helped the Crown to keep the nation moving forward. The Reverend Samuel Pullein took time from his publications on silk cultivation to write the poem "On the Taking of Louisburgh," published in *Owen's Weekly Chronicle* on 9 September 1758 as well as in the *Gentleman's Magazine*. Pullein saw the capture of the fortress, which was believed to be the key base in the French outer defenses of Canada, as a decisive moment in world history and presented the war as part of a struggle against tyranny and superstition presided over by the unlikely figures of the elderly George II and the sickly Pitt:

> Hail Western world! begin thy better fate,
> Hence let thy annals take a happier date...
> George, feared in arms, beloved for gentle sway,
> And Pitt, the vestal guard of freedom's ray;
> Prompt to consummate heaven's supreme decree,
> They give the mandate, and thy realms are free...
> Thus liberty, released by heroes hands...
> gives the new-known worlds a second birth...
> when the fated ages shall have run,
> And shown new empires to the setting sun,
> Each rising era shall its date restrain
> To Pitt, and Liberty, and George's reign.

The capture of Montréal and the destruction of French forces in Canada followed in 1760, and John Pingo's medal *Canada Subdued* (1761) showed George II's head on the reverse. Indeed, the progress of the conflict helped ensure that George II became, in the eyes of many Britons, more British and less German. This was paradoxical, as he remained greatly concerned about Hanover, but also underlines both the shift in public perception of George II and the need, particularly in wartime, to see the country as a united state.

Considering the Seven Years' War in the light of the contested character of national interests, there is a potent suggestion of comparison on which to close. In Britain, the extent to which political contention and politics make strategic culture a means of debate, rather than a category that encompasses it, could probably be reproduced elsewhere in contemporary Europe were the politics to be as well recorded and, in part, as public as in the case of Britain. This underlines contingency and thus the importance of campaigning to the consistency of policy and, therefore, the fate of the conflict.

In this case, a key element of contingency was the rapidly changing nature of the war, both in Europe and overseas. This was true for Britain and for the other powers, and their interaction created a system that was also unpredictable. War, its presence, changes and consequences, thus set the pace for the diplomacy of France and other states. Much of this diplomacy became a matter of keeping the rival coalitions together. Thus, their defeats in late 1757 destroyed early French enthusiasm, leading the French Foreign Minister Bernis, at the start of 1758, to see the alliance with Austria as a failure. These problems obliged the allies to consider new options. The French government sought that spring to persuade Austria to make peace with Prussia. However, Austria, for its part, was determined to fight on against the Prussians, increasingly relied on Russia, and displayed limited interest in the French war.

Similarly, relations between France and Spain affected those between each and Britain. At the same time, they also underlined the role of individuals. Ferdinand VI of Spain (r. 1746–1759) resisted French pressure to act aggressively as well as ignoring warnings from his allies that the Spanish colonies would follow those of France in falling into British hands.[35] His attitude is a reminder of the dangers of adopting a schematic approach to international relations. Far from being driven to align with France from fear of British expansion or by dynastic links, Ferdinand was reasonably close to Britain. In contrast, his half brother Charles III (r. 1759–1788) was concerned about a fundamental shift of maritime power to Britain. This shift in Spanish policy greatly encouraged French firmness in abortive Anglo-French peace negotiations in 1761 because it gave it point.

Meanwhile, British successes helped transform attitudes not only throughout the United Kingdom but also among Britain's opponents. This sense of strategic culture as dynamic is one that needs to be captured. It is particularly appropriate when considering the later years of the war, for the parameters of debate in Britain were very different from those at the outset. In part, this reflected the consequences of campaigning, but there were also key external developments in the shape of the new political environment surrounding the accession of a new king who was determined to see changes.

Those changes directly affected political relations with Prussia and Spain. George III and his key adviser, John, 3rd Earl of Bute and Newcastle decided to seek to revive the "Old System" of prewar alliances. This entailed distancing themselves from Prussia. However, as a powerful reminder of the impact of ideas, and thus of conjunctures and contingencies in opinions, George III and Bute did not envisage repeating the extensive and costly commitment of Newcastle's prewar diplomacy. In particular, the defense of

[35] AE. CP. Espagne 517 fols 26–28, 192–93, 281–85; A. Bourquet, *Le Duc de Choiseul et l'Alliance Espagnole* (Paris, 1906), pp. 6–7, 25.

Hanover was no longer to be a central feature of Britain's Continental policy. Conversely, the argument that the Anglo-Prussian alliance was unlikely to have survived the war throws new light on the policies of Bute, who can be seen as an intelligent and effective minister forced to deal with the commitments of war, including the Prussian alliance, and obliged to adapt policy to the peacetime exigencies of domestic political and financial constraints.[36]

A sense of strategic culture as dynamic makes sense not only of the politics of the period – for example, the response, narrowly defined, to George III's wish to end the commitment to Hanoverian expansionism and to the deployment of British forces in Germany – but also of politics in the more widely defined sense of attitudes towards state and country. The consequences of the Seven Years' War in this respect were more profound in France, where public debate became more prominent. In Britain, the key change was a greater salience for imperial issues, which led to postwar attempts to make empire work. These, however, were the very attempts that led to the American Revolution.

[36]   K. W. Schweizer, ed., *Lord Bute: Essays in Reinterpretation* (Leicester, 1988).

4

Strategy as character: Bismarck and the Prusso-German question, 1862–1878

MARCUS JONES

Germany, situated at the heart of Europe, is Europe's heart. Europe cannot "live" without a sound, strong heart. I have devoted much attention to Bismarck in recent years, and his stature as a diplomat grows continually in my eyes. It is deplorable what a false picture we ourselves have created of him in the world – the politician of force wearing cuirassier's boots – in our childlike pleasure that someone had finally made Germany count for something again. He had a unique skill at creating trust in the world, just the opposite of today. In truth, his great gifts were diplomacy of the highest order, and moderation.[1]

Otto von Bismarck – "the greatest master of diplomacy in the modern era" – is nearly too massive a subject for the modern historian.[2] No historical figure bears more responsibility for the state of great power politics in the long period between 1815 and 1945, and few, if any, in history have managed the strategic policy of their states with such virtuosity. His decisions and policies established the groundwork for the most important geopolitical events of the twentieth century, and his principal creation, a German nation-state at the heart of Europe, endures in truncated form after a half-century of painful adaptation to the world without his guidance.

A man of puzzling contradictions and vast ambitions, as well as a grandiose sense of his own importance, Bismarck's career presents each new generation with a fresh set of problems and perspectives. Rather like

---

[1] Ulrich von Hassell, *Vom anderen Deutschland: Aus den nachgelassenen Tagebüchern 1938–1944* (Frankfurt a.M., 1964), p. 319; from Michael Stürmer, "Bismarck in Perspective," *Central European History* 4 (1971), p. 292.

[2] A. J. P. Taylor, *Bismarck: The Man and the Statesman* (New York, 1967), p. 111. The literature on Bismarck is exceeded by that on no other figure in German history save Hitler. The best syntheses remain Otto Pflanze, *Bismarck and the Development of Germany*, 3 vols., 3rd ed. (Princeton, 1990); Lothar Gall, *Bismarck: Der weisse Revolutionär*, 2 vols. (Berlin, 1980); and Ernst Engelberg, *Bismarck: Urpreusse und Reichsgründer* (Berlin, 1985).

Abraham Lincoln for Americans, Bismarck and his legacy are interpreted afresh by each generation of Germans, who nurse a penchant for viewing his career through the prism of their own perceived anxieties and virtues.[3]

Quite apart from the complexities of Bismarck's personality and ideas, the historian must reckon with the numberless ways his scholarly forerunners have come to terms with the subject. Almost every contemporary document relevant to a consideration of Bismarck and his policies has long been in print. In its totality, the historiography is so vast as to require more than one scholarly lifetime to survey. Particularly for that period most essential for understanding Bismarck as a strategic thinker – the era of Prussian consolidation and German unification spanning 1862 to 1871 – there can be no question of uncovering critical new source material or developing radically original insights. It was in those pivotal years that Bismarck recast the German question – understood by statesman since 1815 and the German public since the revolutions of 1848 as the status of the incipient German nation – in terms of Prussian autocracy and militarism, on one hand, and middle-class economic and social emancipation, on the other.[4]

Given the scale of that accomplishment, it is remarkable to consider that it was largely unintentional. Contemporaries, and particularly succeeding generations of German patriots, hailed the twin victories in 1866 and 1871, and the realization of a Prussian-dominated German nation at the heart of Europe, as the fulfillment of Bismarck's genius, born of his clear strategic intention to realize precisely these outcomes. Bismarck himself worked diligently throughout much of his subsequent career in politics to reinforce the same impression, encouraging the growth of a cottage industry devoted to his totemlike status as the father of the modern German nation. Indeed, and not unexpectedly, doing so frequently proved useful for a statesman gifted at manipulating impressions and mobilizing popular sentiments for what were, under any other circumstances, decidedly unpopular purposes.

But the need of succeeding generations to adulate Bismarck, and Bismarck's own occasional distortion of his role in the unification process, should not obscure the novel means whereby he actually realized his strategic triumphs. Put differently, Bismarck's great genius as the founder of a Prussian-dominated German nation lay not in his adherence to a systematic

---

[3]   Most recently, see Karina Urbach, "Between Saviour and Villain: 100 Years of Bismarck Biographies," *The Historical Journal* 41/4 (1998), pp. 1141–60; see also Michael Stürmer, "Bismarck in Perspective"; and Wilhelm Schüssler, "Die geschichtliche Standort Bismarcks," in Lothar Gall, ed., *Das Bismarck-Problem in der Geschichtsschreibung* (Köln, 1971); and Hans-Günther Zmarlik, *Das Bismarckbild der Deutschen – gestern und heute* (Freiburg, 1967).

[4]   For an overview, see Wolfgang J. Mommsen, *Das Ringen um den nationalen Staat: Die Gründung und der innere Ausbau des Deutschen Reiches unter Otto von Bismarck 1850 bis 1890* (Berlin, 1993); and Harm-Hinrich Brandt, *Deutsche Geschichte 1850–1870: Entscheidung über die Nation* (Stuttgart, 1999).

program or plan but in his expert navigation of uncertain events through intuition and broad experience.

Perhaps no example in his long career demonstrated this better than his masterful handling of the conflict with Austria and the crisis over the duchies of Schleswig-Holstein in 1863–1964, when he deftly maneuvered the Austrian crown from a position of strength to one of defensiveness in German affairs and laid the groundwork for a decisive military showdown at Königgratz in 1866.[5] His carefully conducted policy reveals a statesman with an uncanny gift for balancing seemingly exclusive alternatives without losing sight of his state's overriding interests.

Bismarck's origins were anything but humble, at least by Prussian standards. The son of a dull father and an intelligent and ambitious mother, the future 'iron chancellor' claimed an ancestry at least as distinguished as that of the Prussian royal house, the Hohenzollerns, and possibly more so. According to custom, each Bismarck in the family tree bore a number in the lineage; Bismarck's was 309.[6] From his mother, he inherited an intellectual disposition and a feminine "sensitivity," as some historians have described it, qualities that distinguished him from his social peers; from his father, Bismarck took the staid, upright bearing of the traditional rural *Junkertum* and its masculine references.

One of his most interesting biographers, A. J. P. Taylor, illustrated how Bismarck drew on both impulses and struggled throughout his life to reconcile their contradictions.[7] Ultimately, together, they formed a sensibility remarkable for its diversity and breadth but also largely unfulfilled until his middle years. He was an indifferent university student, first in Göttingen and then in Berlin, where he spent much of his time in carousing and drinking. After his studies, he took up a modest position in the Prussian civil service. Not surprisingly, Bismarck found bureaucratic service stultifying and resolved never again to find himself marching to somebody else's tune.

After his mother's death, he took over the management of his family's estates at Kniephopf and Schonhausen in Pomerania, where the tedium of rural existence brought forth latent tendencies to debauchery and

---

[5]   The basis for the present assessment is Eberhard Kolb, "Großpreussen oder Kleindeutschland? Zu Bismarcks deutscher Politik im Reichgründungsjahrzehnt," in Dieter Langewiesche und Klaus Schönhoven, eds., *Umbrüche deutscher Geschichte 1866/71, 1918/19, 1929/33: Ausgewählte Aufsätze* (München, 1993), pp. 11–33; an earlier articulation of the argument is found in Andreas Kaernbach, *Bismarcks Konzepte zur Reform des Deutschen Bundes: Zur Kontinuität der Politik Bismarck und Preußens in der deutschen Frage* (Göttingen, 1991); the starting point for an assessment of Bismarck's dualist and conservative solution to the German problem is Rudolf Stadelmann, *Das Jahr 1865 und das Problem von Bismarcks deutscher Politik* (München, 1933).

[6]   Marianne Heuwagen, "Der Clan der Großen Nummer 309," *Süddeutsche Zeitung* 5/6 (1996), p. 3; from Urbach, "Between Saviour and Villain," p. 1143.

[7]   Taylor, *Bismarck*, pp. 11–12.

womanizing. He met his future wife through the Pietist circles of the Prussian Protestant nobility and quickly adopted her religious views, which he held earnestly for the rest of his life and which historians ever since have struggled to reconcile with his political career.[8]

In 1847, he entered Prussian politics nearly by accident, after agreeing to stand in for an ill colleague in the Prussian *Landtag*. That experience, along with the revolutions of 1848 in Europe, confirmed Bismarck's basically reactionary social tendencies, even as they made necessary in his mind a revision of the Prussian monarchy's hidebound approach to its interests at home and abroad. He attacked the Frankfurt parliament as 'the German swindle' and counseled the Prussian monarch to reassert his traditional rights against the contemptible middle classes in the cities. As he later put it:

> I would prefer that Prussia remain Prussia. As such it will always be in a position to prescribe its laws to Germany and not to receive them from others. I therefore feel duty bound to oppose a motion designed to undermine the edifice cemented by the blood of our fathers. The crown of Frankfurt may seem very brilliant but its luster is to be obtained by smelting it with that of Prussia and I do not think that this will succeed.[9]

From his earliest days, Bismarck exhibited intellectual traits that set him apart not only from his pedestrian *Junker* counterparts in Prussian government and society but also from the broad run of statesmen through the ages. He quickly developed a gift for seizing on the most salient aspects of a critical question or issue and abstracting them from the less important. Among the best letter writers in the German language, he crafted his personal and official correspondence in a style that was forceful, direct, and nothing short of elegant, with analogies and metaphors that exhibited a rigorous internal grasp of his arguments and context. Throughout his life, he was a skilled linguist and lover of foreign cultures, having spent years of his diplomatic career in St. Petersburg and Paris and traveling with relish and frequency; he spoke and wrote well in Russian, French, English, Italian, and Latin.

As becomes apparent to any student of his strategic policy, his success was inseparable from his broad knowledge of European cultures and societies, linguistic talents, and diplomatic conventions, and his exceptional gift for analysis and prose.[10] It was also reflective of a cast of mind born of a deeply and intuitively humanistic understanding of political affairs, a cautious patience, and humility about the extent of one's own knowledge

---

8   No biography would be complete without such speculations, but see esp. Ulrich Kühn, *Die Grundgedanke der Politik Bismarcks* (Dettelbach, 2001); earlier and famously, see Arnold Oskar Meyer, *Bismarcks Glaube: nach neuen Quellen aus dem Familienarchiv* (München, 1933).
9   Horst Kohl, ed., *Die politischen Reden des Fürsten Bismarck: Historische-kritische Gesamtausgabe*, vol. 1 (Stuttgart, 1892), 9 June 1849, pp. 93–94.
10   Gordon A. Craig, "Bismarck: Diplomacy as a Vocation," in Gordon A. Craig, *From Bismarck to Adenauer: Aspects of German Statecraft* (Baltimore, 1958), pp. 6–11.

and influence, the hallmark of his much-touted realism. Nearly all statesmen consider themselves realists, even those imbued with romantic and idealistic visions of destiny. Bismarck's realism was in the tradition of Richelieu and Talleyrand and was rooted in a sensitive awareness of his own capacities – which were prodigious – and those of the state he headed.

In his political utterings, one can see what set Bismarck apart throughout his career from his contemporaries on the right and left alike: his nuanced grasp of the vast landscape of European relations, coupled with a Machiavellian flexibility in marrying unorthodox, even revolutionary, means to conservative ends.[11] "Politics is neither arithmetic nor mathematics," he wrote on several occasions. "To be sure, one has to reckon with given and unknown factors, but there are no rules and formulae with which to sum up the results in advance." Without losing sight of long-term goals, he focused resolutely on the urgent needs of the moment, planning with a careful eye on the "imponderabilia," as he called them – uncertainties, accidents, and oversights.[12] Despite his superficial excesses – his great size and girth, monstrous appetites, arrogance, and ferocious temper – his most pronounced feature as a strategic actor was his moderation and prudence. Bismarck never set his country on a course that his mind had not cautiously explored beforehand.

When called to the minister-presidency of Prussia in September 1862 by a king who had reached the point of despair in his deadlock with parliament over army reforms, Bismarck had a reputation as a hidebound conservative and was perceived as too much of a political outsider to be effective. But he enjoyed a unique degree of support from his monarch. Wilhelm took seriously his oath to the Prussian Constitution and wished to govern constitutionally, but he also encouraged a more muscular and assertive foreign policy for Prussia and supported initiatives designed to leverage the country's advantages.[13] In this, Bismarck was his ideal complement.

Despite his conservative credentials, Bismarck demonstrated early on a willingness to traffic with forces viewed with suspicion by conservative interests and create new political constellations for furthering the interests of the crown. In doing so, he revealed his guiding light: an unbending loyalty to the

---

[11] The basis of Henry A. Kissinger's well-known interpretation of Bismarck's place in the broad sweep of European diplomacy: "The White Revolutionary: Reflections on Bismarck," *Daedalus* 97 (Summer, 1968), pp. 888–924; for the historian, his interpretation is necessarily compromised by his overt idolization of Bismarck and his desire to give contemporary geopolitics a quasi-Bismarckian cast: Rudolf Augstein, *Otto von Bismarck* (Frankfurt, 1990), from Urbach, "Between Saviour and Villain," p. 157n148, and Freidemann Bedürftig, "Kissinger und das Kissinger-Diktat," *Süddeutsche Zeitung* 12 (July 1998), p. 12.

[12] Norman Rich, *Great Power Diplomacy, 1814–1914* (New York, 1992), p. 189.

[13] Franz Herre, *Kaiser Wilhelm I: Der letzte Preusse* (Köln, 1980), and Karl-Heinz Börner, *Kaiser Wilhelm I., 1797 bis 1888: deutscher Kaiser und König von Preussen: eine Biographie* (Köln, 1984).

Prussian state and its interests in Germany, a loyalty much greater than any he felt for the specific monarch at whose pleasure he served or the abstract idea of a unified German people or nation. The conception of nation so cherished by broad swaths of the emerging German public resonated little with Bismarck, and he viewed it in a cynical light. "There must be some special magic in the word 'German,'" he argued at one point. "One can see that each person calls German whatever suits him and whatever suits his party's standpoint. Thus the use of a word changes according to requirements."[14]

While he was willing to bargain with Prussian liberals as they pursued their national dream, the idea of unification was meaningful to Bismarck only insofar as it served as a vehicle for the protection of the Hohenzollern throne and its prerogatives. As Bismarck argued early in his political career:

> Prussia has become great not through liberalism and free-thinking but through a succession of powerful, decisive, and wise regents who carefully husbanded the military and financial resources of the state and kept them together in their own hands in order to throw them with ruthless courage into the scale of European politics as soon as a favorable opportunity presented itself.[15]

The structure of the new German nation-state after 1871 – wherein the Prussian king functioned as German kaiser and both the Prussian and imperial governments served at his pleasure – bore the unmistakable imprint of Bismarck's Prussian particularism.[16]

As the director of Prussian and German strategic policy for nearly three decades, Bismarck proved a shrewd and imaginative statesman and daring risk taker, but always with the recognition that Prussia remained but one European power among several.[17] For a state so geographically exposed and politically conservative, strategic vigilance and imagination of the highest order were essential. Bismarck demonstrated consistent moderation in defining and pursuing Prussian interests; his decisions were shaped throughout his career by an anachronistic vision of Prussia, traditional and poor, enveloped by larger, wealthier neighbors, especially France. He was convinced that military and diplomatic hubris could result not just in failure

---

14   Bismarck in a speech to the Prussian Landtag, 1864, from J. Breuilly, "The National Idea in Modern German History," in J. Breuilly, ed., *The State of Germany* (London, 1992), p. 3.

15   Otto von Busmarck, *Die Gessammelten Werke (GW)*, vol. 1, Hermann von Petersdorff, et al., eds. (Berlin, 1923–1933), p. 375.

16   Bismarck's authority as minister-president of Prussia and later chancellor of the German Empire depended on the support of the Prussian king. Wits in Berlin described Bismarck as the king's "last mistress, for only such a creature can wield so magic a power over an old man." Otto Pflanze, *Bismarck and the Development of Germany*, vol. 1, *The Period of Unification, 1815–1871* (Princeton, 1963), p. 301.

17   See also Marcus Jones, "*Vae Victoribus*: Bismarck's Quest for Peace in the Franco-Prussian War, 1870–1871," in Williamson Murray and Jim Lacey, eds., *The Making of Peace: Rulers, States, and the Aftermath of War* (Cambridge, 2009), pp. 179–80.

but also in disaster. In this view of his strategy, Bismarck's detachment from the prevailing social forces of the bourgeois nineteenth century, especially romantic nationalism or idealistic liberalism, distinguished him from most of his political contemporaries.[18]

An impression of a man mindful of his own limitations is at odds with much of the historical literature on Bismarck, particularly in English, which binds the most significant events of his career – the war with Austria for supremacy in German central Europe and the unification of the German empire through the war with France – into a cogently articulated plan, a process understood and controlled masterfully, step by step, by a strategic genius. According to this notion, Bismarck entered the minister-presidency of Prussia in 1862 with a clear intention to assert Prussian sovereignty in the northern German lands and eliminate traditional French prerogatives in southern Germany.

One can read the subsequent history of his strategic policy as the fulfillment of successive stages in that program, an impression that Bismarck himself was content to perpetuate, especially late in life. While he was quite frank in private about the limitations of both statecraft and the individual statesman, in his own lifetime he purposely cultivated the public image of a statesman with a clairvoyant grasp of strategic affairs and nearly perfect control over their development. Indeed, Bismarck cast his principal literary legacy, the remarkable *Gedanken und Errinerungen*, as "the ideal handbook," as Gooch put it, "for a statesman with Machiavellian intentions."[19]

This is a fundamentally misguided picture and is easily revised by a cursory look at the most important events and decisions of his life as a statesman. These reveal a formidable statesman, to be sure – indeed, if one believes the likes of Gordon Craig and Henry Kissinger, perhaps the greatest strategist of the modern age. But they also point out that Bismarck entered office without any sort of concrete program but rather only with a collection of priorities, with but a vague conception of Prussian capabilities and with an entirely uncertain outlook on Prussia's future in Central Europe. His great achievements as a strategist lay in his methodical and circumspect approach to the ends of state, an approach based as much on his character, background, and intuition as on a systematized theory of international affairs.

On 13 June 1890, only a few weeks after his dismissal from the chancellorship of Imperial Germany by the impetuous Kaiser Wilhelm II, Bismarck met with an Austrian historian, Heinrich Friedjung, for an interview about the origins of the 1866 Austro-Prussian War. That conflict had served to

---

[18]   Gerhard Ritter, *The Sword and the Scepter: The Problem of Militarism in Germany*, vol. 1, *The Prussian Tradition, 1740–1890* (Coral Gables, 1969), pp. 239–40.
[19]   Quoted in Hans Kohn, *The Mind of Germany: Education of a Nation* (London, 1961), p. 182; from Urbach, "Between Saviour and Villain," p. 1143.

bring the lesser northern states of Germany under Prussian influence in the North German Confederation of 1867 and had set Prussia on the path to unifying all of Germany apart from Austria in the imperial settlement of 1871. During the interview, Friedjung asked whether Bismarck had resolved on war with Austria from the beginning of his term as minister-president of Prussia in 1862 as the only way to resolve the question of leadership in German Central Europe. Bismarck's answer neatly sums up his understanding of statecraft and warfare in a manner surprising, perhaps, to those inclined to view him as the arch-exponent of iron and blood:

> In politics you cannot focus on a long-range plan and proceed blindly in accord with it. All you can do is draw the broad outlines of the directions you seek to follow. This you must keep unswervingly in view, even though you may not know the precise route that will get you there.... The war with Austria was indeed difficult to avoid. He who feels even in slight measure responsibility for the lives of millions will shrink from beginning wars until all other means have been explored. It has always been a shortcoming of the Germans to seek all or nothing, and to focus exclusively on a particular method. In contrast I was always pleased if I managed to come three steps closer to German unification, by whatever means. I would have grasped at any solution that led to the expansion of Prussia and German unity without war. Many paths led to my goals, and I had to arrange them one after the next, with the most dangerous last. Uniformity in business was not my way.[20]

What stands out in Bismarck's formulation is his emphasis on a conscious flexibility in achieving his ends, and quite possibly flexibility in framing the ends themselves – in short, a coldly unsentimental understanding of the state's interests and how to pursue them. Basic as well to Bismarck was an abhorrence of warfare, of the risks and costs associated with it, and a genuine desire to avert it, not quite at all costs but to the greatest possible extent without sacrificing the state's core needs and priorities. And, surprising for a man who struck almost all who knew him as supremely prideful and arrogant, he exhibited a modest view of his own capacities, a recognition of just how limited was the understanding and agency of statesmen.

Bismarck was only 36 in 1851, when Friedrich Wilhelm IV appointed him Prussian delegate to the German Confederation, arguably the most important post in the Prussian Foreign Service at the time, and from the beginning, Bismarck showed himself eager to buck convention. Since 1815, Prussia had staunchly upheld the Holy Alliance with Austria and Russia as the bastion of conservative power in Europe. Practically, the alliance entailed Prussian deference to the traditional primacy of Austrian power in

20 Heinrich Friedjung, *Der Kampf um die Vorherrschaft in Deutschland 1859 bis 1866*, 9th ed., vol. 2 (Stuttgart, 1912–13), p. 579; from Eberhard Kolb, "Großpreuß oder Kleindeutschland?," p. 11.

the German Confederation. As a delegate, Bismarck took every opportunity to assert Prussian equality with Austria in that body, going so far as to smoke ostentatiously during meetings, a right traditionally enjoyed only by the Austrian president of the chamber. Bismarck had become convinced that Prussia had grown beyond the constraints of the balance of power established in 1815 and had a far larger role to play in Central Europe, perhaps equal to that of Austria. He resolved to employ all practical means, to "hold open every door and every turning," to seek advantage.[21]

By and large, the balance of power between the major European states since 1815 had remained stable for several reasons, not least among them the terrible memory of what the long era of the French Revolution and the Napoleonic Empire had wrought and a desire not to relive those experiences.[22] Apart from a handful of relatively minor issues that aroused public passions, statesmen crafted policy and engaged in diplomacy without much regard for public opinion, in the reactionary spirit of Metternich's view that "foreign affairs is not for the plebs."[23] The economic systems of the major powers had yet not developed organized lobbies of the scale and influence necessary to exercise a decisive influence on diplomacy, although Prussia's economic potential was beginning to make itself felt, and one could disentangle British commercial and imperial interests only with difficulty.

Likewise, military establishments throughout Europe remained reasonably content with their level of armaments and readiness and were either too lazy or too fearful to pressure their governments in ways that would unravel the peace. Although the major powers divided loosely into liberal and conservative camps after the revolutions of 1830 (so loosely that they frequently proved willing to cooperate across ideological lines), the internal complexions of the different states bore little on the way they understood and pursued their interests. Finally, all the powers, with the obvious exception of France, seemed both content with their lot and willing, as a group, to work together against any who would alter it.[24] Without major changes in the ideological complexion or economic, military, and demographic power of the states themselves, there seemed little reason to think that the comfortable settlement of 1815 could not persist indefinitely.

---

[21]   *GW*, vol. 14, p. 473; on his conception of history, see Helmuth Wolff, *Geschichtsauffassung und Politik in Bismarcks Bewußtsein* (München, 1926).

[22]   Christian Steinmetz, *Deutscher Bund und europäische Friedensordnung: die Krise der Wiener Ordnung 1848–1850* (Frankfurt, 2002).

[23]   Gordon A. Craig, "Europe and the Balance of Power," in Bruce Thompson, Carolyn Halladay, and Donald Abenheim, eds., *Tact and Intelligence: Essays on Diplomatic History and International Relations* (Palo Alto, CA, 2008), p. 93; see also Richard B. Elrod, "The Concert of Europe: A Fresh Look at an International System," *World Politics* 28 (1976), pp. 159–74.

[24]   Craig, "Europe and the Balance of Power," pp. 93–95.

Of course, international affairs are never static, and Bismarck perceived that the rise of Prussia in the mid-nineteenth century was among the most important factors making a revision of the Metternichian settlement necessary. He reasoned that the most likely source of leverage in a competition with Austria was the neoimperial France of Napoleon III. This set him at odds with his conservative sponsors in the Prussian political system, especially the clique of ministers and advisers around the king. The conservatives tolerated his chancellorship as necessary to preserve their social privileges but saw in his inventive foreign policies a disagreeable populism and a willingness to run roughshod over traditional attitudes.

As events showed, the conservatives were partially correct. Bismarck was anything but a traditional conservative, in foreign or domestic affairs. He had neither an instinctual deference to Austrian primacy in European affairs nor any sentimental devotion to the solidarity of the three monarchies of Central and Eastern Europe. In a series of exchanges with one of the king's confidants about his overtures to France, Bismarck rejected monarchical "legitimacy" as a basis for Prussia's alliances and argued that the identity and ideology of the French ruler was irrelevant in the "chess game of politics." Napoleon's secular interests would dictate a logical course of action in relation to Austria and Prussia, which Bismarck could anticipate and from which the French ruler could deviate only at great cost.[25] Bismarck had spent time in Paris in 1855, where he met Napoleon III and established the background for what would later become his strategy to isolate Austria in European affairs.[26] Not a few of his countrymen found his opportunism abhorrent: Bismarck liked to talk with the "devil," as one historian rather prosaically put it later, and was fond of pointing out that "we have to work with the realities, not with fiction."[27]

Bismarck's self-conscious rejection of the Metternichian order, even as it had expended itself in a series of wars and crises in the 1850s, threatened to create for many "the prospect of an iron age of wars and revolutions, of breaking with moral principles and of ruthless striving for power."[28] For him, the necessity for action was obvious. He proceeded with a primary view of the Prussian state in his strategic orientation, meaning that the driving elements of his policy derived from a concern for specifically Prussian interests and priorities.

---

[25]   Otto Pflanze, "Realism and Idealism in Historical Perspective: Otto von Bismarck," in Cathal J. Nolan, ed., *Ethics and Statecraft: The Moral Dimension of International Affairs* (Westport, 1995), pp. 46–47; see also E. Ann Pottinger, *Napoleon III and the German Question, 1965–1866* (Cambridge, 1967); and William E. Echard, *Napoleon III and the Concert of Europe* (Baton Rouge, 1967).

[26]   Pflanze, *Bismarck*, I, pp. 102ff; from Sheehan, *German History*, p. 861.

[27]   Wilhelm Mommsen, *Bismarck: Ein politisches Lebensbild* (München, 1959), p. 35; from Urbach, "Between Saviour and Villain," p. 1154.

[28]   Stürmer, "Bismarck in Perspective," p. 297.

Bismarck's objective was to expand and secure Prussian *Handlungsspiel-raum*, or freedom of maneuver in international affairs, articulated through the Prussian crown and his own management of policy. This is not to dismiss the importance of the German question in his thinking but merely to place it in context. His occasional nods to national pieties notwithstanding, Germany remained throughout Bismarck's life either a convenient excuse for pursuing Prussian priorities or a pretext for political opponents to undermine his initiatives.[29] For him, the larger German interest was inseparable from the particular Prussian interest, an idea summed up best in a famous formulation of 1858: "There is nothing more German than the pursuit of particular Prussian interests, correctly understood."[30] Only in this light do the vagaries and fluctuations of his later approach to Austria and the southern German states become understandable. The autonomy of Prussian interests and the need to secure them above other priorities constituted the *conditio sine qua non* of his strategic policy.[31]

Bismarck also upheld the idea of Prussia as a European power above all, and only secondarily as the leading state in the German Confederation. Consistent with his view of German nationalism, unification of the German states under Prussian direction served as a convenient form of strategic force multiplication, to abuse a modern concept, and not as the final objective. It is important not to work backward from outcomes to intentions in this case: unifying Germany served in the end as the necessary alternative to his failure to elicit Austrian recognition of Prussia as a peer.

Since 1850, the German Confederation had imposed itself on Prussia, in Bismarck's view, as an engine of Austrian and southern German particularism – in other words, as a way of containing and limiting Prussia. For Bismarck, this was unbearable, and the succession of strategic triumphs that distinguish his career must be seen in this light. The unification of Germany and fulfillment of the German national ideal were purely instrumental measures to enhance Prussian power at the heart of Europe (and, by implication, the security of the Hohenzollern crown within Prussia). If Bismarck could have achieved parity with Austria without drawing the other German states into a unified nation in 1867 and 1871, through some other means such as an alliance with Austria that broke the power of the southern states in the Confederation, he would have done so.

In fact, Bismarck worked purposefully between 1862 and 1866 to prevent the war with Austria that redounded so strongly to Prussia's benefit. In the

---

[29] Egmont Zechlin, *Bismarck und die Grundlegung der deutschen Großmacht* (Darmstadt, 1960), p.148; Heide Barmeyer, "Bismarck zwischen preussischer und nationaldeutscher Politik," in Johannes Kunisch, ed., *Bismarck und seine Zeit* (Berlin, 1992), pp. 311–22.

[30] "Einige Bemerkungen über Preußens Stellung am Bunde" – Denkschrift für Prinz Wilhelm, Ende März 1858: GW, vol. 2, pp. 302ff, here p. 317; from Kolb, "Großpreussen oder Kleindeutschland," p. 16.

[31] Kolb, "Großpreußen oder Kleindeutschland?," pp. 16–17.

German Confederation as then constituted, Prussia and Austria interacted on an unequal footing, and Bismarck's problem was to persuade Austria to accommodate the unmistakable growth of Prussia as an equal partner. To that end, he needed either to isolate Austria and recast its close relations with the southern German *Mittelstaaten* – a course which would force him to traffic closely with the nationalist movement in Prussian politics, which, for that reason, was unappealing – or bring Austria around to a reform of the Confederation that offered Prussia greater stature and influence.

Prussian power was immutable and growing, in Bismarck's estimation; either Austria would peacefully come to terms with the growing power and influence of Prussia and treat with her as an equal within the Confederation, or Bismarck would force events to a head and risk outright military confrontation.[32] The latter was the least desirable alternative for a range of reasons, not least among them the risks, both known and unknown, inherent in warfare. A successful Prussian war effort was sure to engender fear and suspicion among the other European powers, while it would provide fresh impetus for German nationalism in Prussian politics. But it is important to emphasize that Bismarck saw no necessary contradiction between Prussian and Austrian power in the German Confederation or Europe at large.

Of course, Bismarck was not the author of the strategic rivalry with Austria. That conflict long predated his arrival in the offices of Prussian minister-president and foreign minister in September 1862. Two major Prussian initiatives to realize greater parity with Austria had foundered on the majority the latter had formed with the middle states in the Confederation, and the effect had been to marginalize Prussia further. For that reason, at the time of his appointment, Bismarck found himself on the defensive (when, again, he faced a major constitutional conflict on the domestic front) against an Austrian push in August 1862 to create a common judicial framework for the Confederation.

Working in his favor was a changing economic balance in Central Europe that was steadily increasing Prussia's industrial power in the region. The Prussian Customs Union (Zollverein) had effectively realigned the economic interests of almost every state in Germany and, through the bold agreement by Bismarck's predecessors in August 1862 to a commercial treaty with France, enormously strengthened Bismarck's hand.[33] Prussia's dizzying economic ascent in the mid-nineteenth century and its prudent application of that newfound power to the strategic calculus presented the middle

---

[32] Ibid., p. 17.
[33] Alfred Meyer, *Der Zollverein und die deutsche Politik Bismarcks: eine Studie über das Verhältnis von Wirtschaft und Politik im Zeitalter der Reichsgründung* (Frankfurt, 1986).

German states with benefits that Austria could not hope to match.[34] Bismarck felt confident enough in his position over the winter of 1862–1863 to extend to Austria offers of a strategic partnership based on Prussian goodwill and influence. Both states, he argued, stood to gain more from a partnership that marginalized the middle states, acknowledged Prussia's new power, and reserved for Austria her traditional presence in German affairs.

Unfortunately for Bismarck, Austrian politics throughout much of this period was dominated by the anti-Prussian Reform Party of Count Anton von Schmerling and Rudolf von Biegeleben, who worked to nullify Prussia's growing status in German affairs by tightening the federal structure and enhancing Austria's already leading role in it.[35] Their initiative of July 1863 foresaw a radical expansion of federal authority at the expense of the individual states, to be guaranteed by the Austrian crown. As Prussia would have had only one vote in the proposed executive board, and only three votes of 21 in the federal council, the plan threatened nothing less than the emasculation of Prussian power in Germany. It was all Bismarck could do to prevent Kaiser Wilhelm from attending an Austrian-sponsored gathering of German princes later that year, at which the reform program was put forth for consideration. It was a close call for Bismarck. The Prussian abstention effectively quashed the measure and bought time for him to work behind the scenes.

The conflict came to a head in the European crisis over Schleswig-Holstein in 1863–1964. To an extent underappreciated in much historiography on the unification period, Bismarck's adroit maneuvering in the crisis proved his greatest strategic masterpiece, as he himself saw it later.[36] Before that, Prussia had waged a rearguard action within the German Confederation

---

[34] Helmut Böhme, *Deutschlands Weg zur Grossmacht: Studien zum Verhältnis von Wirtschaft und Staat während der Reichsgründungszeit 1848–1881* (Köln, 1966), remains the classic treatment of the economic aspects of this process; see also Eugen Franz, *Der Entscheidungskampf um die wirtschaftspolitische Führung Deutschlands (1856–1867)*, vol. 12, *Schriftenreihe zur bayrischen Landesgeschichte* (München, 1933); and Franz, "Graf Rechbergs deutsche Zollpolitik," *Mitteilungen des Instituts für österreichische Geschichtsforschung* 46 (1932), pp. 143–87; an interesting comparative dimension is provided by Andreas Etges, *Wirtschaftsnationalismus: USA und Deutschland im Vergleich 1815–1914* (Frankfurt a.M., 1999).

[35] See Roy Austensen, "Austria and the 'Struggle for Supremacy in Germany,' 1848–1864," *Journal of Modern History* 52 (1980), pp. 195–225; Enno E. Kraehe, "Austria and the Problem of Reform in the German Confederation, 1951–63," *American Historical Review* 56 (1951), pp. 276–94; and Heinrich Ritter von Srbik, *Deutsche Einheit: Idee und Wirklichkeit vom Heiligen Reich bis Königgrätz*, 4 vols. (München, 1938–32), esp. vols. 3 and 4.

[36] Kolb, "Großpreußen oder Kleindeutschland?," p. 22; Moritz Busch, *Bismarck: Some Secret Pages from His History*, vol. 1 (London, 1898), p. 130. The classic account of the crisis is Lawrence D. Steefel, *The Schleswig-Holstein Question* (Cambridge, 1932), p. 95; the best short treatment is the chapter in Pflanze, *Bismarck*, vol. 1, pp. 237–67; the documentary basis is reproduced in *Die auswärtige Politik Preussens, 1858–1871: diplomatische Aktenstücke*, vol. 4, Reichsinstitut für Geschichte des neuen Deutschlands, ed. (Oldenbourg,

against Austrian efforts to contain her. In the events surrounding the leadership succession in the duchies of Schleswig and Holstein, Bismarck demonstrated an extraordinary talent for political and strategic manipulation and
for managing events skillfully to Prussia's advantage. The effect of the crisis
was to expand widely the strategic space within which he could resolve the
question of the Prussian monarchy's primacy or parity in German affairs.
After working feverishly in early 1863 to fend off bold Austrian plans to
restrict Prussia, Bismarck managed to swing the initiative back in his direction. Austria never regained it.

As Lord Palmerston was famously said to have quipped, only three people
fully understood the Schleswig-Holstein question: the prince consort (who
was dead), a Foreign Office clerk (who went mad), and he himself (who had
forgotten). The duchies had long belonged to the Danish crown through the
accident of one of their dukes having become king. They were not, however,
formal territories of Denmark. Their anomalous status was guaranteed by
the London Protocol of 1852, wherein the major European powers guaranteed their retention by the Danish crown provided their local autonomy
remained intact. Holstein, by virtue of its large German population, was a
member of the German Confederation, while Schleswig, with an only slightly
smaller proportion of Germans in its population, was not.

The Danish minority strongly desired the incorporation of the territories
into Denmark, a wish realized by the passage of the Danish Constitution of
November 1863, which declared the duchies integral to that country. The
German Confederation seized on this nationalist provocation and ordered
the forces of its member states to halt the incorporation of the duchies. It
also voiced a desire to support a rival claimant, the Duke of Augustenburg,
and bring both territories into the Confederation as German federal states.[37]

The windings of Bismarck's thinking during the crisis will probably always
remain obscure. But his objectives were reasonably clear and certainly broad
enough to permit several possible outcomes, always while reserving for himself discretionary room for maneuver.[38] Ideally, he favored the annexation
of the duchies by Prussia and thereby the consolidation of Prussia's position

1933–45); and Heinrich Ritter von Sbrik, ed., *Quellen zur deutschen Politik Österreichs
1859–1866*, vol. 3 (Osnabrück, 1967).

[37] Dieter Wolf, *Herzog Friedrich von Augustenburg: ein von Bismarck 1864 überlisteter
deutscher Fürst?* (Frankfurt a.M., 1999); for a fascinating glimpse of the genealogical
background to the fray, see Karl-Otto Hagelstein, *Die Erbansprüche auf die Herzogtümer
Schleswig und Holstein 1863–64* (Frankfurt a.M., 2003); for a general treatment that
stresses the role of the Habsburg monarchy in the dispute, see Gerd Stolz, *Unter dem
Doppeladler für Schleswig-Holstein: anlässlich des 140. Jahrestages der Gefechte bei Jagel,
Oberselk, am Königshügel 3. Februar 1864 und Oeversee/Sankelmark, 6. Februar 1862*
(Husum, 2004).

[38] On Bismarck's objectives, see Arnold Oskar Meyer, "Die Zielsetzung in Bismarcks
schleswig-holsteinischer Politik von 1855–1864," *Zeitschrift für Schleswig-Holsteinischer
Geschichte* 53 (1923), pp. 103–34; Pflanze argues that Bismarck was unlikely to have had

in northern Germany, an objective at odds with those of every other major party in the dispute but the only one in his estimation which justified war.

The Danish government sought the incorporation of the territories into an expanded national state; the British sought to uphold the prerogatives of the legitimate Danish crown; the Austrians wished the problem to go away by a return to the status quo ante; and Bismarck's own monarch, along with the greater part of German political opinion, favored upholding the claims of the minor dukes in the succession and creating a new confederate middle state.[39] The only meaningful source of international support for Bismarck's program was the notoriously fickle Napoleon III, hardly a heartening crutch on whom to lean. Given the constellation of these interests, Bismarck's eventual success in securing the duchies for Prussia and leveraging their status to achieve a position of Prussian parity with Austria amounts to "one of the amazing feats in the history of politics."[40]

Bismarck described his approach in retrospect:

> The nuances which seemed attainable in the Danish question, each of which providing for the duchies a path to improvement in comparison to prevailing conditions, culminated, in my opinion, in the acquisition of the duchies for Prussia.... If the most ambitious goal could not be reached, then we could have, despite all renouncements from Augustenburg, entertained the installation of this dynasty and the creation of a new *Mittelstaat*, as long as Prussian and German national interests were secured.... If even this, on account of the European situation and the will of the King could not be accomplished without the isolation of Prussia by the great powers, including Austria, then the question arises by what means a bargain could be struck, be it in the form of a personal union or something else, which would in any case have been an improvement in the situation of the duchies.[41]

As Bismarck saw it, the alternatives for Schleswig and Holstein were annexation by Prussia, incorporation as middle states into the German Confederation (where, like the other second-tier German states, they would likely flirt with Austria against Prussia and vice versa), or acquiescence in their continued affiliation with the Danish crown. Under the diplomatic circumstances, he could not simply come out in favor of annexation. Confident of his capacity to massage events toward his preferred goals, he seized on the Danish attempt to annex the territories as a violation of the London Protocol of 1852 and therefore cast Prussian policy as staunchly defending

a rigid order of preference between the second and third choices: Otto Pflanze, "Bismarck's *Realpolitik*," *The Review of Politics* 20 (1958), p. 505n49.

[39] Pflanze, "Bismarck's *Realpolitik*," p. 504; Pflanze, *Bismarck*, vol. 1, pp. 238–40.
[40] Pflanze, *Bismarck and the Development of Germany*, vol. 1, p. 242.
[41] GW, vol. 15, p. 254, from Kolb, "Großpreußen oder Kleindeutschland?," pp. 22–23; credit for the translation, with minor alterations, goes to Professor Donald Wallace of the Department of History, U.S. Naval Academy.

international law, which impressed the British. He persuaded Austria to do the same, thus ignoring the pleas of the Confederation to incorporate the duchies as German states. When the Danes stood firm, Prussia and Austria declared war.

In addition to quashing Danish efforts to behave as a significant power in European politics, the War of 1864 heralded the arrival of the Prussian Army as a major force on the international scene.[42] The experience was a valuable test of the organization and leadership that would prevail so stunningly in wars against Austria in 1866 and France in 1871. To be sure, the badly overmatched Danes fought valiantly, and the Prussians, in league with a sizable Austrian force, stumbled before numbers told. But the final outcome could not have been in doubt. The preliminary peace treaty of August 1864 ceded Schleswig and Holstein to the kings of Prussia and Austria, making no mention of the German Confederation and effectively narrowing the scope of the strategic competition between Austria and Prussia. Because the treaty left the fate of the territories to the major German powers, Bismarck had greater leverage than would have been possible had the duchies become a collective European problem. He used that reality to his advantage during subsequent talks between the German monarchs and their chief ministers in Schönbrunn, Austria, from 20 to 24 August 1864.

The talks revealed that Bismarck seriously entertained the possibility of an arrangement with Austria that would have united the two as joint leaders of a federal German structure on the basis of parity. But the Austrians favored the creation of a separate Schleswig-Holstein state, a proposal for which Bismarck, marking time and mindful of the geographical advantage that Prussia enjoyed in the dispute, demanded major concessions as the price of Prussian agreement. The outcome of the talks soured his monarch, who had come to believe that the victory in 1864 was won primarily by Prussia, on the traditional relationship with Austria. Bismarck recognized that the growing rift had opened the door to a tougher Prussian line.

Nevertheless, the evidence suggests that he remained cautiously optimistic that the two states would find a basis for parity and peaceful coexistence. As detailed by an Austrian historian in the 1930s, the Austrian foreign minister, Count Johann Bernhard Rechberg, recorded in a draft proposal dictated to his secretary a commitment by Prussia to support Austria's recovery of Lombardy in northern Italy in the event of a war with France.[43] In exchange, the Austrian emperor vowed to renounce any claims to the northern duchies

---

[42]   See Arden Bucholz, *Moltke and the German Wars, 1864–1871* (New York, 2001); and Anneliese Klein-Wuttig, *Politik und Kriegführung in den deutschen Einigungskriegen 1864, 1866 und 1870–71* (Berlin-Grunewald, 1934), who strives inordinately to justify and embellish Bismarck's role.

[43]   Richard B. Elrod, "Austria and the Venetian Question, 1860–66," *Central European History* 4 (1971), pp. 149–70.

and consented to their annexation by Prussia.[44] As Eberhard Kolb points out, it is highly improbable that Bismarck would have restricted his options with so strict a promise to Austria or "put himself in the position of being the towline for Austria's Italian policy."[45] The failure of the monarchs on the morning of 24 August to agree to anything so unambiguous may also serve as confirmation that Rechberg misinterpreted Bismarck's intentions.

But Rechberg's notes presumably had some basis in discussions with Bismarck which, even if not binding Prussia to Austrian policy in other venues, foresaw a dual-state solution to the problem of German federalism. It is also probable that any such proposal would have foundered eventually on Austrian intransigence with respect to Bismarck's demands for concessions in the north and within the Confederation. At this point in the strategic standoff, Bismarck appears to have considered the position of the Habsburg monarchy more precarious than did the Austrians themselves; in his view, a simple guarantee of Austria's future position in Italy might have had a value for Austria that merited concession of Schleswig and Holstein to Prussia. As one historian has put it, "Bismarck was not about to pay for what he hoped to get for nothing."[46] But what is noteworthy, again, is that Bismarck continued to nurse serious hopes of outcomes other than war even as relations with Austria deteriorated.[47]

After the conference, both powers were content to overlook the uncertain position of the duchies until external circumstances forced the issue. But Bismarck was clearly more inclined to view the risks involved in a war favorably. In the Gastein Convention of August 1865, intended by both sides to ameliorate tensions, Austria unwittingly played into Bismarck's hands by agreeing to administer the territories separately, which allowed him to undercut the Austrian position to the Prussian king and goad the Austrians into a harder line. It also afforded him the latitude necessary to prepare Prussia's state finances for war.[48] Bismarck's clever handling

---

44 Heinrich Ritter von Srbik, "Die Schönnbrunner Konferenzen vom August 1864," *Historische Zeitschrift* 153 (1936), pp. 43–88; Walter Lipgens, "Bismarcks Österreich-Politik vor 1866: Die Urheberschaft des Schönbrunner Vertragsentwurfs vom August 1864," *Die Welt als Geschichte* 10 (1950), pp. 240–62; Otto Becker, "Der Sinn der dualistischen Verständigungsversuche Bismarcks vor dem Kriege 1866," *Historische Zeitschrift* 169 (1949), pp. 264–98; see also the short transcript of the classic lecture by Hajo Holborn, "Über die Staatskunst Bismarcks," *Zeitwende* 3 (1927), pp. 321–34; and Richard B. Elrod, "Bernhard von Rechberg and the Metternichian Tradition: The Dilemma of Conservative Statecraft," *Journal of Modern History* 56 (1984), pp. 430–55.
45 Kolb, "Großpreußen oder Kleindeutschland," p. 24.
46 James Sheehan, *German History 1770–1866* (Oxford, 1989), p. 892.
47 The Schönbrunn Convention is reproduced in Ernst Rudolf Huber, ed., *Dokumente zur deutschen Verfassungsgeschichte*, vol. 2, *Deutsche Verfassungsdokumente, 1851–1918* (Stuttgart, 1964), p. 175.
48 See John C. G. Röhl, "Kriegsgefahr und Gasteiner Konvention: Bismarck, Eulenberg, und die Vertagung des preußisch-öosterreichischen Krieges im Sommer 1865," in Bernd-Jürgen

of the Gastein Convention facilitated the path to conflict between Austria and Prussia without ensuring it.[49] The desirable result, Bismarck reasoned, was to fabricate minor pretexts for a conflict that Prussia could choose if circumstances proved favorable and Austria intractable. After Gastein, Bismarck left open the chance for Austria to sell her rights over Holstein to Prussia and resolve the growing rift peacefully. But he also embraced the possibility of war and actively prepared for it.

Bismarck's preparations proceeded on both foreign and domestic fronts. Safe in the assumption that neither Britain nor Russia would likely intervene, he met with Napoleon III at Biaritz in October 1865 to secure his neutrality and Prussia's flank. Much more devious was Bismarck's pact with the government of Italy of April 1866, by which the Italians agreed to fight against Austria – if war came within three months – and receive the province of Venice in return. In this, Bismarck sought only to hedge his bets: "We cannot commit ourselves at this time to wage an offensive war against Austria, only to make acceptable those obligations which will be necessary in the event of that war."[50] The pact with Italy was a watershed; in making it, Bismarck violated Prussia's obligations as a member of the Germanic Confederation not to make agreements against other members, certainly one of his more cynical machinations in a career full of them.

In Germany, he also advanced a program for the creation of a popular assembly within the Confederation, a reform to which the Austrians could not agree under any circumstances, and began his long courtship with the befuddled partisans of German liberalism.[51] Of course, his reform proposal to the Confederation mentioned no explicit exclusion of Austria, and one should see it as an attempt to raise the stakes in the standoff. That the staunch defender of traditional Prussian prerogatives contemplated so popular and dangerous a political measure is surprising; that German liberalism may well be said never to have recovered from the association is less so.

Bismarck had boxed the Austrians into a corner. Their clumsy attempts to negotiate with Napoleon III, whose duplicity, if not sagacity, was matched only by Bismarck's, resulted in the effective forfeiture of their Italian holdings in the event of war, regardless of the outcome. In June 1866, sensitive to that loss and their failure to secure a reliable ally, the Austrians raised the

Wendt, Peter-Christian Witt, and Imanual Geiss, eds., *Deutschland in der Weltpolitik des 19. und 20. Jahrhunderts: Fritz Fischer zum 65. Geburtstag* (Düsseldorf, 1973), p. 89, for an interpretation at odds with the one advanced here.

[49] Stadelmann, *Das Jahr 1865*, p. 52; from Kolb, "Großpreußen oder Kleindeutschland," p. 26.

[50] *GW*, vol. 5, p. 395ff; from Kolb, "Großpreußen oder Kleindeutschland," p. 28.

[51] Kaernbach, *Bismarcks Konzepte zur Reform*, pp. 217ff; Harald Biermann, *Ideologie statt Realpolitik: kleindeutsche Liberale und auswärtige Politik vor der Reichsgründung* (Düsseldorf, 2006); also Jürgen Müller, *Deutscher Bund und deutsche Nation, 1848–1866* (Göttingen, 2005).

unresolved status of Schleswig and Holstein in the Confederation, which Bismarck could decry as a violation of the Gastein Convention and use as a pretext for deploying Prussian troops in Holstein. The Austrians saw no way out and declared war.

Few foresaw the outcome: a series of stunning victories for Prussia that culminated in the Battle of Königgratz in 1866.[52] The Austrian Army, despite important advantages, could not overcome grave deficiencies in doctrine and transportation. The Prussian Army was capably led. Helmuth von Moltke was more scholar than soldier in temperament and appearance and an officer who understood better than any of his contemporaries the intellectual nature of preparation and leadership in war. Moltke had deployed his forces along a massive 600-mile crescent, which allowed him to neutralize the German middle states before the Prussian armies converged against the bulk of the Austrian Army under Benedek. In light of subsequent events, Königgratz may well have been the most decisive battle of the modern era. More narrowly, its consequences proved fateful for German nationalism. Bismarck capitalized on the Prussian victory by establishing the North German Confederation, the constitutional structure of which presaged the imperial settlement of 1871 and amounted to the first iteration of a modern German nation-state.

Bismarck's strategic management of the war against Austria brought him into direct conflict with the senior leadership of the Prussian military, most notably Moltke and the "demigods" who made up the core of the latter's staff.[53] Already imbued with a conception of warfare as total – fed by a penchant for allowing operations and tactics to drive strategy, instead of the other way around, and for viewing as illegitimate any imposition of political concerns into military decision making while operations were under way[54] – the officers favored prosecuting the war against Austria to the utmost, driving on Vienna, dictating terms to the defeated empire, and staging a triumphal march through Austria's capital.

---

[52] On the war, see the recently rereleased edition of Gordon A. Craig, *The Battle of Königgrätz: Prussia's victory over Austria, 1866* (Philadelphia, 2003); a more recent account is Gerd Fesser, *1866, Königgrätz-Sadowa: Bismarcks Sieg über Österreich* (Berlin, 1994); and from a perspective more appreciative of the Austrian position, Geoffrey Wawro, *The Austro-Prussian War: Austria's War with Prussia and Italy in 1866* (Cambridge, 1996).

[53] After more than a half-century, the most sensible treatment of the issue remains Gordon A. Craig, *The Politics of the Prussian Army 1640–1945* (Oxford, 1955).

[54] Historiography on the Prusso-German origins of modern strategic and operation theory is extensive, as is that dealing specifically with Moltke and the German General Staff. On what became the grosteque German perversion of warfare as an instrument of statecraft, see the outstanding study by Isabel V. Hull, *Absolute Destruction: Military Culture and the Practices of War in Imperial Germany* (Ithaca, 2005); useful contexts, wherein contrasts are inevitable, are found in Reinhard Stumpf, ed., *Kriegstheorie und Kriegsgeschichte: Carl von Clausewitz, Helmuth von Moltke* (Frankfurt, 1993).

Bismarck found himself taxed to persuade the king that such a course was strategically foolish. It would needlessly lengthen the war; multiply its uncertainties and the chance of an unfavorable outcome; provoke the involvement of the other major powers, who remained wary of Prussia's growth and Austria's decline; and alienate the Austrians, whom Bismarck thought an indispensable source of stability in Eastern Europe and a key counterweight to Russia. "I have the thankless task of pouring water into the bubbling wine," he wrote to his wife six days after Königgratz, "and pointing out that we are not the only inhabitants of Europe but live in it with three other powers that detest and envy us."[55] Throughout his running disputes with the general staff, he understood the strategic utility of the war in terms of Prussia's potential and comparative strengths and resisted the hubris resulting from success in the field. His intellectual posture in 1866 was a model of coherent strategic thinking, understood here as the process of understanding military affairs in terms of how wars are begun, managed, and ended advantageously.

But by involving himself in affairs thought to be the prerogative of the military, Bismarck earned the lasting enmity of Moltke and many of his senior generals, who chafed at his success and vowed never again to let him suborn them. Their antagonism persisted through the Franco-Prussian War of 1870–1871, and the critical counsels that defined Prussian policy during that conflict came to be the textbook example of modern distinctions between political and military discretion in strategic affairs.

Much later, Bismarck bitterly recalled the conflict in terms reminiscent of Clausewitz, whom he apparently never read:

> The task of the army leadership is the destruction of enemy forces; the purpose of the war is the realization of peace under conditions which conform to the policies pursued by the state. The assertion and bounding of the goals to be achieved through war, and advising of the monarch as regards the same, is and remains during the war a political task, and the manner of its resolution cannot but influence the prosecution of the war. The ways and methods of the latter will always be dependent on whether one sought the actual outcome or more or less, whether one demands annexations or renounces them, whether one wishes indemnities and for how long.[56]

Bismarck understood more clearly than most statesmen and officers of his era the overriding relevance of political considerations for every level of military activity. Like few others, he possessed the intellect necessary to view those interactions critically across the entire strategic landscape. His circumspection made the risks and uncertainties inherent in a clash of arms

---

[55] Rich, *Great Power Diplomacy*, p. 204.
[56] *GW*, vol. 15, p. 313; from Kolb, "Kriegführung und Politik 1870/71," in *Umbrüche deutscher Geschichte*, p. 140.

intuitively distasteful, and he devoted much attention throughout his chancellorship to containing hostilities in a manner consistent with his aims. The subsequent military history of Germany in two world wars demonstrated that such concerns were inherently at odds with the German approach to total warfare, wherein conflict assumed a scale and dynamic unchecked by extraneous considerations such as politics or strategic realities.

The prospect of prosecuting the war against Austria after Königgratz threatened negotiations, running since July, with Napoleon III, who was wary of Prussian success and eager to gain what he could from the situation. The talks focused on Bismarck's intention to bring the minor German states north of the Main River into a new confederation dominated by Prussia, a grave concern for any French statesman, to say nothing of one as mercurial as the French emperor. Napoleon eventually assented on the condition that the southern states of Baden, Württemberg, and Bavaria remain independent and that parts of Saxony remain intact, nominal concessions that did little to prevent Bismarck from exerting other, less overt forms of influence on them. The Southern States would find it difficult in the ensuing years to resist the North German Confederation of July 1867, which marked the advent of Prussian strategic influence on a scale truly commensurate with that of the other major European powers.

Bismarck assembled the 22 German states north of the Main River into a political confederation headed by the Prussian king and with a bicameral legislature elected by universal manhood suffrage.[57] Although the new Reichstag had the right to debate and vote on laws, it had no right of legislative initiative and no control over the executive; moreover, a federal council comprising representatives appointed by the federal states, and in which the royal Prussian regime held a preponderance, could veto laws passed by the Reichstag. These political arrangements, which Bismarck later adapted into the imperial constitution of 1871, represented an ingenious mechanism for ensuring the dominance of Prussia in German affairs and addressing the political aspirations of the middle classes, all the while ensuring the unchecked constitutional prerogatives of the Prussian monarchy. Although Bismarck notionally upheld the sovereignty of the southern states in this scheme, he saw to it that they understood that their strategic fortunes were bound closely to those of Prussia through an intricate network of treaties and obligations and that they recognized the new and immediate weight of Prussian strength against defeated Austria and distracted France.

The domestic consequences of Bismarck's successes were as meaningful as his gradual consolidation of Prussia's position abroad, perhaps more so

---

[57] On these arrangements, see Ernst Rudolf Huber, *Deutsche Verfassungsgeschichte seit 1789*, esp. vol. 3, *Bismarck und das Reich*, and vol. 4, *Struktur und Krisen des Kaiserreichs* (Stuttgart, 1957).

in light of unified Germany's troubled political experience thereafter. The stunning military victory over Austria emasculated the liberal movement, which had struggled for years for both a unified German nation and political emancipation. In the end, military victory impresses, and rarely more so than in 1866. Swept up in the fervor of a successful military campaign, the Prussian parliament passed an indemnity bill in September 1862, effectively exonerating the king's government for flouting the constitution and running an independent budget for several years.

The liberal movement itself split into Progressive and National Liberal parties, in the process sacrificing its social idealism to the conviction that progress – in whatever form – was to be realized more through strength and decision than through the tiresome mechanisms of deliberative democracy and participatory politics. The split dealt a blow to the budding confidence of the middle classes as the standard-bearer of modern government and social emancipation, and Bismarck adroitly manipulated the liberal rump into becoming a popular bulwark of the authoritarian Prusso-German regime for the next 20 years. What Bismarck sowed all of Europe later would reap. Middle-class glorification of military sensibilities and habits would pervert the social and cultural complexion of the German Empire and pave the way to the calamities of the early twentieth century.[58]

French nationalists and statesmen had few illusions about Prussian power in the aftermath of the victory over Austria, and many regarded the growth of German national confidence as inimical to the interests of their own country. Napoleon III, notionally committed to some version of the principle of national self-determination, could address these concerns only through weak attempts to secure territorial compensation for Prussian expansion. The threat of war over Napoleon III's request for Luxembourg in 1867, and Bismarck's brusque refusal to entertain it, revealed this approach as leading to little more than antagonism. Later Napoleon III attempted to build a diplomatic bulwark against Prussian overtures to the southern German states by inflaming southern Catholic prejudices and regional sentiments, which were admittedly abundant, and by courting Austria and Italy to form an alliance.

The latter initiative was doomed from the start. The Austrians after 1866 were struggling to define a new place for their country in Europe and a new sense of purpose, and the Germans in the empire were, in any event, unlikely to win the support of the Magyars in reclaiming Austria's lost influence. The Italians could not bring themselves to support the strategic policy of

---

[58]　Worthwhile starting points for this critical facet of Bismarck's legacy are Wolfgang J. Mommsen, "Wirtschaft, Gesellschaft und Staat im deutschen Kaiserreich 1870–1918," in Wolfgang J. Mommsen, *Der autoritäre Nationalstaat: Verfassung, Gesellschaft und Kultur des deutschen Kaiserreichs* (Frankfurt a.M., 1990), and Geoff Eley, "Army, State and Civil Society: Revisiting the Problem of German Militarism," in *From Unification to Nazism: Reinterpreting the German Past* (Boston, 1986).

France, which retained a military garrison in the heart of their grandest city. Bismarck in the meantime, bought Prussia an insurance policy against the prospect of an Austrian-French accommodation in the form of a Russian alliance, which guaranteed a concentration of Russian troops in Galicia to divert Austrian attention in the event of a Franco-Prussian conflict. He nursed hopes that French statesmen would come to accept the inevitability of Prussian power in Germany and adapt agreeably to the resulting changes in the European balance.

Given Germany's troubled history in the twentieth century, Bismarck's intentions on the eve of the Franco-Prussian War have been a source of profound contention among historians throughout the past century. The idea that Bismarck – and by implication, Prussia and Germany in some interpretations – bore responsibility for the outbreak of war in 1870 was long thought to have weighty consequences for the legitimacy of the German nation and its identity. German responsibility for the outbreak of the wars in 1914 and 1939 (the former itself an issue on which historians have spilled enormous amounts of ink) led some to delve even further into the past and write of factors militating against Germany's ability to manage a 'normal' strategic policy ranging from geopolitical and geographical constraints to a uniquely militaristic and expansionist Prusso-German mentality.[59] The most powerful interpretation of 1870 along these lines focuses on Bismarck's eager embrace of war and manipulation of domestic sentiment for the purposes of constructing an authoritarian national state. As the German public's hopes for national unification faded after the founding of the North German Confederation in 1867, so this argument runs, Bismarck deliberately exploited circumstances foreign and domestic to provoke a crisis over the succession to the Spanish throne and a confrontation with France.[60]

More sober assessments present a view of Bismarck's policy more consistent with his actions and decisions over the preceding eight years. Without losing sight of his larger goal of a greater and more secure place for Prussia in the European system, as had been true with respect to Austria, Bismarck demonstrated characteristic flexibility in negotiating the shifting diplomatic sands of Prussia's relationship with France. A provisional government in Spain had searched since 1868 for a replacement for the deposed Queen Isabella II, finally settling on Prince Leopold of Hohenzollern, a distant southern German and Catholic relation of the Prussian king. Bismarck sought to balance the possibility of a conciliatory French line against a desire

[59] Jost Dülffer, "Foreign Policy," in Roger Chickering, ed., *Imperial Germany: A Historiographical Companion* (Westport, 1996), pp. 420–21.
[60] The leading exponent of this interpretation is Josef Becker, "Der Krieg mit Frankreich als Problem der kleindeutschen Einigungspolitik Bismarcks 1866–1871," in Michael Stürmer, ed., *Das kaiserliche Deutschland: Politik und Gesellschaft 1870–1918* (Düsseldorf, 1970), pp. 75–88.

to push the situation toward a resolution favorable to Prussian interests and German unification.

Publicly, Bismarck refrained from endorsing Leopold's candidacy until the French plebiscite of May 1870, in which Napoleon III received a decisive majority and resolved, in Bismarck's view, to pursue a much less agreeable policy toward Germany. Privately, he worked behind the scenes to stimulate sentiment in the Prussian leadership against French opposition to the Hohenzollern candidacy. His motives appear to have been twofold: first, he believed that Napoleon would shrink from a decisive confrontation, as he had in 1854 against Russia and in 1859 against Austria.[61] Second, he was moved by the need to prevent the defection of Bavaria to Austria and France, which would have postponed any further move to unify Germany on his terms and made his political position in the Prussian government precarious.[62]

What Bismarck could not have counted on was the grotesque incompetence of Agénor, Duc de Gramont, at the time French foreign minister and a man bent on scoring political points for the faltering Bonapartist regime, however cheaply.[63] After the gifted French ambassador to Prussia, Count Benedetti, convinced King William, then vacationing at Ems, through gentle persuasion to drop the Hohenzollern candidacy to the Spanish throne, Gramont – to achieve a political triumph sufficient to "efface the memory of previous retreats" – insisted that the Prussian king promise that the candidacy would never be renewed. This was obviously impossible, and the king courteously refused. But he telegraphed a description of the conversation to Bismarck, who massaged the text to make Wilhelm's response to Benedetti seem much harsher and categorical, and then leaked it to the press.[64]

The resulting firestorm of publicity inflamed public passions in Germany and France and made reasoned negotiations between the respective

---

[61] David Wetzel, *A Duel of Giants: Bismarck, Napoleon III, and the Origins of the Franco-Prussian War* (Wisconsin, 2001), p. 94.

[62] Paul Schroeder, "International Politics, Peace, and War, 1815–1914," in T. C. W. Blanning, ed., *The Nineteenth Century* (Oxford, 2000), p. 180; on the character of that crucial strategic relationship, see Wolf D. Gruner, "Bayern, Preussen und die süddeutschen Staaten 1866–1870," *Zeitschrift für bayrische Landesgeschichte* 38 (1974), pp. 799–927; David Wetzel, "Bismarck, South Germany, and the Problem of 1870," in David Wetzel, ed., *From the Berlin Museum to the Berlin Wall: Essays on the Cultural and Political History of Modern Germany* (Westport, 1996); the source and larger argument are in Wetzel's review of Josef Becker, "Bismarcks spanische 'Diversion:' 1870 und der preussisch-deutsche Reichsgründung," *Central European History* 37 (2004), p. 610.

[63] See Gramont's famously provocative declaration of 6 July, reproduced in Pierre de la Gorce, *Histoire du Second Empire*, vol. 6 (Paris, 1905), p. 227.

[64] Debate exists as to both Bismarck's manipulation of the telegram and the significance it had in the French declaration for war in 1870; see William L. Langer, "Red Flag on the Gallic Bull: The French Declaration for War in 1870," in Otto Brunner and Dietrich Gerhard, eds., *Europa und Übersee: Festschrift für Egmont Zechlin* (Hamburg, 1961), pp. 135–54.

governments impossible. Pressed by angry mobs in the capital, the French government declared war on Prussia on 19 July 1870, a decision that served Bismarck's end of isolating France from the other powers and providing a basis for a national German settlement under Prussian auspices. Under the circumstances, the southern German states could do no less than cast their lot with Prussia and mobilize against France. In this view, the French provoked the crisis that Bismarck then manipulated deftly to drive both countries into war on terms beneficial to Prussia.[65]

In the war, now famous for its brutal reintroduction of the complexities of modern asymmetric conflict to Europe, the Prussians held all the advantages. Despite the fact that the French Army was notionally greater in size, the Prussians had long anticipated a major conflict against the French and had provided for both a rapid, well-organized mobilization and a well-articulated operational strategy. After a series of hard-fought battles early in the war, the Prussians succeeded in trapping the main French armies first at Metz and then at Sedan. They rapidly bottled up the first in Metz, and Moltke smashed the other at Sedan, that ill-fated provincial town in northern France, when it attempted to relieve the first.

The imperial regime of Napoleon III quickly collapsed, and a new republican regime under the leadership of Leon Gambetta was organized in Paris to continue the fight, using new levies of raw troops raised in the distant provinces. French stubbornness in the face of conventional defeat confounded German war planning and infuriated Moltke, whose talents for planning and orchestrating operations were unmatched by the standards of the day but who chafed at challenges to his military proprieties. But French initiative could not overcome France's basic military deficiencies. The fall of French forces at Metz and the surrender of Paris in January led to the declaration in January of the Second Reich and the crowning of Wilhelm as German emperor. It also brought about elections to a new French National Assembly in February 1871, which elected Adolphe Thiers as chief executive and empowered him to negotiate a peace with the new empire. But the most lasting consequence was the peace treaty itself. The Treaty of Frankfort of May 1871 was a heavy burden on France and a source of French enmity against Germany for generations.[66] Thiers was compelled to accept a massive war indemnity of five billion francs against a German occupation of large parts of the country.

The most onerous condition, however, was the forced surrender of Alsace and Lorraine. The German decision to annex the territories, which virtually

---

[65] An interpretation capably expressed in Eberhard Kolb, *Der Kriegsausbruch 1870: Politische Entscheidungsprozesse und Verantwortlichkeiten in der Julikrise 1870* (Göttingen, 1970).

[66] Robert I. Giesberg, *The Treaty of Frankfort; A Study in Diplomatic History, September, 1870–September, 1873* (Philadelphia, 1966); see also Jones, "*Vae Victoribus.*"

guaranteed deep and bitter French resentment against the German empire, was formulated shortly after the beginning of hostilities. One historian has argued that the Prussian leadership conceived of annexation as a specific goal to inflame public sentiment for national unification, an interpretation much at odds with the contours of Bismarck's decision making in the years prior to the war and certain to constrain his future diplomatic options.[67] The prevailing view is less categorical: careful consideration of the sources reveals that the demand for annexation arose in the popular media long before Bismarck raised the issue in a substantive way.

In debates with the crown and military leadership, Bismarck was ultimately compelled to reckon a host of variables that favored the step. These included the basic appeal of seizing territory after a victorious war; the military argument that the territories, as the traditional avenues of invasion from Western Europe into Central Europe, were basic to the security of the new Reich; and finally, Bismarck's own lurking sense that European stability required the weakening of France. Given the other results of the war, he reasoned, future French hatred was not to be avoided in any case. The latter is a rather striking instance of prejudicial thinking by a man whose strategic plans were usually devoid of it and undoubtedly reflected resignation to an outcome that he was probably helpless to prevent.[68]

At the same time, Bismarck understood that German security depended as strongly on France as it did on every other European great power. His conception of international politics was that of a balance on the level of interests and strategic potential, with constant gradual adjustments as required to maintain a steady equilibrium. The collapse of France or the too-thorough subordination of her power in a lost war threatened to upset the European constellation into which he had worked so hard to fit Prussia and now Germany.[69]

Thus, Bismarck's principal strategic challenge after 1871 was "to protect the German empire from the dangerous consequences of its own founding."[70] Absolute security is a foolish illusion in the history of strategic

---

[67]   Walter Lipgens, "Bismarck, die öffentliche Meinung und die Annexion von Elsaß und Lothringen 1870," *Historische Zeitschrift* 199 (1964), pp. 31–112.

[68]   Lothar Gall, "Zur Frage der Annexion von Elsaß und Lothringen 1870," *Historische Zeitschrift* 206 (1968), pp. 265–326.

[69]   Note of 25 February 1887, in *Die Große Politik der europäischen Kabinette 1871–1914*, vol. 6 (Berlin, 40 vols. 1922–27), pp. 177ff.

[70]   Andreas Hillgruber, *Bismarcks Außenpolitik*, 3rd ed. (Freiburg, 1993), p. 131. The history of Bismarck's strategic policy after 1871 is a chapter in his career very different from the one that preceded it and can be dealt with only briefly here. A good introduction is Klaus Hildebrand, "System der Aushilfen'? Chancen und Grenzen deutscher Außenpolitik im Zeitalter Bismarcks 1871–1890," in Kunisch, *Bismarck und seine Zeit*, pp. 121–40. Early worthwhile studies include Nikolas Japikse, *Europa and Bismarcks Friedenspolitik* (Berlin, 1927); Ulrich Noack, *Bismarcks Friedenspolitik und das Problem des deutschen Machtverfalls* (Leipzig, 1928); more recently, Wolfgang J. Mommsen, *Großmachtstellung*

affairs. The reality, as Bismarck understood, and other Germans soon learned, is an ever-shifting patchwork of threats and challenges that require constant vigilance and a readiness to recast one's interests. The German Empire after 1871 faced the threat, which had been improbable against Prussia alone, of hostile coalitions of states that feared German power or saw opportunity to gain from her loss. To allay fears, Bismarck was at pains to demonstrate that Germany was a satiated state, without ambitions or intentions against her neighbors or territories abroad.

This was already clear in the case of France, from which no additional strategic dividend could be realized. Elsewhere, Bismarck saw great risks, with slight rewards, to any bid to win control of Denmark or the Netherlands. He also felt that Germany stood to gain nothing from a reduction of Austria through incorporation of her German minority. The Habsburg Empire, however decrepit, was essential to the stability of the multiethnic regions of Eastern Europe and a crucial bulwark against Russia. Any diminution of Austria would leave imperial Germany with enormous strategic liabilities. An expansion abroad was another possible outlet, but Bismarck never seriously entertained the prospect, and his strivings along these lines in the 1880s were halfhearted and ultimately inconclusive.[71] The existing state of affairs in Europe served Germany's interests adequately, in his judgment. For as long as Bismarck steered it, the new German state was the peaceful upholder of the existing European order, the maintenance of which relied more on trust and mutual dependence than fear.

Devils are always in details. Bismarck revived the traditional coalition among Austria, Russia, and now Germany, the three conservative monarchies of Europe, with an eye to stabilizing the neighboring states and building on their basic fear of social revolution.[72] The weakness of the coalition was revealed by the War Scare of 1875, when Bismarck made one of the gravest mistakes of his career. The French paid off their war debt in the astonishingly short span of two years and began to rebuild their military, leading key senior members of the German military to argue for a preventative war to

---

und Weltpolitik: Die Außenpolitik des deutschen Reichs 1870–1914 (Frankfurt, 1993); George Kennan, *The Decline of Bismarck's European Order: Franco-Russian Relations, 1875–1890* (Princeton, 1979); William Langer, *European Alliances and Alignments 1871–1890*, 2nd ed. (New York, 1950); and Imanuel Geiss, *German Foreign Policy, 1871–1914* (London, 1976).

71 See A. J. P. Taylor, *Germany's First Bid for Colonies, 1884–1885: A Move in Bismarck's European Policy* (Hamden, 1967); an interpretive context is provided in Henry Ashby Turner Jr., "Bismarck's Imperialist Venture: Anti-British Origin?," in Prosser Gifford and William Roger Lewis, eds., *Britain and Germany in Africa* (New Haven, 1967); and Paul M. Kennedy, "Bismarck's Imperialism: The Case of Samoa," *The Historical Journal* 15 (1972).

72 Ulrich Lappenküper, *Die Mission Radowitz: Untersuchungen zur Rußlandpolitik Otto von Bismarcks 1871–1875* (Göttingen, 1990), provides a thorough review of Bismarck's foreign policy in the early years of the new empire.

head off an inevitable French campaign. Bismarck, who once had brilliantly derided the notion of preventative war by comparing it to suicide from fear of death, was initially at pains to curb the war fever in Berlin.

But he was just as alarmed at the virulence of French hostility and diplomatic efforts against Germany and so fanned the flames of journalistic rumblings for war. In the resulting crisis, the French portrayed themselves successfully as victims of rampant German militarism and managed to tilt a broad swath of European official and public opinion against a chastened Bismarck. The new German empire had come perilously close to another war, this time under circumstances far less amenable to Bismarck's control.

The crisis in 1875 was a fateful crossroads for Bismarck and Germany, serving to underscore for Bismarck just how unreliable a crutch for German security the alliances with Russia and Austria were; how limited were Germany's options; and how essential to a durable peace was a broad, systemic approach to the European order. His deliberations in the aftermath of the crisis marked the beginning of his long-term program to ameliorate tensions on the Continent and create a lasting basis for German security. This Bismarck realized consummately as the president and inspiration behind the Congress of Berlin in 1878, where he managed, through the creation of a Russian-Bulgarian satellite state and reallocation of Balkan territories, to foreclose the necessity of choosing between Russia and Austria in his strategic plans.[73]

Instead, each became integral to the security of the other, and both became dependent on the central pivot of Germany. His role in the talks as the 'honest broker' headed off a major European conflict from which Germany could not have but suffered, even as it stoked Russian resentment over what was later seen as a diplomatic humiliation. The manifold challenges of juggling Germany's shifting relations with a range of conflicting powers across a continent taxed even Bismarck's capacities, and he was compelled to resort to increasingly arcane expedients to balance the European states. Bismarck's great success in the 1880s was to embed the European states in an interlocking network of defensive treaties and alliances in which no aggressor could be assured of support and for which all bore some degree of defensive responsibility.

The great virtue of the resulting system was the very complexity that soured Bismarck's successors. It offered a vested interest in stability to each of the major European powers. But it also assumed a general contentedness with prevailing strategic arrangements and required ongoing vigilance and inventiveness by its creator to adapt to new developments as they arose and

---

[73]   Bruce Waller, *Bismarck at the Crossroads: The Reorientation of German Foreign Policy after the Congress of Berlin, 1878–1880* (London, 1974); Karl Otmar Freiherr von Aretin, *Bismarcks Aussenpolitik und der Berliner Kongress* (Mainz, 1978).

to overcome them. By the time of Bismarck's departure from the political scene in 1890, even his own public was growing increasingly critical of his moderate conception of Germany as a satiated power and was clamoring increasingly for greater status in world affairs. The resulting policies cast Germany headlong down a path that led to the slaughter of the First World War and defeat.

Historiography on Bismarck and the unification period often makes much of the evidence pointing to his ready and early embrace of war as a solution to the German question. Particularly from Austrian and French perspectives, Bismarck seemed a figure not merely willing to contemplate but actually bent on violent confrontation to assert Prussia's influence and power in the Confederation and beyond. The summary of events presented here should qualify that perspective and point to what made Bismarck one of the great statesmen and strategists of the modern age. Much depends on how one interprets his intentions and objectives. Historians frequently confuse the enormous increase in power and stature that Prussia, and then Germany, realized after the wars in 1866 and 1871 with Bismarck's objectives before those conflicts. That he seriously entertained the possibility of a peaceful resolution in the months and years before each war should underscore that his intentions were far less systematic and permitted a host of outcomes. Particularly as regards Austria before 1866, some form of parity and dominion over northern Germany seemed reasonable and peacefully achievable, particularly early in his political career as foreign minister.

As time passed, however, and the circumstances governing the contest shifted, Bismarck came to embrace more expansive aims. The dispute over Schleswig and Holstein, which Bismarck could not be said to have precipitated, afforded him the leverage necessary to extract far more potentially from Austria than would otherwise have been possible. Bismarck's most remarkable strategic accomplishment thus resulted more from skillful opportunism than from deliberate manipulation, a hallmark of his overarching beliefs about agency and intention in history. "The future is a land of which there are no maps," one of his most sensitive biographers wrote, "and historians err when they describe even the most purposeful statesman as though he were marching down a broad high-road with his objective already in sight." Bismarck himself put it even more prosaically: "Man cannot create the current of events. He can only float with it and steer."[74]

It also is important to point out that the necessary counterpoint in almost every case of noteworthy strategic success in history is some form of failure. In this light, it is appropriate to qualify a description of Bismarck as brilliant and capable by pointing out that Austrian and French policies in the critical phases of his career were largely inept. Historians have been severe with the

[74] Taylor, *Bismarck*, p. 70.

mercurial Napoleon III and savage with Gramont, and there can be little doubt that both were badly overmatched by Bismarck on the chessboard of strategic policy.[75]

In contrast, Bismarck's standoff with Austria was longer lasting and far more complex. His efforts to define a new strategic presence for Prussia in Europe and the German Confederation through an accommodation with the Habsburg Empire were undermined by the Austrians' basic inability to follow a consistent policy as well as by regular overestimations of their own capabilities and potential. Austrian statesmen in the 1850s and 1860s vacillated continually between acceptance of Prussia as a peer in German affairs and a comfortable idea of Austrian preeminence based on her traditional stature in German affairs and as the bulwark of the Metternichian system.

Few, particularly in the reform party, saw a compelling need to compromise with Prussia, while most nursed great faith in Austria's ability to contain Prussia and manage the changing character of the Confederation. Particularly after 1865, there prevailed in Austrian politics a faction of diplomats and officers deeply hostile to strategic parity with Prussia. They viewed any increase in Prussian stature as a corresponding decrease in Austria's, with what in retrospect can only be called broad illusions about the strategic carrying capacity of Austrian power.[76] With figures like these in charge, so grossly oblivious to the brute realities of their situation, it is no wonder that events came to a head as they did.

It was Bismarck's achievement to translate the miscalculations of his counterparts into Prussian advantage, the process at the heart of any competent strategic policy. This he did with an acumen that typified his decisions throughout the long period of conflict and unification, an acumen born not of a master plan unfolding inexorably but rather of Bismarck making the most prudent decisions at each successive stage of the process. As he put it pithily in a memorandum in 1868: "It is illusory to attach decisive importance for the politics of the present to factors that lie in an uncertain future."[77]

In a world in which outcomes are indeterminate, competent strategy consists not in establishing long-range goals and systematically structuring policies and procedures to fulfill them but rather in a clear understanding of one's principles and priorities and a flexible, creative approach to realizing incremental gains in the short term. Local successes, diligently husbanded, led gradually to favorable overall outcomes.

Bismarck understood the international environment in which he had to craft Prussia's grand strategy well enough to have a clear notion of Prussian

[75] See esp. David Wetzel, "A Reply to Josef Becker's Response," *Central European History* 41 (2008), pp. 117–24.
[76] Kolb, "Großpreußen oder Kleindeutschland?," p. 32.
[77] Erlaß Bismarcks an Goltz, 26 February.

interests, while long experience as a diplomat and deep understanding of the cultural and historical identities of the other major European states permitted him to make intelligent assumptions about their own principles and interests. As a strategist, Bismarck was born and educated, not trained. Flowcharts, formulas, and systematized theories were not ingredients in his success. While it is inspiring to note how strongly strategic success depends on character and judgment, it is also dismaying to realize how accidental these qualities are in history.

But even as great a strategic actor as Bismarck displayed blinding short-comings. As the shifting sands of scholarship on the creation and first years of the new German state have shown so clearly over the past century, one needs to assess Bismarck's legacy not only in terms of foreign and strategic policy but also in terms of his divisive domestic policy.[78] As stridently as Bismarck himself may have sought to compartmentalize his strategic and domestic policies from one another, particularly in his declining years, his long tenure as Reichskanzler left in its wake a constitutional structure ill suited to responsible stewardship of Germany's growing power, a political system infantilized by his condescending leadership style, and a nation steeped in admiration of military achievement. War was an instrument of limited utility for Bismarck and carried with it grave risks and uncertain consequences. His comments on war throughout and after his career betray an apprehension of the phenomenon remarkable for its intellectual responsibility and maturity.[79] But he succumbed all too willingly after 1871 to the allure of manipulating public memories of the unification wars to cement the fractious constitutional façade of the new Kaiserreich. For the generation of Germans who rose to public prominence in the Wilhelmine era,

the newly created Reich was secure and permanent, and its creator and the political leadership in general were the objects of a settled confidence. Once this generation had accepted the new authoritarianism as an accomplished fact, it turned its attention outwards and, from its securely established German base, began to observe the thrilling play of forces among the great powers, which Bismarck's artistry had successfully controlled on so many occasions.[80]

[78] Influential for much subsequent interpretation of Bismarck's strategic policy has been the sensitive and balanced appraisal of Hans Rothfels, "Zum 150. Geburtstag Bismarcks," *Vierteljahrshefte für Zeitgeschichte* 13 (1965), pp. 225–35; also W. Bussmann, "Wandel und Kontinuitäat der Bismarck-Wertung," *Die Welt als Geschichte* 2 (1955), pp. 126–36.
[79] See particularly Karl-Ernst Jeismann, *Das Problem des Präventivkrieges im europäischen Staatensystem, mit besonderem Blick auf die Bismarckzeit* (Freiburg, 1957); and Michael Salewski, "Krieg und Frieden im Denken Bismarcks und Moltkes," in Roland G. Foerster, ed., *Generalfeldmarschall von Moltke: Bedeutung und Wirkung* (München, 1991), pp. 67–88.
[80] Ludwig Dehio, "Ranke und der deutsche Imperialismus," in *Deutschland und die Weltpolitik im 20. Jahrhundert* (Frankfurt a.M., 1961), p. 34; from Stürmer, "Bismarck in Perspective," p. 316.

To those who hold naively that one can prosecute a strategic policy in isolation from the robustness and stability of its domestic foundations, Bismarck's
bequest is a cautionary lesson in the perils of glorifying successful wars for
political purposes.

Similarly, one may argue that the tragic flaw of Bismarck's genius lay in
his failure to create enduring institutions capable of perpetuation by talents more modest than his. In his reflections on Bismarck as the towering
statesman of the modern era, Henry Kissinger remarked on his failure to
"transform the personal act of creation into institutions that can be maintained by an average standard of performance."[81] Certainly his policies and
political style contributed much to the dysfunctionality of German political
institutions in the Wilhelmine period and to the stunted political maturity
that prevented successive generations from improving them.

But to lay responsibility for all the catastrophes of modern German history at Bismarck's feet is to overlook the sheer contingency of history. The
imperial regime of Wilhelm II was no more a necessary result of historical
circumstances than was the Nazi seizure of power in 1933, and the sheer
multiplicity of possible outcomes to the Bismarckian era underscores the
hazards of overinterpreting his responsibility for what followed.

[81] Henry A. Kissinger, "The White Revolutionary: Reflections on Bismarck," *Daedalus* 97
(Summer 1968), p. 890; see also Dankwart A. Ruston, ed., *Philosophers and Kings: Studies
in Leadership* (New York, 1970), pp. 317–53.

5

About turn: British strategic transformation from Salisbury to Grey

RICHARD HART SINNREICH

On a crisp morning in December 1905, a British general by the name of James Grierson and a French major by the name of Victor Huguet had what both later claimed was a chance encounter while horseback riding in London's Hyde Park. Grierson, however, happened to be the British War Office's director of operations and a passionate Francophile, while Huguet happened to be the French military attaché in London. Whether accidental or not, that encounter was followed by another less accidental meeting the following day, and a few weeks later by the inauguration of informal but officially sanctioned Anglo-French "staff conversations" that would continue off and on until the outbreak of World War I in August 1914.[1]

Those conversations, and their contribution to Britain's subsequent decision to participate in a great power conflict on the European continent for the first time since the defeat of Napoleon a century earlier, continue to fascinate diplomatic and military historians. Most agree that, whatever their direct impact on that decision, the conversations themselves reflected a fundamental transformation of British foreign policy, the culmination of more than a decade of mounting concern about the British Empire's continued security and prosperity and the strategic arrangements needed to sustain them.[2]

---

[1] Samuel R. Williamson Jr., *The Politics of Grand Strategy: Britain and France Prepare for War, 1904–1914* (Dublin, 1990), pp. 65–66.

[2] Although, for at least one historian, what took place was less a shift in strategy than the inauguration of one. "In 1890," in John Gooch's view, "Britain was a great imperial power without an imperial grand strategy." See "The Weary Titan: Strategy and Policy in Great Britain, 1890–1918," in Williamson Murray, MacGregor Knox, and Alvin Bernstein, eds., *The Making of Strategy: Rulers, States, and War* (Cambridge, 1997), p. 305.

Because one of mankind's most destructive and consequential wars followed, few such strategic transformations have prompted more comprehensive scholarly research or more disagreement about how to interpret it. The one conclusion with which nearly all historians agree is that during the last decade of the nineteenth century and the first decade of the twentieth, British political and military leaders' perceptions of their strategic circumstances changed profoundly, and with them Britain's relationships with the world's other major powers. Just when the change occurred; who was most responsible for it; whether the appraisal it reflected was accurate; and even if it were, whether the resulting strategic response was necessary and appropriate remain matters of historical debate. But agreement on the extent of the strategic transformation is nearly universal.

Although the change ultimately reconfigured British foreign and defense policies in a number of ways, four predominated. One can perhaps best appreciate them by comparing Britain's strategic circumstances at the beginning and end of the two decades in question:

> In 1890, Britain's principal great power antagonists were France and Russia, while her friendliest relations were with Germany and its Triple Alliance partner Austria-Hungary. Twenty years later, precisely the opposite relationships prevailed.
>
> In 1890, Britain's imperial possessions and the lines of communication connecting them with the mother country dominated her strategic concerns, wholly overshadowing her interest in Continental affairs. Twenty years later, those priorities had reversed.
>
> In 1890, British foreign policy continued to reflect the resistance to peacetime alliance commitments that had characterized it ever since Canning. Twenty years later, Britain had entered into formal alliances or ententes with Japan, Russia, and France and had negotiated what amounted to a permanent *modus vivendi* with the United States.
>
> Finally, in 1890, as had been true ever since the Battle of Trafalgar in 1805, Britain remained predominant at sea. Twenty years later, confronted with the aggressive expansion of German naval power and the emergence of Japan and the United States as serious naval competitors, the British effectively had abandoned global naval supremacy. Meanwhile, the British army, in 1890 postured almost exclusively as a colonial constabulary, by 1910 had begun to reconfigure itself for large-scale Continental warfare with Germany as the most likely adversary.

Sweeping as they were, these changes reflected no comprehensive strategic reappraisal but rather emerged from a succession of diplomatic and military adaptations to developing circumstances and events, adaptations that were often politically and sometimes publicly contentious. Throughout, far from ratifying any broad strategic consensus, they tended instead to reflect

John Kenneth Galbraith's acid description of politics as the business of choosing between the disastrous and the unpalatable.[3]

Nor should one conclude that the changes at issue led Britain ineluctably into war. On the contrary, nearly to the moment of decision, it remained far from clear whether Britain finally would jettison altogether the deliberate detachment that had governed her Continental behavior for the better part of a century in favor of going to war alongside the very two nations to which she had spent much of that century opposed. However, without much fear of error, one can argue that, but for the strategic adaptations punctuating the last decade of the nineteenth century and the first decade of the twentieth, such a commitment would have been much less likely. While not compelling Britain to go to war, in short, those adaptations certainly were essential precursors of that decision.

America's current circumstances differ materially from those of late Victorian and Edwardian Britain. Nevertheless, many argue that the United States today confronts a similar problem of strategic overstretch in an environment of growing economic and military competition. As was true in Britain at the turn of the twentieth century, however, debate persists about both the magnitude of that problem and how the United States should respond to it.[4] An examination of the *fin de siécle* transformation of British grand strategy cannot resolve that debate, but it may at least help to inform it.

THE CHANGING OPERATING ENVIRONMENT

However profoundly they may have disagreed about the remedy, late-nineteenth-century Britons of all political persuasions were widely conscious of confronting change so rapid in virtually every aspect of life – social, economic, political, technological, and military – that merely gauging their extent and impact was difficult. As one historian commented: "For [Britons] of an activist frame of mind, it seemed as though everywhere they looked Britain's position was crumbling, in Africa, in the Near East, and in the Far East, the challenges were mounting, and an isolated Britain... appeared to have no strategy for dealing with it."[5] Noted another: "Countries are not often faced with so many global dangers and changes in so short

---

[3] Gooch, "The Weary Titan." For a more elaborate argument, see Aaron L. Friedberg, *The Weary Titan: Britain and the Experience of Relative Decline, 1895–1905* (Princeton, NJ, 1988).

[4] Fareed Zakaria offers a compelling statement of the case in *The Post-American World* (New York, 2008). Paul Kennedy discusses some military implications in "When Your Foreign Policy and Your Military Capacity Diverge, Beware!" (http://www.leighbureau.com). For a contrary view, see Robert Kagan, "Still No. 1," *The Washington Post*, October 30, 2008, p. A23.

[5] John Charmley, *Splendid Isolation? Britain, the Balance of Power, and the Origins of the First World War* (London, 1999), p. 232.

a time. Now all this was happening to Britain just at a period when a number of Englishmen began to feel that the 'British Century' was passing away."[6]

At the price of oversimplification, one can describe the most visible and compelling of those changes in what today's strategic planners would call Britain's "operating environment" in terms of four roughly concurrent developments. The first was the looming collapse of the European Concert, first brought into existence after the defeat of Napoleon and preserved during the early years of the nineteenth century by the Vienna settlement, then during its later years by Bismarck's extraordinary diplomacy.[7] Throughout most of this period, with the exceptions of the Greek War of Independence and the Crimean War, Britain had remained largely aloof from Continental concerns. Geographically isolated, unchallenged at sea, and preoccupied with industrialization, an expanding global trade, and domestic political reform, Britain was free for the better part of a century to pursue her own interests essentially undisturbed by events on the Continent.

By the last decade of the nineteenth century, however, Continental political relationships were beginning to fray. In France, stubborn unwillingness to accept Germany's annexation of Alsace and Lorraine after the 1870–1871 Franco-Prussian War produced periodic outbursts of anti-German feeling, on which more than one French government was willing to capitalize for domestic political benefit. In Russia, growing pan-Slavic pressures and lingering designs against a weakening Ottoman Empire's occidental territories merely compounded resentment at Russia's perceived diplomatic mistreatment by the other great powers, chiefly Germany, in the wake of the Russo-Turkish War of 1877–1878. In Austria-Hungary, rising Balkan nationalism threatened to exacerbate long-suppressed restlessness among the Hapsburg Empire's polyglot ethnic and linguistic minorities. And in Germany itself, public and political dissatisfaction was increasing with what some perceived as the failure of Germany's growing economic and military power to earn it appropriate international deference, not least from Britain.[8]

Throughout the 1880s, Bismarck was able to keep a lid on these tensions, in part by negotiating a series of interlocking alliance commitments so complicated that even his own subordinates had trouble keeping track of

---

[6] J. A. S. Grenville, *Lord Salisbury and Foreign Policy: The Close of the Nineteenth Century* (London, 1970), p. 4.

[7] For a brief discussion of the earlier period, see Richard Hart Sinnreich, "In Search of Military Repose: The Congress of Vienna and the Making of Peace," in Williamson Murray and Jim Lacey, eds., *The Making of Peace: Rulers, States, and the Aftermath of War* (Cambridge, 2009). For the later period, see D. G. Williamson, *Bismarck and Germany 1862–1890* (London, 1998), chap. 12.

[8] Barbara W. Tuchman, *The Proud Tower* (New York, 1972), p. 388.

them.[9] In 1890, however, with Bismarck's bitter resignation, the German ship of state "dropped its pilot,"[10] abandoning the empire's strategic direction to Kaiser Wilhelm II, a vain and mercurial personality whose ambivalent attitudes toward his mother's homeland and grandmother's empire only aggravated his idiosyncratic strategic behavior.[11] During the next 20 years, encouraged by overambitious political advisers and overaggressive military leaders, he would jettison Bismarck's carefully nurtured European balance, driving autocratic Russia into an unlikely partnership with republican France; Italy from formal if nominal alliance to effective military neutrality; and Britain from tolerant friendship to outright hostility.[12]

The second development, itself contributing to the progressive diminution of European comity in the last years of the nineteenth century, was accelerating colonial competition, initially in Asia Minor and Africa and eventually extending through central Asia to the Far East. In the Mediterranean, Ottoman provinces along the entire southern littoral of the sultan's decaying empire progressively succumbed to European occupation or control: Algeria by France in 1830, Cyprus by Britain in 1878, Tunisia by France in 1881, Egypt by Britain in 1882, Morocco by France in 1911, and Libya by Italy in 1912.

In Africa south of the Sahara, Britain's and Portugal's long-standing colonies at the Cape and in Angola and Mozambique respectively were joined early in the 1880s by the Belgian Congo, French West Africa, and German colonies in Togoland, the Cameroons, and East and Southwest Africa, and later by French Equatorial Africa and Italy's seizure of Eritrea and Somaliland. Jostling against each other, with their boundaries often unclear, and invested with national egoism rarely justified by their typically dubious economic value, these competing colonial claims led to increasing friction among their great power sponsors and occasionally threatened outright war.

In Central Asia, meanwhile, successive Russo-Persian Wars in 1812–1813 and 1826–1828 had given Russia virtual control of Transcaucasia. Between 1865 and 1870, the czar's armies overran one Central Asian khanate after another – Tashkent, Khodjend, Djizak, Samarkand – and, by 1885, had conquered and annexed the Transcaspian region. Soon only Afghanistan,

---

[9] As his successor Caprivi later explained to justify his recommendation to shelve Germany's Reinsurance Treaty with Russia, "Bismarck was able to juggle with three balls. I can only juggle with two." Robert K. Massie, *Dreadnought: Britain, Germany, and the Coming of the Great War* (New York, 1991), p. 114.

[10] "Dropping the Pilot," *Punch: Or The London Charivari*, March 29, 1890, pp. 150–51.

[11] Massie, *Dreadnought*, p. 106.

[12] Henry Kissinger, *Diplomacy* (New York, 1994), p. 171. For a more comprehensive and detailed account by still another distinguished diplomat, see George F. Kennan, *The Decline of Bismarck's European Order* (Princeton, NJ, 1979).

tribal, combative, and notoriously unstable, would separate British India from advancing Russian power.

Finally, in the Far East, the last half of the nineteenth century saw the beginning of the progressive dismantling of imperial China. Weakened by opium and its own corrupt bureaucracy, devastated by the 14-year Taiping Rebellion, and estimated to have slaughtered as many as 30,000,000 of its own people, China in the late 1800s was an attractive prey, not only to the European powers but also, by the century's end, to a newly modernized and acquisitive Japan. Russia annexed Outer Manchuria in 1860, followed in 1864 by French seizure of Cochin China. Twenty years later, France seized northern Indochina, Britain took Burma, and Russia annexed Chinese Turkestan. Then, in 1895, following its victory in the First Sino-Japanese War, Japan forced China to relinquish control of Korea and Taiwan and occupied the Liaodong Peninsula and Port Arthur. Although subsequently compelled by the European powers to restore control of the peninsula to China in exchange for an increased war indemnity, Japan, by its victory, announced unmistakably its arrival as a significant Far East power with which its European counterparts thenceforth would have to reckon.

In the Far East, as in Africa and Central Asia, the penetration of other great powers into a region in which Britain for decades had enjoyed virtually unchallenged military and economic predominance threatened a sprawling British Empire that, by the turn of the century, controlled nearly a quarter of the earth's land surface and population. Whether or not, as British historian Sir John Seeley famously suggested, that empire had been acquired in "a fit of absence of mind,"[13] and despite the opposition of anti-imperialists from Adam Smith to J. A. Hobson, most Britons' national self-image had by now become inseparably bound up with the empire, a connection to which Queen Victoria, military ambition, mercantile interests, "muscular Christianity," and cultural chauvinism all contributed.

As the century waned, however, Britain's continued grip on that empire confronted an accelerating redistribution of global economic and military power. Its principal features included the loss of agricultural self-sufficiency, making Britain hostage for the first time in her history to the importation of food; an inevitable but nonetheless disturbing decline in her industrial and technological comparative advantage, particularly with respect to Germany and the United States; growing protectionist pressures on her global trade balance; the modernization and enlargement of Continental armies and, thanks to railroads, a radical increase in their operational mobility and strategic reach; and last but perhaps most disturbing, a mounting challenge to Britain's worldwide maritime supremacy.

---

[13] Sir John Robert Seeley, *The Expansion of England: Two Courses of Lectures* (London, 1914), p. 10.

A few numbers suggest the magnitude of the challenge. During the 1880s, under the twin pressures of domestic industrialization and cheap, principally U.S., imports, British grain cultivation diminished by nearly 30 percent. By 1890, Britain was importing between 45 percent and 65 percent of her food cereals.[14] Meanwhile, from 1870 to 1910, her share of world manufacturing production declined from more than 30 percent to less than 15 percent.[15] In key strategic resources, such as coal and steel, the relative decline was even greater: British coal extraction, in 1870 three times that of its nearest competitor, by 1910 had been equaled by Germany and exceeded by the United States. British steel production, similarly, was surpassed by the United States by 1890 and by Germany ten years later.[16] Perhaps even more distressing for a nation long the world's preeminent financier and wedded more passionately than any other to free trade, the last two decades of the nineteenth century witnessed a sharp decline in Britain's balance of trade, her share of international commerce falling by one estimate by nearly 5 percent from 1880 to 1900, with most of the loss accruing once again to Germany and the United States.[17]

Military power presented a similarly worrisome picture. Reflecting Britain's moated geography and long-standing antagonism to conscription, the British Army had never been very large. Throughout the nineteenth century, Britain's regular forces rarely exceeded 300,000 troops, most of them stationed abroad. Reserves, such as they were, were even less prepossessing; until 1881, they were limited to "county regiments" usable solely as local militia. Both regulars and reserves were manned exclusively by volunteers, the former typically recruited from the lowest economic strata of society.[18] In terms of organization, equipment, and tactics, the British Army was glacially slow to change, and what Rudyard Kipling called the Victorian period's "savage wars of peace" were a litany of recurring military disasters, often subsequently redeemed by determination, discipline, and firepower but rarely by brilliant military innovation.[19]

[14] R. C. K. Ensor, *England 1870–1914* (Oxford, 1968), pp. 115–18.
[15] Friedberg, *The Weary Titan*, p. 26.
[16] Paul Kennedy, *The Rise and Fall of the Great Powers* (New York, 1989), p. 200. It is possible to overstate this problem. After the Second Boer War, exports surged as imperial markets heavily compensated for reduced exports to Europe and the United States. See Zara S. Steiner and Keith Neilson, *Britain and the Origins of the First World War*, 2nd ed. (London, 2003), pp. 13–15. But the *relative* change was still significant.
[17] Friedberg, *The Weary Titan*, p. 24.
[18] Although officered largely from the aristocracy and landed gentry even after the Cardwell reforms of 1871 finally abolished commission by purchase. See Harold E. Raugh, *The Victorians at War, 1815–1914: An Encyclopedia of British Military History* (Westport, CT, 2004), p. xiv.
[19] Byron Farwell, *Queen Victoria's Little Wars* (New York, 1972) is a pleasantly readable account.

Nor, until the final years of the century, did many Britons worry over-much about that institutional lethargy. For most, until the Second Boer War disabused them, prevailing sentiment tended to reflect Hilaire Belloc's cynical ditty, "Whatever happens we have got the Maxim gun, and they have not."[20] The occasional enterprising journalist might throw embarrassing light on some military deficiency or other, as did William Russell during the Crimean War and "Noggs" Norris-Newman during the Zulu War of 1879.[21] But not until well after Prussia's decisive victories over Austria in 1866 and France in 1871 did it begin to dawn on some observant Britons that an army adequate to suppress primitive natives armed with assegais might not suffice to deal with much larger European armies equipped with the latest products of weapons makers like Germany's Krupp and France's Schneider. As Lord Salisbury pointed out grimly to Queen Victoria in July 1886: "As land forces go in these days, we have no army capable of meeting even a second-class Continental Power."[22]

At the same time, the development and construction of railroads threatened to deprive the British Army of its one unambiguous advantage: the ability to be transported by sea farther and faster than any of its adversaries could deploy by land. The railroad particularly affected Britain's ability to deter Russian expansion, deterrence based since the Crimean War on Britain's ability via the Black Sea to threaten Russia's eastward communications. By 1890, Russian railroad construction permitted the virtually unassailable transport and sustainment of military forces as far eastward as today's Uzbekistan.[23] Within a few years thereafter, lines would reach the borders of Afghanistan. Then, in March 1891, Russia began construction of the Trans-Siberian Railroad. When completed, it would furnish Russian armies with relatively rapid overland access to the Pacific, access that British military and naval power would be unable to interrupt or even seriously threaten.

Finally, and most worrisome for British leaders, there was mounting pressure on the Royal Navy, the keystone of Britain's security and a major reason for the complacency with which many Britons continued to view Continental military developments. Between 1881 and 1890, Russia and France alone added 233,144 tons of new naval construction against Britain's 196,440.[24] In response, pursuant to the 1889 Naval Defense Act, which authorized a

---

20   H. B. and B. T. B., *The Modern Traveler* (London, 1898), p. 41.
21   Phillip Knightley, *The First Casualty: The War Correspondent as Hero and Myth-Maker from the Crimea to Iraq* (Baltimore, MD, 2004), chap. 3.
22   Charmley, *Splendid Isolation?*, p. 207.
23   The Transcaspian Railroad, later renamed the Central Asian Railway, reached the Amu Darya in 1886 and Samarkand in 1888. See G. Patrick March, *Eastern Destiny: Russia in Asia and the North Pacific* (Westport, CT, 1996), p. 150.
24   "British Naval Policy 1890–1920" (http://www.globalsecurity.org/military/world/europe/uk-rn-policy2.htm).

significant expansion of naval construction, Britain adopted what became known as the "Two–Power Standard," requiring the Royal Navy to be maintained indefinitely at a strength superior to the combined strengths of its nearest two potential adversaries.

From the outset, the two-power standard was beset with ambiguities ranging from the definition of 'superiority' to the metrics by which one should measure it. But the principal problem with the standard, and the one that finally would have the most significant impact on strategy, was determining to which potential adversaries it should be applied.[25] At the time of its adoption, of course, France and Russia were its principal targets. During the next decade, however, that clarity diminished as the Japanese and U.S. navies modernized; and it evaporated altogether after 1900, when Germany, impelled by the kaiser's jealous ambition, also began to build capital ships that, for naval thinkers mesmerized by Alfred Thayer Mahan, could have no other strategic purpose than to challenge the Royal Navy. Given the breadth of Britain's dominions and her increasing dependence on seaborne commerce to feed her people as well as her factories, this expanding worldwide naval competition presented a challenge to which the two-power standard furnished an increasingly inadequate answer.

Together, the erosion of the European Concert, the expansion of colonial competition, and the changing global balance of power presented British statesmen at the turn of the century with the challenge of preserving an empire that many believed to be increasingly imperiled with means that they feared were becoming progressively less adequate.[26] As one writer described the problem, at the end of the nineteenth century, "Britain was a *mature* state, with a built-in interest in preserving existing arrangements or, at least, in ensuring that things altered slowly and peacefully."[27] Acknowledgment of the difficulties involved was by no means uniform, however. Not least of the problems besetting British foreign and defense policy from 1890 to 1910 was intense disagreement about Britain's actual strategic condition, disagreement only complicated by powerful political and emotional investments in Britain's international preeminence. Suggestions that the latter might be unsustainable were unwelcome, hence, unsurprisingly, by no means uniformly accepted.

Which produced the final strategic complication: for, as the nineteenth century waned, the domestic political effects of Britain's Industrial

[25] Friedberg, *The Weary Titan*, pp. 144–52.
[26] Arguably, the problem itself was not new. In relative terms, by Queen Victoria's Golden Jubilee in June 1887, Britain's power already had peaked and begun to recede. Hence what really changed in the 1890s was that perceptions finally began to catch up with strategic reality. See, e.g., Kennedy, *The Rise and Fall of the Great Powers*, p. 226; and Friedberg, *The Weary Titan*, p. 82.
[27] Kennedy, *The Rise and Fall of the Great Powers*, p. 231.

Revolution were beginning to exert unprecedented influence on Britain's foreign and defense policies. As the center of gravity of Britain's economy shifted from agriculture to manufacture, as basic education became increasingly universal, and as information media proliferated, the political grip of Britain's traditional landowning elites inevitably weakened.[28] The resulting democratization of public policy making increased both domestic competition for budgetary largesse and the influence of public opinion on foreign affairs, and vice versa.

Concerning the latter problem, one historian notes: "At best, diplomacy could be kept out of its ken ... but it always hovered in the background, a far from nameless shadow which constricted, constrained and confined the work of the aristocratic diplomatist."[29] Nor did all British statesmen find that uncongenial. As politicians always have, some saw in foreign policy a means by which to influence domestic political arrangements, whether for personal or ideological purposes, and in the manipulation of public opinion, a means by which to influence foreign policy. By 1890, in sum, the days were ending when a Pitt, Palmerston, Disraeli, or Gladstone could commit Britain abroad or decline to do so subject only to the support of the monarch and the approval of a small, socially cohesive, and politically self-referential elite.

EMERGING STRATEGIC CHALLENGES

All four of the developments just outlined played out against an accelerating stream of strategic challenges. While these involved nations as distant as China, South Africa, Japan, and the United States, most involved Britain's three principal European competitors. The first was its traditional enemy France. By 1890, having recovered with astonishing rapidity from its disastrous defeat in 1870–1871, France once again was a great power. While its principal strategic preoccupation remained Germany and the recovery of Alsace-Lorraine, as the century waned, France's expanding colonial interests, principally in West Africa and Southeast Asia, increasingly butted up against Britain's. Colonial competition thus began to compound traditional Anglo-French antagonism as well as more recent sources of friction, from French resentment over disputed fishing rights off Newfoundland to Britain's continued occupation of Egypt.[30]

Britain's second and more pressing concern during most of the period in question was Russia. Even during the final coalition against Napoleon,

---

[28] As late as 1900, fewer than 3,000 Britons had annual incomes exceeding £3,000, while 16,000,000 earned less than £50. Reform, thus, had profound class consequences. Tuchman, *The Proud Tower*, p. 30. See also Steiner and Neilson, *Britain and the Origins of the First World War*, pp. 6–11.

[29] Charmley, *Splendid Isolation?*, p. 196.

[30] A dispute that reached back to the middle of the eighteenth century.

British statesmen had been wary of their Russian ally, and restraining Russia had proved among the more difficult challenges confronting the Congress of Vienna's plenipotentiaries.[31] The Crimean War transmuted Anglo-Russian relations from mutual wariness into outright hostility. Ordinary Britons detested Russia as the land of the knout and secret police. For its part, Russia under successive czars viewed Britain as a persistent obstacle to its claim of suzerainty over the Balkans' Slavic peoples and its ambition to wrest control of the Turkish Straits from the Ottoman Empire and thus gain unfettered access to the Mediterranean.

Above all, from Britain's perspective, Russia's nineteenth-century expansion into Central Asia and her potential escape from the confines of the Black Sea threatened both India and Britain's overland lines of communication south to Africa and east through Persia to India and the Far East. That concern only mounted as Russian rail lines began to reach eastward and Russian penetration into Manchuria multiplied the potential loci of Anglo-Russian confrontation. And it became even more acute when, in 1894, Russia abandoned its former association with Germany in favor of alliance with France, an increasingly potent Mediterranean power.

Finally, there was Germany. Britain had observed with relative equanimity Germany's unification and subsequent consolidation by Bismarck. Preoccupied with democratization, empire, and Ireland, successive British governments by and large were only too happy to leave the management of the Continent's fractious powers to Bismarck. The marital connection of Britain's and Germany's royal families predisposed both nations to mutual tolerance, and Bismarck himself was careful, apart from one brief departure, to avoid disturbing British maritime and colonial sensitivities.[32] Both nations, moreover, shared an interest in restraining French and Russian ambitions.

All that began to change with the accession of Wilhelm II in 1888 and Bismarck's retirement two years later. Freed of the Iron Chancellor's ruthless but conservative discipline, Germany's foreign policy increasingly began to reflect the mercurial attitudes of its young kaiser. As one historian put it: "A man who could state publicly that Bismarck was a ... pygmy' ... was clearly more than usually susceptible to the megalomaniacal tendencies to which monarchs are subject." Those tendencies, moreover, both reflected and contributed to a growing militarization of German society at large. For a time, British leaders could and did discount Wilhelm's rantings about *Weltmachtpolitik*. Indeed, Britain initially welcomed the kaiser's colonial

[31] Murray and Lacey, *The Making of Peace*, pp. 144–47.
[32] As he famously commented in relation to the Scramble for Africa, "My map of Africa lies in Europe." A. J. P. Taylor, *The Struggle for Mastery in Europe, 1848–1918* (Oxford, 1954), p. 294.

adventures – but not his naval ambitions.[33] As Admiral Alfred Tirpitz's efforts to build a German battle fleet began furnishing an increasingly disturbing backdrop to Wilhelm's repeated diplomatic indiscretions, from the 1896 Kruger telegram to the provocative 1905 visit to Tangier that inaugurated the First Moroccan Crisis, even those like Colonial Secretary Joseph Chamberlain, who had long sought to ally the two nations, abandoned hope of reconciling their interests.

THE POLITICAL CONTEXT

Britain's strategic response to the preceding challenges can be divided into three periods, corresponding roughly with the tenures of the three men who principally managed British foreign affairs from 1890 to 1910: Robert Cecil, 3rd Marquess Salisbury, prime minister, with one brief interruption, from 1886 through 1901, who also acted as his own foreign secretary for all but the last year of his tenure; Henry Petty-Fitzmaurice, 5th Marquess Lansdowne, foreign secretary during that last year and through the subsequent ministry of Arthur Balfour, Salisbury's nephew and successor; and Sir Edward Grey, who succeeded Lansdowne on the Liberal Party's return to power in late 1905 and was still in office when World War I broke out nine years later.[34] As each surrendered responsibility to the next, Britain's foreign policy mutated gradually but inexorably from unilateral efforts to shore up Britain's imperial commitments, to alliance with Japan and reconciliation with France and Russia, to eventual albeit reluctant alignment with the last two against Germany and Austria-Hungary.

That evolution was by no means uncontroversial. In examining it, one should bear in mind that turn-of-the-century British foreign policy was the product of cabinet government, in which the prime minister merely was first among equals. Both domestic and foreign policy reflected a collective decision-making process among players with their own political views and Parliamentary allies, who did not hesitate to take positions at odds with each other and their prime minister. That was especially true of the final Salisbury government and its successor, both of which held office on the strength of an unusual coalition in which Liberal Unionists held key cabinet posts even while continuing to sit on the opposition front bench in Parliament.[35]

---

33 "No issue was as likely to turn Great Britain into an implacable adversary as a threat to its command of the seas. Yet this was precisely what Germany undertook, seemingly without realizing that it was embarking on an irrevocable challenge." Kissinger, *Diplomacy*, p. 185.

34 His eleven-year tenure would be the longest in the history of the office.

35 Liberals who broke with Gladstone's Liberal Party in 1886 over its endorsement of Irish home rule. They eventually either rejoined the Liberal Party or merged with the Conservatives outright to form the modern Conservative Party.

Chief among these was Joseph Chamberlain, colonial secretary from 1895 to 1903, a Birmingham industrialist and much-admired populist who was among the first to raise alarms about Britain's imperial decline and who became the most vocal and determined advocate for abandoning what both those who approved and opposed it referred to as Britain's "splendid isolation."[36]

Reflecting their diverging appraisals of Britain's strategic challenges, the last years of the nineteenth century thus witnessed an intensifying contest between Salisbury, on one hand, who, while acknowledging those challenges, considered them manageable through the nation's own efforts, resisted peacetime alliance commitments as both unnecessarily confining and incompatible with Britain's constitutional traditions, and believed the empire's long-term interests best served by cabinet diplomacy and military self-restraint[37]; and on the other, those like Chamberlain who were fearful that Britain's economic and military supremacy was eroding, were prepared to act more aggressively to protect and expand the empire, and were convinced that doing so required partnering militarily with another great power or powers. Noted one historian: "Far from inaugurating a period of Salisburian control, what followed [the Conservative/Liberal Unionist electoral victory of 1895] was a struggle for mastery over British foreign policy, at the heart of which were two different perceptions of how to react to the new circumstances facing Britain."[38]

It is worth emphasizing that throughout this lengthy contest, there was relatively little disagreement about ultimate strategic aims. With the fracture of the Liberal Party in 1886, the long battle between Disraeli and Gladstone over the broad objectives of British foreign policy had at least temporarily been suspended. Salisbury and Chamberlain and their respective allies were equally committed to preserving the empire.[39] Where they differed was about what diplomatic, economic, and military behavior its preservation would require. The resulting debate conditioned British strategic behavior in a series of crises that migrated from the Mediterranean to Africa to the Far East to Central Asia and back to Europe. Many took place more or less

---

[36] A phrase, ironically, that Chamberlain himself employed as a term of approval, not contempt. See Steiner and Neilson, *Britain and the Origins of the First World War*, p. 25.

[37] Salisbury himself famously likened sound foreign policy "to float[ing] lazily downstream, occasionally putting out a diplomatic boat-hook to avoid collisions." T. G. Otte, "'Floating Downstream': Lord Salisbury and British Foreign Policy, 1878–1902," in T. G. Otte, ed., *The Makers of British Foreign Policy: From Pitt to Thatcher* (London, 2002), p. 98.

[38] Charmley, *Splendid Isolation?*, p. 230. See also Steiner and Neilson, *Britain and the Origins of the First World War*, p. 19; and Avner Cohen, "Joseph Chamberlain, Lord Lansdowne and British Foreign Policy 1901–1903: From Collaboration to Confrontation," *The Australian Journal of Politics and History*, 22 June 1997.

[39] Graham D. Goodlad, *British Foreign and Imperial Policy, 1865–1919* (London, 2000), p. 54.

concurrently, each influenced the others, and all were affected by events that often were entirely beyond Britain's control.

TROUBLE – EAST, WEST, AND SOUTH

The first to arise concerned what had become known as the Eastern Question. Ever since the Crimean War, Britain had supported the Ottoman Empire as a vital bulwark against Russian expansion south and east. Hence, when Russian troops threatened Constantinople during the Russo-Turkish War of 1877–1878, Britain sent the Royal Navy's Mediterranean Fleet through the Dardanelles and, ten years later, signed formal agreements with Italy and Austria-Hungary to maintain the status quo in the Mediterranean. Welcomed by Bismarck as a deterrent to both France and Russia, the Mediterranean Agreements proved in retrospect to be the high point of Britain's relations with the Triple Alliance,[40] but their implementation presumed continued British willingness to commit naval power against any Russian effort to breach the Dardanelles. By the early 1890s, however, Britain could no longer ignore France's growing naval strength in the western Mediterranean. With a potentially hostile fleet at their backs, British admirals became increasingly unwilling to contemplate operations against Russia in the eastern Mediterranean.[41]

After 1894, with France and Russia formally allied, such operations became even less attractive. Just such a prospect arose in 1895, when Turkish atrocities against the Ottoman Empire's Armenian Christians threatened to prompt Russian intervention. Unwilling to risk war with France, the cabinet refused to sanction deployment of a British naval squadron to the straits.[42] In the end, the European powers arranged a diplomatic solution. However, the following year, when a now-suspicious Austria demanded an explicit British commitment to defend Constantinople as a condition of renewing the 1887 agreements, Salisbury felt compelled to allow them to lapse, later admitting that, in propping up Turkey to deter Russia, Britain might have "put all our money on the wrong horse."[43] Nonrenewal ended any further connection between Britain and the Triple Alliance. And when, in 1897, the cabinet similarly refused to sanction British intervention in the Greco-Turkish War, so also ended any effective British influence on Balkan affairs.

---

40 "Robert Davis, "Mediterranean Agreements (1887)," in Carl Cavanagh Hodge, ed., *Encyclopedia of the Age of Imperialism, 1800–1914* (Westport, CT, 2008), p. 465. See also Gordon A. Craig, *Germany, 1866–1945* (Oxford, 1978), p. 131.
41 Friedberg, *The Weary Titan*, pp. 154–55.
42 Such an effort would have been hugely unpopular in any case given public outrage over the massacres.
43 Otte, *The Makers of British Foreign Policy*, p. 115.

Meanwhile, even before the Armenian crisis was resolved, two other problems confronted Britain halfway around the world from each other. In July 1895, the United States demanded that Britain submit a boundary dispute between Venezuela and British Guiana to impartial arbitration. When Salisbury initially ignored what he considered an unjustified and pretentious American demand, President Grover Cleveland, invoking the Monroe Doctrine, made veiled threats of war. After considerable back-and-forth, the Arbitration Treaty of 1896 finally resolved the matter amicably. As one of Salisbury's biographers admits, the entire affair was something of a tempest in a teapot, presenting little likelihood that actual hostilities would ensue.[44] But the incident cast in sharp relief Britain's growing inability to protect its dominions in the western hemisphere in the face of active American hostility without incurring unacceptable risks closer to home. As an Admiralty memorandum later argued: "Britain unaided can hardly expect to be able to maintain ... squadrons sufficiently powerful to dominate those of the United States and at the same time to hold command of the sea in home waters, the Mediterranean, and the Eastern seas, where it is essential that she should remain predominant."[45]

The other concurrent crisis only accentuated that problem. On 29 December 1895, a force of colonial mounted police and volunteers led by Dr. Leander Jameson, administrator of the chartered British company in Matabeleland, invaded the Transvaal, independent since the First Boer War.[46] The immediate objective of the British raiders was to incite expatriate *uitlander* workers who had been denied political rights to rebel against the Transvaal's Boer government.[47] The raid failed almost before it began. Pursued by superior Boer forces and surrounded on January 2, Jameson and his crew prudently surrendered, and after a brief sojourn in Pretoria's jail, he and his countrymen were remanded to Britain for trial.

Apart from embarrassing Her Majesty's government and further alienating the Boers, the only direct cost of the raid was a native uprising in the area depleted of police by their participation. What transformed what otherwise would have been a comic opera into an international incident, however, was the intervention of Kaiser Wilhelm, who unwisely sent Transvaal President Paul Kruger a telegram congratulating him on his successful defeat of foreign invaders "without appealing to the help of friendly powers" – implying that

[44] Grenville, *Lord Salisbury and Foreign Policy*, p. 66. Ironically for Venezuela, the arbitration commission established by the treaty ended by sustaining Britain's position nearly without exception. Ibid., p. 72.
[45] Friedberg, *The Weary Titan*, p. 171. See also Kennedy, *The Rise and Fall of the Great Powers*, p. 251.
[46] Today part of Zimbabwe.
[47] Their ultimate goal, of course, was reunification of the Transvaal with Cape Colony under British rule.

Germany might have responded positively to such an appeal had it been made. Having thus established his diplomatic obtuseness, the kaiser then compounded the problem by releasing his telegram to the press, earning praise in Berlin but prompting fury in Britain. "The *Times* spoke for the rest of the press," notes one account, "when it [called] the telegram 'as deadly and unprovoked an insult as was ever offered by the head of a European nation to one of equal rank.'"[48] Both the raid and the subsequent public uproar were particularly embarrassing to Chamberlain, widely suspected of having incited the episode through Cape Colony's president and Jameson's patron, Cecil Rhodes.[49]

In combination with the Venezuelan dispute, the more far-reaching effect was to multiply questions about how Britain should or could respond were another great power to challenge the empire in a geographically remote region in which Britain previously had enjoyed relative freedom of action. Salisbury's immediate response was to direct formation of a naval "flying squadron" to be in readiness for distant commitment in the event that words led to war. Just where the squadron might be employed was unclear, and after nearly a year attached to the Mediterranean Fleet, it was disbanded.[50] But the Jameson raid and its aftermath were still another indication of Britain's growing strategic overstretch, increasing the pressure on Salisbury to abandon his "freehand" approach to diplomacy.[51]

COLONIAL FRICTION

That pressure only intensified as colonial competition in the Middle East and Africa migrated to the Far East. Japan's 1895 defeat of China inaugurated a series of European impositions on China's decaying Qing Empire. In 1897, Germany demanded and received a treaty port at Kiaochow and mining rights in Shandong Province, while Russia seized Port Arthur. In response, in 1898, Britain leased a treaty port at Wei-Hai-Wei and France annexed Kwang-Chou-Wan. Efforts by the United States and Britain to secure great power agreement to an open-door policy guaranteeing China's territorial

[48] Charmley, *Splendid Isolation?*, p. 239.
[49] Probably erroneously, although at least one contemporary writer accused Chamberlain of having blatantly lied his way out of involvement. See Deryck Schreuder and Jeffrey Butler, eds., *Sir Graham Bower's Secret History of the Jameson Raid and the South African Crisis, 1895–1902* (Van Riebeeck Society, 2002).
[50] The Venezuela dispute still had not been resolved, and some speculated that it might be dispatched to the Caribbean. "Talk About the Flying Squadron," *The New York Times*, 18 January 1896, p. 1.
[51] As an American diplomatic successor later would write: "In some respects, Salisbury's position was not unlike that of President George Bush, though he served longer in his nation's highest office. Both men bestrode a world which was receding by the time they came to power, though that fact was not obvious to either of them." Kissinger, *Diplomacy*, p. 177.

integrity, while assuring equal commercial access to all interested foreign powers, proved unsuccessful in dampening colonial rivalry. In China, as in Africa and the western hemisphere, that rivalry merely compounded liberal imperialists' growing strategic unease, an unease soon reflected in public opinion. Although Salisbury publicly scorned complaints that the arrival of other powers threatened British economic interests in China, neither the press nor the public were mollified and voices multiplied urging him to pursue some sort of formal alignment with another great power.[52]

For Chamberlain and his supporters, the obvious candidate was Germany.[53] In fact, during the 1880s, Bismarck had tried more than once to induce Britain to join the Triple Alliance, efforts frustrated by Gladstone's refusal to commit Britain to any permanent Continental relationship and Salisbury's skepticism that such a proposal to commit future governments would be constitutional in any case.[54] Now, confronted with essentially the same proposition by his own cabinet, Salisbury's view remained unaltered: if isolation was dangerous, alignment with either of Europe's alliance systems would be even more so, especially one led by a ruler whose prudence he distrusted and belligerence he detested. Indeed, notes one writer: "Negotiating with Germany, whether over the Portugese Empire or Samoa, simply confirmed Salisbury in his belief that there were not only no grounds for an alliance, but that Berlin would use any sign that Britain wanted one as an opportunity to engage in a little extortion and blackmail."[55] Instead, he insisted, the vital need was to restore Britain's strategic freedom of action by repairing relations with Russia and France.

During the final years of the decade, he attempted to do precisely that, initially by attempting to defuse tensions with Russia. Speaking at London's Guildhall in November 1896, he had insisted that it was a "superstition of antiquated diplomacy that there is any necessary antagonism between Russia and Great Britain."[56] Early in 1898, he proposed to the czar's government that the two empires directly negotiate their relative spheres of influence in Persia, Central Asia, and the Far East. The proposal went nowhere. Instead, the Russians continued to gobble up more of Manchuria and, in March, coerced the Chinese government into granting them a 25-year lease on the same Port Arthur from which they had helped evict Japan only two years earlier. The resulting adverse domestic reaction compelled Salisbury, with

---

[52] Charmley, *Splendid Isolation?*, p. 254.
[53] The United States was another but too distant and still regarded as too immature to be considered helpful outside its own hemisphere.
[54] Sidney B. Fay, *The Origins of the World War* (New York, 1966), pp. 124–25.
[55] Charmley, *Splendid Isolation?*, p. 272.
[56] Ibid., p. 246. As Charmley notes: "Salisbury was not worried about an Anglo-Russian war for its own sake – geography ensured that the two could inflict little direct harm on each other – but he feared the collateral damage; it might offer France the occasion for revenge, and an Anglo-French war would be extremely serious." Ibid., p. 213.

considerable reluctance, to accede to cabinet demands to establish a countervailing British foothold on the Chinese mainland at Wei-Hai-Wei. But
relations with Russia, it was apparent, were likely to get worse before getting better.

The same unfortunately proved true of France. Britain and France had
clashed over colonial issues more than once during the 1880s, in Siam and
Africa, but the most serious dispute dividing them in the early 1890s was
Britain's continuing occupation of Egypt. Arising out of Disraeli's decision
in 1875 to purchase Egypt's shares in the Suez Canal Company, compelling
France to share control of the Canal, the occupation itself followed British
military intervention in 1882 to quell a nationalist revolt against the Egyptian government. Although explained to the French as a temporary measure to safeguard the Canal, the occupation persisted over France's bitter
objection even after the revolt had been suppressed, and relinquishing it
became even less feasible when, in 1883, a religious zealot known as the
Mahdi launched an uprising in neighboring Sudan, claimed by Egypt, seizing Khartoum and killing British General Charles "Chinese" Gordon in the
process. In the ensuing public uproar, there could be no question of evacuat-
ing Egypt; and although Gladstone successfully resisted pressure to conquer
the Sudan outright, his own liberal imperialists eventually compelled him to
reinforce the British garrison in Egypt.

His Conservative successor was no fonder of the Egyptian commitment
than Gladstone. As Otte notes: "[Salisbury] was not inspired by romantic
notions of an imperial mission [or] driven by some sense of Anglo-Saxon
superiority."[57] On the contrary, writes another historian: "Egypt was like a
noose around the British neck, which any Great Power could tighten when it
wished to wring a diplomatic concession from the Mistress of the Seas."[58] All
things equal, Salisbury would have been delighted to end Britain's presence
in Egypt and so remove a persistent Anglo-French irritant.[59] Unfortunately,
Britain's surrender of maritime control of the eastern Mediterranean only
increased Egypt's strategic importance. "Liquidation of the British occupation of Egypt, the main French demand, was now more unlikely than
ever. With the Ottoman Empire being circled by the vultures, it made no
sense to give up a firm base from which Britain could defend her interests
in the Mediterranean."[60] In addition, the Nile was an essential continental connector to British East Africa and the Persian Gulf, particularly after
Britain's annexation of Uganda in 1894. Reflecting that concern, in 1898,
on the unconvincing excuse of the Mahdi's successors' internal despotism

[57] Otte, *The Makers of British Foreign Policy*, p. 101.
[58] Fay, *The Origins of the World War*, p. 126.
[59] David Gillard, "Salisbury," in Keith M. Wilson, ed., *British Foreign Secretaries and Foreign
Policy: From Crimean War to First World War* (London, 1987), p. 129.
[60] Charmley, *Splendid Isolation?*, p. 247.

and external aggressiveness, Lord Cromer, Britain's consul-general in Egypt, turned General Herbert Kitchener's Anglo-Egyptian army loose to shatter the Dervishes at Omdurman, recapture Khartoum, and avenge Gordon.

Kitchener's victory certainly eliminated the Mahdist threat to Egypt and the Suez, but it merely aggravated tensions with the French. Even before Omdurman, France had set out to establish its own rights to the upper Nile, launching an expedition eastward from Libreville on the Atlantic coast to the Sudanese village of Fashoda, with a view to linking French Equatorial Africa with the Nile basin. The expedition reached Fashoda in July 1898 and raised French colors over a small fort beside the Nile. Allowed to become permanent, the French presence would neatly sever Egypt from British East Africa and the Indian Ocean. Accordingly, two months later, arriving upriver from Khartoum with a flotilla of gunboats, Kitchener demanded that the French evacuate.

Although heavily outgunned, Marchand, the French commander, courageously refused. To avoid hostilities, both commanders prudently chose to refer the dispute to their respective capitals, Marchand in the meantime agreeing to fly French, British, and Egyptian colors. Overheated newspaper reports in London and Paris enflamed both nations' jingoists, however, and the British and French Mediterranean squadrons began mobilizing. Fortunately, confronting superior naval power, preoccupied with the Dreyfus affair, and needing no additional military complications, France's newly appointed foreign minister, Théophile Delcassé, ignored his own ultranationalists, and in November 1898, after some face-saving diplomatic horse trading, Paris authorized Marchand to haul down his colors and withdraw. That averted war, but France's embarrassing retreat did nothing to improve Anglo-French relations.

INFLECTION POINT: THE SECOND BOER WAR

The Fashoda crisis was less than a year in the past when Britain found herself at war once again in South Africa. There is no need here to review the long history of tensions between Britons and Boers that preceded the Second Boer War. More important for the purposes of this discussion is that the war erupted, not in aid of some far-ranging strategic purpose, but rather, on Salisbury's part at least, as a reluctant response to what a majority of his cabinet and countrymen believed to be repeated Boer provocations. Historians today still argue about how to apportion responsibility for the conflict among Transvaal President Paul Kruger, Cape Colony president Cecil Rhodes, Sir Alfred Milner, Britain's high commissioner for South Africa, and Milner's allies in the cabinet, principally Joseph Chamberlain. Whatever the truth of the matter, Kruger's ultimatum on October 9, 1899, demanding that British troops withdraw from his border, produced a combination of official disbelief and public outrage that no British government could easily ignore.

The war itself lasted more than twice as long as anyone had expected, however, and cost Britain much more heavily in lives and treasure. An alarming series of early British defeats revealed serious military weaknesses, and, while a heavily reinforced expeditionary commitment finally defeated the last regular Boer force in August 1900, what followed was not peace but rather a bitter insurgency that dragged on for two more years. In the end, the British managed to bring both the Transvaal and the adjacent Orange Free State under control but only through methods, the harshness of which exacted a terrible cost from the Transvaal's civilian population, outraged Britons in and out of government, and earned Britain widespread international obloquy.[61]

Both the war itself and the international reaction to it had wider strategic ramifications. To begin with, the duration and difficulty of the struggle severely damaged the confidence of both British leaders and ordinary citizens in the nation's military competence. "A kind of paranoia seized the national mood," writes one historian. "The army had been so thoroughly humiliated by its long-suffering attempts to deal with what at first was called by the press 'a tea-time war' that Whitehall feared that some essential élan had disappeared from the English race and that some weaknesses had been exposed which other countries were eager to exploit."[62] The disturbing sense of a world passing away only deepened with Queen Victoria's death in January 1901 and her succession by a prince previously notorious only for his personal excesses.

Contributing to that unease, throughout the war, the British government was haunted by fears of intervention by other great powers. Nor were those fears entirely fanciful. During the early months of the war, there were persistent reports that Russia was attempting to draw Germany and France into an anti-British coalition to assist the Boers, reports given additional credence by Kaiser Wilhelm's injudicious comments to the French ambassador in Berlin.[63] Compounded by the virtual depletion of home-stationed

---

61 It was in South Africa, for example, that the concentration camp was born in an effective, but also widely condemned, effort to deprive the insurgents of concealment and support by the civil population. See Denis Judd and Keith Surridge, *The Boer War* (London, 2003), chap. 12.

62 Cecil D. Eby, *The Road to Armageddon* (Durham, NC, 1987), p. 28. Another writer put it more epigrammatically: "The Boer War," he declared, "knocked the gilt off the Victorian Age." Grenville, *Lord Salisbury and Foreign Policy*, p. 268.

63 Grenville, *Lord Salisbury and Foreign Policy*, p. 272. Grenville argues that these were prompted in part by the continuing Anglo-German dispute over Germany's desire to partition the Samoan Islands. That being settled in November 1899, the kaiser reverted in subsequent dealings with British officials to his habitual mixture of bonhomie and bombast.

regular army forces to feed the war, such reports prompted a resurgence of the invasion paranoia that had been a recurrent phenomenon in Britain ever since Prussia's defeat of France in 1871. As one commentator notes: "During the four decades immediately prior to the outbreak of the Great War of 1914–18, the Impossible Event was described so many times by such an array of military experts (official as well as self-appointed), journalists, and popular writers that it clearly reflected a grave national psychosis."[64] From Lieutenant Colonel George Chesney's "The Battle of Dorking," published in *Blackwood's Magazine* in May 1871, to Erskine Childers's *The Riddle of the Sands*, published in 1903 (and still in print today), Britain was invaded so often in popular fiction that officials from Prime Minister Gladstone to future First Sea Lord Prince Louis of Battenberg were moved to complain publicly.[65]

TURMOIL IN CHINA

Meanwhile, even while the fighting in South Africa continued, China descended into chaos. During summer 1900, a movement of violently antiforeign Chinese, called Boxers by Europeans, spread rapidly from Shantung to Peking.[66] There, openly supported by China's empress dowager and joined by elements of the imperial army, they murdered the German ambassador and besieged the British diplomatic compound, in which the Japanese, American, and most European legations had taken refuge. During the next two months, they roamed unchecked through northern China, pillaging missions and killing both Europeans and Chinese missionaries, until finally, in August, an eight-nation invasion force fought its way to Peking, relieved the legations, and captured the imperial family.[67]

For a British government already worried about Russian penetration into Manchuria, and fearful that China, like Africa, would wind up partitioned among the great powers, the Boxer Rebellion could not have come at a less propitious moment. Embroiled in South Africa and with an election impending, the Salisbury government had few means of exerting leverage on Russia. Nor, while sharing Britain's concern, were Japan or the United States in a position to offer material support. Only Germany conceivably could do so if it wished. Accordingly, under pressure from the cabinet, Salisbury swallowed his distaste and approached Berlin with the proposal that Britain and Germany jointly guarantee China's territorial integrity.

[64] Eby, *The Road to Armageddon*, p. 11.
[65] Ibid., chap. 2.
[66] The Boxers got their name for their passion for the martial arts.
[67] For a lengthy, but readable, treatment of the Boxer Rebellion, see Diana Preston, *The Boxer Rebellion: The Dramatic Story of China's War on Foreigners that Shook the World in the Summer of 1900* (Berkeley, CA, 2001).

The resulting negotiations led, in October 1900, to the Yangtse Agreement, committing the two governments to "consult" if a third power threatened China's territorial integrity. When pressed, however, Berlin refused to apply the accord retroactively to Russia's penetration into Manchuria. As one historian notes: "The reality was that Germany's trade with China did not justify the risk of a clash with Russia, whose entanglement in the Far East was pure gain from Berlin's point of view."[68] Berlin's attitude merely confirmed Salisbury in his long-held conviction that any effort to seek closer alliance with Germany would carry a price tag heavier than Britain was prepared to pay, in return for little real support where most needed.

Salisbury's continued ability to enforce that conviction was eroding rapidly, however. Even as the military situation in South Africa deteriorated, the Russians continued their advance on Persia and Afghanistan, and Germany, having replaced Britain as Turkey's great power sponsor, was negotiating construction of a Berlin – Baghdad railway that, when completed, would give Germany direct rail access through the Ottoman Empire to the Persian Gulf. Writing from Delhi, Lord George Curzon, viceroy of India, complained that London was ignoring these threats. By mid-1900, Salisbury's government was in disarray. "Faced with numerous crises all over the world, the Cabinet disintegrated. Important issues were insufficiently discussed and too much time was wasted on trivial and irrelevant questions."[69] While the "Khaki Election" of 1900 increased the Conservative/Unionist majority, Salisbury's control of the cabinet continued to weaken under pressure from his increasingly rebellious younger colleagues.[70] At last, in November 1900, 71 years old and in ill health, he surrendered the Foreign Office to Lansdowne, then secretary of state for war. A year and a half later, he would relinquish the government altogether to Arthur Balfour.

With him passed an era in British foreign policy.[71] Like Chamberlain, Lansdowne was a Liberal Unionist and shared the colonial secretary's belief in Britain's eroding strategic position.[72] During his five-year tenure, the British government would conclude three crucial diplomatic negotiations. The first two would produce Britain's first explicit peacetime military alliance in more than a century and effectively cede permanent supremacy in the

---

[68] John Lowe, *The Great Powers, Imperialism, and the German Problem, 1865–1925* (London, 1994), p. 116.

[69] Zara S. Steiner, *The Foreign Office and Foreign Policy, 1898–1914* (Dublin, 1969), p. 25.

[70] Ibid., p. 27.

[71] Although some argue that there was more policy continuity from Salisbury to Lansdowne than the former's critics and latter's admirers (and vice versa) have been willing to acknowledge. See, e.g., Charmley, *Splendid Isolation?*, pp. 280–82; Grenville, *Lord Salisbury and Foreign Policy*, pp. 435–37.

[72] As Grenville comments: "After five years at the War Office, he was convinced that Britain's military weaknesses necessitated the abandonment of her traditional policy of eschewing alliances in time of peace." Grenville, *Lord Salisbury and Foreign Policy*, p. 326.

western hemisphere to the United States. The third would begin reshaping Europe's continental balance.

The first of these originated in a renewed effort, instigated by Chamberlain and supported by his War Office and Admiralty colleagues, to enlist Germany in restraining Russia. Early in 1901, over Salisbury's continuing opposition, Lansdowne drafted a proposed secret agreement for Anglo–German–Japanese cooperation and mutual defense.[73] Both its secrecy and its terms, which visualized Anglo-German support of Japan in any clash with more than one other power, represented a sharp break with Salisburian diplomacy. Although approved by the cabinet in March, the proposal during the next several months prompted what amounted to a dialogue of the deaf between London and Berlin, a discourse further confused by competing and often conflicting private discussions among various representatives of the two governments.

Then, in August 1901, Empress Frederick, Wilhelm II's mother and Edward VII's sister, died of cancer. During Edward's visit to Germany to attend her funeral, the kaiser hectored the king concerning Britain's foreign policy generally and her refusal to align herself with the Triple Alliance in particular. Inasmuch as Edward already detested his nephew, whom he considered a loudmouth and bully, this exchange was diplomatically unhelpful, to say the least.[74] By year's end, it was apparent even to Chamberlain that no Anglo-German alliance was in prospect.[75] Quite apart from mutual royal repugnance, no one reasonably could misperceive any longer the fundamental incompatibility of the two empires' strategic aims. London's overriding concern was braking Russian expansion in the Far East, a preoccupation Germany secretly welcomed; while Berlin's only interest was in Britain's acknowledgment of Germany's imperial equality and her support in a potential conflict with France and Russia in Europe, a contest in which London had no desire whatever to participate. Each government thus sought what the other had no intention of conceding.

Instead, Lansdowne turned to Japan. Earlier that year, he had broached the possibility of an Anglo-Japanese alliance with the Japanese ambassador but, hoping for German participation in a tri-nation alliance, had allowed the matter to lapse. Now, seeing no hope of agreement with Berlin, he

---

[73] In what was perhaps Salisbury's definitive statement of the strategic and constitutional objections to any formal alliance with Germany. Ibid., pp. 353–54.

[74] A sentiment warmly reciprocated by Wilhelm, along with acute envy. Fay, *The Origins of the World War*, pp. 140–41. See also Barbara Tuchman, *The Guns of August* (New York, 1962), p. 2.

[75] Indeed, attacked by Germany's foreign minister for implied criticism of the Prussian Army's behavior during the Franco-Prussian War, Chamberlain publicly and unembarrassedly abandoned his long-standing inclination toward Germany. Massie, *Dreadnought*, pp. 307–9. See also Cohen, "Joseph Chamberlain, Lord Lansdowne and British Foreign Policy 1901–1903."

reopened that discussion and, despite Salisbury's continued resistance to any agreement committing Britain in advance to a possible war, convinced the cabinet to support him.[76] On 30 January 1902, the two nations signed the Anglo-Japanese Treaty, committing Britain for the first time since the Triple Alliance of 1788 to a formal defensive alliance with another power. Meanwhile, concurrent with the Anglo-Japanese negotiations, Britain also had been discussing several lingering issues with the United States, ranging from Alaska's boundary with Canada to control of the future Panama Canal.[77] With the U.S. Senate's approval of the Hay-Pauncefote Treaty on 16 December 1901, the two nations had resolved virtually all outstanding disagreements between them. Thereafter, the security of Britain's hemispheric interests would rely on the maintenance of America's good will.

Entente Cordiale

Together, the Anglo-Japanese and Hay-Pauncefote treaties helped relieve pressure on Britain at the periphery of empire. The third key negotiation did so closer to home. Although other factors played a role, the immediate inspiration was French Foreign Minister Delcassé's ambition to enlarge France's predominance in North Africa, using its foothold in Algeria to gain influence over an increasingly unstable Morocco. In 1900, he concluded a secret agreement with Italy, recognizing the latter's colonial interests in Tripoli in return for Italian recognition of French interests in Morocco.[78] Aware that Morocco also touched British, Spanish, and German interests, and having his own domestic enemies, he was careful not to push too hard or too fast. But growing instability in the Moorish kingdom convinced Delcassé that sooner or later, one or another of the European powers would have to secure Morocco, and he was determined that it should be France.[79]

The Anglo-Japanese Treaty complicated that ambition. Given France's Dual Alliance with Russia, it increased the risk that any war in the Far East between their respective allies might end by embroiling Britain and France.

---

[76] Strongly supported by Selbourne at the Admiralty, who saw in the alliance the possibility of reducing the Royal Navy's Far East commitments. P. J. V. Rolo, "Lansdowne," in Wilson, *British Foreign Secretaries and Foreign Policy*, p. 162. In sharp contrast, Salisbury warned that the treaty would commit "without reserve into the hands of another power the right of deciding whether we shall or shall not stake the resources of the Empire on the issue of a mighty conflict." Charmley, *Splendid Isolation?*, p. 303.
[77] Agreed in the 1850 Clayton-Bulwer Treaty to be shared by the two nations, an arrangement, by 1900, no longer satisfactory to the United States.
[78] And a few years later, a secret agreement to remain neutral in any war with a third party, in effect repudiating Italy's obligations under the Triple Entente. Williamson, *Politics of Grand Strategy*, pp. 5–6.
[79] Ibid., p. 5.

Reacting in part to these pressures, and in part to growing unease with Germany's mounting belligerence, Delcassé and Paul Cambon, his ambassador in London, began early in 1902 quietly exploring the possibility of Anglo-French rapprochement. The conclusion of the Second Boer War, which had further antagonized a French public opinion still smarting about Fashoda, helped remove one major obstacle to such a reconciliation.

Edward VII helped even more. A Francophile from childhood, in May 1903, he visited Paris on a tour of European capitals and, in four bravura days of public and private appearances, captivated even the notoriously cynical Parisians. "He has won the hearts of all the French," reported a Belgian diplomat.[80] His visit was reciprocated a few months later by French President Émile Loubet, during which Lansdowne and Delcassé, who had accompanied Loubet, explored the full range of Anglo-French differences, from Egypt to Newfoundland. More deliberate discussions followed between Whitehall and Quai d'Orsay. Eventually, trading a concession here for a concession there, the two nations resolved their outstanding issues and, on 8 April 1904, to widespread European and especially German astonishment, signed what became known as the Entente Cordiale.[81]

Formally, the Entente was no more than a settlement of colonial differences, with no implication of any mutual security commitments. Its most important provision traded explicit French acceptance of Britain's continued dominion in Egypt and the Sudan for British recognition of France's ambitions in Morocco and diplomatic support should they be challenged. Other clauses acknowledged Siam (Thailand) as a neutral buffer between British-dominated Burma and French Indochina, abandoned British claims to Madagascar, and resolved the long-standing dispute over fishing rights off Newfoundland. But nowhere in the agreement was there the slightest suggestion of any defense relationship. On the contrary, despite France's formal guarantee not to fortify the coast opposite Gibraltar, neither the Admiralty nor the War Office was entirely comfortable with the Entente's Moroccan concession. For their part, Delcassé's critics were no happier with his abandonment of France's position in Egypt.

Both sides' doubts were exacerbated when, in February 1904, the long-simmering antagonism between Russia and Japan erupted into war.[82] As it would again 37 years later, Japan preempted its enemy's receipt of a formal declaration of war, mounting a surprise naval attack on Port Arthur.

---

[80] Tuchman, *The Guns of August*, p. 5. Anyone who doubts the impact that an individual personality can exert on historical events need look no further than Edward VII's visit to Paris. See also Williamson, *The Politics of Grand Strategy*, p. 9.

[81] And no little chagrin: Berlin had been complacently confident that a reconciliation of two such traditional adversaries simply was not possible. Tuchman, *The Guns of August*, p. 7.

[82] A war, ironically, the likelihood of which Lansdowne had discounted while negotiating the Anglo-Japanese treaty. Grenville, *Lord Salisbury and Foreign Policy*, p. 423.

When the assault failed to secure the port outright, the Japanese invested it by land and sea. In October, in an effort to relieve its beleaguered garrison, Russia dispatched its Baltic Fleet on an eighteen-thousand-mile voyage around Africa to China.[83] On its way across the North Sea, however, reacting in dirty weather to false reports of hostile torpedo boats, the Russian fleet fired on the Hull fishing fleet off Dogger Bank, sinking one British trawler and damaging four more.[84] Prompt Russian apologies averted a British military response, but the incident only increased British and French nervousness about their newfound relationship.

It was German maladroitness that managed to solidify that relationship and, in the process, begin its transformation into something more significant than merely a settlement of colonial differences. Although surprised by the Entente, Berlin initially had registered no particular concern about its provisions concerning Morocco. A year later, the Germans changed their minds.[85] Annoyed at not having been consulted by the French, and hoping to expose the infirmity of the new Anglo-French relationship, German Chancellor Bernhard von Bülow convinced the kaiser to visit Tangier, where, on March 31, 1904, he made a series of inflammatory statements in effect accusing France of aggression and promising support of Moroccan independence. Taken aback, elements in the French government and press reacted by attacking Delcassé for incurring German hostility at Britain's behest.

The crisis presented Balfour and Lansdowne with a quandary: "Despite the rising tide of anti-German feeling, Lansdowne . . . continued to believe in the vanishing possibility of an Anglo-German understanding. The German challenge in Morocco therefore came as a shock to many and strengthened the Anglo-French entente in an unexpected manner."[86] At first, the cabinet was inclined to discount the Tangier visit as another of Wilhelm's ill-considered faux pas.[87] However, as pressure on Delcassé mounted, British leaders began to worry that he might feel compelled to buy his way out of his difficulties by agreeing to German acquisition of a Moroccan seaport, a prospect that gave the Admiralty the vapors. The British press, meanwhile, were in no doubt whatever that the kaiser's démarche represented a deliberate effort to torpedo the Entente, a conviction reinforced by Wilhelm's caustic comment to Prince Louis of Battenberg on the day after his visit

---

[83]   Britain having refused to allow it passage through the Suez Canal.

[84]   For a brief but fascinating account of this epic but doomed voyage, see "Dogger Bank – Voyage of the Damned" (http://www.hullwebs.co.uk/content/l-20c/disaster/dogger-bank/voyage-of-dammed.htm).

[85]   Assisted by the sultan, who, goaded by local German representatives, decided in December to object to French proposals for administrative and financial reforms. Williamson, *The Politics of Grand Strategy*, pp. 28–29.

[86]   Steiner, *The Foreign Office and Foreign Policy*, p. 48.

[87]   "Lansdowne's first reaction to the German initiative in Morocco was to dismiss it as 'an extraordinarily clumsy bit of diplomacy.'" Charmley, *Splendid Isolation?*, p. 319.

to Tangier that "as to France . . . they should remember no fleet can defend Paris."[88]

Accordingly, Whitehall launched a concerted effort to assure Delcassé of Britain's diplomatic support for whatever stance France might adopt vis-à-vis Berlin. Distrustful of British motives and resolve, and fearful of a war with Germany for which it was unready, the French government nevertheless accepted Germany's demand for an international conference on Morocco, at which point Delcassé resigned in protest. But the contrast between Britain's determined support and Germany's increasing arrogance gradually impressed even Anglophobic Frenchmen. When the conference convened at Algeciras in January 1906, just to make Britain's support clear, a squadron of the Home Fleet deployed to Gibraltar, anchoring in clear view of the Algeciras conferees, who thereupon largely repudiated Germany's objections.

By that time, the Conservatives, who, apart from one brief interlude, had dominated Britain's foreign policy for two decades, were no longer in office. On 4 December 1905, confronted with a cabinet fractured over tariff reform and other issues, Balfour resigned, and the election that followed shortly thereafter produced a Liberal landslide. Replacing Lansdowne at the Foreign Office was Sir Edward Grey. Like Lansdowne a Liberal Imperialist, Grey shared his disillusion with Germany: "'Isolation' haunted his imagination in much the same way it had Joseph Chamberlain. Grey feared the effects on the balance of power if Britain left France 'in the lurch': there would be 'a general feeling that we had behaved meanly;' America 'would despise us;' Russia 'would not think it worthwhile to make a friendly arrangement with us about Asia;' Japan would 'prepare to insure herself elsewhere and . . . Germany would take some pleasure in exploiting the whole situation to our disadvantage.'"[89]

Installed at Whitehall, Grey lost no time in reassuring France that the change in government would in no way alter Britain's support of France in Morocco. Initially, both he and the government for which he spoke intended that support to be exclusively diplomatic. Then Grierson and Huguet had their fateful Hyde Park encounter. The following month, Grey authorized informal discussions between British and French general staffs. Dispute persists about when Grey informed the cabinet of those discussions and to what extent he revealed their purpose.[90] Whatever the case, it is apparent that while their nominal purpose was to coordinate the two nations' possible responses to any German military challenge in North Africa, it was not long before they began to focus on where and how British troops could

[88] Williamson, *The Politics of Grand Strategy*, p. 32.
[89] Charmley, *Splendid Isolation?*, p. 337.
[90] Williamson, *The Politics of Grand Strategy*, chap. 3.

assist their French counterparts in a war with Germany on the European continent.

MILITARY TRANSFORMATION

In part, that crucial development reflected changes in the military and naval environments. In 1902, in response to the military deficiencies surfaced during the Second Boer War and the heightened fears of invasion it had prompted, Balfour had revitalized the Committee of Imperial Defense (CID), making it a cabinet committee with himself as *ex officio* chairman and a permanent staff, thus for the first time giving Britain a formal venue for civil-military planning and coordination.[91] Its first major study, completed in 1903, concluded that Britain could safely rely on the navy to safeguard her shores from invasion by a Continental power. Although the army would be reformed and reequipped to eliminate the defects identified in South Africa, its primary orientation would continue to be the maintenance of imperial security, especially the defense of India. As late as 1905, British leaders still viewed Russia as the empire's preeminent military threat with its expansion in northern Persia and south central Asia seen as endangering India.

All that changed with Russia's decisive defeat at the hands of the Japanese. Of Russia's prewar navy, only its relatively weak Black Sea Fleet survived. Its position in the Far East virtually collapsed, with control of Korea and Port Arthur relinquished to Japan and Manchuria evacuated. In Russia itself, finally, defeat abroad produced revolution at home. Capitalizing on those events, it took Grey little more than a year to achieve what had evaded both Salisbury and Lansdowne. In St. Petersburg, on 31 August, 1907, Russian Foreign Minister Alexander Izvolsky and Sir Arthur Nicolson, Britain's ambassador to Russia, signed an agreement demarcating the two empires' spheres of influence in Persia and guaranteeing Russian non-interference in Afghanistan and Tibet, ending half a century of "The Great Game." Like the Entente Cordiale, its formal provisions were purely colonial in character. However, by simultaneously relieving Britain of a persistent threat and France of a potential embarrassment, the agreement removed the last obstacle to reconciling the Dual Alliance with the Entente Cordiale. As one writer put it: "The entente meant an end to the assumption that an Anglo-French war was always likely; Japan's defeat of Russia did the same for assumptions of Anglo-Russian conflict ... the British [thus] were able to face the international scene with more equanimity than they had been able to muster in a decade."[92]

---

[91]   The Cabinet Committee of Defense, the CID's lineal predecessor, originally was established by Salisbury in 1895 but, restricted to cabinet members and without staff or charter, became little more than a forum for debating army and navy budgets. See Grenville, *Lord Salisbury and Foreign Policy*, p. 18.

[92]   Charmley, *Splendid Isolation?*, p. 314.

The Anglo–Russian Convention was still another blow to German diplomacy, which, as with the Dual Alliance and the Entente Cordiale, had scorned the possibility that traditional enemies could bury the hatchet and thus helped enable them to do so. "Convinced that Russia and Great Britain desperately needed Germany, German policymakers thought they could drive a hard bargain with both of them simultaneously without specifying the nature of the bargain they were seeking or ever imagining that they might be pushing Russia and Great Britain closer together."[93]

From a military standpoint, meanwhile, the Anglo-Russian accord relieved the British Army of what until then had been its principal potential commitment. Armies are uncomfortable without some contingency against which to plan, however, and the Anglo-French staff talks furnished a timely and convenient alternative. They also helped resolve a persistent dispute between the navy and army about how the latter should be employed in the event of war with Germany, a dispute ultimately resolved as much by the changing naval balance as by the army's reorientation and reform.

Far more than the army, the Royal Navy had found itself transformed during the last third of the nineteenth century.[94] By 1880, warships already had progressed from sail to steam and from wood to steel. During the next two decades, similarly radical developments followed in naval weaponry, fire control, and communications. Virtually none of these developments originated in Britain, however. Indeed, as late as 1886, the navy continued to depend for development of its ordnance on the army's Royal Artillery arsenal at Woolwich.[95] HMS *Collingwood*, launched in 1886, was Britain's first modern battleship, built entirely of steel and mounting breech-loading rifled cannon in barbette turrets. By that time, such ships had been in service with foreign fleets for nearly a decade.

If the Royal Navy before 1900 was little more innovative than the army, however, it was much quicker to acquire new capabilities once they appeared. The problem was that they were appearing at an accelerating rate, and as each appeared, it tended to render earlier warship designs obsolete. In such an environment of rapid qualitative change, the Royal Navy's quantitative supremacy actually worked against it. With more ships to replace, each technological change cost Britain proportionately more than it did its competitors. Naval expenditures more than doubled between 1886 and 1900, putting serious pressure on budgets already strained to meet growing domestic demands.[96] Meanwhile, imperial commitments were adding their own burden. Whereas emerging naval competitors – Germany, Japan, the United States – could orient almost exclusively on their own regional

[93] Kissinger, *Diplomacy*, p. 179.
[94] Perhaps the best single-volume study of that transformation is Andrew Gordon's *The Rules of the Game* (London, 1996).
[95] Ensor, *England 1870–1914*, p. 122.
[96] Ibid., p. 289.

waters, the Royal Navy's responsibilities were global, a burden before 1900 shared only to a limited extent even by France and Russia. The resulting dispersal increasingly troubled Admiralty leaders imbued with the Mahanian belief in the decisive clash of battle fleets as the ultima ratio of maritime supremacy.

The first indicator of that concern was the Admiralty's reluctance, by 1895, to conduct operations in the eastern Mediterranean in the teeth of a growing French fleet at Toulon. Soon thereafter, the Venezuelan dispute surfaced the similar risk associated with diverting enough naval power from Europe to the western hemisphere to assure superiority in a potential contest with the U.S. Navy, and the growth of Japanese naval capabilities augured a similar problem in the Far East. By 1900, in short, the two-power standard as originally articulated in 1889 had become anomalous. As Lord Selbourne, First Lord of the Admiralty, pointed out in a cabinet memorandum in January 1901: "It does not seem to me that this basis of calculation is one that will any longer serve, considering that within the last five years three new navies have sprung into existence – those of the United States, Germany, and Japan."[97] In later papers, he went on to argue that squadrons on distant stations such as the Far East or North America would be of little value were Britain to be defeated at sea in the channel or the Mediterranean by France and Russia or, even if victorious in such a contest, emerge with the Royal Navy so weakened as to lose control of the North Sea to a rapidly growing German fleet.

Abandoning the two-power standard outright, however, would be a tacit but public admission that Britannia no longer ruled the waves. As Grenville comments: "In 1892 the Admiralty had declared that the fleet could no longer on its own force the Dardanelles if the Sultan of Turkey chose to oppose its passage. Now nine years later the Admiralty was maintaining that British interests could not be defended in the Far East without running the risk of losing control of home waters."[98] Growing German naval power only aggravated the problem. From the moment of his appointment as naval secretary in June 1897, Tirpitz had agitated vigorously for a navy commensurate with Germany's growing economic power. Now, with Britain preoccupied in South Africa, he convinced the Reichstag to approve the second in a series of Naval Laws, this one authorizing a fleet of 36 battleships and commensurate smaller warships, on expansion justified explicitly as a deterrent and wartime counter to the potential threat posed by the Royal Navy.[99]

[97] Friedberg, *The Weary Titan*, pp. 172–73.
[98] Grenville, *Lord Salisbury and Foreign Policy*, p. 404.
[99] For the peculiar reasoning that led to creation of the German battle fleet, see Holger H. Herwig, *Luxury Fleet: The Imperial German Navy, 1888–1918* (London, 1987).

In a Britain still recovering from the costs of the Second Boer War, a response relying solely on new naval construction would have been a fiscal (and political) nightmare.[100] Instead, in December 1904, Selbourne advised the cabinet that the time had come to redistribute Britain's naval forces. Rather than dispersing its fleet globally, he argued, Britain should concentrate the bulk of its naval power in European waters, a conclusion strengthened not long thereafter by a memorandum from Admiral Sir John Fisher, commander in chief Mediterranean, advancing a similar view.[101] In the redeployment that followed, British squadrons in the Pacific, South Atlantic, and western hemisphere were withdrawn, and those in the Far East reduced in number and consolidated at Singapore. In their place, Selbourne reorganized most of the navy's capital ships into three battle fleets: a Mediterranean Fleet based at Malta, an Atlantic Fleet based at Gibraltar, and a Channel Fleet operating from home ports.[102] The new arrangement was by no means universally popular either with the navy, especially those station commanders who lost major assets, or with the army, which feared that British garrisons from Canada to Cape Town would be deprived of the naval support to which they had been accustomed. But it had the advantage that all three fleets were close enough for mutual support.

Between expanded naval construction, the diminution of distant threats associated with Russia's defeat by Japan and improved relations with France and the United States, and the consolidation of Britain's naval power in European waters, the next few years witnessed a significant improvement in Britain's overall naval posture. Then, in 1906, Britain surprised the world with HMS *Dreadnought*, the first all-big-gun battleship. While an undoubted technological triumph, *Dreadnought* instantly rendered all existing capital ships – including Britain's – effectively obsolete.[103] Germany was not slow to respond, and the result was a reheated naval race. Two earlier disarmament conferences at the Hague in 1899 and 1907 had failed to restrain the growth in naval armaments. The 1908 London Naval Conference was no more successful in arresting what had now become an unambiguous Anglo-German contest for European naval supremacy. Its failure compelled Britain to accelerate its own battleship construction at considerable cost to other

---

[100] "Despite the rise in naval expenditure in the 1890s, the total tax burden per head of population had declined since the 1860s, and an increase to meet Britain's naval commitments would certainly have been possible, but that would have meant an increase in taxation. To raise indirect taxes would have affected the cost of living; to raise income taxes was even less desirable." Charmley, *Splendid Isolation?*, p. 298.

[101] Friedberg, *The Weary Titan*, p. 183.

[102] Dispositions aimed, not coincidentally, at the Russian, French, and German navies, respectively.

[103] One critic complained that "the whole British Fleet was ... morally scrapped and labeled obsolete ... when at the zenith of its efficiency." Massie, *Dreadnought*, p. 487.

Liberal budget priorities, and popular hostility toward Germany mounted commensurately.

However, the increase in German naval power also had another more significant strategic consequence. It demolished the navy's long-standing insistence that, in the event of war with Germany, the army be restricted to operations on the Continental periphery. For Fisher, appointed First Sea Lord in October 1904, the army was merely "a projectile to be fired by the navy."[104] His preferred employment of the army, were it to be employed on the Continent at all, was in an amphibious assault on Germany's Baltic coast. Such diversionary operations, needless to say, held little attraction for a French Army expecting to be fighting for its life between Belgium and Switzerland. Nor, as the size and capability of Tirpitz's High Seas Fleet increased, could the Royal Navy guarantee mounting such an operation safely in time to affect the outcome of a Franco-German struggle. By 1910, even those who, like Grey, were reluctant to envision commitment of British troops to the Continent were resigned to the reality that, to make any difference, the British Army would have to fight alongside its French counterpart, a view adopted officially at a CID meeting on 23 August 1911.[105]

AFTERMATH

On 1 July 1911, the German gunboat *Panther* anchored off the Moroccan port of Agadir, dispatched by Berlin in a quixotic effort to erase the humiliating results of the 1906 Algeciras conference, obtain colonial compensation for France's retention of Morocco, and above all, break up what by then had become the Triple Entente in effect if not yet in name.[106] The resulting crisis had precisely the opposite result. Together with the subsequent failure of Lord Haldane's effort to dissuade Germany from further naval expansion, it forged the final link in the chain of strategic transformation begun by Salisbury nearly twenty years earlier.[107]

Thereafter, the staff discussions, begun during the First Moroccan Crisis, resumed and accelerated, planning for commitment to the European continent of what eventually would become known as the British Expeditionary Force. The following year, in order to concentrate Britain's naval strength in the North Sea and thus ensure its ability to bring the German fleet to battle before it could penetrate the channel, the British and French governments exchanged notes in effect guaranteeing the Royal Navy's protection of

---

104 Williamson, *The Politics of Grand Strategy*, p. 107.
105 Steiner and Neilson, *Britain and the Origins of the First World War*, p. 213.
106 Kissinger, *Diplomacy*, p. 197.
107 Haldane's unsuccessful mission to Berlin took place early in February 1912. Fay, *The Origins of the World War*, chap. 4.

France's Atlantic coast in the event of war with Germany in return for corresponding French naval protection of Britain's Mediterranean lifeline.[108]

Two years later, Britain was at war with Germany, a war the ultimate magnitude and duration of which even the most apocalyptic Victorian scarcely could have imagined. Dispute persists to this day even among British historians, especially younger British historians, about the extent to which Britain's decision to enter the struggle contributed to that outcome.[109] We need not address that issue here, nor the related argument that an earlier British demonstration to Germany of its resolve to do so might have deterred the war altogether.[110] Instead, for the purpose of this inquiry, the central question is whether the lengthy series of strategic decisions that began with Britain's abandonment of the eastern Mediterranean in 1895 and culminated in the Anglo-French Naval Agreement of 1912 made the decision to fight Germany inevitable.

The record suggests otherwise. Certainly before 1905, few of those responsible for British foreign and defense policy envisioned such a result. On the contrary, throughout the lengthy process of diplomatic and military readjustment, inaugurated however reluctantly by Salisbury and carried forward more enthusiastically by Lansdowne and Grey, successive British leaders made repeated efforts to avoid antagonizing Germany and to find some formula that would satisfy Berlin's mounting ambitions without sacrificing British interests. Notes one writer: "The Anglo-French entente did not make Lansdowne anti-German and he was still eager to improve relations with Germany . . . for him, the deterioration of relations with Germany, following [the First Moroccan] crisis, was a matter for regret rather than for congratulation."[111] Even Grey, by far the most Germanophobic of the three, took pains to avoid gratuitously offending the kaiser's tender sensibilities, discouraged use of the term "triple entente," and, until the very outbreak of war, stubbornly resisted French efforts to convert the Entente into a formal defensive military alliance.[112]

Like his predecessors, however, Grey was a realist. By 1906, his confidence largely had evaporated that Britain could placate the Reich barring outright abandonment of the accords with France and Russia that he and his predecessors finally had achieved after decades of mutual hostility. "If there is a war between France and Germany, it will be very difficult for us to keep out of it," he wrote to a correspondent in February. "The Entente and still more the constant and emphatic demonstrations of affection (official,

[108] Tuchman, *The Guns of August*, p. 53.
[109] For diametrically opposed views, see, e.g., Michael Howard, *The Continental Commitment* (London, 1974), and Niall Ferguson, *The Pity of War* (London, 1999).
[110] Kissinger, *Diplomacy*, p. 212.
[111] Cohen, "Joseph Chamberlain, Lord Lansdowne and British Foreign Policy 1901–1903."
[112] Steiner and Neilson, *Britain and the Origins of the First World War*, pp. 50–51.

naval, political, commercial and in the Press) have created in France a belief that we shall support them in war.... If this expectation is disappointed the French will never forgive us."[113] Perhaps even more compelling to Grey was the fear, shared by many, if not all, of his contemporaries, that in seeking to add a navy equal to Britain's to an army already acknowledged to be the most powerful in Europe, Germany would be satisfied with nothing less than outright Continental hegemony, a condition the prevention of which had governed British strategic behavior at least since the days of Marlborough.[114]

Neither of these concerns, however, governed strategic transformation before 1905. Instead, looking backward from the perspective of a century, the decisions resulting in that transformation have an almost inescapable "house-that-Jack-built" quality. At each crucial juncture, British statesmen found themselves reacting to circumstances that, as their own contemporary views make abundantly clear, most would have much preferred to avoid. Responsible for an empire they had inherited as much as created, but which they uniformly felt obliged to preserve, they were like a boy with ten fingers trying to plug eleven holes in the dike. The dilemma they confronted was perhaps best illustrated, ironically, by a cartoon in a wartime anti-British German book entitled *Gott Strafe England!* showing a British Tommie sprawling awkwardly across a huge map of Africa and southern Eurasia, with one foot on England, the other on South Africa, and one hand each on Egypt and India.[115]

It may be true in an academic sense that at each such juncture, statesmen and political leaders might have chosen other diplomatic, economic, and military alternatives.[116] But even where those were decipherable without improbable foresight, it is still not clear that other courses of action would have proven more convincing or that they would have been more successful in resolving the tension between mounting strategic pressures and relatively declining capabilities. That was especially true with respect to relations with Germany, the leaders of which, from the kaiser on down, managed throughout the period to set new standards of arrogance, folly, and duplicity.[117]

---

113 J. Paul Harris, "Great Britain," in Richard F. Hamilton and Holger H. Herwig, eds., *The Origins of World War I* (Cambridge, 2003), p. 271.
114 A fear captured most eloquently in a 1907 "Memorandum on the Present State of British Relations with France and Germany" by Sir Eyre Crowe, Grey's senior clerk, comparing Germany's hegemonic ambitions to those of Napoleonic France. G. P. Gooch et al., *British Documents on the Origins of the War*, vol. 3 (London, 1928), Appendix A.
115 "God Punish England!" Eby, *The Road Armageddon*, p. 158.
116 Friedberg makes the case perhaps most explicitly. Friedberg, *The Weary Titan*, chap. 7.
117 As Kissinger points out, having helped drive first Russia and France, then Britain and France, and finally Britain and Russia into each other's arms, "Germany's reaction to the looming encirclement was to accelerate the same diplomacy which had brought about the danger in the first place." Kissinger, *Diplomacy*, p. 190.

Moreover, like today's American leaders, British statesmen at the turn of the twentieth century were by no means free agents. Patricians most may have been, with the engrained attitudes and prejudices of a favored class. But by the end of the nineteenth century, the political impact of an aroused public opinion informed (and as often misinformed) by an uncontrollable and energetic press no longer could be ignored. No one understood that better than Salisbury, the most patrician of them all, who had complained during a speech at the Guildhall in November 1887 that, far from conducing to a balanced foreign policy, "if there is any possible danger in the future, it rather arises . . . from possible gusts of passionate and ill-informed feeling arising from great masses of population."[118] British policy making during the last decade of the nineteenth century and the first decade of the twentieth was handicapped repeatedly by popular reactions to events ranging from the Armenian massacres to the kaiser's careless interventions. Even more constraining, at least until the Second Boer War, was the widely held public conviction, however unjustified, in Britain's cultural superiority, economic predominance, and military – especially naval – invincibility.

In short, examining their decisions in context, one can only admire the extent to which Britain's statesmen were able to devise policies that by and large were remarkably successful in resolving the immediate strategic problems to which they were directed. If one can fault British policy making between 1890 and 1910, it is only for the persistent failure of successive British governments to consider in any comprehensive way the interactive effect of those policies on great power relations, and especially their effect on an increasingly precarious Continental balance.[119] Not until the First Moroccan Crisis did the latter prompt serious discussion, and even then, British leaders' instincts were to seek some way of insulating both the crisis and its resolution from any Continental ramifications.

In large part, the failure explicitly to address linkage – how a response to problem A is likely to affect problems B and C, to which it may seem only distantly related – reflected the absence of any developed mechanisms through which to refine and reconcile competing appraisals of the strategic environment. Particularly given the impact of public sentiment on policy making in a democracy, nothing is more essential to strategic success than political consensus on the geopolitical, economic, and military conditions in which statesmen must pursue grand strategy, and nothing tends to be more difficult to achieve or to maintain over time. The controversies that repeatedly afflicted British policy making at the turn of the twentieth century almost invariably reflected controversial and underdeveloped strategic appraisals.

---

[118] Charmley, *Splendid Isolation?*, p. 223.
[119] Indeed, as late as 1920, a Foreign Office memorandum for the Committee of Imperial Defense admitted that "for the last century the policy of H.M. Government has been inductive, intuitive and quite deliberately opportunistic" (http://encarta.msn.co.uk/encyclopedia_1481591028/British_Foreign_Policy_Since_1800.html).

Similarly, no grand strategy is likely to be formulated coherently, and certainly none can be implemented consistently, without some means of compelling the bureaucracies on which all modern governments depend to share information and coordinate policy actions. In Britain throughout most of the period examined here, only the cabinet itself furnished a forum for such discussions, and typically at only a superficial level. Below cabinet level, the actors and agencies responsible for executing (and occasionally ipso facto formulating) strategic decisions – the Foreign Office, Admiralty, War Office, imperial viceroys, colonial commissioners, and remotely stationed military and naval commanders – operated largely autonomously and with little coordination. Not until the resurrection of the CID in 1902 was there any formal mechanism through which to coordinate foreign and defense policy. Even then, as the impact of the kaiser and Edward VII revealed, the process always will remain hostage to the unpredictable, but often decisive, impact of powerful personalities outside the bureaucratic arena.

Above all, the more numerous the strategic challenges with which policy makers must cope, the more complicated the linkages among them, hence the more difficult it becomes to develop sensible policy responses. Over-ambition thus is the mortal enemy of effective grand strategy, and not the least important of diplomatic tasks is reducing the strategic problem set to manageable proportions. However, as British statesmen throughout this period discovered, and American experience during the past half-century has confirmed, perceived threats develop their own constituencies. Whether motivated by conviction, institutional self-interest, or some combination of both, such stakeholders tend to insist on the primacy of their own preferred concerns. Not all threats are created equal, however, and a crucial prerequisite of successful strategy is distinguishing those that are existential from those that are merely annoying. In short, economy of force applies as much to strategy as to military operations and requires the same willingness by political leaders to discipline their appetites. For American leaders today, as it was for Britain's at the turn of the twentieth century, accepting that invariably troublesome and occasionally painful self-discipline may be the most difficult but also most essential strategic challenge.

6

British grand strategy, 1933–1942

WILLIAMSON MURRAY

My chief impression was one of impending change and fears. Fear: individual, racial, national, and economic. Munich has withdrawn the lynchpin which held Eastern Europe together and the fragments are preparing to resort themselves.... Everyone is apprehensive as to how this process will affect him individually. Everywhere there is the pathetic hope in the breasts of these ignorant people that England will somehow save them from the fate she did nothing to avert from Czechoslovakia.[1]

There is no doubt that throughout the 1930s the British Empire confronted diverse threats on the periphery: in the Pacific with the rise of an antagonistic and aggressive Japan, in the Mediterranean with Benito Mussolini's and Italy's overweening ambition, and directly across the North Sea with the rise of Adolf Hitler's Nazi Germany and the increasing lethality of air power. Indeed, if there is such a thing as imperial overstretch, this was the ultimate case.[2] Yet, all great powers throughout history have confronted the danger of overstretch in considering their national interests. Above all, grand strategy demands a willingness to weigh and balance risks: those of the present against those of the future, those of the immediate neighborhood against those of distant provinces, and those of the more dangerous against the lesser.

Unfortunately for their nation, their allies, and the course of history, British leaders consistently failed to address in their grand strategy in the 1930s the hard realities of the international environment. The best one can say about their approach was that they placed defense of the periphery over

[1] Public Records Office (PRO) FO 371/21676, C 14810/132/18, Nigel Law to Sargent, 29.11.38.
[2] For a brilliant discussion of the deep, underlying causes for the rise of Hitler and Mussolini, see MacGregor Knox, *To the Threshold of Power, 1922/33: Origins and Dynamics of the Fascist and National Socialist Dictatorships* (Cambridge, 2007).

concerns about the more direct threat that the Third Reich represented. Then, when the latter threat became too obvious to miss in 1938, they dithered and hoped that platitudes of peace and cooperation would work to defuse an explosive international situation. Thus, when Churchill came to power on 10 May 1940, he confronted a situation where his predecessors had jeopardized the existence not only of the empire but also of Britain itself. Even in retrospect, only political and strategic genius could have saved Britain from catastrophe, and that is precisely what Churchill possessed. But it was too late to save the empire. The story of disastrous miscalculation and the almost miraculous recovery of Britain is our tale.

THE INFLUENCE OF THE PAST AND IDLE HOPES

Any understanding of British grand strategy in the period between 1933 and 1942 must begin with recognition of the catastrophe that had ended barely a decade and a half earlier and its baneful influence on virtually every action the British were to undertake in this period in molding a grand strategy. The First World War had shattered the comfortable illusions of the early twentieth century. It had overthrown the European order in a fashion not seen since the Reformation.[3] In its aftermath, the Bolshevik regime in Russia proclaimed its determination to toss the capitalist regimes of the world into the dustbin of history; an unrepentant German people glowered in the economic and political consequences of their defeat; the small successor nations to the empires of Austria-Hungary and czarist Russia displayed no other desire than to quarrel with each other over frontiers; and finally, the British and French regarded the economic and psychological consequences of the most destructive war in history with despair, while the United States withdrew into a self-imposed and self-indulgent isolation from the affairs of Europe and the world.

For the French, the problem was that Germany, though perhaps defeated for the short term, remained an economic and political colossus that in the long term represented a lethal threat to the republic's security as well as that of its allies. Marshal Ferdinand Foch noted shortly after the signing of the peace treaty at Versailles:[4] "The next time remember the Germans will make no mistakes. They will break through northern France and seize the Channel ports as a base for operations against England."[5] The British perspective was quite different. For them, the German problem, even during

---

[3] Before 1914, one did not need a passport to travel across the borders of the European nations; that would not again become true until the 1990s.

[4] At the actual signing he commented that the treaty represented no more than a twenty-year truce with the Germans – prophetic words indeed.

[5] Quoted in Margret MacMillan, *Paris, 1919, Six Months that Changed the World* (New York, 2001), p. 459.

the darkest days of 1918, had never seemed as desperately threatening as to the French, whose northern provinces had been ravaged and then occupied by the Germans during the course of the conflict.[6]

Several factors developed that were to influence British grand strategy through to the opening of the next great war. The first and perhaps the most important was a developing sense throughout the 1920s that somehow the war had all been a terrible mistake and therefore Britain should never again involve itself in another great Continental conflict; rather, many believed the British government should serve as an "honest broker" to mediate quarrels in Europe and preserve the peace. Such attitudes were soon reinforced by a massive disinformation campaign waged by the German government both internally and externally that emphasized the theme that the Reich had been no more at fault for the outbreak of the war than any of the other great powers (patently untrue) and that the treaty of Versailles had mistreated the German people in an outrageously unfair fashion.[7] In fact, given German war crimes and behavior during the war, the treaty had been surprisingly soft on the Germans.[8]

Reinforcing German efforts to suggest that the war had just been a terrible mistake was a deep pacifist movement that swept Britain in the late 1920s, one reinforced by a flood of extraordinary novels and poetry that rank among the greatest literature of the twentieth century.[9] What most in Britain missed was the substantially different reaction to the war across the channel, where Ernst Jünger's ferocious, enthusiastic, and brilliant memoir of his service from 1915 to 1918 as an officer in a frontline Hanoverian regiment was typical in tone, if not in quality, of most German commentators on the

[6] In fact, when the Germans asked for an armistice in October 1918, Field Marshal Douglas Haig was willing to grant them terms that would have only required a withdrawal to the German frontier and the surrender of the High Seas Fleet.

[7] For the German disinformation campaign that substantially warped the understanding not only of the German people but also of many prestigious Anglo-American historians as to the origins of the conflict and Germany's conduct of the war, see Holger H. Herwig, "Clio Deceived, Patriotic Self-Censorship in Germany after the Great War," *International Security*, Fall 1987.

[8] The Treaty of Brest Litovsk, imposed by the Germans on a broken Russia in March 1918, suggests what a harsh Treaty of Versailles might have looked like. For a discussion of German behavior toward occupied areas, see Isabel Hull, *Absolute Destruction, Military Culture and the Practice of War in Imperial Germany* (Ithaca, NY, 2005); for an evaluation of the Treaty of Versailles, see Williamson Murray, "Versailles: The Peace without a Chance," in Williamson Murray and Jim Lacey, eds., *The Making of Peace, Rulers, States, and War* (Cambridge, 2009).

[9] Among the list of novels are Frederick Manning, *The Middle Parts of Fortune, Somme and Acre 1916* (London, 1929); Robert Graves, *Goodbye to All That* (London, 1929); Siegfried Sasoon, *Memoirs of a Fox-Hunting Man* (London, 1928) and *Memoirs of an Infantry Officer* (London, 1930); and Guy Chapman, *A Passionate Prodigality* (London, 1933); C. S. Forester, *The General* (London, 1936); and for a woman's perspective on the pain caused by the war, see Vera Brittain, *Testament of Youth* (London, 1933).

war.[10] A British national mood, exemplified by the infamous 1934 debate in the Oxford Union on a resolution that its members would fight for neither king nor country, dominated the conventional wisdom at the very moment that Hitler came to power in Germany.

It was not just that the great majority of Britain's political leaders felt that war was a nightmare; it was that they simply could not conceive that anyone else could hold such old-fashioned opinions as to believe that conflict might have some utility. For them, as for too many American leaders in the 1990s, history had ended. Thus, military power, strategic concerns, and concepts such as the balance of power no longer mattered compared to settling international disagreements peacefully – usually at someone else's expense. In summer 1938, the British ambassador to Berlin expressed this deep-seated belief in a letter dealing with the Runciman mission to settle the supposed dispute (one entirely manufactured by the Nazis) between the Czechs and their Sudeten German population:

> Personally I just sit and pray for one thing, namely that Lord Runciman will live up to the role of an impartial British liberal statesman. I cannot believe that he will allow himself to be influenced by ancient history or even arguments about strategic frontiers and economics in preference to high moral principles. The great and courageous game that you [Lord Halifax, Britain's foreign secretary] and the Prime Minister [Neville Chamberlain] are playing will be lost in my humble opinion if he does not come out on the side of the higher principles for which in fact the British Empire really stands.[11]

Such naïve beliefs were firmly entrenched among the senior leaders of the government throughout the 1930s. There was a deep-seated assumption that no matter how crass and bullyish the Nazis and Fascists appeared, both Hitler and Mussolini were men of reason – certainly men who rejected the idea that war was a useful tool – with whom Britain could deal in a reasonable fashion.[12] Neville Chamberlain commented to the Soviet ambassador shortly after becoming prime minister in spring 1937 that "if we could only

---

[10] Jünger, one of the two or three greatest German novelists of the twentieth century, was wounded innumerable times on the Western Front and won a *Pour le Mérite* for combat heroism, one of the few infantry officers to win the award, Erwin Rommel being one of the others. Jünger's memoir, *Storm of Steel*, trans. Michael Hofmann (London, 2004), is particularly worth reading because it has been newly translated in this far more accurate edition.

[11] *Documents on British Foreign Policy (DBFP)*, 3rd Ser., vol. 2, Doc. 590, 6.8.38., letter from Henderson to Halifax.

[12] Hitler had been a highly decorated corporal in the war who had served extensively in battles on the Western Front from 1914 to 1918. He used his supposed distaste for war on innumerable occasions in his discussions with foreigners. His comments to German audiences, and especially within the confines of discussions with his advisers and generals, pursued a different line altogether.

sit down at a table with the Germans and run through all their complaints and claims with a pencil, this would greatly relieve all tensions."[13]

In a world in which most British leaders believed that good intentions and reasonable discussions under the aegis of the League of Nations would remove the causes of war, money spent on Britain's military establishment appeared to be no more than simply throwing good money away. To make matters worse, Winston Churchill, of all people, invented the ten-year rule in the 1920s – admittedly in more peaceful times – which posited that there was no prospect of a major conflict for the next ten years. Every year, the rule rolled over and renewed the assumption. The clear result was that throughout the late 1920s and well into the 1930s, Britain provided its soldiers, sailors, and airmen barely sufficient funding to train and maintain their rapidly aging equipment, much less invest in new and more modern weapons systems.

The third great factor in British strategic policy had to do with the severe economic problems occasioned by the Great Depression, problems which the near collapse of sterling in 1931 and Britain's entire financial position had further exacerbated. Thus, throughout the middle to late 1930s, British leaders worried seriously that overspending on defense would cause a financial collapse, which would place the country in a desperate economic situation. Thus, every decision with regard to defense expenditures until March 1939 reflected the economic and financial calculations of the Treasury rather than the estimates and advice of the chiefs of staff, who became increasingly alarmed at Britain's strategic position as the 1930s drew to a close.

Quite simply, we might describe British grand strategy in the decade of the 1930s as grounded in three assumptions:

First, financial security should override all other concerns, including those of national security.

Second, Britain confronted no external threat requiring a substantial rethinking of its defense policies in regard to resourcing the services.

Third, the troubled situation on the Continent did not presage another major conflict, especially if Britain were to lead the way in appeasing the qualms and claims of the dictators.

Few in the three main political parties disagreed with these basic assumptions.[14]

---

[13] Martin Gilbert and Richard Gott, *The Appeasers* (New York, 1967), p. 52.
[14] After the war, the Labour Party was to claim that it had opposed Fascist and Nazi expansionist moves throughout the 1930s. That was indeed true, but how the British government was supposed to oppose such moves is not clear because the party voted against every single defense appropriation bill that came before the House of Commons in the 1930s.

THE UNRAVELING OF EUROPE

One can best sum up the challenges of the 1930s for British defense planners by noting that the entire defense effort was consistently and willingly underfunded, while the international environment underwent a series of massive and swift changes that provided British politicians little opportunity to adapt. As Paul Kennedy has noted:

> Perhaps the greatest difference between British net assessment in the 1930s and American net assessment in (say) the 1960s was the extraordinary fluidity and multipolarity of the international scene in the earlier period.[15] At the beginning of the 1930s, the British widely regarded the Soviet Union as the greatest land enemy of the Empire, while in naval terms the chief rivals were the United States and Japan; they saw Mussolini's Italy as temperamental, France as unduly assertive and difficult (but not hostile), and Germany as still prostrate. Five to eight years later, Japan appeared as a distinct challenge to British interests in the Far East, Germany had fallen under Nazi rule and was assessed as the "greatest long-term danger," and Italy's policies appeared aggressive and hostile, whereas the United States was more unpredictable and isolationist than ever, Russia had become somewhat less of a direct strategic threat . . . , and France's weaknesses were more manifest than its strengths.[16]

The rise of Nazi Germany represented the overarching change in the European balance of power in the 1930s. From the moment Hitler gained power as Germany's chancellor, the British government followed a policy of appeasement – one aimed explicitly at bringing the Reich within the European community. During this early period, Hitler walked and talked warily in the international environment. But his actions indicated a wholly different direction. As he told Germany's senior military leaders four days after assuming office, rearmament would begin immediately, with the express purpose of overthrowing the European system entirely. Moreover, he warned, if France had any leaders, she would act now and not wait for Germany to regain its power.[17]

Thus, massive German rearmament was soon under way in complete contravention of the Treaty of Versailles, the military receiving a blank

---

[15] When Paul Kennedy wrote these words in the late 1980s, the United States still found itself involved in the Cold War. Nevertheless, Andrew Marshall, who sponsored the conference from which these words are drawn, had already recognized how much the world already was changing. In fact, the world the United States confronts at present is beginning to resemble the world Britain's strategic planners confronted in 1901.

[16] Paul Kennedy, "British 'Net Assessment' and the Coming of the Second World War," in Williamson Murray and Allan R. Millett, eds., *Calculations, Net Assessment and the Coming of World War II* (New York, 1992), p. 35.

[17] "Aufzeichnung Liebmann," *Vierteljahrshefte für Zeitgeschichte* 2, no. 4 (October 1954).

check.[18] Germany withdrew from the League of Nations in 1933, announced rearmament and the creation of the Luftwaffe in 1935, and remilitarized the Rhineland in 1936 – all of these actions immediately followed by speeches from Hitler claiming that the Reich was only interested in peace. There was no response to these German actions by either the French or the British, those with the most to lose by the destruction of the provisions of the Treaty of Versailles.

Admittedly, none of this behavior made the British government particularly happy, but no one was willing to declare that Germany represented a serious danger to Europe's peace. In 1934, the Bank of England not only provided the Germans with loans that allowed them to escape a serious credit crunch but then allowed them a substantial break in the clearing agreements between the two countries.[19] Not surprisingly, about the only person to see Nazi Germany for what it was – a moral and strategic danger to the United Kingdom – was Winston Churchill. In a column published in summer 1934, Churchill warned:

'I marvel at the complacency of Ministers in the face of the frightful experiences through which we have so newly passed. I look with wonder upon our thoughtless crowds disporting themselves in the summer sunshine,' [and all the while across the North Sea], a terrible process is astir. *Germany is arming*.[20]

However, to the great majority of Britain's politicians and cognoscenti, Churchill was an old-fashioned dinosaur, a dinosaur who believed in military power, strategic considerations, and the possibility that war might be necessary at some time in the future.

Nevertheless, the international environment had grown so alarming by the mid-1930s that the British government had to make some response. Japan was assuming an increasingly threatening posture in the Far East; the Italians invaded Ethiopia in 1935; then civil war broke out in Spain, which almost immediately attracted the ideologically committed on the Left as well as the Right. The Germans and the Italians supported Franco's Nationalists; Soviet advisers supported the Spanish Republic, when they were not pursuing Trotskyites, anarchists, and other enemies of revolutionary forces. The democracies sat on the fence wringing their hands.

In Britain little changed. In 1934, after an eight-month-long period of bureaucratic haggling, the Defense Requirements Committee agreed to a

[18] For the economic problems the buildup occasioned right from the start as well as the difficulties the German economy had in fulfilling military orders throughout the 1930s, see Williamson Murray, *The Change in the European Balance of Power, 1938–1939: The Path to Ruin* (Princeton, NJ, 1984), pp. 4–30.
[19] Adam Tooze, *The Wages of Destruction: The Making and Breaking of the Nazi Economy* (New York, 2006), p. 87.
[20] Quoted in Martin Gilbert, *Winston Churchill*, vol. 5, 1922–1939 (London, 1976), p. 550.

minuscule upward adjustment in British defense spending of approximately
15 ¹/₂ million £s per year.[21] Three years later, it still was arguing that Britain's
rearmament effort must not interfere with internal or external trade. "From
the production point of view this greatly complicates the matter, but any such
interference would adversely affect the general prosperity of the country."[22]
Some of the more cynical among British officers suggested that the government was preparing to pay the indemnity when Britain lost the next war.[23]

   Translated into comparative figures, the British only caught up to Italian
spending on national defense as a percentage of gross domestic product in
1937 while taking until 1938 to reach the level Germany had attained in
1935.[24] While the Baldwin and MacDonald governments simply drifted,
refusing to make tough decisions in regard to defense or grand strategy,
Neville Chamberlain, on becoming prime minister in 1937, made clear he
was going to limit defense spending come what might. In a cabinet meeting
shortly before he assumed the reins of power, he announced the course of
action his government would pursue. As the cabinet minutes record:

> He [Chamberlain] could not accept the question at issue as being a purely
> military matter. Other considerations entered into it. He himself definitely did
> challenge the [proposed] policy of their military advisers. The country was being
> asked to maintain a larger navy than had been the case for very many years: a
> great air force, which was a new arm altogether: and in addition, an army for
> use on the Continent; as well as the facilities for producing munitions which
> would be required not only for our forces but also for our Allies.[25]

From his point of view, the British government should reject the advice
of its military advisers, and that is precisely what the new prime minister
proceeded to do. The main effort would go to building up the Royal Air
Force (RAF), but not along the lines of what the air staff recommended.
Instead of bombers, the RAF would receive fighters and light bombers, one
of the few correct defense decisions the Chamberlain government would
make, but for the wrong reason: in its calculus of assessment, fighters were
cheaper than bombers.[26] The navy received some additional funding: the
army got nothing, a fact that would contribute mightily to the disaster of
1940.

   Quite simply, Chamberlain and his ministers made the conscious decision
to minimize military preparations in the belief that Hitler and Mussolini

[21] PRO CAB 24/247, CP 64 (34), 5.3.34.
[22] PRO CAB 24/259, CP (36), 12.2.36.
[23] Sir John Slessor, *The Central Blue* (New York, 1957), pp. 160–61.
[24] See Table 1-5 in Murray, *The Change in the European Balance of Power*, pp. 20–21.
[25] PRO CAB 23/88, Cab 20 (37), Meeting of the Cabinet, 5.5.37.
[26] John Terraine, *The Right of the Line: The Royal Air Force in the European War, 1939–1945*
     (London, 1985), pp. 50–51.

were rational men, who, however crass their behavior, abhorred war and consequently would agree to a reasonable settlement. Moreover, British leaders appear to have believed that Britain's economic situation, as well as that of France, was precarious, feelings that the economic meltdown of 1931 had served to reinforce. At the same time, they completely failed to recognize that the Germans confronted a far more serious economic situation.[27]

Chamberlain's assumptions about the potential for reaching a peaceful settlement with Hitler were reinforced by one of the most incompetent ambassadors His Majesty's government ever assigned to the Berlin embassy – or any other embassy, for that matter. As Britain's ambassador to Berlin in the late 1930s, Nevile Henderson consistently reinforced the prime minister's assumptions and preconceptions about the Germans in large numbers of missives that repeated "a hundred times the same ill-founded views and ideas. Obtuse enough to be a menace, and not stupid enough to be innocuous he proved *un homme néfast.*"[28]

But the harsh reality was that Britain confronted three great strategic threats in three very different theaters. In Europe, the rise of an aggressive Nazi regime posed great danger to Britain's position on the Continent as well the possibility of direct air attacks against the British Isles. In this case, the need was for Continental forces and air defense forces. In the Mediterranean, Mussolini's pretensions threatened Britain's lines of communication to India, which demanded a naval and air buildup. And in the Pacific, Japanese expansion demanded a great naval buildup. Nevertheless, the new Chamberlain government continued to base Britain's grand strategy on hopes of good behavior by powers which were providing no evidence that they had any intentions of such moderation.

From a purely military perspective, such a grand strategy represented a nightmare of possibilities. In March 1938, the chiefs of staff warned the government: "Without overlooking the assistance we should hope to obtain from France and possibly other allies, we cannot foresee the time when our defense forces will be strong enough to safeguard our territory, trade and vital interests against Germany, Italy, and Japan simultaneously."[29]

The chickens came home to roost in early 1938. Confronting the most serious civil-military crisis in his career, Hitler took the internal pressure off his regime by moving against Austria in March 1938. The *Anschluss* united Germany and Austria and immensely strengthened the Reich's position in

---

[27] Tooze's *Wages of Destruction* is particularly good on the systemic difficulties that the German economy confronted, difficulties that the Nazi regime's rearmament programs only served to exacerbate.

[28] L. B. Namier, *In the Nazi Era* (New York, 1952), p. 162.

[29] PRO CAB 53/37, COS 698 (Revise), CID, COS Sub-Committee, "Military Implications of German Aggression against Czechoslovakia," 28.3.38, p. 152.

central Europe.[30] For Chamberlain and his advisers, the German throttling of the Austrian state was an embarrassment, but only in the sense that the Germans had negotiated with no one. On 12 March 1938, as German forces roared into Austria, Chamberlain complained to the cabinet that Hitler's methods had shocked the world "as a typical illustration of power politics," which had unfortunately made appeasement more difficult.[31] Three days later, he informed his colleagues that the German occupation of Austria had only confirmed that he was on the right course.[32]

As early as November 1937, at a meeting with his senior military and diplomatic advisers, Hitler had declared his intention to move in the near future against Austria and Czechoslovakia. If the meeting in the Reich's Chancellery did not produce a specific timetable for future conquest, it did spell out the first destinations for the Third Reich's expansion.[33] After Austria, Czechoslovakia was next on the Führer's list. The difficulty for the British and French was that, unlike the Austrians, the Czechs had an alliance with France. Thus, any German attack on Czechoslovakia would demand that France declare war in support of its ally. Over summer 1938, Hitler increased pressure on the Czechs with the demand that they allow the Sudeten Germans to exercise the right of "national self-determination." However, any exercise of self-determination that turned the mountainous fringes of Czechoslovakia, where the Sudeten Germans lived, over to Germany would leave the remainder geographically indefensible.

In effect, the Germans were throwing back in the faces of the democracies their own liberal principles of allowing peoples to decide their nationalities. But it was all an enormous sham. In early June 1938, Hitler had decided on war against the Czechs. He ordered that German forces be ready to attack Czechoslovakia by the beginning of October 1938. The Wehrmacht's preparations for an invasion now proceeded full speed ahead. Meanwhile, the Western Powers engaged in a desperate Kabuki dance. The French had no intention of living up to their obligations to Czechoslovakia. Therefore, they encouraged every effort the British made to decouple France from its alliance with Czechoslovakia. The British, on their part, feared the French would drag them into a European war. Chamberlain's anxiety was such that in September, as the crisis atmosphere peaked, on his instructions, the British chiefs of staff, in a meeting with their French counterparts, informed General Maurice Gamelin, commander in chief of the French Army, that

[30] For the benefits the Germans derived from the Anschluss, see Murray, *The Change in the European Balance of Power*, pp. 149–54.

[31] PRO CAB 23/92, Cab 12 (38), Meeting of the Cabinet, 12.3.38, pp. 349–50.

[32] PRO CAB 27/623, FP(36) 25th Meeting, Meeting of the Foreign Policy Committee, 15.3.38.

[33] For the minutes of the meeting kept by Hitler's military aide Colonel Friedrich Hossbach, see International Military Tribunal, *Trial of Major War Criminals*, vol. 25 (Nuremberg, 1946), pp. 403–13.

they had no authorization to discuss strategic plans with representatives of the French government.[34]

Throughout spring and summer 1938, the chiefs of staff had reiterated their worries, given the general state of inadequacies in the training and equipment of their forces. Yet, in almost every respect, their appreciations represented worst-case analyses of the overall military balance.[35] Chamberlain used such analyses to buttress his policy of appeasement against opponents, like Churchill, who argued that the Western Powers possessed a distinct military advantage over Germany should war break out over Czechoslovakia.

In reality, Chamberlain and his chief supporters in the cabinet do not appear to have feared overly for Britain's strategic position in a war. As Lord Halifax commented: "he had no doubt that if we were involved in war we should win it after a long time," but the key point was that "he could not feel we were justified in embarking on an action which would result in such untold suffering."[36] Thus, the crucial issue for the leaders in the Chamberlain government was the prevention of war, not the protection of Britain's vital interests. As the great historian Lewis Namier commented on the volume of the Documents on British Foreign Policy series that dealt with the Czech crisis: "In the 1250 large pages of the British pre-Munich documents, the question of Europe's political and strategic configuration after Czechoslovakia had been obliterated is nowhere dealt with: amazing mental reticence.... On the British side a blind wall is raised against the future, at least by those vocal in the documents. All they know is that war must be averted."[37]

In fact, the Germans were no better prepared for a major war in 1938 than were the British and the French. In a series of strategic appreciations, the chief of the general staff, General Ludwig Beck, warned that Germany was in an almost hopeless military position should a major war break out over Czechoslovakia in 1938.[38] Hitler was entirely unwilling to listen to such realism. For the only time in its twelve-year history, there was a serious strategic debate in the Third Reich. But it was one that Beck could not win, for most of the senior military leaders were unwilling to confront Hitler. In

---

[34] At least they were embarrassed. *Documents Diplomatiques Français*, 2nd Series, vol. 11, Doc. 376, 26.9.38, "Compte Rendu des Conversations techniques du Général Gamelin au Cabinet Office 26 septembre 1938."

[35] The best example of such reports is PRO CAB 53/37, COS 698 (Revise), CID, COS Sub-Committee, "Military Implications of German Aggression against Czechoslovakia," 28.3.38.

[36] PRO CAB 23/95, Cab 39 (38), Meeting of the Cabinet, 17.9.38., pp. 98–99.

[37] Namier, *In the Nazi Era*, p. 162.

[38] For Beck's strategic appreciations, see Beck's Nachlass, Bundesarchiv/Militärarchiv (BA/MA), N 28/3,4.

late August 1938, Beck resigned from his position as chief of the general staff.

Nevertheless, word of the German military's qualms about their prospects in a war leaked from the Reich to Britain. Thus, there was a rather stunning reversal of British military appreciations of the strategic situation in September. On 23 September the chiefs of staff reported: "Until such time as we can build up our fighting potential we cannot hope for quick results. Nevertheless, the latent resources of the Empire and the doubtful morale of our opponents under the stress of war give us confidence as to the ultimate outcome."[39]

However, no one in either the cabinet or among the government's leading military and diplomatic advisers raised the crucial strategic question about what would happen to the strategic balance should Czechoslovakia be surrendered and Britain confront a major war against the Third Reich in 1939. Only in mid-September 1938 did Oliver Stanley, president of the Board of Trade, raise the question, and by that point in the crisis, it was too late for a coherent answer from the chiefs of staff.[40]

Hitler almost got the war he was so desperate to start. But at the last moment, Mussolini stepped in to propose a meeting of the heads of state of Germany, Italy, France, and Britain. The result was the surrender of Sudeten Czechoslovakia, with its considerable industrial, military, and financial resources, at the Munich conference at the end of September.[41] Considering the painful memories of the First World War, it is not surprising that the British public enthusiastically greeted Chamberlain and his declaration on his return from the Munich Conference at the end of September that he had brought "peace with honour" and "peace in our time." There were, however, several resignations from the cabinet, while Churchill, in one of the greatest speeches in his career, bitterly denounced the results of the Munich surrender:

> All is over. Silent, mournful, abandoned, broken Czechoslovakia recedes into the darkness. She has suffered in every respect by her association with France, under whose guidance and policy she has been actuated for so long.... [But the British people] should know that we have sustained a defeat without a war, the consequences of which will travel far with us along our road; they should know that we have passed an awful milestone in our history, when the whole equilibrium of Europe has been deranged, and that the terrible words have for the time being been pronounced against the Western Democracies: 'Thou art weighed in the balance and found wanting.' And do not suppose that this is the

---

[39] PRO CAB 53/41, COS 773, COS Committee, "The Czechoslovak Crisis," 24.9.38.

[40] PRO CAB 53/41, COS 766, COS Committee, "Appreciation of the Situation in the Event of War against Germany: Minute by the Minister for the Coordination of Defense," p. 10.

[41] For an examination of the strategic impact of the surrender of Czechoslovakia to the Germans, see Murray, *The Change in the European Balance of Power*, chaps. 7 and 8.

end. This is only the beginning of the reckoning. This is only the first sip, the first foretaste of a bitter cup.[42]

Churchill's speech was greeted with derision in the House of Commons, while even his constituency considered withdrawing its support. On the other hand, Chamberlain believed that he had achieved a lasting success. As he announced to the cabinet on his return from Munich, diplomacy had triumphed; representatives of the four major powers – the Soviet Union obviously did not count in his calculus of major European powers – had met and settled the Sudeten matter peacefully.[43] To the prime minister, Munich represented the fruition of his grand strategy to settle Europe's differences by diplomacy and goodwill rather than by military power and strategic concerns about the balance of power. On the morning of his departure from Munich, he and Hitler had signed an innocuous agreement to further good relations between the two powers, which the prime minister believed had put the seal on his success in bringing peace to Europe.[44] Yet within three weeks, Hitler was to denounce the warmongers in London for their obdurate, anti-Nazi stance.

GRAND STRATEGY AND THE ROAD TO WAR

While the Chamberlain government basked in the upswell of popular opinion, it confronted two knotty problems: how to deal with the problem of rearmament and how to build on what the prime minister believed to be the rapport he had established with Hitler over the course of their three meetings in September. On both issues, he stumbled badly. And the mistakes and miscalculations that the British government would make in the six months after the signing of the Munich Agreement would have a profound impact on the first years of the Second World War.

The problem with rearmament flowed from Chamberlain's exploitation of the chief's of staff gloomy picture of the state of British defenses during the summer's debates about how to treat the growing crisis between Czechoslovakia and Germany. Thus, many of the prime minister's most fervent supporters were pressing for a speedup in rearmament as an insurance policy, should the Germans turn out not to be amenable to reason. Nevertheless, Sir Horace Wilson, the senior civil servant in Britain and one of the prime minister's closest advisers, argued strongly in a private note to the

---

[42] Winston S. Churchill, *The Second World War*, vol. 1, *The Gathering Storm* (Boston, 1948), pp. 327–28.

[43] PRO CAB 23/95, Cab 47 (38), Meeting of the Cabinet, 30.9.38.

[44] The French premier Edouard Daladier had no such illusions. He had his plane circle the Paris airport to insure the crowds below were not there to hang him for surrendering Czechoslovakia.

prime minister that Britain should make no changes in its defense policies.[45] He need not have taken the trouble because Chamberlain had no intention of increasing the defense budget significantly. On the contrary, he informed his colleagues in early October that ever since his term as the Chancellor of the Exchequer, he had felt that "the burden of armaments might break our back." Because of that fear, he had embarked on a foreign policy of appeasement to resolve the conflicts that had caused the armaments race.[46] Thus, whatever the dangers of the international environment, the government would make only minimal adjustments to its defense policies.

The government now proceeded to stonewall any attempt by the services to increase their defense budgets. Sir Thomas Inskip, minister for the coordination of defense, clearly enunciated the government's position. Did Munich call for revision of the scope of authorized programs? And did "the financial implications even of the current problems... threaten that [economic] stability which is, after all, in our experience probably our strongest weapon of war?"[47] All this provided a wonderful smokescreen for doing nothing, which is precisely what the government proceeded to do.

After innumerable meetings, the special committee on defense requirements recommended, and the cabinet eventually approved, an increase of 20 escort vessels and 12 small mine sweepers, the dredging of Dover and Rosyth harbors, the building of an airfield at Scapa Flow, and orders for armor plate from Czechoslovakia for the navy. The army received a few antiaircraft guns and nothing else despite the fact that it could barely have put two divisions on the Continent in September 1938. In other words, the government's strategic policy remained firmly committed to a refusal to prepare the army for a role on the Continent. The most dishonest of its efforts to persuade the public that something was being done for defense, however, came with respect to the Royal Air Force. The government announced that it was increasing the number of fighters on order by 50 percent. It achieved this goal by the expedient of extending the two-year contracts for the production of Hurricanes and Spitfires for a third year.[48] Thus, there would be no increase in planned fighter production for either 1939 or 1940.[49]

---

[45] PRO PREM 1/330, p. 43. Note from Wilson to Chamberlain: "Notes made by Sir Nevile Henderson," 20.10.38. Wilson was the senior civil servant at the Treasury as well as for the whole government and, in that position, had enthusiastically supported the prime minister's efforts to minimize Britain's defense expenditure while pursuing a policy of appeasement.

[46] PRO CAB 23/95, Cab 48 (38), Meeting of the Cabinet, 3.10.38, p. 304. It is hard to see what armaments race was occurring because Britain was not participating in any race.

[47] PRO CAB 24/279, CP 234 (38), 21.10.38, "Defense Preparations Forecast."

[48] PRO CAB 23/96, Cab 53 (38), Meeting of the Cabinet, 7.11.38, Conclusions, pp. 168–71; and PRO CAB/143, DPR 285, 14.10.38, CID 24th Progress Report: "Week Ending 1,10,38"; DPR 291, 14.12.38, 25th Progress Report.

[49] The events of March 1939 would change production targets for fighter production, but by then, the British had lost six crucial months, during which time the German industry had been cranking out increasing numbers of new aircraft for the Luftwaffe.

Nevertheless, the government soon found itself hoist on its own petard. Goebbels immediately seized on the discussions of rearmament in Britain to denounce Perfidious Albion for a rearmament program that was "on a scale which far exceeds the security requirements of the Island Kingdom and cannot remain without serious repercussions upon the powers against whom the main British armament efforts are directed."[50] Of course, such nonsense, spouted from the propaganda ministry in Berlin, was a smokescreen for the fact that German rearmament was continuing at full speed. Hitler, on his part, had immediately considered occupying all of Czechoslovakia but had held back because he realized that such a move might be too much even for the British to swallow. Nevertheless, within three weeks after the Munich Conference, he ordered the planners in the Oberkommando der Wehrmacht (OKW, Germany's armed forces high command) to begin preparations to occupy the remainder of the Czech state. Further directives followed in November and December.[51]

For Chamberlain and the appeasers in London, the winter of 1938–1939 was a most uncomfortable one. To begin with, Henderson was diagnosed with cancer and immediately returned from the Berlin embassy for treatment in London. This left the embassy in the hands of responsible members of the Foreign Service, who proceeded to deluge London with more accurate and consequently gloomy reports of the darkness descending on the Continent. The first savage outpouring of Nazi anti-Semitism on Krystalnacht added further to a sense throughout Britain that things were going badly wrong in Nazi Germany.[52]

The British also made no effort to reassure the French, who now viewed their position on the Continent as verging on desperate with the removal of the Czech military from the balance of power. Many in the Foreign and War offices worried about growing French disillusion with their British ally. Moreover, Mussolini mounted a strong attack on the continued French rule over Tunisia and implied that Italy was more than ready to assume its neighbor's position as the preeminent Mediterranean power. Nevertheless, none of this disturbed Chamberlain's blasé attitude toward the French. In December, he announced in the House that Britain would not necessarily come to the aid of France if the Italians were to attack her.[53] Britain's casual treatment of her French ally explains much of the deep antagonism that

---

[50] Quoted in a dispatch from Berlin. PRO FO 371/21658, C 12816/42/18, Ogilvie-Forbes to Halifax, 21.10.38.

[51] *Akten zur deutschen auswärtigen Politik (ADAP)*, Series D, vol. 4, Doc. 81, 21.10,38, "Weisung des Führers Obersten Befehlshabers der Wehrmacht."

[52] "Crystal Night" – a reference to the windows of Jewish businesses and synagogues smashed and broken by Nazi thugs throughout the Reich during anti-Jewish riots on the night of 9 November 1938.

[53] PRO FO 371/21593, C 15630/13/17, 12.12.38.

Marshal Pétain's Vichy regime would display toward Britain from summer 1940 through Vichy's collapse in 1942.

Chamberlain soon found the shoe on the other foot. It appears that in January 1939, anti-Nazis in the higher levels of the German government, appalled by the failure of the Western Powers to stand up to Hitler at Munich, spread rumors that the Führer was about to seize Holland and use Dutch naval and air bases to attack the British Isles. The French now hinted that in such a case, they might not be able to come to the aid of the British, given the surrender of Czech military power to the Germans and the fact that they could count on no British ground forces to aid them should major fighting occur in Western Europe. They now made it clear that only a buildup of British ground forces could guarantee French support in case of a German attack on Holland.

Most of the ministers in the cabinet were appalled, and by February, even Lord Halifax, the foreign secretary and Chamberlain's strongest supporter, had to admit that because Britain could not hold out if France were to fall, the British government would have to come "to the assistance of France on land on a larger scale and within a shorter time than has hitherto been contemplated."[54] Thus, in mid-February, Chamberlain was finally forced by the reality of the strategic situation to agree to a significant ground commitment to the defense of France with a concomitant increase in the army's budget.

However, in mid-February, Henderson returned to Berlin, and reports from the embassy again took on a rose-colored tinge.[55] Optimism crashed and burned, however, on 15 March 1939, when German troops occupied the remainder of Czechoslovakia in direct contravention of the Munich Agreements. Nevertheless, at first, Chamberlain displayed little desire to alter his course of appeasing the dictators. Rather, on the same day German troops occupied the remainder of Czechoslovakia, the prime minister suggested to his colleagues in the Cabinet:

> the state whose frontiers we had undertaken to guarantee against unprovoked aggression had now completely broken up.... He thought therefore that military occupation was symbolic more than perhaps appeared on the surface.[56]

Almost immediately, however, the government discovered that neither the House nor the country viewed the German action so blithely. Instead, a

[54] PRO FO 371/22922, DP (P) 47, CID, "Strategic Position of France in Relation to the Role of the British Army in War," Note by the Secretary of State for Foreign Affairs on Report (COS 833) by the COS Subcommittee.
[55] On February 18, e.g., he reported: "I believe in fact that [Hitler] would now in his heart like to return to the fold of comparative respectability," DBFP 3rd Series, vol. 4, Doc 118, 18.2.39., Henderson to Halifax.
[56] PRO CAB 23/98, Cab 11 (30), Meeting of the Cabinet, 15.3.39, pp. 7–8.

series of furious denunciations of Germany's actions and demands that the government take action, erupted across the political fences that separated the British parties. Facing elections within the year, Chamberlain radically altered his tune and with it the whole direction of British policy.[57] In a speech in Birmingham several days later, he plaintively asked whether the occupation of rump Czechoslovakia represented a "step in the direction of an attempt to dominate the world by force."[58]

The domestic political storm, together with European-wide reaction to German actions, now led to a number of fundamental military, political, and strategic decisions, which, to a great extent, reflected an ill-thought-out attempt to avoid war by drawing a diplomatic line in the sand. The first and most dramatic action was a British guarantee of Poland's territorial integrity, a guarantee that the British had no chance of fulfilling. Chamberlain extended the guarantee in the belief that the Germans were set to invade Poland in the immediate future, and thus, he meant the guarantee to deter Hitler from undertaking any rash act. In fact, the Germans were not prepared to invade Poland in the immediate future.

Further expanding its diplomatic offensive, the Chamberlain government, followed by the somewhat appalled French, then extended guarantees to a number of the other states in Eastern Europe. Winston Churchill caught the reversal in Britain's grand strategy best in his memoirs:

> And now, when every one of these aids and advantages has been squandered and thrown away, Great Britain advances, leading France by the hand, to guarantee the integrity of Poland.... There was sense in fighting for Czechoslovakia in 1938 when the German Army could scarcely put half a dozen trained divisions on the Western Front, when the French with their sixty or seventy divisions could most certainly have rolled across the Rhine or into the Ruhr. But this had been judged unreasonable, rash, below the level of modern intellectual thought and morality. Yet now at last the two Western Democracies declared themselves ready to stake their lives upon the territorial integrity of Poland. History, which we are told is mainly the record of the crimes, follies, and miseries of mankind, may be scoured and ransacked to find a parallel to this sudden and complete reversal of five or six years' policy of easy-going placatory appeasement, and its transformation almost overnight into a readiness to accept an obviously imminent war on far worse conditions and on the greatest scale.[59]

In fact, the British government still refused to accept the reality that war was inevitable. Instead, British grand strategy had switched to a policy of diplomatic confrontation with Germany only in the conviction that Hitler

---

[57] The last major election had occurred in 1935. Thus, unless war were to intervene, the Chamberlain government would face an election sometime in early 1940.
[58] Quoted in Murray, *The Change in the European Balance of Power*, p. 285.
[59] Churchill, *The Second World War*, p. 347.

would back down. Fundamental to the new assumption, still based on the belief that Hitler could not possibly want war, was the judgment that the Germans must be bluffing. If that were so, then a strong diplomatic coalition of great and small powers could deter the Nazis. Illustrating such idle hopes, Sir John Simon, Chancellor of the Exchequer and a fervent Chamberlain supporter, argued that it was important that the "attitude which we [Britain] took be...known in Germany before Germany's act of aggression took place." If this were done soon enough, the impact on the German public might "prevent the war from starting."[60]

That new assumption could not have been more faulty. Hitler's response to the British guarantee to Poland was straightforward and immediate. The head of German intelligence, Admiral Wilhelm Canaris, heard the Führer shout that he was going to cook up a stew for the British that would make them choke.[61] In early April, Hitler ordered the OKW to begin planning for an invasion of Poland. The target date for Fall Weiss (Operation White) would be 1 September 1939.[62] This time, believing that Munich had robbed him of his chance to smash the Czechs in retaliation for their arrogant behavior, Hitler was not to be dissuaded from his decision. A major European war thus was inevitable from the moment that Britain extended its guarantee to Poland.

Meanwhile, Chamberlain made a number of other decisions aimed at deterring the Germans. Despite howls of protest from the Treasury about the need for financial responsibility, the prime minister finally opened the economic floodgates for massive rearmament of Britain's military forces.[63] In the short term, of course, it was going to be too little too late. In the long run, it would have impact, but only after Britain had lost its position on the Continent. Unfortunately, the Chamberlain government had entirely wasted the six-month period after Munich in its dilatory policy toward rearming.

In equally desultory fashion, Chamberlain introduced peacetime conscription for the first time in British history. The decision certainly represented a part of the prime minister's campaign to deter the Germans, but in practice, it set back the army's rearmament program considerably. Only two months earlier, the government had taken steps to expand the regular army, a measure which had barely gotten off the ground. Now the army confronted the prospect of being deluged by a mass of conscripts which it possessed neither the trainers nor the facilities to handle. Meanwhile, a cabinet paper

[60] PRO CAB 23/98, Cab 12 (39), Meeting of the Cabinet, 18.3.39, p. 52.
[61] Alan Bullock, *Hitler: A Study in Tyranny* (London, 1964), p. 445.
[62] *ADAP*, Series D, vol. 6, Doc. 149, 3.4.39., "Weisung des Chefs der Oberkommandos der Wehrmacht."
[63] Among other documents indicating the Treasury's continued resistance to any speed up in rearmament, see PRO CAB 16/209, SAC/4th Meeting, CID, Strategic Appreciations Subcommittee, p. 75; and PRO PREM 1/296, Letter from Simon to Chatfield, 17.4.39.

made clear that "it was not proposed either that the scheme for Compulsory Military Training should supersede our traditional methods of voluntary service or that it should become a permanent feature of our system."[64]

Perhaps the greatest weakness in the government's effort to establish a fundamentally new strategy lay in its almost pathological unwillingness to deal with the Soviets. In hindsight, of course, we know that Stalin would soon leap at the chance to reach an accommodation with Hitler. An alliance with the Western Powers would inevitably have involved the Soviet Union in a major European war, a war that the Red Army was not ready to fight given the devastating purges that had wiped out many of the most competent members of its senior leadership.[65] In contrast, Hitler was in a position to offer the Soviets peace, large portions of Poland and Rumania, and the chance to remain on the sidelines while the capitalist powers destroyed themselves in a bloody conflict.[66]

Hence, the point is not that the British and the French missed a great opportunity to strike a deal with Stalin, a deal that was never in the cards; rather the reluctance of British leaders to align themselves with the Soviets confirmed their inability to recognize that now was the time to prepare for war. And when, eventually, Western negotiators finally went to Leningrad in August 1939 to seek an alliance with the Soviets, they literally traveled by slow boat.[67] The German foreign minister, Joachim von Ribbentrop, would fly to Moscow to negotiate the nonaggression pact on which the two powers agreed.

Even as relations between the Soviets and Nazis warmed in July 1939, neither Chamberlain nor Lord Halifax displayed much worry. That month, Halifax remarked that a failure of negotiations with the Soviets "would not cause him very great anxiety, since he felt that whatever formal agreement was signed, the Soviet government would probably take such action as best suited them, if war broke out."[68] One month later, when the news of the Nazi-Soviet Non-Aggression Pact exploded on the European scene, the foreign secretary discounted the agreement as being of little importance, although he did admit that it would have considerable moral effect. What its strategic effect would be on the military balance, he did not hazard a guess.[69]

---

[64] PRO CAB 23/99, Cab 22 (39), Meeting of the Cabinet, 24.4.39., p. 6.
[65] Still the Red Army was about to demonstrate that it was still capable of dealing out lethal blows. In August 1939, a reinforced Soviet corps under the future marshal of the Soviet Union, Gregori Zhukov, would wipe out, almost to the last man, a reinforced Japanese division in the Battle of Nomonhan. The best discussion of the battle is Alvin Coox's extensive study *Nomonhan: Japan against Russia*, 2 vols. (Stanford, CA, 1985).
[66] Gerhard L. Weinberg, *The Foreign Policy of Hitler's Germany*, vol. 2, *Starting World War II* (Chicago, 1970), pp. 550–52, 570–71.
[67] Murray, *The Change in the European Balance of Power*, p. 304.
[68] PRO CAB 23/100, Cab 38 (39), Meeting of the Cabinet, 19.7.39, p. 186.
[69] PRO CAB 23/100, Cab 41 (39), Meeting of the Cabinet, 22.8.39, p. 320.

By mid-August, as the German war machine gathered on the plains of Silesia, Pomerania, and West Prussia, the British and French confronted the reality of an inevitable war. On 1 September the Wehrmacht began its lightning campaign against the Poles. The Germans began their massive and ruthless assault with major air attacks against targets throughout Poland, including so-called military targets in Warsaw. German forces quickly broke through the ill-prepared Polish defenses and drove deep into the Polish hinterland.

Even then, Chamberlain dithered in London in a desperate search to avoid war. On the evening of 2 September the House assembled, fully expecting the prime minister to declare war on the Germans. He did no such thing. Instead, he cataloged the efforts His Majesty's government was making to stop hostilities. Immediately after a furious House of Commons had broken up, the Conservative Party's chief whip warned the prime minister that if he did not declare war the next day, his government would fall, such was the mood of the Conservative members of Parliament. Henderson delivered the British government's ultimatum to the German foreign minister at eleven o'clock the next morning, and one hour later, Britain and Germany were at war.

GRAND STRATEGY ON THE OUTBREAK OF WAR

Britain and France went to war with Nazi Germany on the straightforward assumption that the war would be lengthy and that, in the long term, the economic and financial strength of the Allied powers would inevitably produce Germany's defeat. In late April 1939, the British chiefs of staff had reported that German territorial acquisitions would not solve the Reich's basic raw material shortages, which remained as pressing as ever.[70] They estimated that whereas the Germans might be able to increase their ground and air forces at the outset of a conflict, their raw material demands would correspondingly increase. A strategic report a year earlier on the potential grand strategy the Western powers might follow in the case of war had indicated:

Our aim therefore should be:

1) The maximum interruption of supplies of these goods in all cases where it is practicable . . . to create a shortage in Germany.
2) Any diminution of Germany's economic resources as a whole. With regard to the former the necessary conditions will be . . . that Germany cannot obtain adequate supplies, direct or indirect, coming from overseas or otherwise within our control.[71]

---

[70] PRO CAB 29/159, AFC 16, 22.4.39, Anglo-French Staff Conversations, United Kingdom Delegation, Annex 1, p. 73.
[71] PRO CAB 47/14, A.T.B. 181, "Plan for Economic Warfare against Germany," 22.7.38.

In fact, the report turned out to be right. The allies would triumph in the end precisely because they possessed access to so much of the world's economic, financial, and industrial power. However, that would be in the long run, and only after a terrible and costly struggle. It turned out that way because the Western Powers brought no military pressure on the German war economy between September 1939 and May 1940.[72] They failed to bring the Italians into the war in 1939, when there was a distinct possibility of moving the Italians off the fence; they failed to cut off the crucial imports of Swedish iron ore that flowed through the port of Narvik in the winter; the French failed even to send patrols against the West Wall or to attempt to shut down the Saar industrial region which lay immediately across the frontier from France.[73]

Instead, Allied actions during the winter of 1939–1940 reflected a bureaucratic inertia bordering on pusillanimity that, combined with military and political inaction, allowed Hitler to marshal the Reich's economic resources for the great throw of the dice that would come with Fall Gelb (Case Yellow) in spring 1940. In every respect, Allied military and political strategy failed to address German weaknesses. A strategic survey in April 1940 underlined the general failure of Allied strategy to address the strategic problems raised by the war in military terms:

> Hence, the Reich appears to have suffered little wear and tear during the first six months of the war, and that mainly as a result of the allied blockade. Meanwhile it has profited from the interval to perfect the degree of equipment of its land and air forces, to increase the officer strength and complete the training of its troops, and to add further divisions to those already in the field.[74]

ON THE BRINK: A NEW GRAND STRATEGY?

On 10 May 1940, Winston Churchill became the prime minister of Great Britain. On that same day, the Germans marched west in a campaign lasting barely five weeks that would crush France and drive the British off the Continent. In this case, Allied grand strategy, shattered because of catastrophic French military miscalculations, allowed what should have been a relatively small success by German infantry in crossing the Meuse to

---

[72] For how serious the economic problems were that the German war economy faced, see Murray, *The Change in the European Balance of Power*, pp. 326–34; see also Tooze, *The Wages of Destruction*, chap. 10.

[73] The failure of Allied military and operational strategy is discussed in depth in Murray, *The Change in the European Balance of Power*, chap. 10.

[74] PRO CAB 85/16, M.R. (J)(40)(s) 2, 11.4.40, Allied Military Committee, "The Major Strategy of the West, Note by the French Delegation." In every respect, this French statement represented an accurate depiction of the overall correlation of forces. For further discussion, see ibid., chap. 10.

jeopardize the entire Allied military situation.[75] As this author has pointed out elsewhere:

> The tired, weary German infantry who seized the heights behind the Meuse and who opened the way for the armored thrust to the coast made inevitable the fall of France, the subsequent invasion of Russia, the Final Solution, and the collapse of Europe's position in the world.[76]

However, although virtually every strategic analyst in the world assumed the Germans had won the war and that Britain also would soon fall to the Wehrmacht, Churchill brought a combination of strategic genius, vision, understanding of history, and a sense of what a German victory would entail not only for the empire but for the very values that underpinned Britain's civilization.[77] Above all, Churchill provided a narrative on which the British people, the Dominions, and even their military allies could hang their efforts. In his first and perhaps greatest speech as prime minister, Churchill announced to the House of Commons:

> You ask, what is our policy? I will say: It is to wage war, by sea, land and air, with all our might and with all the strength that God can give us; to wage war against a monstrous tyranny, never surpassed in the dark, lamentable catalogue of human crime. That is our policy.

> You ask what is our aim? I can answer in one word: it is victory, victory at all costs, victory in spite of all terror, victory, however long and hard the road may be.[78]

This, of course, represented a fundamental break with Chamberlain's unwillingness to confront the essential strategic problem raised by Hitler's Germany: the need to meet force with force. Yet, the mismatch between British resources and the defiance expressed by Churchill after the shattering collapse of France was all too clear. It seemed now that Britain's strategic position had reached a point of complete overstretch, from which there could be no return, given not only the immediate German threat but also the Italian threat in the Mediterranean and the looming threat presented by

[75] General Maurice Gamelin had moved nearly all of the French reserves from Rheims, where they would have been ideally placed to counterattack the German push through the Ardennes, to the far left of the Allied line, in March 1940. On 15 May, Churchill had asked Gamelin where the French reserves were, and the general had laconically replied, "*Aucoun*" (none). There are few greater admissions of military bankruptcy in history.

[76] Williamson Murray and Allan R. Millett, *A War to Be Won: Fighting the Second World War* (Cambridge, MA, 2000), p. 75.

[77] The astonishing school of British historians who have argued in recent decades that Britain could have kept its empire had she made a deal with Hitler in summer 1940 misses the entire nature of the Nazi regime. But none of them appear even to be able to read German or understand the nature of the Nazi regime, which explains their view of history. In this regard, see esp. the works of John Charmley.

[78] *Hansard*, 13 May 1940, cols. 1501–2.

the Japanese in the Far East. Yet, in one of the ironies with which history redounds, the more desperate Britain's situation, the more the British people rallied behind the prime minister and his stirring words.[79]

And Britain's position *was* desperate. Even Churchill understood perfectly well that though Britain could hold in the short term, in the long term, she would need allies to defeat the Third Reich. The prime minister's determination reflected an implicit (and accurate) calculation that the United States and the Soviet Union could not and would not countenance German hegemony over the Continent.[80] Moreover, he believed that Hitler could not resist the opportunities offered by the defeat of France to further aggrandize his burgeoning empire nor Mussolini to increase Italy's colonial empire in North Africa, and that both such efforts would eventually lead to their downfall.

In his first 55 days as Britain's leader, Churchill confronted one of the most difficult set of strategic, political, and military problems ever faced by the leader of a great state. During that period, above all, it was Churchill's personality and extraordinary capabilities that were key to the survival of Britain and its eventual victory. Hastings Ismay, Churchill's personal military adviser throughout the war, best described Churchill's strengths to Field Marshal Claude Auchinleck, commander in chief in the Mediterranean theater from summer 1941 to summer 1942:

> The idea that [Churchill] was rude, arrogant, and self seeking was entirely wrong. He was none of those things. He was certainly frank in speech and writing, but he expected that others would be equally frank with him. To a young brigadier from Middle East Headquarters who had asked if he might speak freely, he had replied: 'Of course. We are not here to pay each other compliments.' ... He had considerable respect for a trained military mind, but refused to subscribe to the idea that generals were infallible or had any monopoly of the military art. He was not a gambler, but never shrank from taking a calculated risk if the situation so demanded. ... I begged Auchinleck not to allow himself to be intimidated by these never ending messages, but to remember that Churchill, as Prime Minister and Minister of Defense, bore the primary responsibility for ensuring that all available resources in shipping, man-power, equipment, oil, and the rest were apportioned between the Home front and the various theaters of war. Was it not reasonable that he should wish to know exactly how all these resources were being used before deciding on the allotment to be given to this or that theater?[81]

---

[79] After the war, Churchill would comment that it was the response of the British people to the terrible threats that they faced that he had only given voice to in his speeches.

[80] Interestingly, Hitler confided to his army advisers in late July that Churchill's hope that the United States and the Soviet Union would intervene was the only thing keeping the British in the war, considering their hopeless strategic situation. The Führer's solution was to decide on Operation Barbarossa, the invasion of the Soviet Union.

[81] Lord Hastings, *The Memoirs of General the Lord Ismay* (London, 1960), pp. 269–70.

Another military assistant characterized the change from Chamberlain to Churchill: "The days of mere 'coordination' were out for good and all.... We were now going to get direction, leadership, action with a snap in it."[82]

During his first 55 days as prime minister, Churchill confronted a series of crises, any one of which could have led to political or strategic disaster. In the immediate days after assuming power, there were two major threats. The first reflected the Churchill government's weak political base, in which significant portions of his own party were immensely suspicious of him – so much so that, when he entered the House of Commons for the first time as prime minister, most of the Conservative benches remained silent and sullen. Only the Labour and Liberal benches cheered him.[83]

The second major threat came with the German breakthough on the Meuse in mid-May that destroyed most of the French units on the Allied left wing and almost swamped the British Expeditionary Force (BEF). Confronted with growing defeatism, Churchill had, on one hand, to attempt to keep the French in the fight and, on the other, to face down an increasingly strong effort, led by Halifax, to seek terms from the Germans. Then, complete disaster loomed when it appeared that the BEF might be trapped on the beaches of Dunkirk. First estimates, as their evacuation began, were that only 50,000 British soldiers would escape from France. In the end, helped by the German failure to realize what was happening until too late, the navy and its civilian auxiliaries brought off 250,000 British and 100,000 French soldiers. But while hailing their preservation as a "miracle of deliverance," Churchill subsequently reminded the House of Commons that "wars are not won by evacuations."[84]

But those who deal with grand strategy must deal not only with the present but also with the future. Two incidents in 1940 emphasize why Churchill was so good at connecting the two. The increasingly dangerous situation in France required the British to make hard choices. Churchill's own sense of obligation to the French because of their sacrifices for victory in World War I was magnified by the mistreatment he had observed various British governments dish out to Britain's most important ally on the Continent during the interwar period.[85] Thus, when French leaders desperately called for more British Hurricane squadrons to cover their troops, hard-pressed by the Luftwaffe, Churchill's instinct was to reply favorably.

[82] General Sir Leslie Hollis, *One Marine's Tale* (London, 1956), pp. 61, 77.
[83] Churchill is reputed to have turned to the Conservative Party's chief whip and commented that one more such demonstration, and he would go to the country (call an election, which the Conservatives were sure to lose).
[84] See http://news.bbc.co.uk/onthisday/hi/dates/stories/june/4/newsid_3500000/3500865.stm.
[85] Throughout his life, Churchill remained a confirmed Francophile, although his efforts to speak his appallingly bad French caused some bemusement among his French listeners.

Here he ran up against Air Marshal Hugh "Stuffy" Dowding, one of the great airpower innovators during the interwar period and combat commanders during World War II.[86] In a brilliant memorandum on 16 May, well before the full extent of the disaster on the Continent had become clear, Dowding laid out the strategic parameters which Britain confronted. Although he "hoped that our armies may yet be victorious in France... we have to face the possibility that they may be defeated" – a reality that was just beginning to sink into the minds of British leaders. He went on to warn:

> I believe that if an adequate fighter force is kept in this country, if the Fleet remains in being, and if the Home Forces are suitably organized to resist invasion, we should be able to continue the war single-handed for some time, if not indefinitely. But if the Home Defense Force [i.e., Fighter Command] is drained away in desperate attempts to remedy the situation in France, defeat in France will involve the final, complete, and irremediable defeat of this country.[87]

THE SQUADRONS STAYED HOME

Churchill has acquired a reputation among some historians for punishing the bearers of bad news or those who thwarted his desires. Nothing could be further from the truth. As Lord Ismay suggested earlier, Churchill was more than open to reasoned, intelligent arguments based on facts. That summer, Churchill not only kept Dowding on to fight the Battle of Britain but also quashed a cabal of senior officers and civil servants in the Air Ministry who were attempting to replace Dowding as commander in chief of Fighter Command before the battle began and only reluctantly replaced the air marshal after the conclusion of the battle.[88]

The second incident involved the estimate of a young 28-year-old scientist working in air intelligence. R. V. Jones had sensed, on the basis of scanty pieces of intelligence, that the Luftwaffe was using intersecting radio beams to guide bombers to targets in bad weather and at night. Churchill's chief scientific adviser, Frederick Lindemann (later Lord Cherwell), who had been Jones's adviser, secured the young scientist a hearing on 20 June before Churchill and a number of leading members of the air ministry and the

---

[86] For Dowding's role as an innovator, see the outstanding article by Alan Beyerchen, "From Radio to Radar: Interwar Military Adaptation to Technological Change in Germany, the United Kingdom, and the United States," in Williamson Murray and Allan R. Millett, eds., *Military Innovation in the Interwar Period* (Cambridge, 1996).

[87] Quoted in John Terraine, *The Right of the Line: The Royal Air Force in the European War, 1939–1945* (London, 1985), p. 185.

[88] Martin Gilbert, *Winston S. Churchill*, vol. 6, *Their Finest Hour* (Boston, 1983), pp. 657–58.

scientific establishment, all of whom thought Jones's theory was nonsense. In the prime minister's words:

> When Dr. Jones had finished [with his presentation on the German radio beams guiding bombers to their target] there was a general air of incredulity. One high authority asked why the Germans should use a beam, assuming that such a thing was possible, when they had at their disposal all the ordinary facilities of navigation.[89]

Churchill overruled the experts. What he understood, and what the so-called experts did not, was that even if there were only a 5 percent chance that Jones was correct, Britain absolutely could not take that risk. He ordered that flights guided by Jones's calculations fly routes to test for the beams' existence. That night, an RAF aircraft detected the beams intersecting over Derby, the main factory town for the production of the Merlin engines that powered the Spitfires and Hurricanes.[90]

Forthwith, British scientists went to work on distorting and jamming the beams. By fall, they had succeeded; the capabilities that they had developed enabled the British largely to thwart the German nighttime blitz offensive and render much of the German nighttime bombing ineffective. Without that ability to jam the German blind-bombing beams, British targets would have lain completely open to direct and accurate German bombing, which would have considerably increased the damage the Luftwaffe would have been able to inflict on the cities of the British Isles.[91]

But the largest problem confronting British grand strategy, if not the most pressing, was how Britain would gain the allies crucial not only to her long-term survival but also to the victory over Germany that the prime minister had promised the British people. Churchill's first move was to send to the Soviet Union as his majesty's representative the left-wing Labour politician Sir Stafford Cripps. The Soviets were not impressed. The German ambassador in Moscow, Count Schulenburg, caught the mood in Moscow with a missive to Berlin:

---

[89] Winston Churchill, *The Second World War*, vol. 2, *Their Finest Hour* (Boston, 1949), p. 384. The British would continue to use totally inadequate means of navigation through to 1941, when they discovered that at least two-thirds of their bombers attacking at nighttime were incapable of dropping their bombs within a target area of seventy-five square miles. In other words, they had a better chance to hit cows and trees than to hit German cities, much less specific targets.

[90] For a full discussion of the intuitive thinking that went into the discovery of the beams and then the arguments that followed until the test flight that confirmed their existence, see R. V. Jones, *The Wizard War: British Scientific Intelligence, 1939–1945* (New York, 1978), pp. 92–105.

[91] The attack on Coventry in November 1940 was accurate and devastating because there was a full moon and no cloud cover to hinder the German pathfinders in their search for the city.

There is no reason for apprehension concerning Cripps' mission, since there is no reason to doubt the loyal attitude of the Soviet Union toward us, and since the unchanged direction of Soviet policy towards England precludes damage to Germany or vital German interests. There are no indications of any kind here for belief that the latest German successes cause alarm or fear of Germany in the Soviet government.[92]

Schulenburg's message was right on target. For the next year, Cripps ran into a complete lack of interest on the part of the Soviets in any improvement of relations between Britain and the Soviet Union. Meanwhile, the Soviets contributed enormously to the German war economy, supplying much of the raw materials and foodstuffs that would support Operation Barbarossa, the German invasion of the Soviet Union in June 1941.[93]

Churchill's warnings to the Soviets through Cripps in April 1941 that Hitler was preparing to invade the Soviet Union met obdurate disdain from a government sure in its ideological conviction that there was no chance the Germans would invade their country.[94] If anything, Churchill's warning further persuaded Stalin that the Germans were not going to invade: obviously the British capitalists were trying to disturb the relations between the two great Continental powers to their advantage. As in 1939, Stalin and Molotov were not about to pull Britain's chestnuts out of the fire.

So the German invasion came in the early morning hours of 22 June 1941. It says a great deal about Churchill's statesmanship that without hesitation, he threw Britain wholeheartedly into an effort to support the Soviet Union in its hour of need. As he told his private secretary, John Colville, on the evening before Barbarossa began: "If Hitler invaded Hell, I would make at least a favorable reference to the Devil in the House of Commons."[95] On the following evening, he broadcast one of his most eloquent speeches to the British people:

No one has been a more consistent opponent of Communism than I have for the past twenty-five years. I will unsay no word that I have spoken about it. But all this fades away before the spectacle which is now unfolding. The past with its crimes, its follies, and its tragedies, flashes away. I see the Russian soldiers standing on the threshold of their native land, guarding the fields which their fathers have tilled since time immemorial. . . . I see also the dull, drilled docile,

---

[92] Raymond J. Sontag and James Stuart Beddle, *Nazi-Soviet Relations, 1939–1941* (Washington, DC, 1948), p. 154.

[93] Molotov plaintively complained to Schulenburg when the latter presented his government's declaration of war on 22 June 1941: "Surely we have not deserved that." Gustav Hilger and Alfred Meyer, *The Incompatible Allies* (New York, 1953), p. 336.

[94] The ideological blinders rested on a worldview that entirely discounted Hitler's focus on Lebensraum (living space) in the east.

[95] Winston S. Churchill, *The Second World War*, vol. 3, *The Grand Alliance* (Boston, 1950), p. 370.

brutish masses of the Hun soldiery plodding on like a swarm of crawling locusts . . .

We have but one aim and one single, irrevocable purpose. We are resolved to destroy Hitler and every vestige of the Nazi regime. . . . Any man or state who fights on against Nazidom will have our aid. That is our policy and that is our declaration. It follows, therefore, that we shall give whatever help we can to Russia and the Russian people.

The Russian danger is, therefore, our danger, and the danger of the United States, just as the cause of the Russian fighting for his hearth and home is the cause of free men and free peoples in every quarter of the globe.[96]

However, the most crucial piece in Churchill's puzzle of grand strategy was the United States and the extent to which he could persuade the Americans, and particularly their president, to support a greatly weakened Britain. Considering that most Americans, including virtually all of the nation's military experts, believed the German onslaught would soon overwhelm the British, this presented a major challenge. Nevertheless, whatever the difficulties in dealing with an American polity that remained greatly divided, Churchill plowed ahead with his usual enthusiasm and political skill.

From the first moments after he had assumed the position of First Lord of the Admiralty on 3 September 1939, Churchill had tested the waters by communicating directly with the American president, Franklin Delano Roosevelt.[97] There is no doubt that the American president was pro-Allied. Almost immediately after the outbreak of the war, he had loosened the strings attached to the neutrality laws that Congress had passed in the mid-1930s. Nevertheless, the president found himself with only limited options. A substantial portion of the American people remained convinced that isolationism was the best course for the United States. Confronting a national election in the immediate future (November 1940), the president was a lame duck because no other president had run for a third term, and only the extraordinary crisis of summer 1940 produced by the fall of France caused the president to change his mind about running for president again.

One might best describe Roosevelt by that wonderful phrase that Churchill used to describe the Soviets: "a riddle wrapped in an enigma." The great American jurist Oliver Wendell Holmes quite correctly described the president, after first meeting him, as possessing "a second class intellect, but first

[96] Ibid., pp. 371–73.
[97] For the Churchill-Roosevelt relationship, see, among others; Warren F. Kimball, *Roosevelt, Churchill, and the Second World War* (London, 2003); Warren F. Kimball, ed., *Churchill and Roosevelt: The Complete Correspondence* (Princeton, NJ, 1987); Joseph P. Lash, *Roosevelt and Churchill, 1939–1941* (New York, 1980); and most recently, Andrew Roberts, *Masters and Commanders: How Churchill, Roosevelt, Alanbrooke, and Marshall Won the War in the West, 1941–1945* (London, 2008).

class character." The president himself played his cards close to his chest – so much so that historians today with access to all the relevant American documents still have difficulty reconstructing exactly what Roosevelt's position was on certain matters or when he actually decided to act. Roosevelt now acted at the crucial moment of the May–June period. Admittedly, the United States was in no position to do anything to aid the French, whose appeals steadily increased in number and desperation as the tide of defeat swept over northern France.

But the collapse of France presented Roosevelt with the frightening strategic possibility that the United States might find itself confronting an entire European continent under German control. Particularly worrisome to American strategists was the possibility that not only the French Navy but also the Royal Navy might fall into the hands of the Nazis, a possibility which would turn the balance of global naval power against the United States.

Thus, as the French situation deteriorated, Churchill and Roosevelt began a delicate dance, Churchill wanting a commitment of American military, financial, and economic support; Roosevelt deeply worried about the fate of the Royal Navy. Unlike the desperate French, Churchill recognized that for the immediate future, U.S. military support could not be direct but would come only in terms of equipment – equipment desperately needed by British ground forces in the post-Dunkirk period and by British naval forces facing a vastly increased threat from German U-boats that soon would possess bases on the coast of Brittany closer to the great Atlantic trade routes than those of the Royal Navy.

For their part, most American military analysts believed that Britain had little chance against Nazi Germany's military might, nor were many Americans convinced that the British would not do another deal with the Germans, as they had done in 1938.[98] In his messages to the president, Churchill played on these American fears. Yes, it was his intention to resist to the bitter end. Yes, his government firmly believed that it could halt the Germans. Nevertheless, the prime minister made clear that he might not remain in charge in Britain and that he could not guarantee what a successor government would do with the fleet.

The dance ended toward the end of June. Roosevelt signaled that Britain could count on American financial and economic aid.[99] At that point, Churchill provided his own signal to Roosevelt. He ordered the Royal Navy to eliminate the strategic threat presented by the Vichy-controlled French

---

[98] And the Americans may well have picked up the rumblings of dissent among the diehard appeasers that it would be foolish for Britain to fight to the end – a message that undoubtedly resonated with the American ambassador in London, Joe Kennedy, who had fully supported such a line.

[99] See, among others, Martin Gilbert, *Winston S. Churchill*, vol. 6, *Finest Hour, 1939–1941* (Boston, 1983).

Navy to the United States as well as Britain. In a meeting with the French
naval attaché shortly before the armistice, Admiral Dudley Pound, First Sea
Lord, had commented:

> The one object we had in view was winning the war and . . . it was as essential
> for them [the French] as for us that we should do so. . . . All trivialities, such as
> questions of friendship . . . must be swept away.[100]

And that is precisely what happened. On the morning of 5 July 1940, the
Royal Navy's Force H from Gibraltar arrived off the great French naval base
of Mers-el-Kebir on the North African coast. The British admiral presented
the French commander with a set of conditions, some more reasonable
than others. The latter refused, and the battleships of Force H opened fire.
When the shooting stopped, the British had sunk the battleship *Bretagne* and
heavily damaged the battleships *Dunkerque* and *Provence*. The total cost of
the merciless attack was 1,300 French sailors killed. The message was clear
to everyone except the Germans: Britain was in the war to the bitter end.[101]

Roosevelt certainly understood the message. By the end of the summer,
the Anglo-American link had solidified to the extent that the Americans had
shipped tens of thousands of "surplus" rifles to Britain, despite the needs
of a U.S. Army that itself confronted the task of equipping and training
the first peacetime conscripted force in American history. A destroyer-for-
bases deal allowed the Americans to build crucial naval and air bases in
Newfoundland, Bermuda, and the British West Indies in return for badly
needed additional escorts for British convoys. Most important, the United
States promised to support Britain financially. That assurance represented
a crucial contribution because Britain had virtually exhausted its currency
reserves and by late fall would no longer be able to satisfy the cash-and-carry
provisions of America's neutrality legislation. These were only the first steps
the Americans would take in supporting the British armament effort. In
March 1941, Roosevelt signed into law the Lend-Lease Act, often described
in somewhat exaggerated terms as the most unsordid act in history but
certainly an act that acknowledged the larger common interests of Britain
and the United States.

In his memoirs of the Second World War, Churchill records his profound
happiness at the news of Pearl Harbor, which meant that the United States
was now in the war:

> No American will think it wrong of me if I proclaim that to have the United
> States at our side was to me the greatest joy. I could not foretell the course

---

[100] PRO ADM 205/4, undated and unsigned memorandum, but the language and discussion
indicates that the discussion took place in mid-June 1940.
[101] For a discussion of the issues involved and the course of the action, see Captain S. W.
Roskill, *The War at Sea*, vol. 1, *Defense* (London, 1954), pp. 242–45, 314.

of events. I do not pretend to have measured accurately the martial might of Japan, but now at this very moment I knew that the United States was in the war, up to the neck and in to the death. So we had won after all! Yes, after Dunkirk; after the fall of France; after the horrible episode of [Mers-el-Kebir]; after the threat of invasion, when apart from the Air and the Navy, we were an almost unarmed people; after the deadly struggle of the U-boat war – the first Battle of the Atlantic, gained by a hands-breadth; after seventeen months of lonely fighting and nineteen months of my responsibility in dire stress, we had won the war. England would live; Britain would live. How long the war would last, or in what fashion it would end, no man could tell, nor did I at that moment care. Once again in our long Island history we should emerge, however mauled or mutilated, safe and victorious. We should not be wiped out. Our history would not come to an end.[102]

Churchill was right, of course, but he now confronted the problem that working with allies presented a huge strain on Britain's overstretched industrial and military resources. Already in the last half of 1941, Britain had added to the enormous overstretch of its military forces by beginning to ship military equipment to the Soviets, to whom the United States already was diverting a portion of its Lend-Lease shipments. Those diversions, especially of Hurricane fighters to Russia, may well have contributed to the disaster that overwhelmed British forces in Malaya and Burma.[103]

In a speech to Parliament on 10 November 1942, Churchill commented that he had not become prime minister "to preside over the liquidation of the British Empire." In effect, however, defeats in early 1942 at the hands of Japanese forces in Malaya and Burma sealed the fate of the British Empire. Above all, it was British statesmen's and military leaders' underestimation of their enemy that contributed mightily to those humiliating defeats. The Japanese had proven that the Europeans possessed no innate superiority over the peoples of Asia – the belief that, more than anything else, had enabled the British to rule their empire with such minuscule numbers of civil servants and military forces. That belief had allowed the British to control a vast conglomeration of territories, which, in aggregate, had made little strategic sense.

In Europe, Stalin proved a thoroughly difficult ally in every respect. Almost from the beginning of the German invasion, the Soviets screamed for the British to open up a second front in France, a second front which, of course,

[102] Winston S. Churchill, *The Second World War*, vol. 3, *The Grand Alliance* (Boston, 1950), pp. 606–7.
[103] Nevertheless one must note that British military incompetence in defending Malaya and Burma was such that one wonders whether the British commanders in Southeast Asia could have held Singapore whatever the extent of the reinforcements they received. For a discussion of British problems in this area, see Williamson Murray, "British Military Effectiveness," in *Military Effectiveness*, vol. 3, *The Second World War*, ed. Allan R. Millett and Williamson Murray (London, 1988).

they themselves had done so much to destroy in 1940 by their inaction. The Communists in the West, aided by large numbers of well-meaning fellow travelers – most of whom would not have to fight the Germans – then echoed Moscow's line. But there was going to be no second front until Allied naval forces, mostly British and Canadian, had won the Battle of the Atlantic, and victory over the U-boats would not come until May 1943.[104] Nor was air superiority to be won over the Continent until May 1944, while the United States would not reach its full military potential much earlier. Nevertheless, in May 1942, in one of his more unguarded moments, Roosevelt actually promised Molotov that the Western powers would launch a second front that year, a promise of which Churchill had to fly to Moscow to disabuse the Soviets.

Meanwhile, whatever aid the Allies gave to the Soviets in their nightmarish fight against the Wehrmacht on the Eastern Front, it was never enough. For Churchill and Roosevelt, the military choices were daunting. Many Americans expected the war against Japan to receive priority at least equal to Europe – a fact that made it exceedingly difficult for the Roosevelt administration to pursue its Germany-first strategy. The British themselves were mounting what was, from their perspective, a major campaign in Burma. The combined bomber offensive against Germany was revealing a voracious appetite for resources.[105]

The Mediterranean was already a major theater of operations requiring the Allies to complete the defeat of Italy simply to open up the SLOCs (sea lines of communication) to Allied shipping and thereby relieve some of the tension on worldwide shipping shortages. And the SLOCs themselves were under dangerous assault by the German U-boat fleet. As Churchill notes in his memoirs: "The only thing that ever really frightened me during the war was the U-boat peril."[106] Fears that the Soviets might cut a deal with the Germans remained real (and justified) among Anglo-American political leaders; thus, Lend-Lease to the Russians remained a major priority. Finally, the Anglo-American Allies had to mount the great invasion of the Continent, the most ambitious amphibious operation ever to take place in history.

Yet, through all these terrible times, Britain remained a democracy. In early 1942, Churchill even confronted a vote of no confidence resulting

---

[104] For a short examination of the longest campaign in the Second World War, which lasted from 3 September 1939, through VE Day in May 1945, see Murray and Millett, *A War to Be Won*, chap. 10.

[105] We now know from the economic analysis of Adam Tooze that the Combined Bomber Offensive, especially Bomber Command's spring 1943 massive attack on the cities and the industrial plant of the Ruhr, began exercising a crucial impact on German war production in the first half of 1943 that severely retarded the ability of the Third Reich to supply its military forces. Tooze, *Wages of Destruction*, pp. 590–611.

[106] Churchill, *The Second World War*, vol. 2, *Their Finest Hour*, p. 598.

from the disasters in the Far East as well as the difficulties British armed forces were confronting in North Africa and in the Battle of the Atlantic. The pressures on the British people were almost overwhelming, considering the burden they were carrying in waging battles across the globe. A report from the senior levels of the bureaucracy in 1944 suggested the strains on the home front:

> The British civilian has had five years of blackout and four years of intermittent blitz. The privacy of his home has been periodically invaded by soldiers or evacuees or war workers requiring billets. In five years of drastic labor mobilization, nearly every man and every woman under fifty without young children has been subject to direction to work, often far from home. The hours of work average fifty-three for men and fifty overall; when work is done every citizen who is not excused for reasons of family circumstances, work, etc., has had to do forty-eight hours a month duty in the Home Guard or Civil Defense. Supplies of all kind have been progressively limited by shipping and manpower shortage; the queue is a part of normal life. Taxation is probably the severest in the world, and is coupled with continuous pressure to save. The scarce supplies, both of goods and services, must be shared with hundreds of thousands of United States, Dominion, and Allied troops; in the preparation of Britain first as the base and then as the bridgehead, the civilian has inevitably suffered hardships spread over almost every aspect of his daily life.[107]

There was no greater servant of British grand strategy than Churchill's eloquent speeches that kept popular morale up not only in the initial dark times but also in the long slog through to victory.

As the war continued, Britain's influence in the coalition slowly but steadily diminished. In 1942 and early 1943, the British were able to exercise an influence equal with the Americans in the decisions about the tough choices that the Allies had to make. By 1944 that was no longer the case; Britain was now clearly the junior partner. In every respect, America's power became overwhelming. What little influence the British exercised over Stalin and his murderous thugs in 1941 and early 1942 rapidly melted away as the Soviets began to overwhelm their German opponents on the Eastern Front. However, unlike his American allies, as the war unfolded, Churchill turned his attention to the postwar world. In that world, the behavior of the Soviets convinced him, Stalin would represent a real danger. But there was little Churchill could do in that respect as long as the Americans looked at the Soviet Union through rose-tinted glasses.

---

[107] Quoted in W. K. Hancock and M. M. Gowing, *British War Economy* (London, 1949), p. 519.

Thus, one can argue that by 1943, Britain was well on the way to becoming a second-class power with little chance of exercising an independent grand strategy. And yet, through Churchill's stewardship, Britain had survived with her values largely intact, a monumental achievement considering her situation in June 1940.

CONCLUSION

The aims of British grand strategy for both the Chamberlain and Churchill governments were in fact the same: the survival of the empire and Britain's position as a great nation. Inherent in such aims was obviously the survival of Britain as an independent, sovereign power. Both confronted the reality of overstretch: the economic, political, and military defense of an empire that faced three distinctly different strategic threats to its territories as well as an economy constrained by the impact of a worldwide depression that had significantly impaired Britain's industrial base.

But if both saw the same problem, their solutions were extraordinarily different, reflecting above all their understanding of and reactions to the past. For Chamberlain, the fundamental basis of international relations in the 1930s was a belief that the world was inhabited by reasonable human beings. Thus, there was no excuse for threatening to use, much less using, military force in the international arena. The corollary was that as a consequence, Britain need only spend the minimum on defense because diplomacy and understanding would remove the danger of strategic confrontations leading to war. One must admit that all approaches to grand strategy must, to a certain extent, rest on assumptions, but leaders must be prepared to adapt those assumptions to the realities they actually confront. Chamberlain adapted only late in the game, when it was almost too late. Halifax, as his arguments in the cabinet in late May underlined, never adapted but luckily met more than his match in Chamberlain's successor.

On the other hand, with his deep historical understanding, Churchill recognized almost immediately the uncompromising nature of the German threat. Ironically, that he remained out of power with no ministerial portfolio in the 1930s allowed him the political freedom in May 1940 to reverse British grand strategy in terms of its understanding of the international arena and of the need for the ruthless use of military force when national survival was at stake.[108] In difficult times, when it is most important, grand strategy demands leadership and political astuteness. It demands the willingness to

---

[108] In September 1939, an RAF officer had taken a proposal to one of Chamberlain's senior ministers that the RAF use incendiaries to set the Black Forest afire. In retrospect, it was a thoroughly unrealistic proposal, but that was not why the minister objected. He objected because much of the Black Forest was private property!

recognize the "other" for what he is, whatever the unpalatable response that recognition may require. It demands a willingness to adapt the path and the means to the effort required. Especially in a democratic state, it demands the ability to convey a convincing and intelligent narrative to its citizens. In all these respects, Churchill measured up as a great strategist.

7

Toward a strategy: Creating an American strategy for global war, 1940–1943

JAMES LACEY

When, in 1940, German panzers overran France and the Low Countries in a matter of weeks, it was apparent to all but the most obtuse that a tectonic shift in the global strategic situation had occurred. With France out of the war, Britain stood alone against the overwhelming might of Germany with seemingly little chance of surviving the Luftwaffe's onslaught. America, however, was slow to formulate a grand strategy. Even though President Franklin Delano Roosevelt fully recognized the extent of the change, he remained constrained by the domestic politics of the United States.

Roosevelt was running for an unprecedented third term in 1940 with the promise that American boys would not die in foreign wars. In spite of his public stand, he took the extraordinarily dangerous step of providing significant military aid to Churchill's beleaguered government, military aid that America's own military forces desperately needed and that could only be released by a declaration that such equipment was surplus to U.S. needs – a declaration that his service chiefs were loath to make, especially considering how bare their cupboards were. And even after Roosevelt had won the election, he still confronted a large, active, and politically influential movement dedicated to ensuring the United States would remain out of the conflict.

It was, therefore, an already worried Roosevelt who, while resting from campaign exertions on aboard the USS *Tuscaloosa* in the Caribbean, received what amounted to a plaintive plea from Prime Minister Winston Churchill for as much military material as possible. Moreover, Britain, on the verge

Segments of this essay are adapted from the author's forthcoming book *Keep from All Thoughtful Men*, scheduled for publication in 2010 by the U.S. Naval Institute Press.

of financial bankruptcy, wished to have this material on the easiest terms possible. As Churchill wrote to the president:

> The moment approaches when we shall no longer be able to pay cash for shipping and other supplies. . . . I believe you will agree that it would be wrong in principle and mutually disadvantageous in effect if at the height of this struggle, Great Britain were to be divested of all saleable assets, so that after the victory was won with our blood, civilization saved, and the time gained for the United States to be fully armed against all eventualities, we should be stripped to the bone.[1]

For several days, Roosevelt mulled over his options. What he came up with startled even his closest aides. As the Neutrality Act forbade just giving the United Kingdom what it needed to continue prosecuting the war, Roosevelt instead decided to "loan" the British what they required. That Britain would never return the proffered equipment, nor would America want it back at war's end, appears never to have been seriously considered, even by those who opposed the plan.

In his own folksy way, Roosevelt sold his Lend-Lease proposal to the American people by explaining that a person does not charge his neighbor for the use of a garden hose if the neighbor's house is on fire. Over the next weeks and months, while continuing to promise to keep America out of the war, Roosevelt sold the American people on the idea that the United States was to become the vast "arsenal of democracy" that would save the world. In spite of having to cope with vicious opposition, such as that of Senator Burton Wheeler, who claimed that helping Britain would eventually lead to seeing "every fourth American boy plowed under," Roosevelt was able to bring the greater mass of the American people to his side.

The president was, of course, aided immensely by Churchill's eloquent words broadcast and reported extensively to the American people as well as to the population of the United Kingdom and the Dominions. As the prime minister reiterated at the height of the German Blitz in August 1940:

> These cruel, wanton, indiscriminate bombings of London are, of course, a part of Hitler's invasion plans. He hopes by killing large numbers of civilians, and women and children, that he will terrorize and cow the people of this mighty imperial city, and make them a burden to the Government and thus distract our attention unduly from the ferocious onslaught he is preparing. Little does he know the spirit of the British nation, or the tough fibre of the Londoners. . . .
>
> This wicked man, the repository of many forms of soul-destroying hatreds, this monstrous product of former wrongs and shame, has now resolved to try to break our famous Island race by a process of indiscriminate slaughter and

---

[1] James MacGregor Burns, *Roosevelt: The Soldier of Freedom* (New York, 1970), p. 13.

destruction. What he has done is kindle a fire in British hearts and all over the world, which will glow long after all traces of the conflagration he has caused... have been removed.[2]

The president understood that the United States could not postpone its entry into the war indefinitely. And even though the tide of public opinion was swinging vehemently against the Axis powers, convincing the American people to enter into the global conflict was still going to require a herculean political effort. Roosevelt was willing to make that effort, but he fully understood the political parameters within which he had to operate. Thus, he was never willing or able to get far out in front of popular opinion. He would shape that opinion as best he could, but when Roosevelt took any measure that increased the belligerent stance of the United States, he first made certain the great majority of the American people were beside or immediately behind him. If the Americans had never gotten to the point where they were prepared to take the final step into the conflict, it is unlikely that Roosevelt would have taken it for them or pushed them into it.

THE JOINT CHIEFS CRAFT A STRATEGY

As Roosevelt worked his political magic, he encouraged both the military and industry to begin planning and preparations for eventual war. Before the 1940 election determined whether Roosevelt would get his unprecedented third term, the military chiefs of the United States were already reappraising their strategy for global war. In September 1939, when Germany had first unleashed its panzers on a hapless Poland, the United States had remained in a strategic haze. Despite years of witnessing the rise of Nazi power and the growing hostility of Japan, U.S. military planners had continued working on a series of outdated color-coded war plans. Among these was Plan Red, which detailed how America would conduct a war against Britain and Canada – a plan not rescinded until after the European war broke out. The most famous of these plans, War Plan Orange, called on the American fleet to marshal off the California coast and then transit the Pacific to engage the Japanese Imperial Fleet in a decisive battle in its own home waters. Other operative war plans included Plan Lemon, war with Portugal; Plan Emerald, an invasion of Ireland; Plan Citron, war with Brazil; and Plan Green, war with Mexico.

However, U.S. strategic direction began to change when the chief of naval operations, Admiral Harold R. Stark, examined the situation and became convinced that Japan was not America's most dangerous enemy. Therefore, he believed, America's entire war-fighting concept was wrong. In early

---

2   Quoted in Martin Gilbert, *Winston S. Churchill*, vol. 6, *Finest Hour, 1939–1941* (Boston, 1983), p. 779.

November 1940, he produced a draft memorandum, which he forwarded to army chief of staff General George C. Marshall for review and concurrence before presenting it to the secretary of the navy.[3] The central point of Stark's analysis was the recognition that American security depended on the fate of Britain. In his opening assertion, Stark stated, "If Britain wins decisively against Germany, we could win everywhere; but that if she loses the problems confronting us would be very great; and while we might not *lose everywhere*, we might, possibly, not *win* anywhere."

The subtext of Stark's memorandum was that Imperial Japan had no hope of defeating the United States in any conflict. Marshall, whose strategic thoughts were still forming, found himself largely in agreement.[4] For Stark, the consequences of a British defeat would be so serious for America that the United States ought to assist Britain in every way possible. Stark also made it clear that he did not believe Britain had the manpower or material to conquer Germany. Thus, it would take direct U.S. military assistance to gain ultimate victory.[5]

In a passage certain to align his thinking with Marshall's, Stark declared, "The only certain way of defeating Germany is by military success on shore and for that, bases close to the European continent would be required."[6] A June 1940 conference between the two men solidified their agreement on a major turn in U.S. strategy. During the conference, Marshall posed the larger strategic question: how would the United States meet simultaneous threats in both the Atlantic and the Pacific? He then answered his own question: "Are we not forced into reframing our naval policy, into one that is purely defensive in the Pacific, with the main effort in the Atlantic?"[7]

America, in Stark's estimation, had to choose between four major strategic options, which he stated as questions:

A. Shall our principal military effort be directed toward hemisphere defense, and include chiefly those activities within the Western Hemisphere which contribute directly to security against attack in either or both oceans?

B. Shall we prepare for a full offensive against Japan, premised on assistance from the British and Dutch forces in the Far East, and remain on the strict defensive in the Atlantic?

---

[3]   Mitchell Simpson, *Harold R. Stark: Architect of Victory, 1939–1945* (Columbia, SC, 1989), p. 66.

[4]   Plan Dog Case File, FDR Library, Safe Files, Hyde Park, New York.

[5]   Louis Morton, *Command Decisions: Germany First: The Basic Concept of Allied Strategy in World War II* (Washington, 2000), p. 235.

[6]   Lawrence Guyer, "The Joint Chiefs and the War Against Germany," an unpublished manuscript which was meant to be a volume in an official history of the joint chiefs of staff. A copy can be found in the National Archives, Record Group 218.2.2.

[7]   Ibid.

C. Shall we plan for sending the strongest possible military assistance both
to the British in Europe, and to the British, Dutch and Chinese in the Far
East?

D. Shall we direct our efforts toward an eventual strong offensive in the
Atlantic as an ally of the British, and a defensive in the Pacific?[8]

As far as Stark was concerned, there was no doubt that option D was
superior to the others (option D is what gave the plan its name, *dog* being
the letter *D* in American military parlance).[9] As he further argued: "I believe
that the continued existence of the British Empire, combined with building
up a strong protection in our home areas, will do most to ensure the status
quo in the Western Hemisphere, and to promote our principal national
interests."[10]

On November 12, 1940, Stark forwarded the plan, with Marshall's concurrence, to Frank Knox, Secretary of the Navy. Knox immediately forwarded it to the White House. There is no record that Roosevelt ever
approved the plan, but from Marshall's and Stark's perspective, what was
important was that the president did not disapprove it. Knowing that Roosevelt had just won an election by promising to stay out of the war, both officers realized he could not officially comment on the memorandum. However,
knowing that the president was never slow to demolish an idea with which he
did not find favor, the two senior American military leaders took his silence
as tacit approval.[11] In retrospect, they had drawn the correct conclusion.

Soon thereafter, Roosevelt approved secret meetings between the American chiefs of staff and their British counterparts. When the first session
of American–British–Canadian (ABC) staff talks got under way on 29 January, 1941, Plan Dog became the basis for agreement among the putative
allies, an agreement which was essentially retitled ABC-1.[12] This agreement,
later integrated into the navy and joint Rainbow 5 Plan, placed Germany at
the center of Allied efforts and became the foundation stone for all subsequent discussions about grand strategy among the Americans and the British
throughout the remainder of the war.[13]

[8] Ibid.
[9] According to Guyer's unpublished history, *The Joint Chiefs and the War in Europe*, the
first drafts of this document had five choices: "(1) war with Japan, in which we have no
allies; (2) war with Japan with the British Empire and the Netherlands as allies; (3) war
with Japan in which she is aided by Italy and we have no allies; (4) war with Germany and
Italy in which Japan would not be initially involved and in which we would be allied with
the British; (5) remaining out of the war and dedicating ourselves exclusively to building
up our defense of the western hemisphere, plus continued material support to Britain."
[10] Ibid.
[11] Simpson, *Harold R. Stark*, p. 72.
[12] "United States–British Staff Conversation Report, ABC-1, March 27, 1941," in Stephen
Ross, *War Plans* (London, 2002), pp. 67–101.
[13] Ibid., pp. 68–69.

Although by early 1941, the United States had cast a new strategic conception of how it would fight a future global war, the planners had yet to match that strategy against national resources and capabilities. It was not until 9 July, 1941 that Roosevelt, heeding the pleas of his industrial mobilization planners, demanded that the secretaries of war and the navy conduct a thorough study to determine exactly what victory in a global war against Germany, Japan, and Italy would require in terms of munitions and equipment. The president also directed the services that these numbers be sufficiently firm so that industrial planners could accurately estimate how much industrial capacity the war effort would require from the American economy.[14]

THE LOGISTICAL SINEWS OF STRATEGY

The response, forwarded to the White House on 11 September 1941, fell short of what Roosevelt had asked for. The strategic plan was, as Roosevelt surely expected, a rewritten version of the Plan Dog memo he had tacitly approved ten months before. As for the munitions and material estimates, the industrial planners judged them as entirely worthless. In fact, those estimates all had to be laboriously redone by an almost unknown economist and statistician, Stacy May, who had recently been brought into government service. What May came up with was the Victory Program, which was to guide U.S. military and industrial strategy throughout the war.

The preceding assertion is sure to make anyone versed in the popular history of World War II mobilization pause. An accurate assessment of grand strategy is often a matter of details. The crucial supporting structure in the development of American grand strategy in World War II had to do with the ability of the United States to (1) project its military power across two great oceans, (2) support two great strategic bombing offensives, (3) create a massive ship-building effort, (4) create massive amphibious and ground forces for both theatres, and (5) provide massive military and economic aid to America's allies. All these operational campaigns, which reflected America's grand strategy for the conduct of the war, thus depended on how effectively and efficiently the United States was able to mobilize its economic potential to support those efforts.

Thus, at this point, it is important to take a short detour to correct one of the more enduring myths of World War II – that Major Albert Wedemeyer wrote the Victory Program. Every history of World War II that takes the time to mention what became known as the Victory Program credits Wedemeyer as it sole author. The basis of this belief lies in a fourteen-page document,

---

[14]   Joint Board Estimates of United States Over-All Production Requirements, FDR Library, Safe Files, Hyde Park, New York.

The Ultimate Requirements Study: Estimate of Army Ground Forces, which
Wedemeyer completed in early September 1941.

At first appearance, it is unlikely that many historians, if any, have ever
bothered to read that document. For if they had, they surely would have
noted it was wrong in almost every one of its particulars.[15] Moreover,
one searches in vain for documents, memos, or letters produced during the
war that reference Wedemeyer's program.[16] In modern terms, Wedemeyer's
version of the Victory Program is analogous to any one of hundreds of
PowerPoint presentations given to Pentagon audiences every month – over
in an hour and just as quickly forgotten.

Churchill's comment that "history would be kind to him because he
intended to write it" was not lost on Wedemeyer. In the aftermath of the Second World War, the latter carefully, patiently, and thoroughly wrote himself
into the historical narrative step by step over the course of 50 years. As a
result, historians have generally accepted that what Wedemeyer called his
Victory Program was central to America's planning in World War II. In reality, Wedemeyer's claims were a scam perpetuated on the history community
for over six decades.

In reality, the estimates for which the industrial planners begged throughout 1940 and 1941 were either not forthcoming or so wildly inaccurate
as to be worthless. Economist Robert Nathan later outlined some of the
frustrations the production people confronted:

> We were trying to find out what the military requirements would be under
> varying assumptions and circumstances so we could have a basis for planning
> what raw materials, what factories, what machinery, what tools and what
> components we would need for the production of armaments. First I went to
> the army and the navy. When I asked them about military requirements, they
> asked 'are we preparing for a land war, a sea war, or an air war, a defensive
> war on the U.S. continent?' I was not in any more of a position to tell them
> what kind of war to prepare for than I was to tell them how to build a bomber

15 An early copy of this document can be found in the Wedemeyer Papers, Box 76, Hoover
Institute, Stanford University. It has been reprinted in Charles E. Kirkpatrick, *An Unknown
Future and a Doubtful Present: Writing the Victory Plan of 1941* (Washington, DC,
1992).

16 There is not a single copy to be found in any of the records of the Office of Production
Management, the War Production Board, or FDR's war files, nor is it mentioned in any of
the early histories of these organizations or their successors. In short, there is no evidence
that any civilian with a major role to play in military production was even aware it existed.
Furthermore, although the Wedemeyer Papers indicate a copy was sent to Secretary of
War Henry Stimson, no record of it can be found in any of Stimson's papers, and his
only mention of Wedemeyer in his autobiography is in reference to operations in China.
Moreover, there appears to be no copy of the document in General Brehon Somervell's
(head of army supply forces) papers or in the papers of Undersecretary of War Robert
Patterson, who was responsible for all army procurement.

or a tank. There seemed to be no way to get those requirements because they indicated that such numbers did not exist.

I remember asking them: 'What are your varying assumptions about defense? You must have some assumptions and some lists of quantities of weapons and planes and ships needed under varied assumptions.' They said, 'We have no estimates of requirements under varying assumptions. If you tell us how many tanks you want, we have tables of allowances and can tell you how many tons of steel or how many pounds of this or that go into a tank, but we do not know whether this is to be a one-million-man army or a ten-million-man army.' I then said, 'Give us the requirements for a one-million-man, and a five-million-man, and a ten-million-man army.' Their reply was: 'We are not going to do all of that work unless we have some indication of what kind of prospective hostilities we will face.'[17]

Despairing of receiving a requirements list from either the war or navy departments, the production organizations took matters into their own hands. May, an economist/statistician working with the supplies production and allocations board (SPAB), became so incensed with the poor quality of the military estimates that he created his own.[18] By using a guess that the country would need a 2,000,000-man army by the end of 1942, May created a template for a functioning army based on that number and then determined if there were sufficient raw materials and industrial capacity to build such a force.

After completing that study, May received permission to go to Britain and make the same assessment of that country's needs and its capability to meet them. The combined tallies made for a 35-pound book that became known as "The Anglo-American Consolidated Statement."[19] If it had not been for Wedemeyer's clouding of the historical record, it would be known today as the true Victory Program.

On his return from London with the "Consolidated Balance Sheet," May undertook to determine the feasibility of asking American industry to produce all of what a global war required. May and his team completed this study in early December 1941, and what they found was extraordinary: *the United States could complete the entire military program as then outlined by military sources no earlier than spring 1944.*[20] In short, three days

---

[17] Robert Nathan, "GNP and Military Mobilization," *Journal of Evolutionary Economics* (April 1994), p. 12.

[18] SPAB began life as the national defense advisory commission and was later to transition into the Office of Production Management. The history and complex evolution of the multitude of organizations created to manage the economic side of the war is well covered in Paul A. C. Koistinen, *Arsenal of World War II: The Political Economy of American Warfare, 1940–1945* (Lawrence, KS, 2004).

[19] W. K. Hancock and M. M. Gowing, *British War Economy* (London, 1949), p. 385.

[20] Memorandum from Stacy May to Donald Nelson, "Feasibility of the Victory Program," National Archives, Planning Committee Document, Records Group 179, Box 1.

before the United States entered the war, a small number of key economists and statisticians within the war planning boards already knew exactly how much of the military and other material called for by the current Victory Plan estimates the economy of the United States could produce and when it would be available.

Thus, all the planning by the joint chiefs and their respective staffs to launch Allied forces onto the European Continent in 1942 or 1943 represented nothing more than a pipe dream. The military could concoct all the plans it liked for its hoped-for invasion of Europe in 1943, but the economists could have told them in December 1941 that the forces they planned for would not be there.

Not that the military was initially prepared to accept the word of mere economists and statisticians that it could not have all that it desired. In fact, for the first half of 1942, the army, following the orders of General Brehon Somervell, chief of the army's service of supply, continued to make munitions demands far beyond American industry's ability to meet them. May, now joined by economist Robert Nathan and future Nobel laureate Simon Kuznets, continued arguing that, asked for more than it was capable of producing, industry actually would produce less than the optimal amount. But converts to their point of view were slow in coming. Throughout the summer, Kuznets refined May's initial work and crafted what he believed was an airtight argument for the case that the military needed to reduce its munitions demands. In the meantime, Nathan, a first-class political infighter, worked the Washington scene to soften up the opposition.

When Kuznets finally delivered his report, Somervell responded in writing: "To me this is an inchoate mass of words.... I am not impressed with either the character or basis of the judgments expressed in the reports and recommend they be carefully hidden from the eyes of thoughtful men."[21]

An angry Nathan replied back: "In view of the gravity of the problem discussed in these documents, I hesitate to take your memorandum seriously." After his own point-by-point refutation of Somervell's points, Nathan concluded with a blistering attack on Somervell's dismissal of Kuznets's estimates:

> I appreciate your frankness in stating that you are not impressed by the character or basis of judgments expressed in this report. Your conclusion... that these judgments be carefully hidden from the eyes of thoughtful men is a non-sequitur. Also, I am obliged to be frank with you in expressing my disappointment in your reply. The problems discussed are important and their intelligent consideration is urgent. The author of the documents is recognized nationally as one of the ablest and soundest authorities on our national economy and upon its ability to

---

[21] As reproduced in Brigante, "The Feasibility Dispute: Determination of War Production Objectives for 1942–1943." This letter is reproduced in its entirety in Appendix 5.

produce for peace or war. I think it would be most unwise to bar these problems, which have been given careful consideration by the staff and members of the Planning Committee, from people who have responsibility for the success of the war effort and the welfare of this country.

The climax came in a showdown between Somervell and Nathan in two well-attended meetings of the War Production Board on 6 October and 13 October 1942. After the most violent confrontation anyone on the board could remember, one in which Somervell was subjected to public and personally insulting scolding by the head of the Office of Price Administration, Leon Henderson, Somervell and the other military representatives finally conceded that May, Kuznets, and Nathan were correct.

Despite conceding that the army's munitions program needed to be cut by almost a third, and agreeing that the joint chiefs be so informed, Somervell hesitated to inform Marshall about the size and significance of the cuts. It was not until the eve of the Casablanca Conference in January 1943 that Marshall learned what the economists had known for a year: the army he counted on to invade Northern Europe in 1943 would not be available until mid-1944. This knowledge was to have a profound impact on how Marshall approached discussions with the combined chiefs and on his conception of how the war needed to be fought.

Crafting a military strategy

As the economists and the army's logistical experts debated the availability of the "sinews of war," the Joint Chiefs and Roosevelt began crafting the strategy for winning the war. Soon after the attack on Pearl Harbor, Churchill and his military chiefs arrived in the United States aboard the battleship *Duke of York* for a prolonged series of discussions.[22] In what became known as the Arcadia Conference, which lasted from mid-December until mid-January 1942, the Allies formally affirmed both the ABC-1 Conference's identification of Germany as the primary enemy and that the most efficient means to defeat the Third Reich was a Continental invasion (although the route was still open for debate).

According to the conference minutes, the combined chiefs recognized that no large-scale offensive against Germany was possible in the immediate future, although they kept open the possibility of a 1942 invasion in the event of a German collapse. Unaware that the production experts had already calculated that it would be impossible to deliver all the military equipment and forces requested for an invasion of the Continent by summer 1943, the chiefs also agreed that 1943 presented the optimal time for a Continental

---

[22] The *Duke of York* was the sister ship of the *Prince of Wales*, which the Japanese had just sunk off Malaya.

invasion. The record further stated that this invasion would be a prelude to
a final assault on Germany itself and went so far as to direct that the Victory
Program "be such as to provide the means by which this can be carried
out."[23]

After the Arcadia Conference, Marshall ordered his chief planner, Briga-
dier General Dwight D. Eisenhower, to prepare a strategic plan focused on
the decisive defeat of Germany. On 1 April, Eisenhower presented the basic
outline of this plan, which Marshall approved and then sold to the president.
The plan consisted of three major potential operations:

BOLERO: The buildup of men and material in England for a
cross-channel invasion

ROUNDUP: The actual invasion of northern France, scheduled
to take place in 1943

SLEDGEHAMMER: A smaller invasion of as few as a half-dozen divisions that Allied forces would carry out in 1942 in
the event an imminent Soviet collapse necessitated a
sacrifice to relieve pressure on the Soviets

After receiving the president's approval of the basic concept, Marshall flew
to Britain with Roosevelt's closest advisor Harry Hopkins, to sell the plan to
the British. After several days of consultations, both Marshall and Hopkins
believed they had British support for a 1943 invasion. In a letter to Secretary of War Stimson dated 15 April, 1942, Marshall noted: "Our proposal
was formally accepted after an oral presentation by me and by Hopkins followed by general comments by members and chief of staff. PM in impressive
pronouncement declared complete agreement."[24] Marshall then turned his
attention to SLEDGEHAMMER in 1942, which, in his opinion, the British
had also accepted, if conditions were right.[25]

Almost immediately after Marshall and Hopkins had returned from
London, Anglo-American conceptions for future operations began to
diverge. Toward the end of May, Soviet Foreign Minister Vyacheslav Molotov visited first Britain and then the United States. While Molotov was in
Britain, Churchill told him that a second front remained a priority, but the
prime minister was vague as to the exact date when such an invasion would

---

[23]   "Minutes and Formal Agreements of the Arcadia Conference," held in Washington, D.C.
22 December, 1941–14 January, 1942. A copy of the minutes for all wartime conferences
can be procured from the joint chiefs of staff history office (Pentagon, Alexandria, VA).
Although these files have been digitized, they have not as of yet been posted to the Internet.

[24]   George C. Marshall, *The Papers of George Catlett Marshall*, vol. 3 (Baltimore, MD, 1991),
p. 162 [hereinafter *Marshall Papers*]. Marshall reiterated this comment in a letter to the
president on 18 April, 1942 (*Marshall Papers*, p. 164).

[25]   Robert Sherwood, *Roosevelt and Hopkins: An Intimate History* (New York, 2001),
p. 515.

prove possible. By the time he arrived in the United States, the Soviet foreign minister was ready to press for a more specific commitment, and he found a receptive audience. During a 30 May White House meeting, the president seemed committed to a 1942 cross-Channel invasion. After getting Marshall's assurance that developments were far enough along to ensure Stalin there would soon be a second front, Roosevelt authorized Molotov to inform the Soviet leader that he could expect a second front that year.[26]

Even before this commitment, Marshall and the Joint Chiefs had begun focusing on the possibility of conducting SLEDGEHAMMER in 1942 with the intention of establishing a lodgement on the Cotentin or Brest peninsula, which the Allies would reinforce by a more massive ROUNDUP the following year. The president, who had earlier appeared supportive of Churchill's conception of a North Africa invasion, no longer supported such an operation and was fully supportive of a rapid BOLERO buildup and the launching of SLEDGEHAMMER sooner rather than later – the sooner being as early in 1942 as possible.

By the end of May, the British had become deeply concerned about American ambitions to invade the Continent in 1942. Churchill, alarmed at the emphasis that the American chiefs of staff appeared to be placing on a possible cross-Channel operation in 1942, decided the time had come to cross the Atlantic to determine how matters stood. By early June the British Eighth Army's situation in Africa was rapidly deteriorating, as Colonel General (soon to be field marshal) Erwin Rommel smashed British forces along the Gazalla Line and then advanced toward Tobruk, which soon fell.

The British chiefs, therefore, were hardly eager to commit to a possible, but doubtful, operation on the European continent in fall 1942, especially because it would use troops and equipment desperately needed in Egypt. Moreover, most of the forces that would hazard such a landing on the French coast would be British rather than American. And, thus far in the war, the British had received a number of nasty knocks from the Wehrmacht, while U.S. commanders, planners, and troops had had no combat experience against the Germans. At the same time, the British chiefs felt that some form of invasion of North Africa might be extremely helpful. Moreover, British planners had not succeeded in developing what they considered an acceptable plan for SLEDGEHAMMER.[27]

Roosevelt received Churchill at Hyde Park, New York, in early June 1942 and patiently entertained all of the prime minister's strategic conceptions. Churchill's primary purpose, though, was to convince Roosevelt that even

---

[26] Ibid., p. 535.
[27] Hayes, "The Joint Chiefs and the War against Japan." The British official history of World War II confirms this British position and how the British chiefs came to accept it. See J. M. A. Gwyer and J. R. M. Butler, *Grand Strategy*, vol. 3, *June 1941–August 1942* (London, 1964), pp. 617–24.

a limited operation in 1942 would lead to disaster. Warning Roosevelt that failure would "expose the French people to Nazi vengeance, would not help the Russians and would gravely delay the main operation in 1943," Churchill concluded by arguing that the Allies should not make any substantial landing in France in 1942 unless they were going to stay there.[28]

Right or wrong, Churchill's arguments appealed to Roosevelt, who was always interested in reducing loss of life.[29] By the time the president and prime minister returned to Washington to continue discussions with their military staffs present, the president was half convinced to scrap SLEDGE-HAMMER. By this point, he was beginning to look at North Africa as the first sphere of combat operations for American forces – an idea that had long appealed to him but that was anathema to Marshall and the new chief of naval operations, Ernest J. King.

The reaction of the American chiefs to such an operation was visceral. King utterly opposed a North Africa invasion. He informed the president that the risks already taken in the Pacific to provide for BOLERO had caused him great anxiety and that an invasion of North Africa would render the Pacific situation desperate by requiring the immediate withdrawal of naval forces from the Pacific for redeployment to the Atlantic. Marshall reiterated that opening another front would "achieve nothing" and that from the military point of view, there was "no other logical course," but to concentrate on BOLERO and drive ahead, while diverting only the minimum of forces elsewhere.[30]

Whatever Roosevelt's attachment to a North African invasion might have been, the arguments of his chiefs convinced him once again to support a 1942 invasion of Northern Europe, both in public and in private discussions with Churchill. Ironically, the American debating success was probably due in large part to the prime minister's and his staff's preoccupation with the news that Tobruk had fallen. This was a huge blow to the British, as Tobruk had withstood a year-long siege the year before. Churchill took its rapid collapse this time as hard as he had the humiliating loss of Singapore to Japanese forces in February 1942. When this thunderclap arrived, the conference rapidly shifted from debates over a cross-Channel invasion to determining how best and most rapidly to ship munitions to reinforce the crumbling British position in North Africa.

As Marshall made emergency plans to move hundreds of new Sherman tanks and modern aircraft to Egypt to reinforce the badly battered British Eighth Army, he was content in his belief that this was a temporary diversion of resources now that the British had finally acquiesced to plans for an

---

[28]   Sherwood, *Roosevelt and Hopkins*, p. 565.
[29]   Ibid., p. 567.
[30]   Ibid; section 5, p. 8.

invasion of the Continent in 1943. The full text of that agreement was brief, but it definitely focused everyone's attention on cross-Channel operations by ordering that: "Plans and preparations for the BOLERO operation in 1943 on as large a scale as possible are to be pushed forward with all speed and energy."

The agreement also continued to hold open the option of a 1942 invasion by calling for "The most resolute efforts to overcome the obvious dangers and difficulties of the enterprise." Despite the emphasis on as rapid a return to the Continent as possible, the agreement did leave some hope for undertaking an operation in North Africa by stating that: "all possibilities of Operation GYMNAST [a north African invasion] will be explored carefully and conscientiously." What was crucial was the fact that the Anglo-American agreement called offensive operations in 1942 essential, while recognizing that such action on the Continent was fraught with risk. Thus, the GYMNAST option would inevitably grow in significance throughout the summer.

However, on July 8, the British chiefs of staff dispatched a message to the joint chiefs of staff (JCS) which was to cause one of the most violent JCS reactions in the entire war. Referring to the June agreement, the British pointed out a number of obstacles that made any 1942 Continental invasion impossible and a 1943 invasion unlikely. During the JCS meeting on July 10, Marshall read the dispatch to his fellow chiefs and informed them that the prime minister had forwarded a similar note to the president, in which Churchill concluded with a suggestion that the Americans reconsider the option of a North African invasion.

According to the JCS minutes, Marshall then announced that if the British position must be accepted, he proposed that the United States should turn to the Pacific for decisive action against the Japanese. He added that this would tend to concentrate rather than to scatter U.S. forces; that it would be highly popular throughout the United States, particularly on the West Coast; and that, second only to BOLERO, it would be the operation that would have the greatest effect on relieving pressure on Russia. Not surprisingly, given his Anglophobia and desire to smash the Japanese, Admiral King expressed total agreement with Marshall's proposal.[31]

---

[31] 24th mtg. of JCS, 10 July 1942, National Archives, Record Group 218. In *On Active Service in Peace and War*, McGeorge Bundy began a long-standing debate as to whether this was a serious proposal on Marshall and King's part. According to Bundy's interpretation of Secretary of War Stimson's biography, the proposal "was designed mainly as a plan to bring the British into agreement with Bolero." However, the actual quote from the Stimson Diary gives no indication that this was a ploy (p. 424). As the diary records: "I found Marshall very stirred up and emphatic over it [the British memo rejecting].... As the British won't go through with what they agreed to, we will turn our backs on them and take up the war with Japan." A person planning a ploy is normally not as agitated as Marshall comes across in this description. Moreover, if this plan were a ploy, it would be critical to involve Stimson in it before it went to the president. However, there is no indication in the

A memorandum to this effect was then sent to Roosevelt, detailing the views of the U.S. chiefs. It concluded by stating: "If the United States is to engage in any other operation then forceful, unswerving adherence to full BOLERO plans, we are definitely of the opinion that we should turn to the Pacific and strike decisively against Japan; in other words assume a defensive attitude against Germany, except for air operations, and use all available means in the Pacific."[32]

Roosevelt immediately called the chiefs' bluff. From his family home in Hyde Park, he responded: "That he desired to have dispatched to him at once, by airplane, a comprehensive and detailed outline of the plans for redirecting the major effort of the United States to the war against Japan – including the effect of such a decision on the Soviet and Middle East fronts during the balance of 1942."

Roosevelt also demanded definite plans for the remainder of 1942 and tentative ones for 1943. He did, however, make clear that dispersions of forces should be avoided and that coordinated use of American and British forces was essential. On the other hand, once again, the president emphasized that "it is of highest importance that U.S. ground troops be brought into action against the enemy [in Europe] in 1942."[33]

In as much as no one had foreseen any possibility of such a radical change in U.S. grand strategy, there were no detailed plans in Washington for major offensives in the Pacific. However, the JCS planners made a hasty survey and

record of this proposal being a ploy. In fact, the JCS minutes, where it was discussed, never mention that this was a ploy. The discussion revolves entirely around why it represented a sound proposal and never once mentions that it was not a real proposal but just a method to pressure the British. This event is covered in the *Marshall Papers* in detail (vol. 3, pp. 269–73). Moreover, when the president pushed back on this proposal, Marshall at first made an effort to defend his and King's position. One would assume, if this were a ploy, that instead of defending his position, Marshall would have informed Roosevelt that it was designed to force Britain's hand and was not a serious proposal. One would also assume that the joint chiefs would have brought the president into their thinking before forwarding such a radical proposal. Roosevelt's reply makes it obvious that he was not so informed. Thus, both Marshall and King were taking a severe risk that the president would lose faith in their ability and judgment. One should also note that at this level of leadership, this kind of game is not played, at least in this way. Moreover, it would have been just as effective a scare tactic, if that is what it was supposed to be, to bring in General Dill and tell him what Marshall and King were thinking and let him back-channel their thoughts to the British chiefs. This could have been done without involving the president and risking his wrath. Although the debate continues, all contemporary accounts indicate that both Marshall and King were serious about the proposal. In fact, Marshall's deputy, General Handy, would return to this idea in November 1942. His unpublished memoirs (Handy File, Military History Institute; Carlisle, PA) demonstrate that this was a serious proposal on the eve of the Casablanca Conference, as was the earlier proposal discussed here. Andrew Roberts, in his new book *Masters and Commanders* (London, 2008), addresses this debate at some length and concludes that this was a serious threat and not a bluff (pp. 230–33).

32   Guyer, "The Joint Chiefs and the War against Germany," section 5, p. 15.
33   Ibid.

drew up a paper outlining in general terms the immediate adjustments that the services could make. Roosevelt rejected these new proposals out of hand and made it clear he was not in favor of transferring the major effort to the Pacific. However, the president realized the matter had to be brought to resolution in the immediate future. To that end, he determined to send Marshall, King, and presidential adviser Harry Hopkins to London for a final showdown with the British.[34]

Before sending the party off to London, Roosevelt presented them with detailed formal instructions to guide the conduct of negotiations. The final points of these instructions formed the crux of the president's agenda. Here Roosevelt spelled out that he was unalterably opposed to an all-out effort in the Pacific against Japan. He reminded all concerned that the defeat of Japan would have relatively little impact on Germany and that American concentration against Japan in 1942 or 1943 would increase the chance of complete German domination of Europe and Africa. The president also asked his representatives to keep three cardinal principles in mind: speed of decision on plans, unity of plans, attack combined with defense, but not defense alone. He concluded by stating to the group traveling to London that he expected U.S. ground forces to be engaged against the Germans in 1942 and, finally, that he wanted this matter settled within a week.

With these instructions, Marshall had lost politically before his mission even began, while Churchill prepared to exploit Marshall's weak hand.[35] According to Marshall's biographer, Churchill sensed that the president had given up the fight. Although he still supported SLEDGEHAMMER and ROUNDUP, Roosevelt had let it be known weeks before that American forces had to be in action against the Germans somewhere before the end of the year.[36] The British were certain they faced a divided delegation. As Field Marshal Alan Broke noted in his diary: "Hopkins is for operating in Africa, Marshall wants to operate in Europe, and King is determined to stick to the Pacific."[37] If the British were to stand firm against the Channel attack, there would be no chance for Marshall to win. In the event, the British did stand firm, while the unity of their American counterparts crumbled.

For Roosevelt, several calculations weighed in his decision to opt for the North African invasion and abandon thoughts of an immediate amphibious assault on the European continent. First, by the time preparations began for the North Africa invasion, the need to do something dramatic on the Continent to keep Russia in the war was waning. Despite spectacular successes in

[34] Sherwood, *Roosevelt and Hopkins*, p. 576.
[35] Ibid, p. 582.
[36] Forest C. Pogue, *George C. Marshall: Ordeal and Hope 1939–1942* (New York, 1966), p. 343.
[37] Alex Danchev and Daniel Todman, eds., *War Diaries: Field Marshall Lord Alan Brooke* (London, 2001), p. 280.

their drive towards the Volga, the Germans appeared to have been stopped by a tenacious Russian defense at Stalingrad. Although that bloody battle would not run its course for a number of months to come, it was clear that Hitler's armies had failed to attain their goal and that Russia would remain in the war.

Furthermore, the president's full attention was not on the Atlantic theater. American marines had landed in the Solomons, on the small island of Guadalcanal. After meeting with initial success, the battle became increasingly desperate. For a while, it appeared doubtful that the marines could hold. If the Japanese succeeded in throwing the marines off the island at great loss of life, it would be hard to justify a buildup in Britain for a 1943 invasion. Americans would justly ask why great masses of troops were sitting idle across the Atlantic while their brothers in arms were being defeated in the Pacific.

This last point leads to another of Roosevelt's primary considerations. When one is leading a democratic nation in war, it is important that the people see their military forces doing something on a large scale every year. This was something on which Marshall, who never truly understood the political dimension of the conflict, commented bitterly after the conflict was over.[38]

In the event, American and British forces invaded North Africa on 8 November 1942 (operation TORCH), and by the end of the first week, Morocco and Algiers were under Allied control. To sound out the joint chiefs as to their ideas for post-TORCH strategic initiatives, the president convened a White House meeting on 25 November. Both the JCS meeting minutes and Harry Hopkins's notes bear out one notable fact – Marshall never brought up the topic of a 1943 cross-Channel invasion.[39] In truth, his, and therefore the president's, strategic conceptions at this point were definitely not anything that could be called a grand strategy. In fact, at the war's end, Marshall admitted that the United States did not have a grand strategy at the time and, in fact, did not really settle on one until after the Casablanca Conference.

By mid-December, however, Marshall had come up with another concept. Rather than the massive ROUNDUP he had previously envisioned for 1943, he proposed a smaller invasion of the Brest Peninsula.[40] This idea

---

[38] Jean Edward Smith, in his book *FDR* (New York, 2007), p. 561, quotes Marshall: "We failed to see that the leader in a democracy has to keep the people entertained. That may sound like the wrong word, but it conveys the thought. The people demand action. We couldn't wait to be completely ready."

[39] Sherwood, *Roosevelt and Hopkins*, p. 630.

[40] Matloff and Snell, *Strategic Planning for Coalition Warfare: 1941–1942* (Washington, DC, 1958).

represented a considerably narrowed scope from anything Marshall had proposed before, and even as he stated it, he understood that its prospects were not great. In fact, he ended up defending the proposal with the claim that the damage a Brest invasion would do to Germany's 1944 defensive prospects justified the possible annihilation of the invading force.[41] It was also a conception that was out of step with what his own army planners were advocating. And it was certainly not something the British were going to countenance because they would have to supply the bulk of the ground forces.

On 11 December, the Joint Strategic Survey Committee (JSSC), an organization Marshall set up under Lieutenant General Stanley Embick to plan long-term strategy, produced its first paper. In Embick's formulation, the earliest practicable date to conduct a strategic offensive directly against Germany was still 1943, but only on the assumption that the Allies would stand on the defensive in all other theatres. As a preliminary to this invasion, the JSSC advocated wearing down German strength by an integrated air offensive from bases in the United Kingdom and North Africa "on the largest possible scale." According to the JSSC, the major effort would go into building up forces in the United Kingdom, including transfers of ground and air units from North Africa, to launch a decisive offensive against Germany in 1943.[42]

This recommendation was directly at odds with what army planners outside the JSSC were advocating. Although they had not abandoned the idea that there must be a decisive campaign in Northwestern Europe, they could not see how or when it could be launched. Resuming plans for ROUNDUP in 1943 meant ignoring that a decisive, large-scale, cross-Channel operation would be logistically infeasible before mid-1944. Accelerating preparations for an invasion of Europe meant sacrificing all the psychological and tangible advantages promised by TORCH. It also meant disregarding the fact that large ground forces were still required in the Mediterranean to safeguard North Africa and the Middle East and the Allied sea lines of communications. In addition, the heavy losses incurred in 1942's disastrous Dieppe raid by Canadian and British troops had made a strong impression on army planners. They, thus, accepted once more the indefinite postponement of ROUNDUP.[43]

The joint chiefs of staff discussed this report in closed session at their meeting of 15 December. Only four copies of the minutes were produced, all of which went to the members of the JSSC, and none apparently survived

---

[41] Guyer, "The Joint Chiefs and the War against Germany."
[42] Matloff and Snell, *Strategic Planning for Coalition Warfare*, p. 363. Grace, "The Joint Chiefs and the War against Japan," and Guyer, "The Joint Chiefs and the War against Germany."
[43] Matloff and Snell, *Strategic Planning for Coalition Warfare*, pp. 365–66.

the war.[44] During this meeting, Admiral William D. Leahy, Roosevelt's chief military adviser, took exception to many of the points in the JSSC study, particularly the idea of orienting the entire strategic direction of the war towards Germany. He agreed that Germany was currently the principal concern, but he was not certain that it was the "primary enemy." Nor was he convinced that making the primary effort against Germany was "acceptable strategy."

King, on the other hand, was willing to accept Germany as the primary enemy in Europe but expressed concern at the offhand manner with which he perceived the chiefs were addressing the Pacific situation. He felt there should be constant pressure applied against Japan not to postpone the end of that conflict indefinitely. He then urged that the chiefs determine a fixed percentage of war effort for the Pacific and suggested that the appropriate proportion would be 25 to 30 percent. When Marshall asked how one would arrive at a percentage of the total war effort, King replied that it was probably not possible to make an exact analysis. However, he believed a reasonable overall estimate would be that only 15 percent of the current war effort was going to the Pacific.[45] In effect, King was slyly putting forth a proposal for doubling the resources sent to the Pacific, a proposal that would surely kill any near-term prospects for a cross-Channel invasion.

Marshall agreed with King that continuous offensive operations in the Pacific were necessary to make progress.[46] Nevertheless, the major thrust of Marshall's remarks concerned the war against Germany. He showed little patience with operations based on North Africa, indicating that he felt landings in Sardinia or Sicily were just what the Germans themselves would recommend. Instead he thought the Allies should build up strong forces in the British Isles as fast as possible and move against the Brest salient in spring 1943.[47]

As Roosevelt had already agreed to meet Churchill in Casablanca to discuss the next phase of the war, the president was greatly bothered by the fact that his own chiefs not only disagreed with the British chiefs on how to prosecute the war but also were divided amongst themselves. On 7 January 1943, Roosevelt convened a final meeting in the White House in an attempt to hammer out the differences among his own military leaders. After

---

[44] The JCS minutes only mention that this meeting occurred, but because of its secret nature, the minutes do not provide any details. Most of this account comes from Hayes, "The Joint Chiefs and the War against Japan." Guyer's unpublished history presents the same version of events. As both authors were senior officers on the joint staff at the time of the meeting, their reports have substantial credibility.

[45] King had made a similar estimate of the total Pacific War effort at a previous JCS meeting. See JCS Notes Taken at the Meeting, 25 November 1942, JCS Minutes, National Archives, Record Group 218.

[46] Both Guyer and Hayes agree on this point.

[47] Hayes, "The Joint Chiefs and the War against Japan."

hearing them out, he proposed a compromise to allow preparations to continue for further Pacific operations, a 1943 Continental invasion and renewed operations in the Mediterranean. Roosevelt knew he was going to meet a British delegation who would be aligned behind a single strategic conception, with which they would mercilessly hammer the divided and unprepared Americans.

CASABLANCA

Before considering the decisions made at Casablanca, it is first necessary to dispose of two enduring myths about the conference. The first is that Marshall went to Casablanca dead set against further operations in the Mediterranean and was determined to force the British to agree to a 1943 invasion of Northern Europe. The second is that the British won most of the key debates because of their superior staff system, which overwhelmed the American planners. Both myths are untrue.

In 2005, the Army Center for Military History published a volume on American military history that included the following statement: "At Casablanca, General Marshall made a last vigorous, but vain stand for a cross-channel operation in 1943."[48] Once again, an "official" history perpetuated a myth that has no basis in fact, a tradition dating back to the first official histories of the war. Ever since the publication of *Strategic Planning for Coalition Warfare: 1943–1944*, all too many historians have accepted that during the Casablanca Conference, Marshall opposed further operations in the Mediterranean and continued to push for a decisive invasion of Northern Europe in 1943. According to Matloff's 1958 official history, "[i]t was extremely important for the American and British leaders to decide on the main plot." To support this line of reasoning, Matloff then quotes Marshall as stating that, "Every diversion or side issue from the main plot, acts as a 'suction pump.'" After this, Matloff presents his own insight into Marshall's thoughts, stating: "It was Marshall's belief that in the diversion to TORCH [the invasion of North Africa] the United States and Great Britain had been abnormally fortunate. He still favored a main British-American effort against Germany in the form of a cross-Channel operation aimed at northern France."[49]

In a single paragraph, the official historian captured two main points: Marshall's revulsion against all diversions from the main effort and his desire for a cross-Channel operation in 1943. Unfortunately, this version of

---

[48]   Richard W. Stewart, *American Military History*, vol. 2 (Washington, DC, 2005), p. 140. This quote is lifted directly from Maurice Matloff's *American Military History*, vol. 2, 1902–1996 (Conshohocken, PA, 1973), p. 419.

[49]   Maurice Matloff, *Strategic Planning for Coalition Warfare: 1943–1944* (Washington, DC, 1959), pp. 21–22.

events has serious flaws. First, the Marshall quote was far from complete. The part the authors left out totally reverses the point they were trying to make. The minutes of the Casablanca Conference reveal that immediately after making the "suction pump" remark, "He [Marshall] stated that the operations against Sicily appeared advantageous because of the excess number of troops in North Africa brought about by the splendid efforts of the British Eighth Army."[50]

Besides neglecting to inform their readers that Marshall was not adamantly opposed to further Mediterranean operations, the official historians categorically stated that Marshall was a strong advocate for a 1943 cross-Channel invasion.[51] This is most certainly wrong. By the time Marshall and the rest of the joint chiefs arrived in Casablanca, a major 1943 invasion was no longer a serious option from their point of view. The joint chiefs' goal in Casablanca was therefore not to persuade the British to commit to a 1943 invasion but rather to get their agreement to an invasion, with the exact date to be determined later.

The belief that at Casablanca, Marshall strongly advocated a 1943 invasion is more a result of the extrapolation of his previous stance on the matter than a reflection of his thinking by late 1942. Before Operation TORCH, the evidence of Marshall's support for a cross-Channel invasion as soon as feasible is beyond doubt. The joint chiefs and the president joined Marshall without reservation in this policy. Moreover, the British chiefs of staff and Winston Churchill fully supported a decisive cross-Channel invasion. However, they did insist that the Allies not launch it before preparations ensured a fair chance of success.[52]

As for the superiority of the British staff system, one can quickly dispose of that canard. According to an unpublished history of the JCS:

> The British chiefs of staff had not changed their view, expressed in the pre-Casablanca interchanges on the question of a strategic concept, that a landing should be made in northern France in 1943 only in the event that Germany already showed definite signs of collapse. Early in the conference the U.S. chiefs resigned themselves to this and concentrated on the problem of which operations in the Mediterranean area would be most desirable.[53]

---

50 Minutes of the meeting held at Anfa Camp, 16 January 1943 are available in digital form from the joint chiefs of staff history office (Pentagon, Alexandria, VA). This resource has not been placed online but is available on CD.

51 Some historians, notably Sir Michael Howard, note that Marshall's commitment to a 1943 invasion was uncertain. However, although some, but no means all, historians of this period addressed this issue properly, their position does not dominate the historical record.

52 For a brilliant explosion of the fallacy that there was a rift between British and American grand strategic conceptions on the wisdom of a cross-Channel invasion, see Richard M. Leighton, "Overlord Revisited: An Interpretation of American Strategy in the European War, 1942–1944," *American Historical Review* 68, no. 4, July 1963, pp. 919–37.

53 Ibid. (emphasis added).

There, in a nutshell, is the Casablanca Conference. The JCS did not roll over at the behest of the British chiefs and their supposedly better-prepared staff work.[54] The American military had already decided to acquiesce to the British strategic viewpoint, as far as the European and Mediterranean theaters were concerned, before they even sat down with their British counterparts for their first combined meetings. It is worth reviewing some of the key points of the JCS meeting at Casablanca, held in the days prior to the combined meetings.

First, as to Marshall's new pet idea, an invasion of Brittany, General Mark Clark, Eisenhower's second in command for TORCH, threw cold water on the plan almost immediately. According to the minutes of the first JCS meeting in North Africa, Clark told the assembled chiefs that operations against the Brest and the Breton Peninsula would be "very hazardous, require overwhelming air support, extensive naval support and immediate heavy follow up."[55] In other words, it was guaranteed to be a military disaster.

Even Marshall took the opportunity to throw cold water on his own plan. He told the assembled chiefs that Eisenhower had changed his viewpoint on the practicality of a European invasion as a result of his experiences to date in North Africa. In preconference conversations, Eisenhower had brought Marshall around to the idea that a successful invasion required that ROUNDUP be organized on a far larger scale than American planners, including himself, had previously envisioned. This meant that the invasion force would have to be double the size contemplated in any previous plan. More important, given the lag in landing craft production, Marshall was disturbed over Eisenhower's belief that it would be unsound to count on more than one trip from the first wave of landing craft as only a small proportion of them were likely to be available for a second trip.[56]

In fact, during the meeting Marshall only mentioned a cross-Channel attack once, and that was hardly a ringing endorsement of the plan for an attack on Brittany. According to the Conference minutes:

> General Marshall said that we wanted to keep the German Army engaged with the Russian Army, and we wanted to make a landing on the Continent. Can we do that in time to support Russia in the summer? Will any other operation destroy our ability to make a Continental landing our main objective? We must insure that it does not. If we do Sicily we might not have the means to

---

[54] As Admiral King is reported to have said, "Every time we brought up a topic those bastards had a paper on it." General Wedemeyer expatiated at great length on the superiority of the British staff system at Casablanca: "They swarmed down on us like locusts... with prepared plans... from a worm's eye's viewpoint it was apparent that we were confronted by generations and generations of experience in committee work, in diplomacy, and in rationalizing points of view. They had us on the defensive practically all the time." Wedemeyer Reports, p. 192.

[55] JCS 50th Meeting, minutes of the meeting held at Anfa Camp, 13 January, 1943, available in digital form from the joint chiefs of staff history office.

[56] Ibid.

do anything on the Continent before October. We must determine what must be done to support Russia this summer. If it is essential that we attack, we must determine where. Everything now building up in the United Kingdom is composed of raw troops, which, however, are better than previous unseasoned troops.

When the joint chiefs met with the president, Marshall not only failed to convince Roosevelt that an invasion of Europe was the next best strategic move but often seemed to be trying to do the opposite by spelling out the difficulties. During meetings with Roosevelt, Marshall pointed out that he and Clark agreed with Lord Mountbatten that there must be a long period of training before Anglo-American forces could succeed in any attempt to land against determined resistance. Moreover, Marshall stressed the British point that the rail net in Europe permitted the movement of seven divisions a day from east to west, which would enable the Germans to reinforce their northern European defenses rapidly.

Startlingly, Marshall also commented to the president that there would be an excess of troops available in North Africa when the Axis powers had been expelled and that "this is one of the chief reasons Operation HUSKY (the invasion of Sicily) appears to be attractive." When the president asked how many American divisions were currently in England, Marshall had to concede that there was only one. However, he told Roosevelt, he was hopeful there would be six more by summer 1943.[57] Finally, Marshall quoted Eisenhower's belief that an invasion of the Continent would require a minimum of 12 divisions in the first days, which he admitted was double all previous estimates.[58]

In sum, despite the claims of official historians that Marshall went to Casablanca determined to fight one more battle for ROUNDUP in 1943, the evidence suggests no such thing. Even with his own president, he emphasized the factors weighing against the invasion without ever examining what proposed benefit a 1943 cross-Channel invasion would possess. By the time the American chiefs had finished with the president and had turned to meet their British counterparts, their major concern was to insure that ROUNDUP remained on the table for 1944.[59]

---

[57] Considering that the original ROUNDUP plan called for 45 divisions to land in 1943, one can see why Marshall's conception of the possible had by this time been radically scaled down.

[58] Minutes of JCS meeting with President Roosevelt held at Anfa Camp, 14 January, 1943, available in digital form from the joint chiefs of staff history office.

[59] Had Marshall strongly backed a cross-Channel invasion for 1943 at Casablanca, as the official historians contended, there were several instances during the meeting when Marshall remained silent when, if he had still been advocating a 1943 invasion, he most definitely would have been on his feet. For instance, at one point, Sir Alan Brooke stated that with the limited ground forces available, he did not believe that the Allies could muster a sufficient threat to Northern France to force the Germans to divert much from the Eastern Front.

What the Allied chiefs did agree on was a firm commitment to land substantial forces on the north coast of France in 1944, and Marshall seemed content with that result. If, however, as the evidence indicates, Marshall agreed with a 1944 cross-Channel invasion date, one still has to explain what turned his mind from his previous fixation on reentering the European continent at the earliest possible date. In fact, earlier in the war Marshall had pushed hard for an invasion in 1942, long before American forces were even remotely capable of such a feat. When that failed, he pushed strongly for a 1943 invasion. But by November 1942, he had become, at best, lukewarm to the idea. By the end of the year he appears to have given up on a 1943 invasion entirely.

Yet, prior to November 1942, Marshall fought tooth and nail against anything he perceived as a diversion from that goal, to the point of threatening to divert the entire war effort to the Pacific if Anglo-American strategy failed to adhere to his plans for a rapid invasion of Europe. In all of this, he had the full support of the Joint Chiefs, if somewhat grudgingly given. Sometime between TORCH and the Casablanca Conference, however, Marshall abandoned his single-minded crusade for a second front in 1943 and supported a major post-TORCH diversion of resources to further Mediterranean operations. In this, too, the other chiefs joined him. The Americans were not overawed or overwhelmed by superior British negotiating skills or staff procedures, as historians have too often suggested. Rather, they had simply changed their minds about the wisdom of a major 1943 invasion, though they do appear to have been more than a bit reticent about announcing their change of heart and thereby admitting that the British had been right from the beginning.

But why the change of heart? Part of the answer is that after TORCH, the American chiefs had sobered up to just how difficult a contested landing in northern France against a determined enemy might be. Eisenhower's doubling of what he considered the minimum number of divisions necessary for a successful invasion had shocked Marshall. That, then, explains his comments on the new requirement for a minimum of 12 divisions several times during the Casablanca Conference and again when meeting separately

---

To this, Marshall made no rejoinder. When Brooke continued that the Germans still had sufficient strength to overwhelm us on the ground or perhaps hem us in to such an extent that any expansion of the bridgehead would be impossible, Marshall still remained silent. Marshall even let slide by without comment a statement by one of the American chiefs, Hap Arnold, to the effect that based on discussions up to that point, it looked very much as though no Continental operations on any scale were in prospect before spring 1944. Arnold even went so far as to include the suspension of any further consideration of the small invasion of Brest without attracting Marshall's ire. Finally, when Admiral King said it was necessary to accept that the Allies could do nothing in France before April 1944, Marshall failed to make any protest (see Minutes of the meeting held at Anfa Camp, 16 January, 1943, available in digital form from the joint chiefs of staff history office).

with the president. Running over second-rate Vichy French divisions had cost the American combat forces involved heavy losses. How much worse would it be facing the battle-hardened Wehrmacht?

Even more important, though, was that just about at the time of TORCH, the production agencies had finally convinced the joint chiefs that the munitions and material the chiefs expected to have on hand in mid-1943 would not be fully available until a year later. Moreover, Marshall discovered that virtually all these cuts were going to fall on the army while the navy and air forces would escape almost unscathed. In fact, the day after TORCH, Marshall sent a bitter memo to the president about troop estimates for 1943, in which he informed Roosevelt that this would cause a reduction of 14 transportable divisions in 1943. Such a reduction would preclude any chance of a 1943 cross-Channel invasion.[60] This reduction eventually turned out to be a misunderstanding that was straightened out after a flurry of notes between Marshall and the president. Nevertheless, Marshall still would face 1943 with significantly fewer divisions then he had assumed the army would possess because the production lines simply could not produce sufficient equipment.

Even as Marshall was in the process of reducing the scope of his strategic planning, Roosevelt was widening his. While the president prodded and guided his military chiefs toward coming up with a unified conception on how best to employ American forces toward immediate objectives, he was already thinking past those debates toward a wider grand strategic goal. During a news conference toward the end of the Casablanca meetings, he announced the fruits of his thinking to the world:

> The elimination of German, Japanese and Italian war power means the unconditional surrender of Germany, Italy, and Japan. That means a reasonable assurance of future world peace. It does not mean the destruction of the population of Germany, Italy, or Japan, but it does mean the destruction of the philosophies in those countries which are based on conquest and the subjugation of other peoples.[61]

At the time, Roosevelt claimed that his call for unconditional surrender had just occurred to him, and he offered it up to the reporters as an offhand comment. Churchill, although he admitted that he had previously discussed the concept with the president, professed that he was also surprised by Roosevelt's announcement. In reality, the matter had been the subject of long discussions back in Washington and had already been endorsed to the president by a State Department advisory group assigned to study the matter. For 60 years, historians have debated the wisdom of this policy.

60 Forest C. Pogue, *George C. Marshall: Organizer of Victory 1943–1945* (New York, 1973), p. 12.
61 Smith, *FDR*, p. 567.

The prevailing attitude has been that the call for unconditional surrender provided the Germans with a propaganda coup with which to rally the flagging morale of their populations. Moreover, many historians believe it hardened both Nazi resistance and that of the German Army and therefore prolonged the war.

However, a closer look at the other side suggests that such arguments were dragged out by the defeated after the war to exculpate themselves for having supported a hopeless cause long after the defeat of their nation and military forces should have been obvious to the meanest intellect. Both Germany and Japan were fully committed to fighting the war through to the bitter conclusion. Therefore, the call for unconditional surrender was just a recognition of reality.

It is also difficult to conceive of what "conditional" terms would have been appropriate to offer societies that had been practicing genocide on a scale previously unimaginable in Europe and Asia. Furthermore, Roosevelt's statement brought with it immediate advantages that helped the war effort. It assured the Soviets, who were severely disappointed that the Casablanca meetings did not agree on a fixed date for the invasion of Northern Europe, that the Anglo-American powers would not abandon them to fight it out alone against the Germans. It also helped to buoy Allied morale at a time when it was still shaky, despite victories at Guadalcanal, at Stalingrad, and in North Africa.

Roosevelt as a strategist

The call for unconditional surrender also demonstrated Roosevelt's one dominating wartime leadership trait – a fixation on what was necessary to win the war. In this regard, James MacGregor Burns's assessment of Roosevelt's strategic qualities and abilities closely mirrors this author's:

> If military strategy, in Samuel Morison's words, is the art of defeating the enemy in the most economical and expeditious manner, Roosevelt must surely rate high as a military strategist. As Commander in Chief he husbanded military resources in both the Atlantic and Pacific until the enormous power, industrial and technological, of the nation could be brought to bear on the military scene. Despite endless temptations to strike elsewhere he stuck firmly to an over-all strategy of Atlantic First, and in Europe, despite the diversions of Africa and Italy, he and his military-chiefs finally delivered the full weight of the Anglo-American effort into France. He helped gain a maximum Soviet contribution to the bleeding of German ground strength and brought Allied troops into the heart of Germany at just the right time to share in and claim military victory; he found the right formula for getting the most militarily from the Russians without letting them, if they so wished, occupy the whole continent. And if he was deliberate and single-minded in Europe, where victory demanded

consistency and continuity of effort, he was opportunistic and flexible in the early stages of the Pacific War. He shifted from a strategy of depending on China and Formosa as huge bases for ground forces to a stepped-up island-hopping by amphibious forces. Compared with the Soviet, German, and even British losses, and considering the range and intensity of the effort and the skillful and fanatical resistance of the enemy, American casualties in World War II were remarkably light.[62]

For a number of reasons, it is more difficult to judge Roosevelt's abilities as a grand strategist than those of Churchill or Stalin. The first and most important factor hampering an appraisal in this regard is that by late 1944, Roosevelt was a desperately sick man who would not survive the war. During the period with which this essay is concerned, the daily exigencies of the war consumed all of the president's attention and energies. Through most of 1942, although his military chiefs were already looking forward to great offensives on the European mainland and across the vast expanse of the Pacific, the bulk of the president's time was taken up with the more immediate imperative – avoiding defeat at the hands of the Axis powers.

Of course, it is the duty of the highest national political leader not only to consider the immediate perils but also to look forward to creating a postwar environment conducive to the long-term security and well-being of his nation. For instance, it is clear that even in the darkest days on the Russian Front, Stalin never lost sight of the fact that complete victory for the Soviet Union would require the destruction of Western Europe's ability to wage offensive war against the east ever again. After the end of the war, Churchill was much castigated by American strategists for his continuing attempts to base many matters of wartime policy on what would best secure the power and privileges of the British Empire at war's end.

Roosevelt, despite the high-mindedness of many of his public speeches and his signing on to such agreements as the Atlantic Charter, never really had a firm idea of exactly what kind of world he wanted to bring forth during the postwar era. For instance, he may have glimpsed the rising power of Asia, but when the island-hopping campaign across the Central Pacific promised a quicker conclusion, he rapidly began drawing down America's military commitment to China. It is too easy, however, to say that Roosevelt was too ready to throw away principle or long-term interest when it was expedient. Nevertheless, the price of ignoring these expedients was always paid with the blood of thousands of Americans.

The president was also only too aware that when it came to grand strategic concerns, there were no guarantees. Even mighty exertions of effort and the expenditure of copious amounts of blood and treasure were not likely to deliver the world for which Roosevelt would have hoped. Such an effort

[62] Burns, *Roosevelt*, p. 546.

would have produced a different world, but there is no surety that it would have been any more peaceful or prosperous than what the world would get at the end of the war. In the meantime, there was a great war to be won. Given that, it is hard to fault Roosevelt for his tendency to focus on what it was going to take to win the greatest war in human history at the least cost in American lives.

8

Harry S. Truman and the forming of American grand strategy in the Cold War, 1945–1953

COLIN S. GRAY

> In the absence of theory, the facts are silent.
> – F. A. Hayek[1]

With more than a little help from his loyal lieutenants, and with some notable assistance from European statesmen and officials, President Harry S. Truman won the Cold War in the brief period from 1947 to 1949[2] – so, at least, the wisdom of hindsight attempts to persuade us today. It is the central purpose of this essay to examine the quality of Truman's leadership of American policy and grand strategy throughout this period. Because the story is both highly complex and eminently contestable, it is essential to be crystal clear about the "plot" for 1945–1953. Lest the complications and the myriad detail which follow these opening paragraphs inadvertently muddy the water of understanding unduly, let the author be quite explicit about the argument he will advance and test. This argument rests on four claims.

First, and most important, Harry Truman got the "big things" right enough. He did sufficiently well what political leaders are supposed to do: he made sufficiently correct judgment calls on the most important issues of the day. The American people do not elect their presidents to run the government in any detailed sense, though from time to time, they must strive to immerse themselves in the details pertinent to particular questions. Rather it is the job of presidents, above all else, to make the decisions that have the largest potential consequences and to police the execution of those decisions. This essay will show beyond reasonable doubt that Harry Truman performed

---

[1] Quoted in John Keegan, *A History of Warfare* (London: Hutchinson, 1993), p. 6.
[2] Vojtech Mastny advances this plausible argument in *The Cold War and Soviet Insecurity: The Stalin Years* (New York, 1996), p. 196.

that task adequately, indeed better than most. Even so, not surprisingly, his record of achievement remains mixed and controversial.

Second, although America's political and strategic advantage leading to ultimate success in the Cold War appears to have made the results inevitable, it is reasonably certain that the emergence of the great Soviet-American Cold War was amply fueled if not quite overdetermined.[3] But the actual course taken by that struggle did not have to approximate a "long peace" terminating in the moral, economic, political, and strategic – though not military – collapse of a genuinely evil empire.[4] This is not to endorse the gratuitous nonsense of what-if-style virtual history. The historical narrative is far too complex to lend itself to interrogation by plausible alternative scenarios. However, the evidence of skill and effort exerted on policy and grand strategy formation and execution by Truman and his senior officials compels the judgment that they were not merely history's pawns, moving as circumstances commanded. The grand narrative of the creation and sustenance of an essentially prosperous and secure West could have ended abruptly with a number of nuclear explosions, among other misfortunes, had Truman and his lieutenants and overseas allies (with apologies to significant Canadians) performed less well.[5] The late 1940s, in particular 1947 to 1949, could have unfolded quite differently. Perhaps some alternative tracks to history would have been compatible with a tolerable security condition for Americans – but then again, perhaps not.

Third, to expand on the first two claims: although Harry Truman made mistakes, both the undeniable and contestable, none proved irretrievable. It would be a challenge to overstate the importance of this claim. All political leaders and strategists make mistakes. However, the key to quality in political and strategic leadership is not the avoidance of error, which is impossible. Instead, it is the ability to make small rather than large mistakes and to err generally in ways for which one can readily find adequate compensation. Even if he makes a major mistake, a generally competent political leader will not commit a literally fatal error. For the most perfect of examples, one scarcely could cite a greater error in grand strategy than the Japanese military's blunder of attacking Pearl Harbor.

---

[3] See Colin S. Gray, "Mission Improbable, Fear, Culture, and Interest: Peacemaking 1943–49," in Williamson Murray and Jim Lacey, eds., *The Making of Peace: Rulers, States, and the Aftermath of War* (Cambridge, 2009), pp. 265–91.

[4] "The long peace" was an infamously misleading concept coined by John Gaddis. See his book, *The Long Peace: Inquiries into the History of the Cold War* (Oxford, 1987), chap. 8.

[5] Dean Acheson, in particular, was eloquent in the cultural construction of an idealized Atlantic community of the West (alternatively the "Free World," capitalization optional). See Robert J. McMahon, *Dean Acheson and the Creation of an American World Order* (Dulles, VA, 2009), pp. 83–84.

To cite a lesser case, though one with the utmost meaning for Truman's conduct of America's grand strategy, Stalin's hesitant decision to license and support Kim il Sung's disastrous invasion of South Korea in June 1950 proved an error of the first magnitude and one from which there could be no Soviet competitive recovery. It served as a "gravity assist" for those in the United States who were pressing for vast increases (between three and fourfold) in the defense effort. Moreover, the Korean War catalyzed the military institutionalization of a North Atlantic Treaty Organization (NATO) that would include a rearmed Germany. The West has ironic reason to be grateful to Stalin for that blunder.

Fourth and finally, Truman was lucky. It is true that he and his most senior officials contributed largely to America and the West's good fortune in what slowly matured into the Cold War rivalry of total competition. Nonetheless, things, events, happenings, processes, and trends could well have gone terribly wrong. The Truman administration believed that it was taking what its members, and now many historians also, are fond of calling calculated risks.[6] In historical practice, it is a fact that statesmen and historians must calculate the risks attached to unique events. Any more than the future is ever foreseeable, however, these can never be more than useful euphemisms. In fact, commentators should replace pseudometric claims for calculation, for risk assessment in statecraft, with the words *guesswork*, *intuition*, and *judgment*. We know that Truman and his advisors guessed well enough. But when one seeks understanding of the whole context of the late 1940s, one can only be astonished by the confidence shown by purportedly prudent people in the correctness of their guesses about Soviet – which is to say, Stalin's – behavior.

To date, the historiography on the Truman administration has been far too forgiving – even kind – with regard to the military risks that might have been lurking given the evidence accessible to Washington and London. Indeed, if anything, contemporary historians have tended to fault Truman for allegedly militarizing the great rivalry needlessly. We must return to this important matter time and again. In brief, the principal thrust of the charges leveled against the president is that, prior to summer 1950, he erred in overrating Soviet political hostility, whereas thenceforth, his main error lay in overarming. Poor Harry could not win, so it seems – at least not in the court of a number of historians half a century on.

---

6 Melvin P. Leffler, *A Preponderance of Power: National Security, the Truman Administration, and the Cold War* (Stanford, CA, 1992), argues that Truman was both prudent and unwise in his statecraft. In other words, Leffler seeks to have it both ways, as perhaps a balanced historian should. Leffler's intellectual drift toward the refuge of complexity, the somewhat commonsensical, if less than thoroughly insightful, view that everyone and everything interactively produced the Cold War, is registered in his revealing essay, "Bringing It Together: The Parts and the Whole," in Odd Arne Westad, ed., *Reviewing the Cold War: Approaches, Interpretations, Theory* (London, 2000), pp. 43–63.

Having provided up front a clear four-pronged argument, it remains only for this introduction to specify the plan for discussion. The text proceeds initially by registering important but somewhat contextual points, mainly of a general character. All have a significant bearing on the choice, course, and performance of American high policy, grand strategy, and military strategy from 1945 to 1953. Next, we identify and analyze the several most important functions and, in complex combination, contexts that enable one to assess the content and historical meaning of Truman's conduct as the leader of what came to be known as the West, and what American politicians delighted in calling the "Free World." The principal contexts are geopolitical (material and perceptual), ideological, human (people and their personalities), and historical (circumstances, events, challenges, and opportunities, planned and otherwise).

From context, the essay moves to examine Truman himself. "Cometh the hour, cometh the man" to fit the needs of the hour, or did he? And just what were those needs? Who says so? And when? With Truman presented center-stage, it will address his leadership performance in policy and grand strategy.[7] This is much a case of competing historical grand narratives. The essay concludes by revisiting the quartet of major claims, first advanced here in the introduction, in light of all the evidence and arguments specified and considered.

BACKGROUND

All too often, histories reveal more about the attitudes among temporally and culturally particular cohorts of historians than what happened, why, and with what consequences. Many, probably most, historians are more honest in reflecting their own attitudes and beliefs than they are toward their historical subjects. The record of the Truman administration in its attempt to manage what became known as the Cold War – which we can date without undue hesitation as fairly characterizing the period 1947–1989 – has attracted successive waves of dominant interpretation by Western historians. Each wave has been true enough to its time, place, and circumstance. It is noticeable that a number of well-respected historians of the Cold War have succumbed to what one might call theory creep and have allowed an idea, an intellectual construction, not an observable, verifiable, empirical historical reality, to shape and even drive their work.[8]

---

[7] The general theory of strategy that is employed en passant in this essay is explained fully, with its key concepts defined, in Colin S. Gray, *The Strategy Bridge: Theory for Practice* (Oxford, 2010).

[8] In quest of a usefully greater self-awareness, historians could venture a little way into the dark forest of international relations theory by reading a founding text of modern constructivism: Alexander Wendt, *Social Theory of International Politics* (Cambridge, 1999).

For a leading example, the somewhat absurd concept of the "national security state" has taken firm root among the market leaders of American Cold War scholarship.[9] This is a classic example of an interesting conceptual weapon with which historians should not be trusted. In the English vernacular, the concept of a national security state overeggs a basically reasonable characterization. Those of us who are scholars of strategy, particularly of strategic theory, know that the national security state is so pejorative and potent a light for grand-narrative making that it lethally biases any realistic assessment by its application. Admittedly, national security represents a valid concept, and as its undisciplined historian-devotees claim, it can be and has been abused by those in power. The trouble is that every state "does" national security.

In a world dominated by Thucydidean relations among states, there is no alternative. Unfortunately, once one has in one's mind that Truman presided over the emergence and maturation of a national security state, rampant, unrealistic theory is in the saddle at the expense of evidence and historical empathy. Thus, it becomes an overreaching concept. Because, historically, the Truman years were so significant a strategic moment, they have attracted exceptionally forceful pendulum swings in interpretation. Scholars are apt to fall in love with their theories at the cost of empirical discipline – the facts, the facts. Of course, it is important to try to explain why Truman and his officials behaved as they did and, with presumable cause and effect working overtime, what the consequences appeared to be. But it is scarcely less important to remember that a hard bedrock of factual historical narrative is accessible, from which one theorises at one's peril for the honourable purpose of explanation. Also, one must insist, caveat emptor.

Looking back from the twenty-first century at the 1940s and early 1950s, it is difficult at times to locate empathically the *dramatis personae* historically, or even simply as individuals. Both context and personality are likely to be distorted by the "otherness" of time, place and circumstance. Personality alone is not destiny; nor are geography and culture. But when reviewing Truman's leadership, it is vital not to short-change the human being behind the rhetoric, decisions, and unique contexts of his time. In the late 1940s, the political leaders of the United States, the USSR, and the exhausted, nearly prostrate polities of Europe and Asia were all graduates of a half-century

---

[9]   The leading case in point is Michael J. Hogan, *A Cross of Iron: Harry S. Truman and the Origins of the National Security State* (Cambridge, 1998), while Arnold A. Offner endorses the thesis of an American national security state in his indictment of Truman's alleged sins as a statesman in *Another Such Victory: Harry S. Truman and the Cold War, 1945–1953* (Stanford, CA, 2000). A relatively early example of the genre is Daniel Yergin, *The Shattered Peace: The Origins of the Cold War and the National Security State* (London, 1980). Yergin's title and thesis comprise a two-pronged assault on history and commonsense. There never was a political peace that could be shattered, and all states confront more or less the problems of national security.

of truly interesting times. Those who made decisions in the late 1940s were the products of their distinctive gene pools, admittedly, but they were also the living legatees of the individual and socially collective experience of two world wars, some bloody lesser conflicts, and an interwar period that, in the 1940s, seemed laden with relevant contemporary lessons.

Truman and his lieutenants had learnt by observation, typically, though not always, secondhand, that it is possible to win a great war and then, significantly for reasons of domestic political mismanagement, lose the peace that follows. The tragedy of Woodrow Wilson's flawed grand strategy was ever present in the minds of America's political leaders. For his part, Joseph Stalin had learnt from the first two decades of the twentieth century that war is the midwife of revolution, a provider of opportunity beyond compare. Moreover, he knew as a matter of faith that the greatest among the capitalist states must quarrel over markets and, one day, probably sooner rather than later, come to blows.

In 1945–1947, West European elites "knew" from experience that America most likely would soon withdraw from its residual postwar involvement in European affairs. America's sincere and oft-repeated intention of bringing its troops home within two years of Germany's surrender in May 1945 was entirely consistent with the record of American behavior following the Great War. It is not surprising that all the major players in the drama of immediate postwar international politics anticipated a greater or lesser measure of American disengagement from the European continent.

As a result, Stalin had considerable grounds for patience in his moves to consolidate the new Soviet imperium in East-Central Europe. Across the Elbe and the Danube (for most of its length), European polities had excellent reason to be anxious lest Truman should prove faithful to American political and strategic culture, as well as to his and others' expressed intention, and disengage entirely. Today, it represents a stretch for many historians to appreciate fully the significance for all the polities relevant to this narrative of the understandable contemporary anticipation of American withdrawal from active engagement on the ground in Eurasia.

One must not forget that those who made the Cold War what it became were the children of history, circumstances, and the fashion in which they interpreted the former to cope with the latter. Their life narratives teamed with their biological and psychological inheritance to produce thought and behavior that did not by any means render them helpless actors in a well-scripted drama. It is compellingly arguable that there was always going to be some Soviet-American rivalry following the total defeat of the Axis Powers.[10] But, the course of history had human drivers who *mattered*.

---

[10]   See John Gaddis, *The Cold War* (London, 2005), and Gray, "Mission Improbable."

Thus, the scholars of modern, and especially contemporary, history need to be educated in temporal depth because little of the greatest significance in matters of statecraft, including peace and war, has altered in its essentials over millennia. The emergence of the great Cold War between 1945 and 1947 must appear entirely unremarkable to anyone familiar with the deeds, and especially the misdeeds, of history's strategic *longue durée*. Although individual and institutionalized human agency counts for much in detail, antagonism among allies, once victorious, is all but a structurally determined certainty in politics, foreign and domestic. Politics at root is always about power in its several nuanced meanings. Human beings, individually and collectively, biologically and psychologically, are programed to compete for advantage for the purpose ultimately of survival, and more typically, for benefit or loss avoidance.

The thoughts and behavior of Harry Truman and Joseph Stalin were of high importance in the period from 1945 to 1946. However, neither could possibly have selected a historical grand narrative characterized for long by consensus and cooperation. One or other, or both, can be faulted for an error here and there, but neither had the structural or contextual freedom to produce a political peace between the only two great powers still standing after the catastrophe of World War II. Allies are partners of convenience. Once the Allies had crushed Nazi Germany and imperial Japan, it became increasingly inconvenient, then difficult, for the United States and the Soviet Union to cooperate in the creation and shared management of some approximation of an agreed international political, economic, and strategic order.

This is not quite deterministic. But it is to claim that the structural prospects for human agency to produce a lasting political peace out of the course and outcome of the Second World War were less than auspicious. It was a notable sign of the times, and a faithful pointer to the future, when Britain's chief of the imperial general staff, General Sir Alan Brooke, confided to his diary on 27 July 1944: "Germany is no longer the dominating power in Europe. Russia is. . . . She . . . cannot fail to become the main threat in fifteen years from now."[11]

It is commonplace to observe that peace is more difficult to make than war.[12] This popular belief is probably true, though it is easy to overstate. Certainly, it is valid for the period 1943–1947. Wartime provides the discipline of military logic, even necessity, and above all else, there is the North Star of an active enemy in the field. Errors in the conduct of warfare are apt to

---

[11] Alan Brooke, as quoted in Tony Judt, *Postwar: A History of Europe since 1945* (London, 2005), p. 111.

[12] G. John Ikenberry, *After Victory: Institutions, Strategic Restraint, and the Rebuilding of Order after Major Wars* (Princeton, NJ, 2001); Colin S. Gray, *Fighting Talk: Forty Maxims on Peace, War, and Strategy* (Westport, CT, 2007), pp. 11–15; and Murray and Lacey, *The Making of Peace.*

be punished immediately, whereas errors pertaining to the postwar political order, whether committed while hostilities continue or soon thereafter, tend not to be revealed as such for some years to come. War accelerates the pace of events and, hence, the appearance of their consequences. At least, the alliance of temporary convenience politely known as the Grand Alliance did not oblige the Allies to squabble damagingly over the terms to be offered Nazi Germany. Blessedly for Allied comity, unconditional surrender was the only option formally on the table for Adolf Hitler to consider from the time of the Casablanca Conference in January 1943 until May 1945. Thus, usefully, no German feet had to be put under the table at a postwar peace conference (which function Potsdam had to serve). However, the multicontextual changes wrought by the course and outcome of the war were so many and traumatic that peacemaking for a new world order could not be anything other than an additional labor that would have taxed the resources of Hercules.

The Second World War had affected revolutionary change in the character, though certainly not the nature, of world politics. In 1945, no one understood – indeed, could have understood – how much international politics had been altered by the war, actually, by two simultaneous great wars waged half a globe apart as well as by the plethora of minor wars within wars, not to mention the postwar hostilities that continued around the world. Only in the simplest of textbooks is the organized and semi-organized politically motivated violence known as the Second World War isolated as a period of war preceded and succeeded by a condition expediently labelled "peace." In point of fact, and this applies no less to the First World War, the greatest of political-military events had nasty outriders, both before and after. In short, in 1945, Truman confronted the historically all too familiar conditions of postwar uncertainty, chaos, and the need to comprehend a cluster of contexts substantially different in detail and broad character from those either experienced before or recently predicted by most observer-participants.

Although peacemaking typically has tested statesmanship at least as severely as has war making, 1945–1947 – arguably 1948, or 1949 – were postwar years of exceptional, though not unprecedented, challenge. In modern times, though, it is hard to locate a precedent for the international circumstances of 1945. Two unusual factors require emphasis. First, there is no modern equivalent to the ideological authority that informed the worldviews of American and Soviet leaders.[13] In practice, both could and did function as cynical, as well as prudent, geopoliticians. But the geopolitical chessboard

---

[13] See the informative comparative discussion of what Odd Arne Westad suggestively terms "The Empire of Liberty: American Ideology and Foreign Policy," and "The Empire of Justice: Soviet Ideology and Foreign Interventions," in *The Global Cold War* (Cambridge, 2007), chaps. 1–2.

also had an ideological dimension that in practice, though not in theory, had been lacking in 1919. Woodrow Wilson's rather naïve democratic idealism did not seriously confuse the delegates from America's erstwhile allies at Versailles.

But in the 1945–1947 period, Harry Truman was not obliged to listen to, let alone try to understand, the *realpolitikal* preferences and views of anyone other than his fellow Americans.[14] When Truman played geopolitics with Joe Stalin, both did so in a manner that blended material and ideological outlooks, values, and interest. There is nothing novel about a great power behaving explicitly in the service of an ideology, but not since the early part of the murderous Thirty Years' War (1618–1648) had two principal adversaries been the sincere – again, albeit tactically cynical – bearers of intensely held, quasi-religious political faiths.

Second, to add to these difficulties in tidying up politically after a murderous conflict that had laid waste the globe, as well the problems of fundamentally antagonistic worldviews of an all but theological nature (i.e., Marxism–Leninism–Stalinism versus democracy-freedom/liberty–open markets/free trade), there was the challenge of "the bomb." Even today, the meaning of the weaponization of atomic physics for international relations remains a contested subject.[15] Did nuclear weapons keep the "long peace," or was the absence of active East-West belligerency overdetermined? Did the bomb prolong the Cold War by making the risks of purposeful political change prohibitive? We do not and cannot know.

The point is that now, 20 years on from the demise of the Soviet imperium, there is much about the warlike peace of the Cold War decades that is not adequately understood. Much of what we have are theories that purport to explain the facts; robust understanding remains elusive. For Truman in 1945, inaugurated as president after only 82 days as vice president, during which time he was very much in the shadows as Roosevelt's crown prince, the atomic bomb presented what literally was a historically unprecedented challenge, first to understanding, then to policy making and strategy.

The atomic bomb appeared to many in 1945–1947 to be the "absolute weapon."[16] But what could and should it mean for American political and strategic choices? In 1945, Truman did not know the answer to this

14 Britain was very important to America in this period, but Truman was not particularly understanding of, or sympathetic to, the British worldview in 1945–1947. See an excellent recent collection of pertinent essays by the dozen of contemporary historians of Anglo-American relations: David Reynolds, *From World War to Cold War: Churchill, Roosevelt, and the International History of the 1940s* (Oxford, 2006).

15 There is unusual merit in Laurence Freedman, *The Evolution of Nuclear Strategy*, 3rd ed. (Basingstoke, 2003); and Michael Quinlan, *Thinking about Nuclear Weapons: Principles, Problems, Prospects* (Oxford, 2009), while some readers may find some value in Colin S. Gray, *War, Peace and International Relations: An Introduction to Strategic History* (Abingdon, 2007), chap. 15.

16 For some contemporary attitudes and opinions, see Bernard Brodie, ed., *The Absolute Weapon: Atomic Power and World Order* (New York, 1946); and Jacob Viner, "The

question, nor, really, did anyone else. How well did the president rise to the atomic-related demands of the new era? How energetically did he pursue the pertinent knowledge? How hard did he drive his lieutenants to find plausible answers to the pressing strategic questions raised by the atomic fact? On the evidence, it is not obvious that Truman tried as determinedly as he could and should have done to make political and strategic sense of the atomic dimension of the postwar era. As Henry Kissinger has written: "The responsibility of statesmen... is to resolve complexity rather than to contemplate it."[17] Truman's entire record of postwar nuclear stewardship shows only a modest presidential interest in the subject, notwithstanding its growing centrality to U.S. national security throughout his years in office.

It is important to recognize not only the exceptional military context of the mid-1940s, occasioned in part by successful development of the atomic bomb, but also the fiercely if flexibly ideological dimension to U.S. and Soviet statecraft. In addition, there was the material preponderance of the United States in the global economy. No polity in modern or mediaeval times had been as economically dominant as the United States of the late 1940s. It is said, and history amply illustrates the claim, that political ambition tends to grow with material potency.

In the "sinews of power," as the popular phrase of the era put it, the United States was the superpower. America's economic capacity, resting notably on high scientific and demonstrated technological prowess, bequeathed the opportunity to play the role of a global hegemon should America's leaders so choose and the people permit. Should America's leaders pick the default option of doing, more or less boldly, what obviously needed to be done? Translated: how difficult were the choices for American statecraft in the middle to late 1940s, given both U.S. strengths and the absence of obviously attractive alternatives? Did it really require great wisdom for an American leader to recognize in late 1945 and 1946 that the Soviet Union was an emerging problem that the United States could not placate into generally cooperative behavior? That Europe was in ruins to such a degree that, as a devastated region with enormous power potential, it must pose an economic, political and, eventually, a strategic challenge to U.S. national security? And that the United States was the only agent capable of effecting some marked improvement in these dire conditions?

There also is no evading recognition of the authority of events, especially military events, in the period from 1943 to 1945. The terms of postwar settlements invariably reflect, albeit somewhat imperfectly, the verdict of

Implications of the Atomic Bomb for International Relations," *Proceedings of the American Philosophical Society* 90 (January 1946), pp. 53–58. Viner read this pathbreaking essay to a conference on 16 November 1945. A voice discordant from those in the "absolutist" chorus was that of William L. Borden, *There Will Be No Time* (New York, 1946). Borden urged preparation for atomic warfare conducted to achieve military victory.

[17] Henry Kissinger, *Diplomacy* (New York, 1994), p. 113.

the battlefield. A brutal but unavoidable reality for Truman was that he must make peace with a Soviet Union formerly a much praised and excused ally. The Red Army had broken the back of the Wehrmacht's ground forces. The Soviets had lost approximately 27,000,000 people in the war against Germany. In 1945, their armies stood on the Elbe in Western Germany and in all the main capitals of recently Nazi central Europe: Berlin, Vienna, Budapest, Prague, and Warsaw. The size of the Soviet (formerly Red) Army had peaked at 603 divisions on 1 December 1943, and, although in 1945–1947, it was demobilising, it still represented a force in being throughout the Truman period.

When, or if, Truman wished to reshape the political landscape of the periphery of postwar Eurasia, he could not ignore the military-strategic, hence, geopolitical, extent of the Soviet victory on the ground. The Soviet Army was where it was and where Stalin could – and largely, though not entirely, would – choose to keep it. It was there by right of conquest as well as by license of explicit and implicit agreement among the Big Three (Roosevelt, Churchill, and Stalin) at February 1945's Yalta summit.[18] A basic fact structuring the geopolitical playing fields of the Cold War was the high tide the Red Army had reached in Germany and prospectively would hold forever.[19]

Truman, indeed, anyone cast into a leadership role, needed only to be good enough to secure an outcome tolerable for his followers. The American electorate does not require, or expect, greatness in its presidents, whatever that elusive and contestable quality is judged to be. One might go so far as to claim: "happy is an America that has no need for great presidents." A president should be great enough to meet and tame adequately, if not vanquish, the more dangerous problems of the day. Just how great, if great at all, Harry Truman needed to be was decided above all else by the quality of character and purpose of leadership shown by America's unavoidable rival-adversary. Inevitably in international relations, a positive record of leadership requires some inadvertent assistance from the adversary. This is not necessarily a matter of luck, or accident alone.

Much as golfers discover that their luck improves when they practice harder, so in politics, it is usually possible to give Dame Fortune a helping

---

[18] See Reiner Marcowitz, "Yalta, the Myth of the Division of the World," in Cyril Buffet and Beatrice Heuser, eds., *Haunted by History: Myths in International Relations* (Providence, RI, 1998), pp. 80–91; David Reynolds, *Summits: Six Meetings that Shaped the Twentieth Century* (London, 2007), chap. 3; and Wilson D. Miscamble, *From Roosevelt to Truman: Potsdam, Hiroshima, and the Cold War* (Cambridge, 2007), esp. chaps. 2–3.

[19] Because the Allied occupation zones had to be negotiated and agreed well ahead of military events, it was inevitable that the actual, let alone the potential, line of contact between the Anglo-American and Soviet armies would not match neatly what had been settled previously. There were some peaceable withdrawals, both in Germany and Czechoslovakia. The occupation zones were agreed in the London Protocol of 12 September 1944.

hand by encouraging the enemy to make mistakes. Happily for the Free World, and certainly for many among the ranks of the unfree, Joseph Stalin labored overtime to help Truman achieve the near-great status that seems to be the current assay of America's historians.[20] Because war and peace – or warlike peace, for that matter – are a continuum wherein rivals and enemies duel, it is not practicable to tell a wholly autistic story of presidential leadership.[21] Truman was not leading against an inert natural world or in a space devoid of an active foe.

Finally, for reasons of parochial professional culture and fashionable theory, many scholars are unduly reluctant to take full and proper account of the historical reality that foreign policy and strategy, though directed abroad, are made at home. International and domestic politics, if not quite one, certainly overlap so significantly that, more often than not, they comprise a gestalt. An American president must lead at home if he is to lead abroad. This elementary, perhaps even banal, truth is of fundamental importance if one is to make a fair assessment of Truman's leadership in developing and conducting America's grand strategy.

If politicians fail domestically, as nearly all do eventually, they lose authority abroad; their foreign policies and strategies are, to a degree, hostage to the enabling strength of public support or at least compliance at home (witness Winston Churchill's sad, somewhat angry and uncomprehending departure from the Potsdam Conference on hearing the unexpected news of his party's *débâcle* in the July 1945 British elections). There are many occasions in the history of most states when domestic circumstances literally drive choice in foreign affairs and their military adjunct. For Truman, sensibly prudent policy options confronted not only the paranoid and probably malevolent Soviets, inter alia, but also a legion of actual and potential foes on the American domestic scene.

FUNCTIONS AND CONTEXTS

Within the total metacontext of the period 1945–1953, to coin a term, though certainly not a concept, the American electorate hired Truman to perform competently in at least four functions key to the nation's

---

20 Vladislav Zubok and Constantine Pleshakov, *Inside the Kremlin's Cold War: From Stalin to Khrushchev* (Cambridge, MA, 1996); Mastny, *Cold War and Soviet Insecurity*; and Yoram Gorlizki and Oleg Khlevniuk, *Cold Peace: Stalin and the Soviet Ruling Circle, 1945–1953* (New York, 2004), do not paint flattering portraits of Stalin the statesman. In the same genre, the title tells all in Constantine Pleshakov, *Stalin's Folly: The Tragic First Ten Days of World War II on the Eastern Front* (Boston, 2006).

21 See Carl von Clausewitz, *On War*, trans. and ed. Michael Howard and Peter Paret (Princeton, NJ, 1976), p. 75; and for a superb extended analysis which privileges the duelling dimension, see Edward N. Luttwak, *Strategy: The Logic of War and Peace*, rev. ed. (Cambridge, MA, 2001).

security.[22] He was required to provide: political, and perhaps moral, vision; policy goals; strategy, grand and military; and executive command, including management.[23] These vital functions had to be addressed and pursued in the metacontext, a setting which may be analyzed helpfully in terms of six identifiable subordinate, but interpenetrating, contexts: (1) political, domestic, and foreign; (2) material, broadly economic; (3) human, embracing key personalities; (4) geopolitical-strategic, including military; (5) cultural, including ideological; and (6) historical, meaning the flow of events, however caused.

This may approach academic pedantry, but the reality of Truman's performance as grand strategist reflected the influence, great and small, of every item just cited as a category of context or of identifiable function. Let us begin by examining the function that Truman sought to perform well enough as national leader. It is prudent to pose the question, "what does leadership entail?" For Truman to be a leader, he had to provide a consistent elevated vision, occasional policy, steady though adaptive strategy, and command and management oversight. The relationship between these four executive functions and leadership is truly reciprocal. One simply cannot lead without them, while they, in turn, cannot be performed adequately, if at all, when leadership is absent or resting. Much of the scholarship on historical leaders and leadership neglects to attend to an inherent ambiguity in the concepts. Strictly speaking, to be a great or even a good or adequate leader, one need not necessarily lead one's followers to what they would be likely to regard as successful outcomes. Leadership is a relational variable; it has meaning only with respect to followership. Great leaders do not need to succeed, though admittedly, failure will tend to limit their historical tenure. All that they require is to be able to attract and satisfy followers.

Given the authority of the warning *caveat emptor*, it is obvious why leadership typically is infused with the implied meaning of "leadership in a just cause" and by ethically widely accepted means and methods. Nevertheless, notions of justice and ethical acceptability with respect to policy goals, strategic objectives, and military and other means have varied widely throughout history. To cite only a most extreme illustration of the problems inescapable in the assessment of leadership, one can ask, "Was Adolf Hitler a great leader?" In the opinion of this author, he certainly was. One could hardly set the bar for greatness in leadership higher than to require the candidate to lead the most powerful nation in Europe to wage ever more predictably suicidal war, and to have the best educated and in some respects

---

22 By metacontext, I refer to the total cluster of identifiably distinctive contexts that all worked together, sometimes in harmony, but often not, to produce what could only be a single actual course of events.

23 See Gray, *Strategy Bridge*, chap. 6.

most cultured country in the world choose to follow and keep following to the point of utter destruction.[24] Even as Hitler withdrew from domestic events during the war, Germans were largely content to "work towards the *Führer*," as British historian Ian Kershaw explains the character of followership in response to Hitler's charismatic attraction.[25]

When we consider Truman's leadership, there is no avoiding the question, "leadership towards what ends?" Historians and social scientists, in common with the rest of mankind, have difficulty separating bare function from the specific historical intent animating that function. Hitler led brilliantly, but toward the abyss, indeed irretrievably so.[26] Truman led America and a growing security gang of more and less dependent allies in what events one day would reveal as having been a superior performance in the conduct of statecraft and grand strategy. At least, that is what the historical record appears to demonstrate.

Some sceptical readers might suspect that Truman's leadership was more fortunate than brilliant. One can argue that much of America's eventual success in the Cold War might well have been unnecessary, had only U.S. leaders been men with a wiser vision to light their country's path. But that is mere speculation. The point in need of emphasis is that leadership skills typically, if not quite logically, are assayed with some regard to both the merit believed to belong to the goals pursued and the measure of success, or otherwise, achieved in that pursuit. Contemporary attitudes towards Truman's leadership remain tied umbilically to one's view of the necessity for American leadership in the conduct of a warlike peace after 1945.

None of the four facets of leadership specified can be slighted. High policy does not emerge in a vacuum, though it can be invented in a hurry without much forethought when necessity presses. Policy requires a North Star for guidance that can inspire, yielding to would-be leaders the fuel they require to recruit and satisfy their followers. For the Truman administration to lead the international security project that was the West, it first required a vision that it could articulate simply and accessibly, if, by necessity, somewhat inconsistently. High policy, beyond the minimal objective of mere political and physical survival, which could serve well enough only in the direst of straits, had to be directed at some superior idea, hence, the role of the concept of the Free World (or the West).

---

24 Which is not to deny the potency of some duress, much desperation and an absence of options.

25 Ian Kershaw, *Hitler, 1889–1936: Hubris* (London, 1998); and *Hitler, 1936–1945: Nemesis* (London, 2000).

26 There is much food for thought in John Lee's judgment that "[g]reat commanders can lead their countries to calamitous defeats." *The Warlords: Hindenburg and Ludendoff* (London, 2005), p. 194.

In turn, policy is necessary to guide strategy, while strategy is necessary if policy is to have any practical consequence. Containment, the conceptual progeny of the State Department's George F. Kennan in 1947, inherently was more than marginally opaque in its implications for policy and strategy.[27] Indeed, was Containment a vision, a policy, a grand strategy, a military strategy, or all of the preceding? This question is not, truly was not, rhetorical. Truman made a record of leading his country, with some specific material means and fairly distinct words, in the light, and sometimes explicitly in the name, of this rather imperial idea. If the concept of Containment were nonsense, then Truman's (and his successors') leadership had to be ill starred. Even if this argument is favored, the history of 1945–1989 reveals incontestably that Truman's legacy was at least tolerable for national security. After all, the great Cold War concluded with only a whimper.

Much of presidential power has to do with the power to persuade, as Richard E. Neustadt insisted many years ago.[28] One might take Neustadt's argument even further and suggest that American presidential potency depends on persuasion in nearly all its aspects. Most especially, it must rest on the willingness of followers to be persuaded to conform to the presidential will. In truth, every one of Truman's leadership functions could be exercised only with and through the compliance of others. Even the supreme command and management function that is the president's by law, in practice can be exercised effectively only when he is obeyed by people who choose to accede to the presidential will with devotion and energy, though not necessarily competence. In other words, obedience is apt to be more than marginally discretionary.

In this endeavor to assess Truman's leadership, it is essential to view that behavior as a whole, over each and all of the broad functions specified earlier. Moreover, one needs to take into account the interdependence of the functions of visionary, policy maker, strategic conceptualizer, and commander and manager. In other words, one needs to connect the dots. Just as policy is not only words and leadership not style alone, so the leadership that Truman needed to exercise had to extend over, and bind together, every function of his office. His policy was guided broadly by the overarching concept of containment of the Soviet Union. This truly was an idea derivative from the proposition that America could not tolerate domination of the Eurasian landmass by a single imperial state or grand coalition.[29]

---

27   The core of "Mr Xs" [pseud. George F. Kennan] *Foreign Affairs* article, "The Sources of Soviet Conduct," is reprinted in Thomas H. Etzold and John Lewis Gaddis, eds., *Containment: Documents on American Policy and Strategy, 1945–1950* (New York, 1978), pp. 84–90.

28   Richard E. Neustadt, *Presidential Power* (New York, 1960).

29   The geopolitical logic behind this commonsense thesis was explained, if not over-explained, in Halford J. Mackinder, *Democratic Ideals and Reality* (New York, [1919] 1962); Hans

This would have been only an interesting, if potentially dangerous, notion, had it not been made manifest in policy guidance for grand and military strategy.[30] Vision, policy, and strategy would have been mere verbiage had they not been translated into, and expressed as, behavior.

As for the contexts of Truman's executive performance, there is the familiar analytical problem that the principal human agent, the president himself, dynamically helped shape those contexts.[31] Yes, Truman found himself constrained at every would-be turn by both domestic and foreign limitations on his ability to impose his will. But – and it is a notable but – the president personally could influence his working environments, his contexts, increasingly as his tenure in office matured. At least, this was the case until the last two years of his presidency. Truman alone, even with the assistance of generally faithful senior lieutenants, could not remake in a preferred American image the structure and working of world order from 1945 to 1953, any more than he could reinvent America domestically.[32]

However, as the leader of by far the most powerful country on the planet, Truman was by no means entirely at the mercy of events. Modern historiography is adamant in insisting, for once persuasively, that East–West relations in the 1940s, indeed as ever is so, effectively must be regarded as a unified whole. Truman, Stalin, and the other players, major and minor, acted on each other simultaneously. Sometimes they behaved in anticipation of feared outcomes, and sometimes they acted to initiate a desired sequence of events. However, regarded overall, Truman's vision, policy, strategy, and actual command and management were reflected, albeit imperfectly, in the incontestable influence they had on Soviet behavior and misbehavior.

It is possible – indeed, it is easy – to identify such complexity in all the factors interacting, typically untraceably, to produce what emerged as the Truman record and legacy, that the baseline of the main plot is lost.[33]

W. Weigert, *Generals and Geographers: The Twilight of Geopolitics* (New York, 1942); Nicholas John Spykman, *America's Strategy in World Politics: The United States and the Balance of Power* (New York, 1942); and Spykman, *The Geography of the Peace* (New York, 1944).

30 American policy and grand strategy documents of the Truman era are seeded with reference to the perils to America of being isolated in North America by a Soviet imperium that controlled Eurasia. The Truman administration both thought and acted explicitly in geopolitical terms. See G. R. Sloan, *Geopolitics in United States Strategic Policy, 1890–1987* (Brighton, 1988), chap. 5.

31 For long and short biographies, see the admiring and massive tome by David McCullough, *Truman* (New York, 1992); and the short, but workmanlike, balanced treatment in Robert Dallek, *Harry S. Truman* (Dulles, VA, 2008).

32 Gray, "Mission Improbable."

33 Dean Acheson said of Harry Truman: "I have never known a man who kept so clearly in mind what were first things. Mr Truman [the Dean invariably spoke respectfully of his leader] was unable to make the simple complex in the way so many men in public life tend to do. For very understandable reasons, of course. If one makes something complex out of something simple, then one is able to delay making up one's mind. And that was something

That is why this essay opened with an elementary but, it is hoped, not oversimple statement of its four-pronged argument. If we are prepared to risk the dangers of reductionism, as we must for the purpose of explanation, then we need to see Truman's performance as America's leader as a historical narrative brewed from the heady mixture of personality shaped by culture, of materially and ideationally constructed geopolitics, and of the uneven flow of history's events. It is time to place human agency where it belongs, in a, if not the only, lead role in this drama. Who and what was Truman?

COMETH THE HOUR, COMETH THE MAN?

Or did he? In 1945, and again in 1951–1952, widespread assessment at home in America certainly did not suggest that Truman was the "man suitable for the hour." Of course, interpretations of the needs of the hour have been ever contestable. Just what did the "hour" of 1945 require of the new president? Was it necessary for Truman, generally believed at the time to have been cruelly and unfortunately dramatically overpromoted by Roosevelt's death on 12 April, to consummate his erstwhile leader's legacy?[34] What was Roosevelt's legacy? Roosevelt as president had made a vice of the virtue of secrecy; in particular, he had neglected to educate his vice president as to his assumptions, let alone his tactics and purposes. Hence, it followed that Truman found himself forced to fly on an exceptionally unreliable autopilot. Even today, more than 60 years on from Roosevelt's performance as one of the so-called Big Three leaders of the anti-German coalition, historians remain desperately short of tangible evidence of the president's true beliefs, expectations, and plotting.

Like Otto von Bismarck, Roosevelt flew much of American grand strategy almost entirely solo in a fashion that could not continue after his departure. As a four-term[35] president, Roosevelt cast a giant shadow over his more modest successor. But it was a shadow that, all too faithful to the metaphor, was short on the substance necessary to help Truman cope with the pressing challenges of the hour. At least for a significant while during the strategic moment of 1945–1946, Truman effectively lacked reliable navigational assistance from the immediate past. Thus, Roosevelt's performance represented an intensely ambiguous legacy. Solid mentoring in the present by senior advisors was not available (with the notable exception of the venerable and exceptionally able Secretary of State for War Henry L. Stimson).

---

that never troubled Mr Truman." Merle Miller, *Plain Speaking: An Oral Biography of Harry S. Truman* (New York, 1974), p. 259. If one wished to be unkind, one could comment that to the simple, all things are simple, even when really, they are complex.

[34] See the first-rate recent analysis of Miscamble, *From Roosevelt to Truman*, on the challenge of the presidential transition period in 1945.

[35] The last perforce severely abbreviated.

Most inhibiting of all, Truman lacked anything resembling careful personal preparation for the conduct of grand strategy.

One might characterize Truman as being charismatically ordinary. He became Roosevelt's vice president for the fourth term because he was broadly acceptable as the default option in 1944, given the unattractiveness of the leading alternatives.[36] With reference to the domestic politics of 1944, Truman was well enough qualified to be vice president, a position which possesses no defined duties save the requirement to be physically able to step into the Oval Office in the unhappy event of the president's material or legal demise. On the evidence available, as well as in history's rearview mirror, Truman appears to have been thoroughly unqualified for his new duties, at least with regard to his practical knowledge of a chaotic, crumbling world order. Whether he could acquire the knowledge, then the understanding, he would need, and whether he would have the personal qualities necessary for that knowledge and understanding to be put to good service, were questions entirely unanswerable in spring 1945.

As the result of Roosevelt's medical condition, Truman found himself propelled into the role of global statesman, if not necessarily the competent performance of global statecraft, in a human context that initially placed him in the company of two giants: Joseph Stalin and Winston Churchill. It is true that America was economically and militarily preponderant, peaking with 12.5 million people in uniform in early summer 1945. However, statecraft and strategy, somewhat akin to poker, are more about how one plays one's cards than about their face value.

Admittedly, Truman held potent cards: literally the world's dominant economy in an undamaged homeland, the reality and legacy of total victory in two distinct great wars half a world apart, and the atomic bomb. But how competent was Truman, the American card player? As much to the point, how competent did he need to be in the context of international security politics in the immediate wake of a mighty conflict that he personally had not helped direct, save in its terminal days (Europe) and months (Asia)?

While there is considerable space for scholars to dispute about Stalin's assumptions, policies, and strategies, the character of the Soviet dictator is as open a book today as is Truman's. In the president's case, unlike Stalin's, however, scholars have found much room to debate the wisdom of his policy and strategic leadership. The historians' verdict on Stalin approaches consensus on a failing grade. Like his fellow dictators Hitler and Mussolini, Stalin himself proved the principal architect of his foreign policy failures. Unfortunately, those failures both contributed to and comprised part of the narrative of the great Cold War. What remains contested is the extent to which Truman's performance in conducting U.S. grand strategy

[36] Dallek, *Harry S. Truman*, pp. 14–16.

may needlessly have exacerbated an inherently conflictual Soviet-American relationship.[37]

In 1945, Truman possessed considerable naïvety as a would-be world statesman, but he was anything but naïve about politics. He was a political professional of distinctly modest achievement and limited and limiting life experience, who had seized his own strategic moment. During the Second World War, he led a long-running, politically prominent, though not especially important, investigation into waste, fraud, and mismanagement in the war effort. Truman was an opportunistic, street-smart senator, whose political career the sleazy Pendergast political machine in Missouri had sponsored.[38] Personally, he was honest, though he owed his career to the goodwill of those who were not. Throughout his career, but especially in its terminal phase in 1951–1952, he found himself beset by rumors and accusations concerning the real and alleged misdeeds of some of his close friends and associates. Personal loyalty was among Truman's more attractive qualities, a fact that served him ill when he remained faithful to those whose misbehavior splashed mud on the presidential office.

A president always remains vulnerable, even hostage, to the behavior of others. At a higher level, this maxim applies also to the relationship between great and less great polities. The Cold War would demonstrate that a supposedly bipolar system of world order could risk perilous disorder by virtue of the conflicting interests and actions of allies.[39] In practice, irresponsibility, or simply different agendas, could endanger superpower safety. In this regard, East Germany, Cuba, South Vietnam, and Israel – and even Britain and France over Suez in 1956 – spring to mind.

Truman did not lack intelligence. Moreover, he had read widely in history and current events. But in 1945, as noted already, he was painfully short of the relevant knowledge, understanding, and any approximation of the training necessary to perform as a president. Truman had to cope with the problems posed by a paranoid Soviet leader blessed with no moral compass beyond expediency and heavily influenced by his own version of a morbid and irrelevant ideology. Moreover, that Soviet leader commanded victorious armies which stood on the Elbe. And almost as challenging to U.S. statecraft as the geopolitical reality of mid-1945 was Stalin's apparent belief that he enjoyed Western understanding and compliance with his postwar political designs. Stalin had read the signals transmitted by Churchill and Roosevelt–most especially, though not solely, at Yalta – as an amber, if not green, light to consolidate a Soviet sphere of interest-as-control in East-Central Europe.

---

[37] For a representative, more than marginally negative, scholarly judgment on Truman the statesman, see Hogan, *Cross of Iron*.

[38] This was the political machine of John Pendergast, centered on Kansas City.

[39] This argument, more accurately a major finding, is a theme in John Lewis Gaddis, *The Cold War* (London, 2005).

What the world saw in Truman in 1945 was indeed the man himself. He was blessed with a strong physical constitution, a robust, quick intelligence, and attitudes, opinions and many habits entirely standard for a person from the deeply interior, insular, and parochial American Midwest. Culturally, Truman was a thoroughly faithful representative of his time, place, and experience. His career as a politician appeared distinctly inadequate for the starring role, but despite a relatively undistinguished record, he possessed solid virtues. While painfully aware of his unreadiness for the White House, he also lacked hubris and excessive ambition. Nevertheless, he was fully confident that he would be able to rise to meet the demands of the presidency. Generally speaking, he was a clever politician, a true professional, not unduly blinkered by ideology. He was, however, prepared to act as a man of principle and to bring wrath down on those whom he believed were not.

Truman made a virtue of plain, even blunt, speaking, while both his contemporaries and historians disagree as to whether he was decisive.[40] On one hand, Truman could be indecisive when he lacked confidence in his understanding of a problem or when he had good grounds to fear negative publicity, as during the crisis with General Douglas MacArthur in 1951. On the other hand, paradoxically perhaps, he arguably could be unduly decisive when his ignorance led him to be overimpressed by the most recent persuasive voice. More to the point, his record demonstrates that he was more than sufficiently decisive, and faithfully steady in command thereafter, about policy and grand strategy.

Truman had no truly extraordinary gifts or life experience prior to 12 April 1945. He was not physically imposing. He was not a great orator. He was not intellectually brilliant. In 1945 he did not possess a dazzling résumé. However, his notably ordinary gifts of clarity of thought, plainness of speech, and solidity of standards, principles, and values were tempered with a political professional's comprehension of how one needed to play the game of (domestic) politics. This ordinary frame proved more than adequate to cope with a genuinely strategic moment for U.S. statecraft.

Significant among Truman's virtues was his frank recognition of his limitations, though he did not believe these to be seriously inhibiting, and his readiness to seek out and employ faithfully (i.e., support reliably) those who possessed the talents and experience which he lacked. Specifically, Truman was sufficiently modest and prudent to tolerate large figures among his senior lieutenants in policy and strategy. In a word, here was a president who could and did delegate. Furthermore, his judgment of some key men and affairs was sufficiently wise for him to identify safe pairs of hands. His

---

[40] See Miller, *Plain Speaking*, in which the former president, as quoted, lives up to his reputation for directness of expression.

dislikes derived from his personality and culture: flamboyant generals such
as Douglas MacArthur and dishonest, grandstanding political demagogues
such as Joseph McCarthy, for example, as well as journalists who dared criticize his beloved daughter Margaret. His animosities were fairly ordinary,
in common with the rest of him.

A thumbnail sketch of this rather ordinary midwesterner, thrust unexpectedly into the presidency on 12 April 1945, is not hard to provide. Truman
was smart, widely and well read, but not deeply educated. He was personally principled, though fairly, indeed unduly, tolerant of others who were
less so. He was firm of purpose, once he had decided on that purpose. He
was not given to complicate further matters that were already complicated
enough; in fact, he was inclined to a questionable reductionism. This was a
virtue for a domestic politician who, through focusing on the essentials, had
little difficulty empathizing and communicating with his politically enabling
domestic base. He was not a profound, let alone an original, thinker, but
then arguably, he did not need to be, given the context of his time, place
and circumstances.

Above all else, perhaps, Truman was comfortable with himself as president. Typically, he was willing and able to make big decisions, while in
nearly every case, he would take sound advice from those whom he came to
trust. Both scholarship and commonsense tell us that the most fundamental
basis of sound leadership is trust. Leader and follower must trust each other
if their relationship is to remain healthy. Truman felt comfortable delegating
roles and missions. He could be a tenacious and strong-willed chairman of
the board, as it were, but he trusted some intellects and résumés greater
than his own, and to a quite remarkable degree, he could cope with the
personalities that possessed them. Truman was fortunate to inherit Stimson
from Roosevelt, albeit briefly, while his ego tolerated delegation of prominent responsibilities, most particularly to General of the Armies George C.
Marshall, as secretary of state and later secretary of defense, and Dean G.
Acheson, as secretary of state from 1949 to 1953.

On occasion, Truman could be ignorant, petty, unwise, and unlucky, but
then, so can we all. His vices, like his virtues, were ordinary. The latter
included a commonsense intelligence, a deep sense of duty and honor, an
ego of ordinary size keyed to realistic self-assessment, an ambitiousness
overfulfilled by his elevation, the ability to listen, a willingness to make
sometimes difficult decisions and then abide by them, and a preference for the
orderly processes of government. Fortunately, his virtues were far stronger
and of much greater significance than his vices.

This essay now turns to the highly contested zone that is the historical
record. By and large, there is no mystery about what happened between
1945 and 1953. The challenge is to explain and understand the verifiable

record and the theory that best explains it, with specific focus on the quality of Truman's leadership.

COMMAND PERFORMANCE: CONTESTED NARRATIVES

For the American side of Soviet-American relations from 1945 to 1953, there is little scope for dispute over what was attempted and done, and why. In contrast, the consequences and wisdom of American behavior continue to fuel scholarly controversy. We can explain the course of history, but how should we understand it? For the Soviet side, by and large, we know what was done and attempted, but there remains considerable room for argument over Stalin's motives. In the opinion of this author, at least, there is only modest space for scholarly disagreement concerning the consequences of Soviet behavior.

It may be helpful to remind readers of the course taken by the *Schwerpunckt* of Western scholarship over the past half century. Historians have predominately ascribed the appearance, intensification, and overt militarisation of the Cold War in the Truman years successively to (1) Soviet misbehavior and paranoia; (2) American misbehavior and paranoia; or (3) the malign synergism of two paranoias and interacting tracks of behavior perceived and misperceived as hostile. Compared with this elementary sequence of thesis (orthodox), antithesis (revisionist), and synthesis (postrevisionist), the argument here might be labelled "3 $\frac{1}{2}$." It is substantially postrevisionist in privileging the evil consequences of toxic interaction, while it returns in some degree to assigning prime responsibility for the long struggle to Soviet assumptions and behavior.

However, unlike a surprisingly large fraction of historical analyses, this essay is not censorious. Neither the Soviet Union under Stalin nor Truman's America misbehaved notably – at least, the two polities did not misbehave when they are assayed according to their own cultural, political, and ideological assumptions. One needs to take sensible account of the contemporary geopolitical realities and perceptions. This is not to say that one could not, or should not, attempt to assign relative responsibility for a costly historical passage of virtual warfare. But one can avoid charging that responsibility with moral content. Truman's America and Stalin's USSR behaved in ways nontrivially pushed by what academic jargon has usefully termed the "systemic backdrop." In other words, the making of policy and grand strategy for world politics of 1945–1953 was by no means an exercise drafted in real time on a tabula rasa. Yes, key individuals and rank happenstance, interacting unpredictably, at least unpredicted, at times did make history. But that history moved broadly along a course systemically well prepared by late 1945 and early 1946.

As we have sought to emphasize, although individuals did make a difference to the course of events, human beings represent only one of the major contexts that, functioning together as a gestalt, produces outcomes. The geopolitical and, hence, military strategic facts of the Soviet Army's conquest and occupation of East-Central Europe (and somewhat beyond) was not really a matter of Soviet policy choice. There had been no practicable, let alone desirable, alternative for Stalin than to chivvy his military machine to pursue the retreating Wehrmacht whither it fled. History and events set the stage for the Cold War.

Two (or three, if Britain is counted) preponderant great states had been victorious allies only of convenience. They were certain to be rivals, and probably enemies, in the postwar world. One must add to that general, eternal, and universal lore of statecraft the specific conflictual geopolitics of continental Heartland versus maritime Rimland.[41] In addition, one needs to take into account the hostility licensed by the distinctiveness of two mutually exclusive ideologies. Furthermore, when one considers the systemic backdrop of a paranoid Stalinist regime and a tough, no-nonsense political professional from Missouri, the postwar historical moment of 1945–1947 was unlikely to witness an outbreak of any semblance of true political peace.

Although one must recognize the essential unity of foreign and domestic politics and policy, it would be a mistake to interpret either Soviet or American behavior in foreign policy in this period as driven primarily by domestic motives, though these were always present. It is the case that domestic and other political insecurity was a significant factor for both sets of leadership, but in the Soviet case, the cause was largely, though not entirely, paranoia. As for the Truman administration, it was sufficiently insecure domestically that most political observers believed its tenure would terminate in the November 1948 elections. Increasingly from 1945 to January 1953, domestic political criticism and vociferous opposition were simply facts of life for Truman and his lieutenants. Stalin's paranoia achieved a clinical intensity by 1952 that manifested itself in the preparation of yet another bloody purge.[42]

Yet, Truman's genuine political vulnerability at home had surprisingly little impact on his course in grand strategy. It should not be forgotten that Truman, though by no means all in his cabinet, shared most of the cultural and other assumptions of midwestern Americans of his generation and experience. He was unusually well read in history; after 12 April 1945, he was exposed to an uncommonly large quantity of information about the world; his political and legal duties obliged him to be more or less

---

[41]   In addition to the works on geopolitics cited earlier, see W. H. Parker, *Mackinder: Geography as an Aid to Statecraft* (Oxford, 1982); and Brian W. Blouet, *Global Geostrategy: Mackinder and the Defense of the West* (Abingdon, 2005).
[42]   The "doctors" plot, a triumph of Stalinist constructivism.

prudent in transferring his beliefs and opinions into America's behavior in the international arena. Nonetheless, to a fundamental degree, Truman had little difficulty in leading America because his vision of the desirable, and in notable measure also his grasp of the practicable, were not usually far out of step with majority opinion in the American electorate.

On the evidence of the verifiable record, Truman took such notice of public sentiments as a politician must, but his pace and vector of evolution and change in high policy typically were popular enough for him not to risk domestic political disablement. Where actual and predictable opposition might have proved lethal to Truman's purpose, for example over the European Recovery Program (ERP) in 1947–1949 (the Marshall Plan) and with respect to America's commitments to NATO, the president and his cabinet officers proved sufficiently energetic and persuasive in coopting or sidelining opponents.

Truman was courageous in adhering to his principles, though not always heroically so (e.g., in denouncing hysterical McCarthyism in 1950–1952). The president did have the politically somewhat disarming habit of speaking his mind more plainly than was typical of most politicians. What helped noticeably to save him from the perils of such frankness was the expedient fact that his core decency and commonsense led him to convictions that truly were mainstream among his fellow Americans.

To assess Harry Truman's leadership in policy and grand strategy, this essay now will pose and answer four questions. Specifically:

1. What was attempted and done, 1945–1953?
2. Why was it done?
3. How well was it done?
4. How dangerous was it to do?

1 *What was attempted and done, 1945–1953?*

During these nine years, the United States led a complex process of reconstruction in Europe and Asia to achieve a condition sufficiently robust in its essentials that it would persist beyond the demise of the Soviet Union and into the twenty-first century.[43] Leaving aside for the moment matters of judgment, the record demonstrates the purposeful building, in succession,

---

[43] For a superb combination of narrative history and analysis, see Judt, *Postwar*, part. 1. Another sound narrative history, this one focused on the major concern in this essay, is George C. Herring, *From Colony to Superpower: U.S. Foreign Relations since 1776* (Oxford, 2008), chap. 14. Readers also should profit from acquaintance with Marc Trachtenberg, *A Constructed Peace: The Making of the European Settlement, 1945–1963* (Princeton, NJ, 1999). Two fine workmanlike student textbooks also warrant honourable mention: Mark S. Byrne, *The Truman Years, 1945–1953* (Harlow, 2000); and Peter Calvocoressi, *World Politics since 1945*, 9th ed. (Harlow, 2009).

of the economic, then the political, and, finally, the military tiers of Western security between 1945 and 1953. Not without good reason did Dean Acheson title his memoirs *Present at the Creation*.[44]

Stated simply as factual accomplishments, for the moment bereft of comment, the United States played the vital role in kick-starting and then accelerating European economic engines with the Marshall Plan, as well as by its management of international finance through the International Bank for Reconstruction and Development (IBRD), the World Bank, the International Monetary Fund (IMF), and the General Agreement on Tariffs and Trade (GATT) – all, save the Marshall Plan, the products of the 1–22 July 1944 Bretton Woods Conference.[45] The United States led the process of political reconstruction in Europe by forging a new (West) German state that, for reasons of force majeure, could be neither neutral nor unified, out of the former American, British and French zones of occupation. It encouraged and pressed hard for measures of European economic – leading hopefully to political – coordination, cooperation, and possibly unification. It underwrote the grand strategic security of the new Free World, or West, by promoting and joining a peacetime alliance, NATO, a peacetime commitment unprecedented in 150 years of American history. It resisted militarily the first post-1945 example of cross-border invasion by a Communist-run polity (North Korea). It vigorously led a cascading process of rearmament and set in motion political steps which, albeit with hesitation on the part of some and with notable changes in strategy, enabled the rearmament of West Germany within NATO.

All of the preceding resulted from the concept, policy, and strategy of Containment. This eminently contestable term yielded coherence to the U.S. national security project from 1946–1947 until the close of the Cold War. This bare recital of facts is noncontroversial. (West) Germany's return to polite (Western) international society in 1954 was the direct product of American political efforts during the Truman years.[46] It is simply factual to

---

[44] Dean Acheson, *Present at the Creation: My Years in the State Department* (London, 1970).
[45] It is worth noting that an important reason why the Truman administration performed as well as it did in the economic and financial, including trade, reconstruction of international order was because it was led by some officials with serious firsthand experience of high finance: examples include Paul H. Nitze, Robert Lovett, and James Forrestal. Given the scale and complexity of the economic and financial challenges in the early postwar years, not to mention the harm wrought by the purposefully negative influence of Soviet agent Harry Dexter White, the number two man in the U.S. Treasury Department, the presence of such outside experts was crucial. See Jim Lacey, "The Economic Making of Peace," in Murray and Lacey, eds., *Making of Peace*, pp. 293–322. For the Marshall Plan, see Greg Behrman, *The Most Noble Adventure: The Marshall Plan and Time When America Helped Save Europe* (New York, 2007).
[46] Inadvertently, many American historians understate seriously the British contribution to President Truman's successes in foreign policy. By way of some corrective to unduly patriotic American historiography on the "creation" of the "West," see the following

state that the Western architecture for international security in the second half of the twentieth century was all but complete by the time Dwight D. Eisenhower took the oath of office on 20 January 1953.

2 Why was it done?

By early 1947, American grand strategy under Truman had settled by prudent default on the idea of resisting further geopolitical gains for Stalin's imperium. The word *Containment*, though assuredly not the concept, entered general public and official currency with authority as a result of the prominence it received in George F. Kennan's "Mr X" article in the *Foreign Affairs* of April 1947 as the plausible, master solution to America's Soviet problem.[47] Truman did not understand that Stalin most probably believed Roosevelt had informally ceded Soviet control over East-Central Europe. We can only speculate as to whether Stalin would have been prepared opportunistically to advance his dominion geopolitically beyond the stop lines of May 1945 had the necessary doors been open and unprotected.

What historians do know for certain is that Stalin consistently required unqualified control at home as well as abroad in polities he regarded as rightfully in his domain (by conquest, by some historical authority, and by agreement, explicit or implicitly inferred). There is no way of knowing what Roosevelt ultimately would have made of, or done about, Soviet behavior in Poland and elsewhere, although we know he was disturbed by reports he received after Yalta in the last days of his life. What is certain, though, is that Truman had not knowingly been party to any signals from Washington that Stalin might have misconstrued as implying compliance with his establishing a satisfactory quality of control.[48] Indeed, Stalin may have taken American inaction over Soviet malpractice in East-Central Europe as meaning tacit consent, though most probably it was appreciated accurately enough in Moscow as reflecting nothing other than incapacity. Viewed in retrospect, it is plausible to claim that, with respect to the establishment of his East European imperium, Stalin did what he was always going to do: secure total

---

British studies with a London focus: John Baylis, *Anglo-American Defense Relations, 1939–1984* (London, 1984); Ian Clark and Nicholas J. Wheeler, *The British Origins of Nuclear Strategy, 1945–1955* (Oxford, 1989); and Paul Cornish, *British Military Planning for the Defense of Germany, 1945–50* (Basingstoke, 1996).

[47] "Mr X" [pseud. George F. Kennan], "Sources of Soviet Conduct." See its author's explanation and disclaimer of some of its consequences, 20 and more years on, in Kennan, *Memoirs, 1925–1950* (London, 1968), chap. 15. Containment became a much contested concept, policy, and strategy, in Cold War revisionist writings in the late 1960s and the 1970s.

[48] Stalin required control in the English-language sense of reliable direction, not in the French sense of *contrôle*, meaning only a general supervision. The latter would have to depend on a quality of trust that was utterly alien to Stalin's nature.

and reliable control, unless something intervened forcefully to prevent him. Given that the United States was the only potential candidate to frustrate his designs, but given also that it lacked the means – political, economic persuasive or punitive, military – physical, and psychological-moral – all that could be in doubt about the Soviet imperium were the details of its process of establishment.

Truman and his advisers almost certainly misinterpreted Soviet behavior in 1945–1949 as aggressive steps taken to advance the course of dominion over much or all of Eurasia.[49] Instead, Stalin was securing in characteristic ways what he had some reasons to regard as rightfully his to dominate and, in effect, to own. Whether Truman and his lieutenants misread Soviet behavior in those years – and there must always be some element of doubt regarding Stalin's motives as well the possibility of historical narratives alternative to the actual record – there is little room for doubt about the motives that drove U.S. policy as well as its grand and military strategy.

As usual, Thucydides' triptych was right: "fear, honor, and interest" were authoritative, alive, and working overtime.[50] Taken in reverse order, Truman's America perceived a vital U.S. interest in the reconstruction of a devastated Europe. That interest was geopolitical, economic, and military-strategic, to differing degrees. The United States had determined to do all it could to insure that a materially and psychologically depressed Europe should be sufficiently restored to prosperity that it could resist the lures of Communism.[51] Such a restoration of economic, then consequently political, confidence would both inoculate fractured and depressed European societies

---

[49]   I am much persuaded by the interpretation of Stalin's behavior provided in Zubok and Pleshakov, *Inside the Kremlin's Cold War*, rather than by the return to almost 1960s vintage revisionist argument presented recently in the somewhat radical pages of Geoffrey Roberts, *Stalin's War: From World War to Cold War, 1939–1953* (New Haven, CT, 2006). The debate continues.

[50]   Thucydides, *The Landmark Thucydides: A Comprehensive Guide to 'The Peloponnesian War*,' ed. Robert B. Strassler (New York, 1996), p. 43.

[51]   George F. Kennan's mid-1940s theorizing and policy advising were long on the vital importance of the psychological reconstruction of depressed European peoples. As a first priority for U.S. efforts, Europeans needed help in regaining confidence in a secure and prosperous future. Kennan, among others, believed that this was the most vital of enabling agents for all that was necessary to follow. In retrospect, it seems to this theorist that Kennan's good argument overreached. It was somewhat akin to the implausible theory that the Confederate States of America lost the (military) war because its people lacked the strength of national identity and moral fibre necessary to sustain their new nationhood in the face of adversity. In the latter case, I believe that many Southerners suffered psychological detachment from their cause largely because their armies were overwhelmed in the field. Military defeat tends to be a potent psychological depressant. See Joseph Glatthaar, *General Lee's Army: From Victory to Collapse* (New York, 2008), esp. chaps. 34–35. As with Confederates in 1864–1865, Europeans were demoralized for good material reasons. In both cases the challenge was to provide concrete evidence of success; only then could morale improve. For Confederates this proved impossible, but for Europeans, the challenge was met.

against the commission of irredeemable political error and contribute in essential ways to America's security.

Next, as a notably ideological polity, the confident, victorious, and prosperous United States of the immediate postwar period believed it had a duty, even a manifest destiny, to shine the light of its values, principles, and practices in some currently dark places. This is not to suggest that the United States has ever been entirely averse to ruthlessly self-interested behavior. America's self-regard and reputation were always bound up in a sense of identity as the exemplar of a better way of life. Considerations of honor, in every nuance of its meaning, suggested the necessity of America's doing good in the world. Truman was an entirely sincere believer in the quintessential goodness of the United States and its values. Ironically, perhaps, according to his lights, Stalin also was a true believer in the merit of his personal, and his polity's, destiny.

The first item in Thucydides' triptych grew slowly from 1945 through 1950, with events seemingly confirming the somewhat speculative perception that Stalin's Soviet Union was an implacable, but cunning and fortunately generally risk averse, enemy engaged in a total struggle with the United States for global dominion. What Americans, not unreasonably at the time, regarded as Soviet misbehavior in East Central Europe – in Poland, then, slowly but still definitively, in Bulgaria, Rumania, Hungary, and, most provocatively of all, Czechoslovakia – hammered nails in the coffin of hopes for a postwar prolongation of the Grand Alliance. The Czech coup in February 1948; the road, rail and water blockade of Berlin from 24 June 1948 until 5 May 1949; and, as the last straw, the invasion of South Korea by North Korea on 25 June 1950 seemed to provide incontestable confirmation that the United States had everything to fear from the Soviet Union. One must add to this cascade of events the first Soviet test of an atomic bomb on 29 August 1949, Stalin's efforts to transform his occupation zone in Germany into a profitable satrapy, and the final success of Mao Zedong Communists in China in 1949.[52] It seemed to many highly intelligent and well-informed persons in North America and Western Europe that Stalin's Russia was a monster on the march.

A major factor explaining why Truman's America behaved as it did was that there appeared to be no superior alternatives to the pursuit of a vigorous, if initially largely nonmilitary, containment of an aggressive Soviet Union. Truman, his counsellors, and indeed the American people through their congressional voices, judged the risks of America not acting to reconstruct Europe (and East Asia, especially Japan) as being far too high to

---

[52] On the Soviet atomic bomb project, see the thus far incomparable book by David Holloway, *Stalin and the Bomb: The Soviet Union and Atomic Energy, 1939–1956* (New Haven, CT, 1994).

be acceptable.[53] America's leaders in the 1940s typically were geopolitically educated in the theories of Halford J. Mackinder and Nicholas John Spykman. They thought in terms of a Eurasian Heartland with peripheral Rimlands.[54] They were genuinely fearful that America might find itself confined to the northern portion of a western hemisphere effectively isolated from, even (depending on the magic in the geopolitical cartography deployed) surrounded by, a hostile, alien, Soviet-led would-be global imperium.[55] A succession of Soviet-authored, or suspected strongly to be Soviet-authored, mishappenings supported initial American suspicions of Soviet intentions. The pattern of events from 1945 to 1947–1948 drove American leaders and their advisers to believe the Soviet Union's intentions malign as well as exhibiting bad faith in reference to Americans' reading of Soviet undertakings at Yalta and Potsdam.

In 1946 and 1947, George F. Kennan became an unlikely prominent prophet for the thesis that there was an existentially implacable Soviet challenge, but he was by no means the first. Harry Truman and his chief advisers had agreed by early 1946 that Stalin's Soviet Union needed to be prevented from enlarging its area of control and influence. However, what was far from obvious in 1946 was how best to achieve that goal, on which there was a growing domestic American political consensus.

---

53 In heated defense of its all but demand for a massive rearmament program, the key policy document NSC-68 of 14 April 1950 was especially eloquent on the subject of risks. The risks inherent in resisting the "inescapably militant" evil Soviet grand design were contrasted favorably with the risks of compliance. In Paul Nitze's words in the document: "There are risks [endangering some of the benefits of 'freedom'] we will invite by making ourselves strong, but they are lesser risks than those we seek to avoid." "United States Objectives and Programs for National Security, NSC-68," 14 April 1950, reprinted in Etzold and Gaddis, eds., *Containment*, p. 415.

54 FDR was conceptually a president much in tune with intellectual fashion. Explaining his basic rationale for opposing the Axis powers, the president had argued that America must not become "a lone island in a world dominated by the philosophy of force." Quoted in Leffler, *Preponderance of Power*, p. 22. The geopolitical image of an isolated America excluded economically and politically from traffic with Eurasia was a constant theme in the logic of American national security policy and grand strategy from the early 1940s until the end of the Cold War. Mackinder introduced the Heartland concept and term in his 1919 book *Democratic Ideals and Reality*, pp. 73–74. Spykman's high contemporary reputation in the early 1940s, and certainly his name recognition by the general public, did not long persist after his early death in 1943. Mackinder biographer Brian W. Blouet has written that: "Spykman was not the author of containment policy, that is credited to George Kennan, but Spykman's book [*America's Strategy in World Politics*], based on the Heartland thesis, helped prepare the U.S. public for a post-war world in which the Soviet Union could be restrained on the flanks [of Eurasia: CSG]." "Halford Mackinder and the Pivotal Heartland," in Blouet, ed., *Global Geostrategy*, p. 6. In his original conception in 1904, Mackinder defined the Heartland, then termed the "geographical pivot area," strictly with reference to physical geography. It was that huge area in the center of Eurasia that was inaccessible to sea power. By 1919, and then in 1943, Mackinder's definition of the Heartland became more inclusive, courtesy of the intrusion of strategic judgment to augment the merely geographical.

55 See the sensible judgments in Dallek, *Harry S. Truman*, pp. 37–46.

3 How well was it done?

A plausible answer to this question requires careful definition of the problem. We know what the Truman presidency attempted and did in the connected fields of policy and strategy. We can answer in an autistic, self-regarding way how well the president and his advisers crafted and effected policy and grand strategy. Rather more difficult to answer is the question whether what was done and attempted was necessary. The intimate follow-on question must be whether Truman's policy and strategy, no matter how elegant and even effective, had negative consequences in their impact on the relationship with Stalin and his Soviet empire-imperium.

To abbreviate what could be told as an excruciatingly complex and detailed narrative, Truman's America succeeded beyond reasonable expectation in reconstructing, indeed, in constructing, a Western Free World. That world was to be security-proofed – economically, politically, and militarily – against everything save the accidental but lethal political train wrecks of history or by major folly in high places. Virtually the entire architecture of international order in its potentially cataclysmic East-West aspects either was in place or its features were well enough anticipated by the end of 1949. The sole exception lies in the vital military field. The West did not begin seriously to recognize military reality until the NATO Council Meeting of 18–19 December 1950.

It is a matter of record that the Marshall Plan, the 16.5 billion-dollar kick-start to European economies requested of Congress by Truman (though only 13.5 billion dollars was spent), proved a runaway success. In today's prices, the value of Marshall Plan aid actually delivered to Europe was approximately $200,000,000,000. The political reconstruction and construction of much of Europe could hardly have been prosecuted more effectively. This creation advanced within the embrace of a permanent North Atlantic Community, institutionalised in NATO, which came to have psychological, geopolitical, and eventually, albeit belatedly, in the opinion of this author, military reality. The EU-Europe of today is the linear descendant of the Europe-rebuilding efforts of the American and European statesmen of the late 1940s and early 1950s.[56] Truman and his advisers led this effort initially, and it was underwritten, as it needed to be, by American power in its several dimensions. This is not to underrate the importance of the contribution by European politicians to the enterprise, an effort junior, but not minor, when contrasted with the American.

---

[56] It is impolite in continental Europe for an Anglo-American scholar to point out that the roots of the EU-Europe of the 2000s should be located in the economic colonialism implemented by the Nazi occupation. Most especially was this true for the creation of the European Coal and Steel Community (ECSC) by the Paris Treaty of April 1951.

The job of reconstruction was done well. But was it the right job? And was such success in and by the West purchased at too high a price in consequent Soviet antagonism?[57] Was much of that antagonism really a consequence of the American-led drive to reconstruct Europe? Perhaps the American drive was the default option among a shortlist of policy and strategy alternatives that, prudently regarded, were not really alternatives at all.[58] For fear of irritating or offending Stalin needlessly, might not the United States have been wise to withdraw its concerns about Europe from the active policy file and instead return to some variant of political and strategic isolation? Alternatively, should Truman have tried much harder, more consistently and persistently, to allay Stalin's suspicions? The questions are many but alas not definitively answerable. However, in the firm view of this scholar, Stalin's suspicions were so firmly based on his personality and ideology that geopolitical triggers could only add fuel to a permanently conflictual condition.

By way of a Parthian shot in answer to this third among my questions, it is at least arguable that the Truman administration overreached on the prudence-imprudence spectrum in its policy and strategy for European reconstruction and was fortunate not to have its record blighted by some lethal historical ambush.

4 *How dangerous was it to do?*

Nearly everyone in Washington whose opinion carried some weight for U.S. policy and strategy from February 1945 (Yalta) to June 1950 (the invasion of South Korea) agreed that the Soviet Union posed no immediate military threat to American interests. The historical record appears to confirm that assumption. After all, there was no movement by Soviet armies in Europe beyond their high tide mark of April–May 1945, and there were even some subsequent withdrawals.

Although now we know better, the invasion of South Korea was heralded as the first postwar case of Soviet-authored overt military aggression across an international boundary, a recognized, if in practice contested, cartographic line of division (the 38th Parallel). Secretary of State Acheson noted in his notes preparatory to a congressional hearing in 1950: "The profound lesson of Korea is that, contrary to every action preceding, the USSR took a step which visited – however remotely – general war. No other action has

---

[57] For a hostile assay of Truman's record in national security, see Offner, *Another Such Victory*, chap. 16.

[58] I recognize that prudence is a virtue that arrives as a guide empty of specific historical content. That granted, it is significant that French sociologist and philosopher Raymond Aron identified prudence as the supreme virtue in statecraft in his masterwork, *Peace and War: A Theory of International Relations* (Garden City, NY, 1966), p. 585.

done this – not even the Berlin Blockade." He went on to emphasise that this was the "all important *new* fact."[59] Seen in retrospect, Stalin's sponsorship of Kim il Sung's adventure was none too enthusiastic and, almost certainly, was not regarded in Moscow as an especially useful step on the high road to world dominion.

In the event, what Stalin achieved with his lukewarm sponsorship of the North Koreans was the military institutionalization of NATO, vital political progress towards West German rearmament within NATO, and an immediate quadrupling, in due course lowered to a medium-term tripling, of the U.S. defense budget and the initiation of a long-term competition the Soviet Union could not win. Truly, one can claim that to be a great statesman or military commander, one requires a needful yet permissive historical context. But in addition, probably above all else, there should be an inadvertently cooperative enemy. As Edward N. Luttwak argues convincingly, strategy is paradoxical and ironic in nature.[60] It is certainly the case that Western perceptions of Soviet misbehavior in 1945–1953 enabled Truman and his lieutenants to demonstrate competence in exceptionally trying times. Nonetheless, it is only fair to observe that most of the architecture of postwar Western security was constructed with the large bricks representing egregious errors by Stalin.

Beginning in 1944 and proceeding inexorably in 1945, Stalin's establishment of the new satellite polities of East-Central Europe, most especially Poland, represented such disdain for what one might call the "decent opinion of mankind" that it all but invited maximum irritation in the West. In 1946, Stalin pressed too hard over base rights in Turkey and was dilatory in withdrawing his soldiers from their occupation of northern Iran. By 1947, cumulative Soviet economic depredations (disguised vaguely as "reparations") and political clumsiness, in the context of British withdrawal from Greece, moved Truman to declare engagement in a global struggle that the Americans elevated subsequently in public discourse to a "doctrine," announced on 12 March. The particular issue of the day was American assistance to the domestically embattled Greeks and an externally threatened Turkey, in place of the bankrupt British.

The general message, however, declared that "it must be the policy of the United States to support free people who are resisting attempted subjugation by armed minorities." Truman rather overreached with the ideological language in which he clothed his request to Congress for $400,000,000 to assist the two menaced polities. We know now that the bloody insurgency in Greece was not of Soviet making and did not enjoy Stalin's support. Its foreign backing primarily was Yugoslavian. But that is not the way it seemed

---

[59] Dean Acheson, as quoted in McMahon, *Dean Acheson*, p. 134 (emphasis in original).
[60] Luttwak, *Strategy*, p. xii.

to American eyes. There is no denying that given an ideologically moderate president, albeit one faithfully a man of his time and place, the unaccustomedly vivid rhetoric in the Truman Doctrine contributed unhelpfully to the theological dimension in the rivalry with Stalin's Soviet Union. Nonetheless, Vojtech Mastny is persuasive when he writes: "Meeting the Soviet threat as a moral challenge was congenial to the American mentality."[61] Significantly, Mastny does not suggest that Truman himself shared in that moralizing mentality, notwithstanding that, in American politics, it is domestically expedient to clothe one's behavior in proclaimed high purpose, especially when the claim is more or less sincere.

Understandably enough, Stalin responded to Truman's declaration of global struggle, or resistance to aggression, as intended in Washington. The aid program for Greece and Turkey, then the Marshall Plan to fuel European economic reconstruction, both in 1947, then the early steps taken toward achievement of a possibly united Germany distinctly friendly to the United States all encouraged Stalin to secure the quality of control he required over Czechoslovakia. Rapid consolidation of the new imperium was the order of the day, most especially in a Prague whose political future remained too open for Stalin's taste.[62] The pro-Soviet coup of 19–25 February 1948 was a genuine shock to American leaders, but it was of great assistance in helping move American and Western European opinion in favor of German political rehabilitation.[63] When the three Western occupying powers introduced a new common currency, the Deutsche mark, in their zones on 20 June 1948, Stalin replied by committing the blunder of initiating a road, rail, and water blockade of Berlin on the 24th of that month. This attempt physically to deny access to the former German capital contributed massively to American and Western European perceptions of a great Soviet threat. In hindsight, it is reasonably obvious that in 1947 and 1948, Stalin principally was reacting

---

61 Mastny, *Cold War and Soviet Insecurity*, p. 196.
62 Stalin's problem with the Western-style democracy that threatened in Czechoslovakia early in 1948, as previously it had elsewhere in East-Central Europe, was that the electorate might make an historically wrong choice. Since Soviet occupation practices were overtly predatory, even somewhat "friendly" voters could not be trusted to elect the candidates who enjoyed Soviet sponsorship.
63 It is important not to forget that George Kennan contributed to U.S. grand strategy not only a potent, if imprecise, concept – Containment – but also the assumption that Soviet hostility was permanent and could not usefully be reduced by persuasion or negotiation. This was the central message of "The Long Telegram" of 22 February 1946. Pending regime change in Moscow, Soviet antagonism would be an unalterable fact of global politics. On the record of the Cold War, wherever else Kennan may have erred, plausibly most especially over the necessary priorities in U.S. grand strategy, he was correct in his postulate of a permanently hostile Soviet Union. Moscow stopped being hostile only when it ceased to be Soviet. Stalin's hostility was an expression of his personality, but absent that factor, plainly the ideological and geopolitical fuel for the antagonism was sufficient to sustain 37 years of a rather warlike peace after the tyrant's demise on 1 (or 2) March 1953.

to American-led initiatives to reconstruct Europe and create a world order tolerable for Americans. But to contemporary observers, Stalin's behavior conformed plausibly to a pattern of measured and opportunistic aggression, one that carried with it dark echoes of Nazi Germany's behavior in the late 1930s. The opportunism at issue was deemed only tactical because the Truman administration believed that the unhealthy melding of Soviet ideology and cynical geopolitical reasoning had produced a dangerous and mortal enemy.

It is fortunate for the Western world that Stalin was so maladroit as to provide the necessary ammunition when most needed for Western European recovery. Stalin's greatest blunder, his giving the green light to North Korea in 1950, enabled the United States and its allies to summon the political will to pay for a truly serious program of rearmament. In retrospect, it is plain that Truman presided over a considerable exaggeration of the Soviet threat. Contemporary official documents bristle with fearsome depictions of the Soviet will to achieve world domination.[64] In those years there was little official understatement of the Soviet Union as the greatest of menaces. But what kind of current and near-menace did Americans understand it to be?

To make political and strategic sense of Truman's statecraft and grand strategy, it is essential to recognize that the dominant official U.S. attitude toward Stalin's Soviet Union from 1945 to 1953, certainly to June 1950, was a combination of political optimism and military pessimism, as Stephen T. Ross has judged in his masterly study of the U.S. war plans of the period.[65] In those years, Truman purposefully waged what amounted to economic and political warfare against the Soviet Union. This endeavour de facto was licensed, fuelled, and decorated by American ideology and was prosecuted by individuals who felt secure in the belief that there was no great near-term military danger to national security. To rewrite a familiar line of 1898 doggerel by Anglo-French writer and historian Hilaire Belloc: "Whatever happens we have got the atomic bomb, and they have not."[66] How could Truman and his fellow construction workers for postwar recovery have been so certain Stalin would tolerate the rebuilding of countries in a manner friendly to American values and material interests, all within the reach of the

---

[64] Most especially, the language of NSC-68 of 14 April 1950 positively boiled with reference to a Soviet "totalitariat"—as frightful a neologism as ever was—mortal challenges, speculation that Moscow might seek a decisive military victory should opportunity knock, and so on, in a similar terrifying vein. "NSC-68," passim. For a retrospective view of the policy document, its provenance, purpose, and consequence, see David Callahan, *Dangerous Capabilities: Paul Nitze and the Cold War* (New York, 1990), chap. 4.

[65] Steven T. Ross, *American War Plans, 1945–1950* (London, 1996), p. 19. "Thus, [by mid-1946] the JCS adopted a position of military pessimism coupled with political optimism."

[66] With apologies to the long late Mr Belloc. His original reads: "Whatever happens we have got the Maxim Gun, and they have not." Quoted in Carlo D'Este, *Warlord: A Life of Winston Churchill at War* (London, 2009), p. 104.

Soviet Army? Why would he not use those canonical (albeit assuredly over-counted by Western Intelligence agencies) 175 line and 35 artillery divisions, at least 31 of which were within a fairly short drive of the Rhine, not to mention his 56 "allied" divisions, to bring the great Western reconstruction project to a crashing and explosive halt?[67]

The numbers just cited come from the estimate submitted by the Intelligence Committee to the U.S. Joint Chiefs of Staff (JCS) in late February 1949.[68] For its part, the United States had deployed "one division and three regiments in Europe and five divisions and five regiments in [North America]." On the other hand, American intelligence estimated "the Soviet Union had 20,100 aircraft, including 1,725 long-range bombers, and the Navy possessed 400 submarines and 3,225 planes."[69] The North Atlantic Treaty Organization[70] fielded the equivalent of ten divisions in the new Federal Republic of Germany. "Planners [in 1949] estimated that eighteen [divisions] were required to conduct an effective fighting retreat to the Rhine."[71] It is easy to see why Britain's "Field Marshal [Bernard Law] Montgomery reported in mid-June [1949] that the Allies had little chance, given current force ratios, of offering effective resistance to the Red Army."[72]

This essay opened with the claim that there is a vital sense in which Truman had won the Cold War by, and in, 1949. Self-evidently, Stalin chose to tolerate the U.S. and British policies that enabled so successful an American-led, albeit European prompted, outcome as the main legacy of the immediate postwar years. But did he have an attractive alternative? Most policy makers in Washington, though not quite all, assumed that Stalin was neither desirous nor capable of waging war successfully against the West. Unlike the gangsters of Nazi Germany, who believed that history was working against them, Soviet leaders knew that adventurism could be a sin against the prudence that their theory of historical change endorsed.

However, confident though he was of eventual victory for his beliefs and geopolitical patrimony—his destination and personal destiny were reliably secure—Stalin was a sufficient realist to know that history can yield nasty surprises. The Soviet near-defeat in 1941 must have been seared into his

---

[67]   Defense communities often seek to compensate for the deep uncertainties of their business by fixating on certain magic numbers. In the early years of the Cold War, 175 Soviet divisions was one such figure which gained in authority from its largely uncritical repetition by officials. It is in no small measure ironic that although the fairly ready order of battle of the Soviet Army was almost certainly overestimated, Western beliefs about Stalin's willingness to employ it, albeit most likely correct, bordered on the complacent when regarded in historical context.
[68]   Ross, *American War Plans*, p. 138.
[69]   Ibid.
[70]   Comprising the twelve countries that signed the North Atlantic Charter on 4 April 1949.
[71]   Ross, *American War Plans*, pp. 38–39.
[72]   Ibid., p. 39.

consciousness; indeed, how could it not have been?[73] Although he could not match the U.S. atomic arsenal mathematically or psychologically in perception and influence for some years to come, Stalin might well have reasoned that his great Western enemy was better bested today than tomorrow.[74] Although the Soviet Union needed time both to recover from the awesome damage and losses of the Great Patriotic War and to acquire an atomic capability, its leader recognized that power is always relative and that one cannot hold it in excess. While the Soviet Union should be absolutely far more powerful by the middle to late 1950s than it was in the late 1940s, so, too, would be its enemies. Overall, what was the character and content of the military – implying the strategic – balance between the United States and the Soviet Union from 1945 to 1953?

It was dynamic, of course. Both countries demobilized: the Soviet Union modestly, the United States precipitately and in obedience to no political or strategic guidance worthy of the name. To tell the military facts of the period could well occupy the whole length of this essay. Naturally, the story evolved year by year, by no means in lockstep with the course of political and economic history, at least not west of the Iron Curtain. Rather than burden the narrative with gratuitous detail, this essay shall confine itself to providing a simple itemized characterization of the most salient military realities of this eight-year period:

1. The U.S. military establishment did not regard its growing atomic arsenal as a guarantee of victory in war with the Soviet Union. Not until the early 1950s did the United States acquire sufficient atomic ammunition, means of delivery (aircraft), and adequate logistical infrastructure to support an atomic campaign.[75]

---

[73] See Geoffrey P. Megargee, *War of Annihilation: Combat and Genocide on the Eastern Front, 1941* (Lanham, MD, 2006); and Chris Bellamy, *Absolute War: Soviet Russia in the Second World War* (London, 2007), chaps. 8–12.

[74] The heroic scale of the Soviet effort to close America's atomic lead is well explained in Holloway, *Stalin and the Bomb*. From a desperately slow start during the war, in September 1945, Beria was ordered to get the job done as soon as possible at any cost.

[75] The U.S. atomic stockpile in the years of most interest for this essay is reported none too reliably as having grown as follows: 1945, six bombs; 1946, 11; 1947, 32; 1948, 110; 1949, 235; 1950, 369; 1951, 640; 1952, 1,005; 1953, 1,436; 1954, 2,063; and 1955, 3,057. The Soviet stockpile is estimated, even less reliably, as having progressed as follows: 1949, 1; 1950, 5; 1951, 25; 1952, 50; 1953, 120; 1954, 150; and 1955, 200. One needs to be sceptical of exact seeming precision, just as one should of round numbers. These particular figures derive from R. S. Norris and H. M. Kristensen, "Global Nuclear Stockpiles, 1945–2002," *Bulletin of the Atomic Scientists*, 58 (2002), pp. 103–4. Alternative, much lower numbers for the early years of the U.S. stockpile may be found in David Alan Rosenberg, "U.S. Nuclear War Planning, 1944–1960," in Desmond Ball and Jeffrey Richardson, eds., *Strategic Nuclear Targeting* (Ithaca, NY, 1986), p. 38. Rosenberg credits the United States with only two bombs in December 1945, nine in July 1946, 13 in July 1947, and 50 in July 1948. "None of these was assembled." A further, more recent source of reference is NRDC (Natural Resources Defense Council), "Nuclear Data: Table of U.S. Strategic Force

2. American planners assumed officially and consistently through all these years that war with the Soviet Union would resemble the Second World War, but with an atomic addition for the West alone until 1950. They anticipated in 1949–1950 that the Soviet atomic counterthreat would mature to lethal proportions by 1954, the so-called year of maximum danger.[76] They believed that when the Soviet Union could deliver 200 atomic bombs against the United States and its principal strategic assets, it would effectively level the East-West playing field, with atomic arms of both sides paralyzed as potent instruments. Logically, they reasoned that a growing Soviet arsenal must negate the U.S. ability to threaten with its atomic arsenal as an asymmetrical offset to Soviet conventional power in Eurasia.

3. However, throughout the period, the American atomic arsenal and long range airpower (along with a navy, albeit for several years after 1945 much reduced from its wartime scale) were the only means available to support Truman's statecraft militarily. In actuality, the nuclear-capable airpower was none too impressive prior to General Curtis LeMay's assumption of command of the Strategic Air Command (SAC) in November 1948. As late as 1949, "the Air Force had only 66 B-29s, 38 B-50s, and 17 B-36s able to deliver atomic bombs, hardly an overwhelming number."[77] The atomic arsenal grew usefully throughout this period, but even by 1951–1952, alone, it was not believed to be the answer to the U.S. dilemma of how to protect its European security dependencies.

4. During the whole Truman era, the U.S. military establishment struggled with the strategic reality that it lacked the ability to deny the European littoral to Soviet conquest. A succession of U.S., British, and later NATO war plans all reflected the same basic, inescapable circumstance, namely, that NATO could not deny Soviet land and air power the ability to occupy the whole of Europe should Stalin choose to flex his muscles. "Plans" (most especially in the form of estimates of what would be needed) to conduct a "fighting retreat" successively to the Rhine, then to the Channel coast (though possibly holding on to a bridgehead in Brittany), then to the Pyrenees, and in the extreme, into Morocco were the order of the day. The U.S. Navy was not overly optimistic that a Dunkirk-style evacuation from Iberia to Morocco would be logistically feasible. This probably would not have mattered

---

Loadings, 1945–2002," http://www.nrdc.org/nuclear/nudb/datab1.asp. This third listing tells us that the U.S. atomic stockpile stood as follows: 1945, six bombs; 1946, 11; 1947, 32; 1948, 100; 1949, 200; 1950, 330; 1951, 500; 1952, 720; 1953, 878; 1954, 1,418; and 1955, 1,755.

[76] "NSC-68," pp. 399–400, 415–17.
[77] Ross, *American War Plans*, p. 13.

because it was unlikely that anything resembling an Allied army could have retreated under fire all the way across Europe from Germany to coastal Andalucia and Gibraltar. At no time prior to 1953, when President Dwight D. Eisenhower unveiled his "New Look" at defense and its strategy, was the atomic bomb hailed *militarily* as the potential savior of Western security.[78]

5. The degree of American and Allied military pessimism varied in detail from 1945 to January 1953, but the dominant scenario anticipated was not in doubt. To be specific: (1) Soviet armies and air forces would overrun most, and probably all, of continental Western Europe and might – or might not – be able to invade Britain; (2) from the periphery of Continental Europe (Britain and the Middle East), the United States would punish the Soviet Union with air strikes, including the use of atomic bombs; and (3) the United States would mobilise and rearm, as it had in 1940–1945, and eventually, as in 1943–1945, U.S. and British military power would surge back in a great counteroffensive to destroy Soviet forces and win the game ashore in Eurasia late in the conflict's second half.

6. The rapid growth in the size of the U.S. atomic stockpile, and the increase in SAC's ability to deliver those weapons after 1949, obviously promised an ever more devastating air-atomic offensive.[79] Unfortunately, though, Western military planners perceived the simultaneous emergence of a Soviet atomic arsenal as having the ability both to negate much of the deterrent value of the SAC's air-atomic potency and, in use, to wreak increasingly serious damage on the all important capacity of domestic America to mobilise the sinews of eventual victory.

7. The strategic context just outlined was overtaken by the consequences of money and technology. U.S. technological success with its programme of research into nuclear fusion, as contrasted with nuclear fission, heralded a revolution in explicit, though not necessarily implicit, strategy. After 1953, the West came to be armed with thermonuclear rather than only atomic striking power, a factor which seemed to

---

[78] The Eisenhower "New Look" was expressed in the document NSC-162/2, "Review of Basic National Security Policy," 30 October 1953. This capstone policy paper can be accessed online, http://www.mtholyoke.edu/acad/intrel/pentagon/doc18.htm.

[79] All authorities agree that the SAC of the late 1940s left a great deal to be desired, if it were to function as the white knight of the West. See Harry R. Borowski, *A Hollow Threat: Strategic Air Power and Containment before Kennan* (Westport, CT, 1982). The story of U.S. air-atomic striking power in the 1940s is not a pretty one. In addition to Borowski's sad narrative, Rosenberg, "U.S. Nuclear War Planning, 1945–1950," and Ross, *American War Plans*, reveal the severe contemporary limitations on America's prospective military atomic prowess in war.

sideline the former critical issue of the gross imbalance in land and airpower available to contest continental Europe.

8. Truman decided to develop the hydrogen bomb that was to retire for many years the deeper anxieties about NATO's nominal in-theatre vulnerability to Continental conquest. However, it is difficult to evade the conclusion that the atomic arsenal was not approached by the president with the intellectual care and attention that it would seem to have merited on several grounds. Given that together with the navy, the Bomb was the only American long(ish) suit of much relevance to an East-West war in the period from 1945 to January 1953, its care, feeding, command, control, and strategy would seem to have deserved far more thought and guidance from the Oval Office than the record indicates they received.

9. We know that Stalin did not choose to fight in these years. Moreover, we know that no war occurred by history's accident or by the catalytic effect of misbehavior by an ally. However, Truman could not know what we know today. What he did know, for certain, was that every net assessment of the current and near-term future military context in Europe predicted a clear victory for Soviet arms. There were no dissenting voices on this matter. Did Truman ignore these steady predictions of hypothetical military disaster in Europe? The answer is no. Instead, he took note of the dire military context, then sought and located more than adequate political and strategic compensation in the comforting assumption that Stalin's Soviet Union did not pose a contemporary military threat, only a political one.

It so happens that Truman and his advisers proved correct in this most vital belief (or was it a leap of faith?). However, on the extant evidence of all kinds, and in light of the president's wide and deep historical reading, not to mention his own life experience, was it a prudent assumption to make and to which to adhere, year after year? Suffice it to say that the combination of military pessimism and political optimism obviously had no small potential to result in catastrophe. But how can one argue with success? The Soviets did not choose violently to preempt the reconstruction of Europe and the creation of the West. Ergo – or was it? – Truman's statecraft was nothing short of a brilliant success.

CONCLUSION: HARRY TRUMAN'S LEADERSHIP – THE ASSESSMENT

Truman did not create the Cold War, though his leadership assuredly had a notable impact on the pace of its emergence and its variable temperature. It is essential to appreciate that there was no gentler, kinder, fundamentally more cooperative Stalin (or Soviet Union) that might have been teased into reality by more skilful statecraft on the president's part. Stalin – his personality, his beliefs, and his state – were what they were, and neither Truman nor anyone else could have altered any of the three. Stalin was a thoroughly convinced Communist, albeit one whose behavior could be almost infinitely flexible for tactical purposes in pursuit of his goal of maximum control over anything and everything that did, or might, menace what he valued. In order, what he valued were (1) the security of his personal power, (2) the security of his state; and (3) distantly and with mixed emotions, progress in the historical process of global Communisation. The three were happily conflated in Stalin's mind. Personality, geopolitics, and ideology truly were one. Stalin was not uncertain or confused about his historical situation or intentions. He knew that he and his personal and ideological vehicle-state, Lenin's monstrous creation, the USSR, were permanently (until ultimate victory) at war, or warlike peace, with capitalist societies, as were the leading capitalist states among themselves. Truman and America were enemies by definition and conviction, period. The detailed implications of this profound belief for Soviet policy, strategy, and tactics would have to vary opportunistically with evolving circumstances and events.

To conclude this analysis, one needs to return to the four claims advanced in the introduction.

First, Truman as leader got the big things right enough. Good leaders need to be sound of judgment about the most important matters. With this in mind, one can plausibly argue that Truman was plainly right, or right enough, on the major challenges to American policy and grand strategy. The president was a relatively early convert to the thesis that Stalin's Soviet Union was a systemic and unappeasable adversary. The historical record underlines that Truman was correct in this belief. Fundamental Russian hostility terminated – albeit temporarily in the view of this author – only when its Soviet dimension melted down between 1989 and 1991. The United States and the West that Truman led for nearly eight years could not, under any circumstances, achieve a political peace with the Soviet Union.

That does not mean that there was a need to anticipate imminent warfare, but it does translate as a general endorsement of Truman's policy assumptions. His grand strategy is more open to question in its military aspect, but the historical record indicates beyond argument that he was successful in pressing forward grand strategic priorities privileging the economic, the political, and the military, in that order. Truman should receive credit both for conceptual prudence, in his broad endorsement of Containment, and for policy effectiveness in his command performance in grand strategy. Each of the main strands of his grand strategy – economic, political, and military – bound together purposefully by the idea of containing, and perhaps rolling back, Soviet power and influence, were handled in practice well enough, especially in their economic and political facets. It is hard to fault Truman's leadership on the basics of the larger security issues of the period.

Second, Truman had to work hard to get it right enough. It is true that Truman was blessed with the assistance of some outstanding people, especially General George C. Marshall as secretary of state (1947–1949) and later (1950–1952) as secretary of defense, and Dean Acheson as secretary of state (1949–1953). But he also possessed a personality that could allow those lieutenants to shine. Truman was a genuinely modest man who frankly recognized his limitations, though he would brook no disrespect to the authority of the office of the presidency, at least not for long, as General Douglas MacArthur discovered to his surprise on 11 April 1951.[80]

Truman as a domestic political professional knew what needed to be done to appeal successfully to the electorate, and he understood in fine-grained detail how political business was conducted in Washington, D.C. He led policy personally when he needed to, but he was content to donate the opportunity to secure glory, admittedly as a matter of political prudence, to the greater among his cabinet officers. As a principal example, the president insisted that Marshall rather than he announce the proposal for what became the Marshall Plan.[81] This may have been shrewd politics, but on the evidence, it would seem to have been one of great generosity as well.[82]

The Republicans were ever more ascendant in Congress as Truman's tenure in the White House lengthened. All but self-evidently, it followed that the president needed to exercise all his political and personal skills if he were to obtain the quantity and quality of political support necessary to enable policy and grand strategic effort and success. Though plain-spoken, and by nature not one to turn the other cheek, the president consistently led his administration in a bipartisan manner concerning the major national security issues of the day. In short, Truman did well enough what presidents need to do in domestic and foreign politics, if their intentions are not to be reduced to mere vanity. It is well to recognize, for example, that neither the Marshall Plan nor Western Europe's political, and later, military reconstruction, including the rearmament of a new Federal Republic of Germany, occurred as natural happenings, by divine fiat, or by some inexorable logic

---

[80] See the fine account of this unsavory episode by John W. Spanier, *The Truman-MacArthur Controversy and the Korean War* (New York, 1965). For an analysis that does not admire what he judges to have been Truman's record of indecisiveness when treating with wayward generals and admirals, see Dale Herspring, *The Pentagon and the Presidency: Civil-Military Relations from FDR to George W. Bush* (Lawrence, KS, 2005).

[81] See Behrman, *Most Noble Adventure*, chap. 3.

[82] Truman is quoted as saying: "It [the Marshall Plan] was called that because I realized that it was going down in history as a very great, very important thing, and I wanted General Marshall to get credit for it, which he did. I said to him, 'General, I want the plan to go down in history with your name on it. And don't give me any argument. I've made up my mind, and, remember, I'm your Commander in Chief.'" Miller, *Plain Speaking*, p. 257.

of history; rather they occurred through sufficiently prudent, typically wise, and more often than not skilfully persistent statecraft. That process was the direct result of a whole complex of interlocking initiatives directed by the man then in the Oval Office: Harry S. Truman.

Third, Truman made no irretrievably damaging mistakes in policy and grand strategy. In support of this claim, one need only refer to the objective facts of Cold War history. By skill, luck, or both, the major decisions taken by this president, a man who identified decision making as the core of his duties, produced no egregious errors in policy and strategy. In this respect, if no other, the history of the Cold War speaks for itself. There was no East–West war directly involving the West and the Soviet Union during the Truman years, or indeed thereafter. The broadest of relevant policy concepts, Containment, served adequately to provide navigational assistance to the whole succession of Cold War presidents. They may not always have implemented the idea prudently, but at least they were not confused as to America's prime responsibility for international order.

Of course, there were mistakes in detail, but to notice that is not to score points in debate against Truman's record. Every president errs. The challenge for competency is not to perform with zero plausible defects but rather, when caught out in error, to behave in ways that can be modified, redirected, or halted before lasting harm results. One can argue that Truman was too slow in rearming America, that he invested the Cold War rivalry unduly and unnecessarily with ideological trappings that rendered cool political judgment more difficult, that he gratuitously fed the suspicions of an already paranoid Stalin, and that he utterly misread the nature and character of Stalin's policy intentions and proximate strategic goals. These are heavy charges indeed, but this writer does not find them convincing, even though, not surprisingly, there is some measure of plausibility in them. The whiff of merit about such points is just sufficient to warrant the particular kind of comment expressed in the fourth, concluding, claim:

Fourth, Truman was lucky. This is neither to praise nor to criticize the president. However, one might incline to generosity, endorsing the maxim that many improve their luck by honing their skills and hard work. Nonetheless, it is hard to avoid concluding that Truman's calculated risk in postponing American rearmament until the press of menacing events foreclosed the alternatives was a judgment call, actually a guess, that verged on the hazardous, perhaps the reckless.[83] In 1945–1947, there was no anti-Soviet or anti-Communist hysteria in America to which Truman had to bow. From wherever the Cold War came, it was not initially from the domestic politics of the United States. The president and his advisers edged into the conflict with some reluctance, hesitation, and denial. Strongly negative assessments

[83] See the concluding judgment in Ross, *American War Plans*, p. 155.

of Soviet (mis)behavior drove Truman cumulatively – as it were, attrition-ally – to accept the necessity for resistance to what was perceived as a pattern of Soviet aggression.

One can criticize the president for some commissions and omissions, but as an overall judgment, it is difficult to disagree with John Gaddis's con-clusion that the Cold War was a struggle necessary for the United States to wage.[84] It did not wage that struggle immaculately, but when could this be claimed for the policy and grand strategy of any leader in any historical era? On the critical side, the U.S. government in the middle and late 1940s may have been somewhat in denial with regard to its Soviet policy and strat-egy. This suggests an apparent paradox. On one hand, America's political leaders assessed Stalin's steady political hostility, as well as his readily mobi-lizable military power, in a fashion that even today appears to have been substantially accurate. On the other hand, despite an explicitly anti-Soviet U.S.-led effort to reconstruct Europe, Washington and London assumed that Stalin would not exercise his military ability to overrun continental West-ern Europe and probably much of the Middle East as well.[85] This resulted in simultaneous military pessimism and political optimism among Western leaders. Threats always are assessed as comprising the compounded result of capability and political intention. American leaders in the late 1940s chose to pick the Soviet political intentions that were most congenial and expedient given Western military unpreparedness and disarray.

This essay has focused on Truman's and America's policy and grand strat-egy, but it is instructive to recognize that most of what has been written here on the military side of threat applies also to the British record in this period. Of course, Britain was bankrupt, massively diverted by the messy process of colonial divestiture, and lacked the atomic bomb. However, London, too, slid only reluctantly and, one could say, halfheartedly into the role of senior lieutenant to America's Cold War generalship. A factor probably short-changed in this essay was the role played by European anxiety over a residual, certainly potential, German menace. It is hard today to empathize as we must try to with a generation of leaders who had only just defeated a superpower Nazi Germany in a terrible, protracted war. This essay, in

[84] Gaddis, *Cold War*, p. ix.

[85] Vojtech Mastny tells us that "the two documents from the Cold War's formative period that the Russian authorities have thus far chosen to release show a strictly defensive posture." "Imagining war in Europe," in Mastny, Sven G. Holtsmark, and Andreas Wenger, eds., *War Plans and Alliances in the Cold War: Threat Perceptions in the East and West* (Abingdon, 2006), p. 16. Before we hasten to conclude that Stalin's intentions were "strictly defensive," it is appropriate to note, as Mastny allows, that "[t]he dark Stalin years still leave us much in the dark about what Soviet strategy really was at that time. The weight of the fragmentary evidence lends support to its defensive rather than offensive character." This may well be true, but it is a truth that is convenient for Russian authorities to have us believe today.

common with nearly all the histories of the period, struggles to grasp the German legacy in the minds of the survivors, even though victorious, of the greatest of history's wars. After all, Germany surrendered only on 8 May 1945, and we have been discussing U.S. policy and strategy, particularly with reference to Soviet intentions toward a devastated Europe, with displaced refugees by the millions on the roads heading in all directions.[86]

In sum, Europe was ruined, truly a disaster zone, and the focus of most in the West, not excluding political leaders, was as much or more on Germany than on some arguable Soviet threat. It is a common trait for politicians, and even some military professionals, to deny probability to possibilities with which they believe they cannot cope. Because the Western Powers could not defend continental Europe successfully against a Soviet invasion, throughout the Truman years, it was convenient to believe that Stalin's political intentions did not match what his armies unquestionably could have achieved.

Obviously, on the unarguable evidence of what the historical record shows did not occur, Truman and his advisers exercised sound judgment. However, we are entitled to conclude that the benign assumption that the Soviets did not pose a contemporary military threat sufficient to warrant Western rearmament prior to June 1950 was more an expedient leap of faith than calculated judgment. For a more generous concluding thought, it needs to be said that political and strategic leadership requires some genius translated into action as educated intuitive judgment. Plausibly, we should recognize that Truman made the right calls when and where it mattered. Moreover, scarcely less important, he led and supervised the command performance that got the most necessary jobs done. This is what leadership is all about.

[86] See Richard Bessel, *Germany, 1945: From War to Peace* (London, 2009).

9

Patterns of grand strategy

RICHARD HART SINNREICH

Readers who have navigated all seven of the cases examined in the preceding pages might be pardoned for doubting whether grand strategy, in the sense of the consistent execution over time of a preconceived strategic design, is even possible, let alone likely. Certainly none of those cases reveal such a pattern. "In fact," as Professor Murray notes in his introduction, "those who have developed successful grand strategies in the past have been very much the exception ... a strategic framework, much less a grand strategy, has rarely guided those responsible for the long-term survival" of the state.

Instead, on the evidence of our cases, grand strategy is much more likely to be imputed retrospectively by admirers and critics than developed and applied self-consciously by the statesmen whom they typically credit or blame. At least two of the statesmen examined in the preceding essays explicitly acknowledged that reality in strikingly similar analogies: Britain's Robert Lord Salisbury likened the business of managing foreign policy to "float[ing] lazily downstream, occasionally putting out a diplomatic boat-hook to avoid collisions," while his great Prussian contemporary, Prince Otto von Bismarck, similarly insisted that "man cannot create the current of events. He can only float with it and steer."

Both certainly were too modest. But history confirms that even in war, in which its explicit formulation is most likely, grand strategy almost never will be executed as conceived. The fortunes of war are too chancy and adversaries too unpredictable to underwrite such prolonged consistency. In periods of peace, consistent strategic behavior is even less to be expected. Quite apart from competition with other policy interests, it would require not only that grand strategy's prompting aims endure essentially unaltered but also that the environment in which they must be pursued alter minimally, or at worst predictably. Instead, as Murray argues, "there is rarely clarity in the effective casting of grand strategy because by its nature, it exists in an environment of constant change, where chance and the unexpected are inherent."

In fact, only two of the seven cases examined here reveal a preconceived strategy grounded in an explicit analysis of the prompting challenge, both not coincidentally involving the United States.[1] The first – Franklin D. Roosevelt's decision to prioritize Europe over the Pacific should the United States be drawn into World War II – reflected not only his own conviction but also that of his senior military and naval advisers that the United States could not tolerate Germany's outright defeat of Great Britain. As James Lacey writes of Admiral Stark, Roosevelt's chief of naval operations, "the consequences of a British defeat would be so serious for America that, the United States ought to assist in every way possible." Seven years later, confronting a Soviet Union apparently aspiring to the same Continental hegemony that the United States had helped fight two European wars to prevent, Harry S. Truman's Containment policy likewise embodied an explicit strategic design reflecting the perceived strengths, weaknesses, and motives of America's Soviet adversary.

Even in those two cases, however, subsequent American behavior scarcely adhered slavishly to the nominal dictates of the relevant strategies. Throughout World War II, Lacey reports, the diplomatic, political, bureaucratic, and resource tensions between America's two principal theaters of war repeatedly threatened both strategic coherence and Allied comity. Similarly, as Professor Gray's discussion of the Truman Doctrine suggests, and as events both during and after the period he examines confirmed, in practice, Containment at best incompletely guided U.S. strategic behavior throughout the Cold War.

For many, Bismarck is the exemplar of the successful grand strategist. As Professor Jones notes, however, even "Bismarck's great genius as the founder of a Prussian-dominated German nation lay not in his adherence to a systematic program or plan but in his expert navigation of uncertain events through intuition and broad experience."[2]

In the other four cases, any preconceived or systematic strategic behavior at all is considerably harder to detect. Pursuit of *la gloire* and French preeminence, Professor Lynn tells us, motivated Louis XIV throughout his

---

[1]   Some would add Churchill's undoubtedly courageous decision in May 1940 to fight on alone after the impending fall of France, and it certainly is true that after the subsequent entry of the United States into the war, Churchill sought repeatedly to steer Allied military strategy – and to a considerable extent, succeeded. However, evidence of any mature Churchillian strategic design prior to that is difficult to identify. Some commentaries on Churchill's stance at the time compare him to *David Copperfield*'s Mr. Micawber, who keeps hoping that "something may turn up" (thanks to the Japanese, of course, it did). See John Lukacs, *Five Days in London: May 1940* (New Haven, CT, 1999), p. 127.

[2]   He is careful to add, however, that "Bismarck never set his country on a course that his mind had not cautiously explored beforehand."

lengthy reign. As Lynn demonstrates, however, the practical expression of those ambitions altered radically as France's military and economic circumstances changed and as the French monarch's incautious pursuit of absolute military security generated reciprocal insecurity among his neighbors. Similarly, during the Seven Years' War, Professor Black argues, "[Britain's] strategic culture was altered considerably, indeed transformed, during and by the war, as much as it caused it, or set its alignment." Eventually, accelerated by the succession of George II by George III, that change produced a virtual reversal of Britain's strategic priorities, with imperial ambitions superseding the Continental concerns that had originally prompted the contest.

Ironically, a century and a half later, precisely the opposite turnabout occurred, as efforts to preserve her empire under growing economic and military pressure increasingly forced a reluctant Britain back into the very Continental engagement from which she had for decades deliberately remained aloof. Finally, as Murray explains in his essay on Britain's interwar strategy, the terrible consequences of that reengagement, together with renewed distrust of her old adversary Russia, would profoundly distort Britain's appraisal of the rise of Nazi militarism and almost fatally delay her response to it.

In short, conditions encouraging even the formulation, let alone the prolonged execution, of grand strategy as deliberate method seem to be uncommon at best, and even then impermanent. Defined more modestly as a broad guiding aim or principle – for example, preservation of a balance of power or prevention of Continental hegemony – grand strategy is more likely to endure. Even then, however, its impact on strategic behavior almost certainly will be episodic and inconsistent. Like a vessel under sail, grand strategy is at the mercy of uncontrollable and often unpredictable political, economic, and military winds and currents, and executing it effectively requires both alertness to those changes and constant tiller correction. In the end, more than an unattainable foresight, it is that essential adaptability – together with, as Gray rightly notes, a good deal of luck – that is likely to determine any nation's strategic success.

Adaptation is by no means synonymous with improvisation, however. Even an imperfect navigational chart is usually preferable to none at all, provided that those who employ it recognize and accommodate its imperfections. To quote Jones once again, "in a world in which outcomes are indeterminate, competent strategy consists not in establishing long-range goals and systematically structuring policies and procedures to fulfill them but rather in a clear understanding of one's principles and priorities and a flexible, creative approach to realizing incremental gains in the short term." Gray advances what amounts to a corollary, arguing that "the key to quality in political and strategic leadership is not the avoidance of error, which is impossible. Instead, it is the ability to make small rather than large mistakes and to err generally in ways for which one can readily find adequate compensation."

On the record of the cases examined in the preceding pages, several factors seem to condition the success with which nations and their leaders have satisfied these requirements. One such prerequisite is the ability to reconcile continuity with change. Spurning the first forfeits consistency; ignoring the second invites irrelevance. As Murray comments, "those who develop a successful grand strategy never lose sight of the long-term goal, whatever that may be, but are willing to adapt to the difficulties of the present in reaching toward the future." None of the statesmen discussed in the preceding pages adhered more closely to that principle than Bismarck. As Jones writes, "what stands out in Bismarck's formulation is a conscious flexibility in achieving his ends, and quite possibly flexibility in framing the ends themselves – in short, a coldly unsentimental understanding of the state's interests and how to pursue them."

In contrast, the failure to discipline near-term behavior with long-term aims almost invariably invites strategic problems. Thus, describing the changes through which French military policies evolved during the 72 years of Louis XIV's reign, Lynn remarks that "Louis abandoned a strategy based on alliances and international agreements for one based on unilateral action that increasingly isolated France... Ultimately, his grand strategy caused him to overstretch the resources of France, which were insufficient to stand against all Europe, and the wars of the Sun King bankrupted the state."

The problem is even greater during war itself, when, as Lacey points out, the immediate priority to win on the battlefield can easily overwhelm efforts to shape the postwar environment. As the late U.S. ambassador John McCloy once commented in relation to U.S. strategic decisions during World War II, "we concentrated so heavily on the actual conduct of the war that we overlooked the need for political thinking."[3] Not the least of the challenges confronting any wartime grand strategy is that of preventing tactics from driving strategy. In turn, that requires harmonizing a military bias toward concrete planning against defined objectives with a diplomatic bias toward retaining maximum political flexibility, a trick that even great nations rarely have managed to master consistently over time.

For democracies, in which periodic political change is structural, reconciling the present with the future presents a special challenge. As one writer

---

[3] John J. McCloy, *The Challenge to American Foreign Policy* (Cambridge, MA: Harvard University Press, 1953), p. 44. A notorious but far from the only example was Eisenhower's decision to halt Anglo-American offensive operations at the Elbe, a decision to which the British strongly but fruitlessly objected. See Forrest C. Pogue, "The Decision to Halt at the Elbe," in Kent Roberts Greenfield, ed., *Command Decisions* (Washington, DC, 1960), p. 479.

recently commented with respect to the British government, "in a society such as Britain, where politics is a spectator sport, with every tackle covered by the breathless and indefatigable media, the bonds between the public and their leaders invariably fray over time."[4] Given the resulting episodic shifts in leadership, maintaining any strategic continuity at all requires not only foresight but also considerable political courage and self-discipline. Indeed, not the least of the challenges confronting strategic leaders is recognizing when *not* to act and, as important, the political stamina to sustain that inaction in the teeth of invariable pressures to "do something." As diplomat and historian George Kennan once noted, "the counsels of impatience and hatred can always be supported by the crudest and cheapest symbols; for the counsels of moderation, the reasons are often intricate, rather than emotional, and difficult to explain."[5] War only exacerbates the problem. In Lacey's words: "when one is leading a democratic nation in war, it is important that the people see their military forces doing something on a large scale every year. This was something on which Marshall, who never truly understood the political dimension of the conflict, commented bitterly after the conflict was over." The same problem continues today to bedevil Marshall's successors.

Still another obstacle to taking the long view is that, while the future impact of current strategic behavior is essentially unknowable, its prompting concerns tend to be all too visible. Britain's efforts at the turn of the twentieth century to adapt her imperial commitments to a changing global power distribution were extraordinarily successful in solving the immediate problems to which they were directed. However, they also contributed subliminally to an accelerating deterioration of Continental relationships, the ultimate consequences of which none of those responsible fully anticipated, or perhaps even could.

As Murray demonstrates, a similar problem afflicted Great Britain's interwar policies. With the benefit of hindsight, it is easy enough today to recognize the futility of Neville Chamberlain's appeasement policy. For Britons of the late 1930s, it was much harder. Writes one commentator, "although today it is considered shameful and craven, the policy of appeasement once occupied almost the whole moral high ground. The word was originally synonymous with idealism, magnanimity of the victor and the willingness to right wrongs."[6] Winston Churchill was a distinct political nonconformist in that regard, calling public attention to the threat of Nazism as early as 1934. Yet, as Murray points out, even Churchill occasionally succumbed to the temptation to subordinate the indefinite requirements of the future to

---

[4]   Catherine Mayer, "Brown's Blues," *Time*, June 22, 2009, p. 30.
[5]   George F. Kennan, *American Diplomacy* (Chicago, 1984), p. 62.
[6]   Andrew Roberts, *The Holy Fox: A Biography of Lord Halifax* (London, 1991), p. 49.

the more pressing demands of the present, as his sponsorship of Britain's notorious ten-year rule constraining military budget estimates revealed.

While British reluctance in the 1930s to recognize Churchill's "gathering storm" in part reflected the public and political disillusionment generated by the horrors of the First World War, it also reflected profound incomprehension of the fundamentally revolutionary character of the Hitlerian challenge, a challenge in that respect wholly different from its predecessor of 1914. As Murray notes, among British leaders, "there was a deep-seated assumption that no matter how crass and bullyish the Nazis and Fascists appeared, both Hitler and Mussolini were men of reason... with whom Britain could deal in a reasonable fashion." As much as anything else, that fundamental misreading explains British leaders' persistent efforts to appease Adolph Hitler despite his repeated lies and betrayals. As too few recognized, not since Napoleon Bonaparte had Europe encountered a similar phenomenon. It was above all the profound sense of history that enabled Churchill to diagnose that terrible similarity and its potential strategic consequences were Hitler not confronted that distinguished Churchill from his less perceptive contemporaries.

From a grand strategic perspective, therefore, the vital lesson of the 1930s may be that in a revolutionary environment characterized by the refusal of one or more international players to abide by informal but generally accepted political and military rules of the road, it becomes far more difficult not only to diagnose the true nature of the strategic challenge but also – equally important in liberal democracies – to achieve political consensus about that diagnosis before events reach the point of crisis. As Henry Kissinger wrote about the earlier Napoleonic challenge: "Coalitions against revolutions have usually come about only at the end of a long series of betrayals and upheavals, for the powers which represent legitimacy and the status quo cannot 'know' that their antagonist is not amenable to 'reason' until he has demonstrated it. And he will not have demonstrated it until the international system is already overturned."[7] That problem has special resonance for today's strategic decision makers, confronting as they do a fractious world in which no broad geopolitical framework has yet emerged to replace its bipolar predecessor, and in which new actors have arisen that are indifferent to, or reject outright, the traditional norms of diplomatic and military behavior.

Not unrelated to the kind of international political environment in which grand strategy must be pursued, moreover, is the intrinsic character of the aims to which it is directed and, in particular, whether they are perceived to be broadly preservative or transformational. Such descriptors, it goes without saying, are at once incomplete and impermanent. For both Louis XIV

---

[7] Henry A. Kissinger, *A World Restored* (Boston, 1973), pp. 13–14.

and Bismarck, for example, transformational aims ultimately mutated into preservative aims – in Louis's case, in grudging response to financial and military overstretch, and in Bismarck's case, reflecting his ruthless determination to avoid war, a resolution regrettably not shared by his successors. In contrast, Britain's aims during the Seven Years' War evolved in the opposite direction. And during the half-century in which Containment formally guided America's strategic choices, the latter vacillated more than once between transformational and preservative objectives.

Because they seek to change the status quo, transformational aims tend inherently to be more vulnerable to strategic overreach than preservative aims. In part, as it did for Louis XIV, that simply reflects the risk that ambition will outstrip resources. However, as several of our cases suggest, it also invites reciprocity. Transformational aims, by definition, are likely to threaten other states' interests or at least be perceived to do so. Hence, they are more likely to generate countervailing behavior. Moreover, because such aims take for granted the future's tractability, they tend to be insensitive to the lingering effects of history. The difference between the Cold War experience of the United States in Europe and in the Pacific is a case in point. In Europe, despite brief rhetorical flirtation with "roll-back," U.S. strategy aimed largely at strengthening and protecting the free nations on the Continental periphery.

In Asia, in contrast, successive administrations sought to erect new security arrangements in an environment almost entirely lacking equivalent socio-economic and political foundations and in which the legacy of colonialism intrinsically fostered mistrust of America's intentions.[8] Unsurprisingly, the Pacific proved a much tougher strategic challenge than Europe. So also, and for much the same reasons, have America's more recent transformational efforts related to the Muslim world.

That said, even preservative aims easily can be misperceived by those affected or who believe they ultimately might be. As Lynn writes of the Sun King's later wars: "[Louis] never appreciated how his quest for absolute security threatened his neighbors; an impregnable France could bully them with impunity. . . . In modern terminology, Louis lost control of the narrative, which portrayed him as a danger to Europe, and his opponents continued to see him as such." In similar fashion, Kaiser Wilhelm II proved impervious to the impact on British sensitivities of Admiral Tirpitz's insistence on building a battle fleet with which to challenge the Royal Navy, a fleet offering little intrinsic advantage to a Germany militarily dominant on land but presenting a threat to the sea-reliant British Empire that no British government could ignore. And it is at least arguable, as Gray suggests, that "the great

---

[8]   For a more robust argument, see Richard Hart Sinnreich, "A Strategy by Accident: U.S. Pacific Policy in the Cold War, 1945–1972," in Williamson Murray, ed., *Conflicting Currents: Japan and the United States in the Pacific* (Santa Barbara, CA, 2009).

Soviet-American Cold War was amply fueled, if not quite overdetermined" at least in part because Soviet insistence on permanently dominating a western *glacis* from which Russia repeatedly had been invaded looked quite different from the other side of the contested geography.

Whence Lynn's argument that "if a state's ultimate goals are essentially benign but others portray them as threatening and aggressive, then honest transparency can serve to correct international perceptions, allay fears among those who need not feel threatened, and put the real foes on notice." In fact, just such a goal seems currently to be motivating the U.S. government's effort to reset strained relations with both traditional adversaries Russia and China and with the Muslim world in general.

There certainly is nothing wrong with such an effort. On the historical evidence, however, one should be wary of expecting too much from transparency alone, especially when it principally involves rhetorical efforts not confirmed by a visible and enduring alteration of strategic behavior on the part of the nation making the claim. By the midpoint of his reign, for example, even a ruler less arrogant than Louis XIV might have had difficulty convincing Europe of his benign intentions, just as Hitler's efforts to portray Germany as the champion of national self-determination finally proved unconvincing even to those least eager to confront him.

As several of our cases suggest, moreover, the communication of strategic intentions is far from merely a matter of diplomacy. Discussing the differences between Britain and France during the Seven Year's War, Black notes that "in Britain, the politics of the conflict drew on the direction of public political concern to an extent that was not matched on the Continent... [The] war helped powerfully to foster ambitions, not only at the governmental level but also in terms of public discussion." Public pressures likewise constrained Britain's strategic choices both before and after World War I.

Indeed, as Jones acknowledges, even Bismarck was not immune from underestimating the impact of domestic politics, noting that "to those who hold naively that one can prosecute a strategic policy in isolation from the robustness and stability of its domestic foundations, Bismarck's bequest is a cautionary lesson." Today, at a time when information is pervasive and gaps between claim and reality tend quickly to become visible, no grand strategy easily can be formulated, and certainly none can be implemented for long, without reference to its domestic political context. In democracies especially, strategic aims and the behavior they underwrite must first be accepted by national publics. As Gray puts it succinctly, "an American president must lead at home if he is to lead abroad."

Some argue that for that very reason, democracies are at an intrinsic disadvantage in pursuing grand strategy, except perhaps during wars viewed as existential, when even democratic governments are tempted to assume some of the peremptory powers of autocracy. The cases examined here do not confirm that view. Louis XIV enjoyed a discretion that even Bismarck might have envied, but it proved no guarantee of strategic success. Bismarck himself, Jones tells us, was scrupulously careful, however cynically, to devise arrangements "addressing the political aspirations of the middle classes, all the while ensuring the unchecked constitutional prerogatives of the Prussian monarchy" and thus "adroitly manipulat[ing] the liberal rump into a popular bulwark of the authoritarian Prusso-German regime for the next twenty years." When, with his departure, Wilhelm II substituted idiosyncratic rule for Bismarck's political caution and diplomatic self-restraint, self-delusion and disaster followed.

In contrast, while it is undeniable that Britain's cabinet politics materially complicated the process of reaching agreement on strategic behavior before both world wars, in each case, the ultimate result was a relatively unified national polity. That the critical strategic decisions in both cases easily could have gone the other way does not diminish the achievement of the respective British statesmen who successfully forged public and political consensus despite the risks that acting on it entailed. As Murray writes of Churchill: "Above all, [he] provided a narrative on which the British people, the Dominions, and even their military allies could hang their efforts... in one of the ironies with which history redounds, the more desperate Britain's situation, the more the British people rallied behind the prime minister and his stirring words."

Similarly, Gray points out that "for Truman, sensibly prudent policy options confronted not only the paranoid and probably malevolent Soviets, inter alia, but also a legion of actual and potential foes on the American domestic scene." Nevertheless, he shows that, in the astonishingly short interval between the announcement of the Marshall Plan in June 1947 and the signing of the North Atlantic Treaty in April 1949, the Truman administration was able to set in motion strategic policies that would guide the U.S. commitment to Europe for the next 40 years and that ultimately would be crowned with precisely the outcome that the authors of Containment had envisioned.

It helped that, as Henry Kissinger has argued:

> During the Cold War, the unique American approach to foreign policy was remarkably appropriate to the challenge at hand. There was a deep ideological conflict, and only one country, the United States, possessed the full panoply of means – political, economic, and military – to organize the defense of the noncommunist world. A nation in such a position is able to insist on its views and can often avoid the problem facing the statesmen of less favored societies: that their means oblige them to pursue goals less ambitious than their hopes, and that their circumstances require them to approach even those goals in stages.[9]

[9] Henry Kissinger, *Diplomacy* (New York, 1994), p. 23.

Even so, the tribulations that afflicted several of Truman's successors attest to the reality that the domestic and, increasingly, international political support essential to strategic effectiveness is not self-perpetuating but rather must be earned anew as strategic conditions change or are perceived to do so.

Above all, grand strategy must reconcile ends however desirable with finite means. It thus must suppress the temptation to seek strategic perfection. Overambition is the mortal enemy of strategic success, not least because it tends to breed strategic antibodies. As Jones writes approvingly of Bismarck: "[he] demonstrated consistent moderation in defining and pursuing Prussian interests.... He was convinced that military and diplomatic hubris could result not just in failure but also in disaster." In contrast, reviewing the lengthy succession of Louis XIV's wars, Lynn notes that "it was not his particular interpretation of glory in itself that damned Louis but rather the blindly arrogant unilateralism it inspired.... The success of one act of force simply convinced him that the next would meet with resignation as well."

A similar arrogance afflicted Adolf Hitler. Discussing German preparations to invade Czechoslovakia in late summer 1938, Murray notes: "In a series of strategic appreciations, the chief of the general staff, General Ludwig Beck, warned that Germany was in an almost hopeless military position should a major war break out over Czechoslovakia in 1938. Hitler was entirely unwilling to listen to such realism." Munich, of course, convinced him that he had been right to ignore his generals' fears. But while a tactical success, Munich led to a strategic catastrophe. Unable to leave well enough alone, Hitler allowed only six months to elapse before gobbling up the rest of Czechoslovakia, and that finally proved too much even for the reluctant British and French.

Given that strategic perfection is unattainable, and that even its pursuit is likely to be self-defeating, prioritizing strategic effort is essential. That is true, moreover, not only because resources are finite but also because strategy becomes exponentially more difficult to manage as strategic commitments proliferate and as the interconnections among them become more difficult to diagnose. Failure to recognize and reconcile the linkages among such commitments is among the most common of strategic errors. Hence a vital requirement of successful strategic design is to bound the universe of objectives, recognizing that desirable is not the same as important, nor important the same as urgent. Bismarck once again may have been the exemplar. Asked why Germany under his direction had refrained from joining the 'Scramble for Africa,' for example, he famously replied, "My map of Africa lies in Europe." His successors unfortunately proved to be less self-disciplined.

One persistent obstacle to enforcing that self-discipline is the difficulty of assessing strategic risk. Indeed, Gray argues, such assessments "can never be more than useful euphemisms. In fact, commentators should replace pseudometric claims for calculation, for risk assessment in statecraft, with the words *guesswork, intuition,* and *judgment."* At best, risk assessments are hypotheses that only action or inaction itself can confirm or refute. The medical adage, "First, do no harm," thus has more than a little application to grand strategy. Better expressed, sound strategy favors policies the consequences of which threaten the least strategic damage should the premises underwriting them prove to be wrong. In that respect, conducting grand strategy is not unlike investing. Indeed, a recent comment by one market adviser captures the challenge of managing strategic risk almost perfectly: "As asset allocators, we always keep in mind that our assumptions could be wrong. . . . Our targets are just that – targets – they are not set in stone."[10]

In practice, however, several obstacles complicate risk management, especially, but certainly not exclusively, by democratic governments. One problem is that one man's threat is another's Fantasy. As our own and Britain's experience reveals, achieving consensus about the state of the operating environment and its potential impact on strategic choices is difficult even when threats are unmistakable and immediate. When they are ambiguous or distant, the difficulties multiply.

Moreover, threat estimates are not just intellectual abstractions. Having fiscal, institutional, and ideological implications, they tend to develop powerful bureaucratic constituencies, among whom the resulting political bargaining all too frequently produces an enlargement rather than a diminution of strategic commitments. The persistent resource battles in and among theaters of war described by Lacey were by no means unaffected by the institutional interests of the military services involved. Much later, examinations of America's strategic decision making related to the Vietnam War revealed a similar phenomenon.[11] Considerable political firmness is necessary to prevent such intramural contests from leading to the dissipation of strategic effort, at best, and dangerous overstretch, at worst.

Allies merely exacerbate the prioritization problem. As several of our cases confirm, the same allies that undoubtedly often empower the execution of grand strategy also complicate its formulation, whence Winston Churchill's wry remark that the only thing worse than fighting with allies is fighting without them.[12] Thus, regarding Louis XIV's shortsighted failure to preserve the alliances that his mentor Cardinal Mazarin had labored so successfully to build, Lynn notes, "the need to honor others' interests incurs

[10] Ron Sweet, "Evaluating Earnings: What's the New Normal?," USAA On-Line Market Commentary, (https://www.usaa.com/inet/ent_utils/MeStaticPages?key=mc_200906_Evaluating-Earnings.

[11] See, e.g., David Halberstam, *The Best and the Brightest* (New York, 1969); and H. R. McMaster, *Dereliction of Duty* (New York, 1997).

[12] Arthur Bryant, *Triumph in the West, 1943–1946* (London, 1986), p. 445.

the inconvenience of unwanted complexity or moderation, but it can also encourage a wisdom that avoids self-deluded policy." "Mazarin," he adds, "demonstrated that alliances between strong and weak players can work best when the former operates as a sponsor of the latter rather than when they act as dispensable junior partners," a lesson his royal student unfortunately never absorbed. Instead, Lynn tells us, "Louis eventually came to see France as powerful enough to fight alone if it had to, and this made him unwilling to accommodate the interests and outlooks of others." The parallel with recent American strategic behavior need not be belabored.

In contrast, determined to insure that Prussia never became strategically isolated, Bismarck was scrupulous to keep Germany's allies reasonably content, even at some cost in flexibility. As Jones notes, "Bismarck's great success in the 1880s was to embed the European states in an interlocking network of defensive treaties and alliances in which no aggressor could be assured of support and for which all bore some degree of defensive responsibility." His successors' cavalier refusal to sustain and nurture those associations contributed materially to the catastrophe of 1914.

In contrast, during successive Moroccan crises, Britain's leaders at the turn of the twentieth century were staunch in their support of France, despite the cost in Anglo-German relations. Winston Churchill similarly, was in no doubt about the strategic price of alliance. As one admirer notes: "If the price of survival of British independence and British democracy was the eventual transference of much of the imperial burden to the Americans, so be it; and if the price of winning the war was the tacit acceptance of Russian overlordship over much of Eastern Europe, that was unavoidable too: for half of Europe (including of course all of Western Europe) was better than none."[13]

Even when their strategic aims are congruent, or at least not mutually antithetical, allies, whether actual or putative, complicate the management of strategy. Black describes at some length the difficulties attending George II's efforts to convince Austria to assist in the defense of Hanover, difficulties paralleled a century and a half later by Britain's unsuccessful effort to secure German support to reverse Russian encroachment in Manchuria. During World War II, British, Soviet, and American differences concerning strategic priorities increased steadily as the war progressed and became even more marked once victory had been achieved and the common danger removed. Throughout the Cold War, finally, our own and our North Atlantic Treaty Organization allies' conflicting strategic priorities more than once strained alliance cohesion and, in the case of France, eventually produced a breach requiring 40 years to repair.

---

[13] Lukacs, *Five Days in London*, p. 214. Of course, Churchill never entirely reconciled himself to either part of that bargain, hence many of the disputes afflicting the transatlantic relationship both during and after the war.

Such difficulties reflect both inevitable differences in history, culture, and geostrategic perspective and, especially in war, the challenge of equitably apportioning cost and risk. As Lacey suggests, both problems underlay the occasionally bitter Anglo-American arguments prompted by Churchill's persistent desire to attack Hitler's soft underbelly in preference to invading directly across the channel. In the end, the two allies were compelled to compromise, but debate persists to this day among historians whether Allied operations in Sicily and Italy contributed to or delayed Hitler's eventual defeat and whether, in any case, they achieved results worth their price in blood and treasure. Equally bitter arguments characterized Allied operations in Southeast Asia, where British imperial interests clashed with American desires to attack Japan from China. Ultimately, in the Pacific as in Europe, the result was a compromise that maintained allied political comity only at the price of dispersing military effort.

In the end, like all the other conditions affecting the formulation and execution of grand strategy, the need to reconcile competing allied interests and risks reflects the quintessentially political character of the strategic enterprise. As Murray comments in the introduction to this volume, "grand strategy demands an intertwining of political, social, and economic realities with military power as well as a recognition that politics must, in nearly all cases, drive military necessity." That political quality, and the concomitant reality that foreign and defense policy are large-scale endeavors, renders grand strategy especially sensitive to the capabilities and idiosyncrasies of national leaders, a sensitivity abundantly evident in each of the seven cases examined here. Moreover, it is clear from those cases that character counts as much as educated foresight. However much they may have differed in intellectual attributes, for example, the men who guided British foreign policy through its turn-of-the-century transformation reflected a common upbringing and shared an equal commitment to the preservation of the British Empire. Similarly, while, as Gray points out, "Truman lacked anything resembling careful personal preparation for the conduct of grand strategy," he nevertheless managed to get "the 'big things' right enough."

Finally, in considering the strategic importance of personalities, it is impossible to ignore the unpredictable but often decisive impact of the quality of one's adversaries. As the saying goes, every Hannibal needs a Varro. In Jones's more elegant words, "the necessary counterpoint in almost every case of noteworthy strategic success in history is some form of failure." Thus, he argues, "it was Bismarck's achievement to translate the miscalculations of his [Austrian] counterparts into Prussian advantage, the process at the heart of any competent strategic policy." Similarly, Gray notes that "to be a great statesman or military commander . . . probably above all else, there should be an inadvertently cooperative enemy" and adds, "happily for the 'Free World,' and certainly for many among the ranks of the unfree,

Joseph Stalin labored overtime to help Truman achieve the near-great status that seems to be the current assay of America's historians." More recently, Saddam Hussein proved a peculiarly feckless adversary for successive U.S. administrations, although with strategic results thus far less than entirely satisfactory.

On the other hand, while grand strategy may well benefit from an adversary's unforced strategic errors, a strategy premised on the expectation that they will occur is an invitation to self-deception and overcommitment. In strategy, serendipitous opportunities are like sunny days in Seattle: something to be relished and capitalized on when they arise but never to be counted on and always to be treated as gifts. Rare indeed is the strategist who can create his own opportunities, as in Bismarck's masterful manipulation of the Schleswig-Holstein crisis. But it is just such achievements that distinguish the most successful strategists.

Before concluding this essay, it might be worth devoting a few lines to the relationship between grand strategy and military power. About the strategic importance of military strength, little need be said. While, as Adolph Hitler proved, it is possible for a time for a nation to execute an effective grand strategy even from a position of relative military weakness, such success is likely to prove fleeting. For better or worse, military power remains the ultimate underwriter of a nation's diplomatic IOUs, and a strategy pursued in prolonged defiance of military weakness thus is intrinsically hostage to fortune, not least the folly or pusillanimity of those toward whom it is directed.

But if the relationship between grand strategy and military strength is relatively self-evident, the same cannot be said about the relationship between strategy and the character of the military capabilities on which it relies. Our cases suggest, however, that that impact can be profound. Thus, Lynn points out, the dependence of armies in the late seventeenth century on fortification for both protection and sustainment heavily influenced Louis XIV's strategic choices. In the Seven Years' War, British military forces at the far end of a lengthy transatlantic lifeline had little choice but to enlist the economic and military assistance of their American colonists, assistance that later contributed both directly and indirectly to the disputes that launched the American Revolution. A century and a half later, Britain's virtually complete reliance on naval power for both military and economic security compelled British leaders to seek means of reducing Britain's imperial exposure that ended by radically reshaping her strategic relationships. And in the late 1940s and early 1950s, as Gray suggests, the atomic bomb was the uninvited but omnipresent guest at every strategic encounter.

All of which suggests that developing and fielding military capabilities without, at the very least, considering their grand strategic implications probably is unwise. At the final session of a recent military exercise conducted to examine a proposed new joint operating concept, one senior participant derided complaints that the concept was being developed absent an agreed grand strategy, insisting that, from his reading of history, military development more often than not precedes such strategy rather than the reverse. In fact, most of the cases examined here tend to support him. Whether we should take comfort from that is another matter. Certainly what passed for grand strategy during America's recent unhappy flirtation with the so-called revolution in military affairs does not bode well for allowing military concepts to drive strategy.

At the same time, we should recall that during both World War II and the Cold War, each more or less governed by an explicit grand strategy, U.S. military capabilities and operating concepts nevertheless evolved repeatedly and dramatically, in the first case driven by the exigencies of war itself, in the second by repeated changes in the strategic and military operating environments. It is hard to avoid concluding that, whether in pursuit of an explicit grand strategy or in default of one, versatility is the essential coin of the military realm. The more adaptable the force, in the end, the greater its inherent strategic robustness and the stronger a nation's hedge against unanticipated strategic challenges.

That by no means implies that grand strategy should rely preeminently on the use or threatened use of military force. On the contrary, to paraphrase Sun Tzu, the acme of successful grand strategy is achieving strategic success without war.[14] Thus, Jones insists that, despite his blood-and-iron reputation, Bismarck considered war an instrument of limited utility "... His circumspection made the risks and uncertainties inherent in a clash of arms intuitively distasteful." Even Churchill, in his later years, admitted that "to jaw-jaw is always better than to war-war." Moreover, the accumulation of military power is never free. As Louis XIV's experience reveals, seeking absolute strategic security through military predominance paradoxically risks both destroying the national wealth on which it depends and creating new enemies where none previously existed. In stark contrast, at the turn of the twentieth century, British leaders' much more successful response to their empire's mounting security dilemma was to transform all but one of the nations considered to be most responsible for that dilemma from potential adversaries into friends and allies.

In short, on the evidence of these essays, military force should be America's least preferred and certainly least precipitately employed strategic instrument. Instead, as Kissinger argues, confronting an increasingly interconnected world in which geographic isolation no longer guarantees her

---

[14] The actual quote is as follows: "Hence to fight and conquer in all your battles is not supreme excellence; supreme excellence consists in breaking the enemy's resistance without fighting." Sun Tzu, *The Art of War*, trans. Lionel Giles (London, 2007), p. 7.

protection, "America, like other nations, must learn to navigate between necessity and choice, between the immutable constants of international relations and the elements subject to the discretion of statesmen."[15] More perhaps than it ever has before, America's future strategic success is likely to require both modesty in defining its strategic aims and patience in achieving them. Reconciling those requirements with modern America's media-driven combination of missionary zeal and limited attention span may be the nation's toughest strategic challenge.

[15] Kissinger, *Diplomacy*, p. 812.

Index

Germany (*cont.*)
geographical position, effect of,
13–14
Imperial Germany, 14, 24, 109
Luftwaffe. *See* Luftwaffe
Morocco, interests in, 136–137, 142
naval competition before WWI and,
141
Nazi-Soviet Non-Aggression Pact
and, 165
Nine Years' War and, 39
North German Confederation and,
86–87, 89, 91–97, 108
Poland, invasion of, 166
post-WWII and, 212, 216–217, 234,
242, 253
rearmament and, 152–154, 161
Second Reich and, 103
Schleswig-Holstein, crisis of, 91–96
Soviet Union, invasion of, 173. *See
also* Barbarossa
Third Reich and,
defeat of, 216–217
Krystalnacht and, 161
rise of, 147, 152–153, 161
Thirty Years' War and, 36
Triple Alliance (1882) and, 112, 124,
127
unconditional surrender and, 207
unification of, 80, 85–86, 89, 107,
121
Wehrmacht. *See* Wehrmacht
Yangtse Agreement and, 131–132
Gibraltar, Entente Cordiale and, 135
Gladstone, William Ewart, 123,
127–128, 131
Goebbels, Joseph, 161
Gordon, General Charles, 128–129
Gramont, Agénor, Duc de, 102, 108
Grand Alliance
Nine Years' War and, 39, 50–51
WWII and, 237
Grand Dauphin, Spanish succession
and, 40–41
Grand strategy
adaptability and, 256–258
alliances and, 25–28, 264–265
bureaucracies and, 146
components of, 3, 8–9
definition of, 5–6, 8
diplomatic strategy and, 3

ends and means, reconciliation of,
263
execution of, 254, 256
geographical position and, 11–14
great states, as matter for, 1–2, 8
history, impact of, 4, 6, 13, 19, 33
Churchill as student of history,
21–22, 25
Lincoln as student of history,
21–22, 25
ideology, effect on, 15–19
leadership and, 2, 19–25, 266–267
military power, relationship between,
267–268
military strategy and, 3
nature of government and, 14–21
overambition and, 146, 263
overstretch and, 2, 13, 147, 257, 260,
264
policy and, 4, 70
preservative aims and, 260
public opinion and, 145, 261–262
revolutionary environment and, 259
risk assessment and, 264, 266
strategic culture and, 63–65
sustainment of, 28–33
transformational aims and, 260
transparency and, 261
uncertainties and, 10, 33, 255
war avoidance and, 6
worldview, impact on, 8
Grant, General Ulysses S., 23
Great Depression, 151
Great Northern War, 14
Greco-Turkish War, 124
Greece
British withdrawal from, 241–242
Greco-Turkish War and, 124
Greek War of Independence and, 114
Mussolini and, 26
Grey, Edward, 122, 137, 142–144
Grierson, James, 111, 137
Guadalcanal, battle of, 198
GYMNAST, operation, 195. *See also*
TORCH

Haldane, Lord Richard, 142
Halifax, E. F. L. Wood, Lord, 157, 165,
170
Hanover, Seven Years' War and, 69,
72–77, 265

CPSIA information can be obtained at www.ICGtesting.com
Printed in the USA
LVOW11s1500280716

498017LV00009B/176/P